CTA

Awareness Paper Workbook
Finance Act 2010 and Finance (No 2) Act 2010

Study Text November 2010 Edition

For exams in May and November 2011

TQT

Tax Qualification Training

Third edition November 2010

Printed Text ISBN 9780 7517 9125 9

e book ISBN 9780 7517 9276 8

British Library Cataloguing-in-Publication Data

A catalogue record for this book
is available from the British Library

Published by

BPP Learning Media Ltd
BPP House, Aldine Place
London W12 8AA

www.bpp.com/learningmedia

Printed in the United Kingdom

Contents

This text is printed on paper sourced from sustainable, managed forests

A note about copyright

Dear Customer

What does the little © mean and why does it matter?

Your market-leading TQT books, course materials and e-learning materials do not write and update themselves. People write them: on their own behalf or as employees of an organisation that invests in this activity. Copyright law protects their livelihoods. It does so by creating rights over the use of the content.

Breach of copyright is a form of theft – as well as being a criminal offence in some jurisdictions, it is potentially a serious breach of professional ethics.

With current technology, things might seem a bit hazy but, basically, without the express permission of BPP Learning Media:

- Photocopying TQT materials is a breach of copyright.
- Scanning, ripcasting or conversion of TQT digital materials into different file formats, uploading them to Facebook or e-mailing them to your friends is a breach of copyright.

You can, of course, sell your books, in the form in which you have bought them – once you have finished with them. (Is this fair to your fellow students? We update for a reason.)

The exam structure

Under the syllabus, candidates must pass four three-hour written papers on taxation which can be taken separately or in any combination. The four taxation papers are as follows:

- One awareness paper
- Two advisory papers
- One application and interaction paper

In addition there are two one-hour e-assessments, one on Professional Responsibilities & Ethics and the other on Law.

E-assessments

The e-assessments can be sat separately or together. Candidates can sit the assessments at a time of their choosing at examination centres throughout the UK. It will, however, be a condition that these assessments must be **passed** before the examination entry closing date for the last tax paper that a candidate will sit (if sitting in a modular way) or before the examination entry closing date if a candidate is taking all the written tax papers at the same sitting.

Candidates must answer **60 questions** from a variety of multiple choice and multiple response questions. Multiple choice questions are where a candidate must identify one correct response from a choice of four. Multiple response questions are where a candidate must identify several correct responses from a choice of up to six.

Candidates must answer 60 questions within the hour permitted for each assessment. **A candidate must provide a total of 40 correct responses out of the 60 questions to pass each e-assessment.** The questions for an e-assessment are randomly selected before candidates start the test and therefore each individual assessment is unique.

A short section is provided before the start of the hour long assessment in order to allow candidates to familiarise themselves with the format of the examination.

Objective

The objective of the Professional Responsibilities and Ethics e-assessment is to test candidates' understanding of the obligations of a Chartered Tax Adviser in the areas of professional responsibilities & ethics. Examinable documents are available for download without charge from the Institute's website www.tax.org.uk.

The objective of the Law e-assessment is to test candidates' knowledge of law within the relevant areas of tax. Questions are drawn from the CIOT's manual Essential Law for the Chartered Tax Adviser (fifth edition examinable to 28 February 2010, sixth edition examinable from 1 March 2010, seventh edition examinable from 1 March 2011) which is available for purchase from the Institute. Candidates are not expected to demonstrate a high level of application and interpretation of law in order to satisfy the requirements to pass the assessment. Candidates who have studied Scots law are allocated alternative questions compliant with that jurisdiction, where required.

TQT materials

To assist your studies TQT have written **market leading i-pass CD Roms** which contain plenty of **questions** including the CIOT's sample questions. We believe that the best way for you to practice for this E-assessment, is to work through these questions provided to you in an E-format. In addition, in order to aid your revision TQT also supply **pocket sized passcards**. These are a handy set of revision cards designed to reinforce, and help you remember, the key examinable topics.

TQT strongly recommends that you purchase the law manual 'Essential law for the Chartered Tax Adviser' from the CIOT as it has been updated for the new syllabus exams and it defines the syllabus. You can purchase this manual by telephoning the CIOT on 020 7340 0550 or 0844 579 6700. Alternatively, you can purchase the manual online at http://www.tax.org.uk/about_the_ciot/shop/Publications

The seventh edition (examinable from 1 March 2011) is available from October 2010.

The Awareness paper

Objective

One of the strengths of the CTA examination is the requirement for candidates to show an understanding of a broad range of taxes. The objective of the Awareness paper is to examine core areas of the various taxes which candidates may not deal with on a daily basis and which do not form part of their chosen Advisory papers.

You can find the Awareness syllabus on the CIOT's website (www.tax.org.uk).

Detail

The Awareness paper comprises one three-hour paper covering five modules. Candidates must choose **three out of the five modules** and answer all the questions on each of their chosen modules. All Awareness modules must be attempted at the same sitting.

The five modules in the Awareness paper are:

- Taxation of Individuals
- Inheritance Tax, Trusts and Estates
- Taxation of Unincorporated Businesses
- Corporation Tax
- VAT Including Stamp Taxes

Candidates choose three modules from the Awareness paper – BEWARE – these cannot be the same as the corresponding Advisory papers chosen, for example candidates who have decided to sit the taxation of Owner-Managed Businesses Advisory paper are precluded from selecting the Taxation of Unincorporated Businesses module at Awareness level.

Each module contains 12 short-form questions. Each question is worth five marks. To obtain a credit, candidates must obtain 50% or more of the total marks awarded for the whole paper at the same sitting. There is no requirement to obtain 50% of the marks in each individual module.

The Awareness paper takes place on the morning of the second day of the examinations.

TQT materials

To assist your studies TQT has prepared an **Awareness Paper Study Text** which you should use in conjunction with the **Awareness Paper Workbook**. These products are completely focussed on the exam you will be facing. Together they contain all the technical material you need plus plenty of questions to practise. In addition, to give you a really good idea of what the paper is like, the CIOT's sample paper is included. Finally, in order to aid your revision TQT also supplies **pocket-sized passcards**. These are a handy set of revision cards designed to reinforce, and help you remember, the key examinable topics.

The Advisory papers

Objective

The objective of the Advisory papers is to test candidates' knowledge at an advisory level, on the areas of taxation which they choose, in accordance with the defined syllabus for each paper.

You can find the Advisory syllabus on the CIOT's website (www.tax.org.uk) in the same prospectus document as the Awareness syllabus (see above).

Detail

Candidates choose **two** Advisory papers. TQT produces material for each of the following four Advisory papers:

- Taxation of Owner-Managed Businesses
- Taxation of Individuals
- Inheritance Tax, Trusts and Estates
- Advanced Corporation Tax

The Advisory papers form the first day of the examinations and are divided into two sessions. The grouping is as follows:

Morning session	**Afternoon session**
Taxation of Owner-Managed Businesses	Taxation of Individuals
Inheritance Tax, Trusts & Estates	Advanced Corporation Tax

It is considered that the groupings as shown accommodate the choices of the majority of candidates who wish to sit the examination in a single sitting. There is no restriction on a candidate choosing two advisory papers from the same group. In such circumstances, however, the candidate cannot sit both papers at the same examination sitting.

Each Advisory paper is a 'stand alone' paper. Candidates receiving a mark of 50% or more of the total marks will receive a credit in that paper.

TQT materials

TQT's innovative approach to the Advisory level is to provide three technical Study Texts:

- Taxation of Businesses & Companies
- Taxation of Trusts & Estates
- Taxation of Individuals

Which of these technical texts you need depends on which Advisory paper you are taking as shown in the table below:

Advisory paper	Technical texts required
Taxation of Owner-Managed Businesses	Taxation of Individuals Taxation of Businesses & Companies
Advanced Corporation Tax	Taxation of Businesses & Companies
Inheritance Tax, Trusts and Estates	Taxation of Trusts & Estates
Taxation of Individuals	Taxation of Individuals

The texts are signposted where necessary to ensure that you only study the material that is relevant to the paper you are sitting.

In addition to the technical texts, there is a workbook for each paper. This workbook guides you through the technical texts. In addition it contains plenty of questions and answers relevant to the paper that you will be sitting. The questions range from introductory to exam standard. Some of the answers to questions in the workbook include marking schemes so that you really can gauge how well you are doing.

The Application and Interaction paper

Objective

The objective of the Application and Interaction paper is to test candidates' ability, to apply to a practical case study, the knowledge gained in sitting the Advisory and Awareness papers and to demonstrate how the various taxes interact.

Detail

The paper consists of a case study, which candidates must answer in three hours. Candidates must answer **one** Application and Interaction case study question. TQT provides material for you to study for any of the following case study questions:

- Taxation of Individuals, Trusts & Estates
- Taxation of Companies
- Taxation of Owner-Managed Businesses

Each case study question is worth 100 marks. The pass mark is 50%.

The subject matter of the case study may include any of the items specified at Advisory level for those topics. It may also include elements of any subject within any of the Awareness modules. For example, the case study on the Taxation of Companies will be mainly corporation tax based but may also include areas such as shareholder issues, VAT and SDLT. Issues involving consideration of professional responsibilities, ethics and/or law should also be expected to feature in the case studies.

This is not a 'time pressured' case study. The emphasis is on allowing the candidates the time to submit a complete answer, thus demonstrating their ability to deal with practical situations.

The Application and Interaction paper takes place on the afternoon of the second day of the examinations.

TQT materials

TQT's material is outstanding. We produce a study text for the application and interaction paper which includes a chapter on **how to use your legislation** (essential for this examination); **guidance on how to approach the case study; guidance on how to use your time in the examination hall; guidance on how marks will be awarded; guidance on how to write reports** as well as **recap of some major technical points** that you will need for this examination. There are some questions in the Study Text for you to attempt at the initial phase of your studies. The pilot paper question and answer is included together with all important guidance on how this question would have been best approached.

Revision phase

Practice and revision kits

For your revision phase TQT publishes practice and revision kits for the Awareness, Advisory and Application and Interaction papers. These practice and revision kits will be available in January 2011.

The practice and revision kits are the **key to your success** in your CTA exams. They are packed full of questions, together with **helpful hints on how to approach the questions**. The answers are **clearly structured** and **supported by hints on how you can maximise your marks in an examination situation**. In addition some answers have **marking schemes** so that you can really gauge how well you are doing. The May and November 2010 questions and answers are also included.

Approaching your studies

The Awareness Modules

We will be introducing the topics in each module to you from first principles. If you have any previous knowledge, perhaps as a result of work experience, or as a result of having studied for other papers within this, the ATT or any other syllabus, you can modify the amount of time you spend on each topic to take account of your knowledge. The main areas of knowledge required for each of the modules given below.

1 **TAXATION OF INDIVIDUALS**

This module tests three main areas of knowledge:

(a) The **income tax liability** arising in connection with various types of income including employment income, income from property and investment income.

(b) The **national insurance** position of employees and their employers.

(c) The **capital gains tax** issues arising when an individual sells both business and non business assets.

2 **INHERITANCE TAX, TRUSTS AND ESTATES**

This module tests three main areas of knowledge:

(a) The preparation of **inheritance tax computations** for both lifetime and death transfers of value.

(b) The understanding of the legal issues surrounding **trusts** and the preparation of computations of tax due by trustees.

(c) The preparation of computations of tax for deceased persons, their executors and beneficiaries of their estates.

3 **TAXATION OF UNINCORPORATED BUSINESSES**

This module tests three main areas of knowledge:

(a) The **income tax and national insurance liabilities** arising in connection with an unincorporated business for its owner.

(b) The **capital allowance** position of an unincorporated business.

(c) The **capital gains tax** issues arising on the sale of business assets including the relief available when a business is incorporated.

4 **CORPORATION TAX**

This module tests three main areas of knowledge:

(a) The **computation of a company's taxable profits** from trading and other activities, such as investments and renting out property.

(b) The **capital allowance** position of a company.

(c) The basic **chargeable gains** issues arising on the sale of assets by a company.

5 **VAT INCLUDING STAMP TAXES**

This module tests four main areas of knowledge:

(a) The **scope** of VAT and the meaning of **supply**.

(b) Calculating the **VAT liability** in simple and more complex situations involving land and buildings, and international transactions.

(c) Accounting for and the administration of VAT.

(d) The **stamp duty** and **stamp duty land tax** implications of the transfer of business assets.

TQT talks to the Examiners

1 **Prospective legislation**

Question When is prospective / new legislation examinable?

Examiner Response: Legislation enacted at least 5 months prior to the exam is examinable in any given exam even if it has yet to come into force ie the legislation may still be prospective at the date of the exam.

However, given the exceptional nature of 2010, only FA 2010 and F(No 2)A 2010 are examinable in 2011. Any subsequent Finance Acts enacted in 2010 will not be examined in 2011.

2 **Availability of actual student scripts**

Question Would the CIOT be prepared to issue actual scripts from the Application & Interaction exams to offer students additional guidance as to the standard that needs to be achieved to pass. Perhaps one first quartile and one marginal pass script could be released?

Examiner Response: Education Department will publish a 'reasonable script' subject to obtaining candidate's permission.

3 **Marking guides**

Question Would the CIOT consider publishing its marking guides for all papers again?

Examiner Response: There are no plans to make these guides available...all marking guides are flexible and credit will always be given to candidates who make relevant comments not within the marking guide/model answer.

4 **Interest rates for unpaid / late tax**

Question Will rates be given in the exam? And where the rate is 0% (eg IHT and repayment supplement before September 2009) presume no point in examining?

Examiner Response: Rates of interest on unpaid and overpaid tax due vary from time to time and in some cases the calculation will span a change of rate date so it would not be appropriate to assume there is no point in examining merely because the current rate is nil. Where relevant the rates will usually be supplied in the question.

5 **New administration and penalties regime**

Question Are both the old and new administration/penalties rules examinable?

Examiner Response: Only the new administration and penalties rules are examinable for the 2011 exams. However, the VAT default surcharge notice is still examinable.

6 **Share pooling**

Question Given the recent changes to the share pooling rules in FA 2008 is it reasonable to assume that the detailed share pooling rules for companies will not be examined?

Examiner Response: Not examinable.

7 **Intra-spouse transfers & indexation**

Question Where an intra-spouse transfer has been made would candidates be given the indexed cost to the spouse or be expected to calculate the relevant amounts from the tables?

Examiner Response: Candidates do not need to calculate the indexation.

8 **Rollover relief – Advisory level**

Question	Rollover relief is on the Taxation of Individuals syllabus – but not all candidates for this paper will have studied for the Taxation of Owner-Managed Businesses paper. Can we expect therefore, that the questions will concentrate more on the other reliefs such as PPR, gift relief and EIS?
Examiner Response:	Rollover relief could be tested on the Taxation of Individuals paper.

9 **Rollover relief – Awareness level**

Question	Rollover relief is not examinable in the Corporation Tax module of the Awareness paper, but groups and transactions within groups are. Can we assume that questions about groups would not include rollover relief? Would this include the potential for rollover of a de-grouping charge?
Examiner Response:	Correct.

10 **March 1982/April 1965 assets**

Question	Are assets held at 31 March 1982 / 6 April 1965 examinable in the Awareness paper?
Examiner Response:	31 March 1982 – yes 6 April 1965 – no

11 **Partnership CGT**

Question	Partnership CGT is on the Taxation of Individuals Advisory syllabus but income tax for partnerships is not. Can we please remove partnership CGT from the syllabus?
Examiner Response:	Partnership CGT is included within the Taxation of Individuals Advisory syllabus so that non-trading partnerships may be examined. We will clarify the syllabus for 2011 so that it confirms that the CGT is limited to non-trading partnerships and that income tax on non-trading partnerships is also examinable. The only partnerships which will be examined in the Individuals Advisory paper are investment partnerships which have no trade or profession, for example property partnerships.

12 **Overseas aspects of CGT**

Question	Is DTR examinable for all papers? It is not clear from the syllabus, as all it says in terms of overseas CGT on the latest syllabus document is 'residence'.
Examiner Response:	The syllabus states: Supplemental matters contained in s.272 to s.291 TCGA 1992 DTR is therefore examinable – see s.277.

13 **CGT administration**

Question	To what extent is CGT administration examinable in the Awareness papers?
Examiner Response:	We would not expect candidates to have a detailed knowledge of the administration of CGT. The thrust of the Awareness papers is to enable candidates to spot issues rather than to be able to deal with the detailed administration of the tax.

14 **IHT planning**

Question: We assume that the more complex planning schemes for IHT such as double flip-flops are not included in the Advisory syllabus for Inheritance Tax, Trusts & Estates.

Examiner Response: We do not specifically expect candidates to be aware of the various complex planning schemes which have been marketed – to do so may unfairly penalise candidates from smaller firms who may be less likely to come across such schemes. However, we would expect candidates to be aware of schemes if they are part of a tax case so that they are then widely known.

15 **PAYE**

Question: The operation and application of the PAYE system is examinable in Taxation of Individuals Awareness module. Can we assume this is from the individual's perspective and so things like due dates for the employer submitting forms, details re PSAs would not be examinable?

Examiner Response: No, this also covers employer aspects.

16 **Unincorporated businesses – Awareness level**

Question: Are we correct to assume that just basic income tax computations involving trading income would be examinable in this paper?

Examiner Response: Yes

17 **Restricted securities**

Question: The syllabus is not clear as to whether the rules on restricted securities are examinable and in which Advisory level papers. Can this please be clarified?

Examiner Response: Yes they are examinable, but only in the Taxation of Individuals paper. Since the rules are so complex, we will not require a detailed knowledge of the rules nor require candidates to prepare detailed calculations. We would expect them to be aware of the concept of restrictions which may attach to shares, to be aware that this affects the value, to be aware of the broad impact this may have in terms of the timing of the tax and to be aware that a s.431 election could be made.

18 **Pension anti-forestalling rules**

Question: Are the pension anti-forestalling rules examinable?

Examiner Response: Yes.

19 **High income excess relief charge**

Question: Please confirm whether the high income excess relief charge is examinable.

Examiner Response: Not examinable.

20 **Accrued income scheme**

Question: Is the accrued income scheme examinable?

Examiner Response: Yes for the Taxation of Individuals Advisory paper.

21 **Remittances of income**

Question: In relation to Taxation of Individual's Advisory paper, what level of detail is required in respect of remittances of nominated income (s.809I-J ITA 2009) and remittances out of mixed funds (s.809Q-R ITA 2007)? In particular will students need to perform calculations under the method statements in both sets of sections?

Examiner Response: Calculations may be required for both sets of sections.

22 **Non-qualifying life assurance policy deficiency relief**

Question: Is Non-Qualifying Life Assurance Policy deficiency relief in the syllabus?

Examiner Response: An awareness only of life assurance policies is required in Taxation of Individuals Advisory and therefore we would expect no more than an awareness that such a relief exists.

23 **Tax credits**

Question: To what extent are tax credits examinable?

Examiner Response: We would expect candidates to know for example:

1) Tax credits exist, are based on joint income and are paid to the claimants rather than adjusted through their income tax computation.
2) A claim can only be backdated for three months.
3) Pension contributions and Gift Aid donations reduce income for tax credit purposes. A person making a large pension contribution every few years could therefore create an entitlement to credits in that year.
4) Losses reduce income in the year or the following year if not used up. When a loss is made, candidates should therefore flag that tax credits may have been available (noting the three month time limit) and to make a claim if in doubt.
5) Notional income (eg income one deliberately deprives oneself of) is added back.

Therefore, what we are looking for is essential knowledge to be able to flag to a client opportunities to claim tax credits (and hence not be sued for failing to mention them). There would never be a whole question on them and candidates would not be expected to calculate them. It is more likely to be an element of a question majoring on another topic and in particular could be included in an A&I question.

24 **Taxation of investor in an offshore fund**

Question: Are the transitional rules in respect of taxation of investor in an offshore fund in the syllabus?

Examiner Response: In Taxation of Individuals Advisory paper candidates should be aware that the distributing/non distributing regime is being replaced by the reporting regime. They should be aware that an election can be made to deem a disposal to be made on the change of status of a fund.

25 **Overseas issues – Advisory level**

Question: The previous Paper IIA exam did not examine overseas issues. Can we assume that this will also be the case for the Taxation of Owner-Managed Businesses paper?

Examiner Response: The syllabus includes, for example transfers of assets abroad and DTR on companies. However, overseas issues will really only feature in passing rather than as a core element of a question. The in depth testing of overseas issues will be in the other papers.

26 **World-wide debt cap**

Question	Is the world-wide debt cap examinable at Awareness level?
Examiner Response:	Not examinable at Awareness level, but is examinable for both the Taxation of Owner-Managed Businesses paper (at a basic level) and Advanced Corporation Tax (in depth) Advisory papers.

27 **CFC ADP and exempt activities holding companies transitional rules**

Question	To what extent are the transitional rules examinable?
Examiner Response:	The rules are examinable in detail for Advisory level Advanced Corporation Tax.

28 **Derivative contracts – disregard regulations**

Question	To what extent are the disregard regulations examinable for derivative contracts?
Examiner Response:	Not examinable.

29 **Bank levy and bank payroll tax**

Question	Please confirm whether the bank levy and / or the bank payroll tax is examinable.
Examiner Response:	Not examinable.

30 **Corporate venturing scheme relief**

Question	To what extent is CVS relief still examinable?
Examiner Response:	Only the relief for losses will be examinable. Candidates will be told that the shares originally qualified for CVS relief and may assume it has not been withdrawn.

31 **Cars transitional rules – leases and capital allowances**

Question	To what extent are the transitional rules for cars in relation to capital allowances and leases examinable?
Examiner Response:	Transitional rules are examinable. Existing expenditure on pre April 2009 cars is therefore examinable as are leases entered into before April 2009.

32 **Capital allowances changes**

Question	To what extent are the old rules examinable?
Examiner Response:	Pre April 2008 first year allowances, the old long life asset pool, and pre April 2008 rates are no longer examinable.

33 **BPRA**

Question	Is the Business Premises Renovation Allowance examinable.
Examiner Response:	Yes – for Advanced Corporation Tax Advisory paper only.

34 **Land remediation relief**

Question	Is land remediation relief examinable.
Examiner Response:	Yes – for Advanced Corporation Tax Advisory paper only.

35 **Share schemes**

Question: Are the examiners prepared to give more guidance to students with regard to the perspective that the exams will take, eg with regards to share schemes (in both Taxation of Owner-Managed Businesses & Taxation of Individuals Advisory papers) is it the intention that Taxation of Owner-Managed Businesses paper will be from the perspective of the employer and the Taxation of Individuals from the perspective of the individual employee?

Examiner Response: This is generally true. The main thrust of a shares question in the Taxation of Individuals paper would be from the employee's perspective whilst the main thrust in the Taxation of Owner-Managed Businesses paper would be from the employer's or owner's perspective.

36 **Owner-Managed Businesses**

Question: What does the CIOT consider to be an owner-managed business? Is it primarily going to be sole traders and partnerships or is it just as likely to be companies? Are groups going to be significant? Small groups only? What about a £100m group owned by wealthy chairman?

Examiner Response: It can be sole traders, partnerships, LLPs and companies. Groups may be tested, but will not form a significant part of this paper. It is not possible to give hard and fast rules about what is and what is not an OMB and size alone will not mean that that the subject matter is more or less complex. As you will know from practice, often the greatest complexities come from relatively small transactions.

Using the Home Study Programme

1 Introduction

This TQT Home Study Programme will guide you through the 2010 edition of the TQT Study Text. If your Study Text does not have that date on the cover, please contact your course provider.

The 2010 edition of the study text has been thoroughly and reliably updated for the first two 2010 Finance Acts, Corporation Tax Act 2010 and Taxation (International and Other Provisions) Act 2010. These Acts will be examined in the May 2011 and November 2011 exams. If you are not taking your exams in 2011 please contact your course provider.

2 Using the Home Study Programme

This Home Study Programme is made up of a number of **Study Periods**, for each of the FIVE Awareness modules. **You must only study for THREE of the Awareness modules**. Identify which modules you will study now and then use the study periods for those modules to take you through the learning phase of your studies.

As every individual studies at a different pace, there is no definitive time period over which the learning phase is designed to be completed. Ideally you should aim to complete the learning phase within six to twelve months, depending on your own learning pace.

Once your 'learning phase' is complete you should move onto the Revision Phase. More detail is given later in this Workbook.

Each Study Period has been graded as high or medium priority and consists of the following elements:

Exam Guidance

This gives you **important** information of how your exam is likely to focus on the particular area you are studying

Introduction to the session

Here you are **introduced** to the subject and the **main issues** that you should understand when you have finished your study of this session.

Guidance through the Study Text

This provides you with **important instructions** on how to work through the TQT Study Text. You must follow the guidance in this table for time efficient study, as you will be told which areas of each chapter must be worked through in detail and which can be skimmed over. It contains **key points**, summarising the most vital areas of the Study Period.

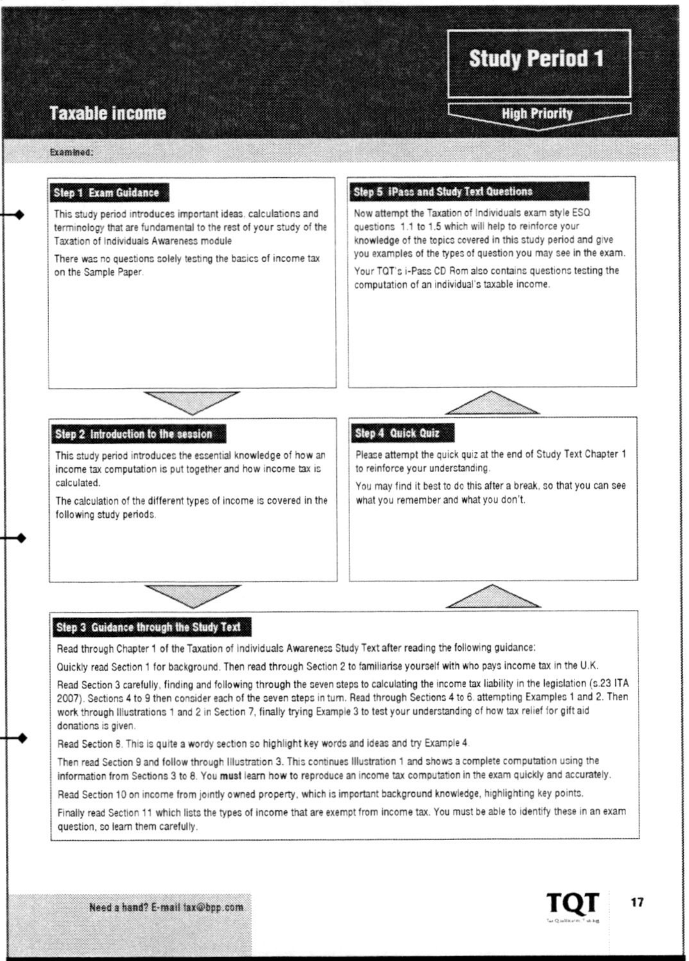
Study Period 1

High Priority

Taxable income

Examined:

Step 1 Exam Guidance

This study period introduces important ideas, calculations and terminology that are fundamental to the rest of your study of the Taxation of Individuals Awareness module

There was no questions solely testing the basics of income tax on the Sample Paper.

Step 2 Introduction to the session

This study period introduces the essential knowledge of how an income tax computation is put together and how income tax is calculated.

The calculation of the different types of income is covered in the following study periods.

Step 3 Guidance through the Study Text

Read through Chapter 1 of the Taxation of Individuals Awareness Study Text after reading the following guidance:

Quickly read Section 1 for background. Then read through Section 2 to familiarise yourself with who pays income tax in the U.K.

Read Section 3 carefully, finding and following through the seven steps to calculating the income tax liability in the legislation (s.23 ITA 2007). Sections 4 to 9 then consider each of the seven steps in turn. Read through Sections 4 to 6, attempting Examples 1 and 2. Then work through Illustrations 1 and 2 in Section 7, finally trying Example 3 to test your understanding of how tax relief for gift aid donations is given.

Read Section 8. This is quite a wordy section so highlight key words and ideas and try Example 4.

Then read Section 9 and follow through Illustration 3. This continues Illustration 1 and shows a complete computation using the information from Sections 3 to 8. You **must** learn how to reproduce an income tax computation in the exam quickly and accurately.

Read Section 10 on income from jointly owned property, which is important background knowledge, highlighting key points.

Finally read Section 11 which lists the types of income that are exempt from income tax. You must be able to identify these in an exam question, so learn them carefully.

Step 4 Quick Quiz

Please attempt the quick quiz at the end of Study Text Chapter 1 to reinforce your understanding.

You may find it best to do this after a break, so that you can see what you remember and what you don't.

Step 5 iPass and Study Text Questions

Now attempt the Taxation of Individuals exam style ESQ questions 1.1 to 1.5 which will help to reinforce your knowledge of the topics covered in this study period and give you examples of the types of question you may see in the exam.

Your TQT's i-Pass CD Rom also contains questions testing the computation of an individual's taxable income.

Need a hand? E-mail tax@bpp.com

TQT

17

Each Study Period should take an average of 3 hours.

Progress Tests

Some of the Study Periods are '**Progress Tests**' which you can use to assess the work you have done on a limited number of Study Periods. You should mark the tests yourself using the solutions in this Workbook.

Course Examinations

If you are a home study student your TQT material contains **Course Examinations**. These should be attempted at the points suggested within the Study Programme (they cover the preceding Study Periods). If you are attending a taught course your course provider may use these exams or they may use different exams. You should follow the instructions given to you by your course provider regarding the sitting and marking of any exams you are told to sit.

To gain the greatest benefit from the exams, you must set aside a period of three hours during which you will have no interruptions.

By sitting these exams, you will increase your chances of passing the real exams by 30%.

Please note that course exams are only available as part of the home study package. They are not available to purchase individually.

Sample Paper

When you have studied all three of the CTA Awareness modules attempt the CTA Awareness Sample Paper. Set aside a period of three hours and attempt the exam in exam conditions. This will help you to assess how you would perform in the real exam.

The Revision Phase

Congratulations

If you've got this far. Well done!

It might not feel like it at the moment, but the hard work you've already put in is about to pay off. You have about a month to go before the exam and you now need to focus your attention on even more question practice.

The final steps

The key to passing this examination is to work as many questions as possible during the revision phase of your studies. You should initially re-work any questions in the Workbook that you may have struggled with in the learning phase of your studies. You will then be ready to make the transition to practising the questions on in the **TQT Practice and Revision Kit**.

The TQT **Practice and Revision** Kit contains:

Exam Standard Questions and Answers. Now is the time to practise as many questions as you can and TQT's material certainly gives you plenty of opportunity to do just that.

Marking schemes: A number of the questions in the Practice and Revision Kit have marking schemes. You should use these when marking your own answers to obtain an idea of your progress in the particular topics being tested. Remember, you do not need full marks to pass!

Passcards are not just a condensed text. Each card is separately designed for clear presentation of the facts. The topics are self contained in a highly visual format, including diagrams and boxes to highlight important points. The Passcards focus on the exam and contain helpful hints to help you pass each chapter.

Revision course

We strongly recommend you book on a revision course – these courses will give you valuable support and guidance on how to approach the questions in the **TQT Practice and Revision Kit** and on how to maximise your marks in the examination hall. **The ability of a tutor to help you prioritise your studies at this stage is vitally important**. Tutors have a wealth of experience of these examinations and they are there to help you. They'll be happy to go through any problem areas and to support you in any other way they can.

Work smart (and hard)

Don't fall into the trap of assuming that if you work for 5 hours a night for the next six weeks, then you will pass the exam. Your brain doesn't work that way – so make sure you factor in the following when creating your revision plan:

- Make sure you get enough sleep – a tired mind won't pass the exam
- Make sure you build in time to relax (your brain needs the time to process the information you're trying to squash in to it)
- You are more likely to retain knowledge if sessions are short and there is a recap session built in to the plan later on
- Keep disruptions to a minimum, and take regular short breaks where possible
- Try to reproduce exam conditions for timed question practice

Stick with it!

There is not long to go now. Don't give up. Remember these exams are hard for everyone and when you finally pass you'll be really pleased that you kept going.

Awareness Paper
Taxation of individuals

TQT
Tax Qualification Training

Study Period Planner
Taxation of Individuals

Use this schedule and your exam timetable to plan the dates on which you will complete each Study Period. The letters 'H' and 'M' tell you whether the topic is high or medium priority.

Study Period	Topic		Due Date
1	Taxable income	H	
2	Savings and dividend income	H	
3	Income from UK land and buildings	H	
4	Tax efficient investments	M	
5	The employed earner	H	
6	Share remuneration	M	
7	Pensions	H	
8	Overseas aspects of income tax	M	
9	National Insurance Contributions/PAYE	M	
10	Administration of income tax	M	

Study Period	Topic		Due Date
11	**Progress Test 1**	**H**	
12	Outline of CGT	H	
13	Computing CGT liability	H	
14	Shares and securities	H	
15	Chattels and wasting assets	M	
16	Principal private residence relief	M	
17	Other CGT reliefs	H	
18	Administration of CGT	M	
19	**Progress Test 2**	**H**	

COURSE EXAM 1

A practice exam covering Study Periods 1 to 10.

COURSE EXAM 2

A practice exam covering all Study Periods.

REVISION PHASE

Your revision phase will begin when **Course Exam 2** is complete. This should ideally be four months before the final exam.

TQT Note: The Course Exams contain questions for all FIVE of the awareness paper modules. In your exam you must answer questions from THREE modules. We suggest that you identify the THREE modules you will study and then work through the Study Period Planners for each of those modules until the point where you are told to take Course Exam 1. When you have completed all THREE modules to that point, sit Course Exam 1. Similarly, you should complete all THREE modules before you sit course exam 2. Course Exam 2 covers all of the Study Periods, although it is weighted towards the second half of your studies.

Taxable income

Step 1 Exam Guidance

This study period introduces important ideas, calculations and terminology that are fundamental to the rest of your study of the Taxation of Individuals Awareness module.

The basics of income tax were tested in:

- Q2 (Sample Paper), Q5 (May 2009), Q5 (Nov 2009) and Q1, Q4 and Q9 (May 2010)

Step 2 Introduction to the session

This study period introduces the essential knowledge of how an income tax computation is put together and how income tax is calculated.

The calculation of the different types of income is covered in the following study periods.

Step 3 Guidance through the Study Text

Read through Chapter 1 of the Taxation of Individuals Awareness Study Text after reading the following guidance:

Quickly read Section 1 for background. Then read through Section 2 to familiarise yourself with who pays income tax in the U.K.

Read Section 3 carefully, finding and following through the seven steps to calculating the income tax liability in the legislation (s.23 ITA 2007). Sections 4 to 9 then consider each of the seven steps in turn. Read through Sections 4 to 6, attempting Examples 1 to 3. Then work through Illustrations 1 and 2 in Section 7, finally trying Examples 4 and 5.

Read Section 8. Highlight key words and ideas and try Example 6.

Then read Section 9 and follow through Illustration 3. This continues Illustration 1 and shows a complete computation using the information from Sections 3 to 8. You **must** learn how to reproduce an income tax computation in the exam quickly and accurately.

Briefly read Section 10 and note those benefits which are taxable and those which are exempt from tax.

Read Section 11 on income from jointly owned property, which is important background knowledge, highlighting key points.

Finally read Section 12 which lists the types of income that are exempt from income tax. You must be able to identify these in an exam question, so learn them carefully.

Step 4 Quick Quiz

Please attempt the quick quiz at the end of Study Text Chapter 1 to reinforce your understanding.

You may find it best to do this after a break, so that you can see what you remember and what you don't.

Step 5 Workbook Questions

Now attempt the exam style questions (ESQs) 1.1 to 1.5 which will help to reinforce your knowledge of the topics covered in this study period and give you examples of the types of question you may see in the exam.

Study Period 2

Savings and dividend income

High Priority

Step 1 Exam Guidance

It is unlikely that you will be able to avoid calculating income tax for individuals in the exam.

The tax rates differ depending on whether the income being taxed is savings, dividend or non-savings income.

You must be able to identify the different types of income and calculate tax at the appropriate rate.

The taxation of dividend income was tested in:

- Question 5 of the May 2009 exam

Step 2 Introduction to the session

Now that we understand how a basic income tax computation is put together, we need to look in more detail at the different rates of tax that can apply to different types of income.

In the income tax computation, we need to be able to split taxable income into savings, dividend income and non savings income, understand the order in which income is taxed and the tax rates that apply.

Step 3 Guidance through the Study Text

Read through Chapter 2 of the Study Text after reading the following guidance:

Read Section 1 quickly as background information. Refer to the Institute's tax tables at the front of the Study Text as you go along so that you know what rates and allowances will be given to you in the exam.

Read through Section 2 and note that interest can be received both gross and net (of 20% tax). Then read Section 3, which covers dividends and items that are treated as dividends. These all come with a 10% *deemed* tax credit. Attempt Examples 1 and 2. You **must** understand that all figures are included **gross** in the income tax computation.

Read through Section 4 on the order in which savings and non-savings income should be taxed and the appropriate tax rates to use. Pay particular attention to the three column format of the computation.

Review the illustration in Section 5 to check your understanding of what has been covered in this study period and how savings and non savings income fit into the income tax computation. Attempt Examples 3 to 7 to check your understanding.

Finally, quickly read Section 6 on other income.

Step 4 Quick Quiz

Please attempt the quiz at the end of Study Text Chapter 2 to reinforce your understanding.

You may find it best to do this after a break, so that you can see what you remember and what you don't.

Step 5 Workbook Questions

Now attempt ESQs 2.1 to 2.7 which will help to reinforce your knowledge of the topics covered in this study period and give you examples of the types of question you may see in the exam.

Study Period 3

High Priority

Income from UK land and buildings

Step 1 Exam Guidance

In the exam, you may be required to calculate the amount of taxable property income or you may be asked factual questions, such as the conditions for a furnished holiday letting or for rent a room relief to apply.

This topic was tested in:

- Q7 (Sample Paper), Q7 (May 2009), Q3 (Nov 2009) and Q2 (May 2010)

Step 2 Introduction to the session

In this study period we learn to calculate how much to include as taxable property income from UK land and buildings in the income tax computation.

Step 3 Guidance through the Study Text

Read through Chapter 3 of the Study Text after reading the following guidance:

Read Section 1 quickly for background then concentrate on Section 2 which covers how to calculate the property income figure. Pay attention to the deductions available, in particular the 'wear and tear' allowance in Section 2.2 and attempt Example 1. Read Section 3 on property losses and the restricted ways in which they can be used.

Section 4 on lease premiums is an important topic, so attempt Examples 2 and 3 to test your understanding.

Read Section 5 on 'furnished holiday lettings' but do not waste time learning the conditions, instead learn where to find them in the legislation. Then read Section 6 which deals with the rent a room scheme. Locate the rent limit in the Institute's tax tables that you will be given in the exam.

Read quickly through Section 7 on non-resident landlords then read Section 8, which deals with Real Estate Investment Trusts (REITs). Contrast how dividends from a REIT are taxed compared to normal dividends. Follow through the Illustration.

Finally read through Section 9 on transactions involving land, following through the relevant part of the legislation.

Step 4 Quick Quiz

Please attempt the quiz at the end of Study Text Chapter 3 to reinforce your understanding.

You may find it best to do this after a break, so that you can see what you remember and what you don't.

Step 5 Workbook Questions

Now attempt the ESQ 3.1 to 3.7 which will help to reinforce your knowledge of the topics covered in this study period and give you examples of the types of question you may see in the exam.

Tax efficient investments

Study Period 4

Medium Priority

Step 1 Exam Guidance

You must be able to identify tax free investments so that you do not include them in an income tax computation. Do, however, always tell the examiner why you have not taxed the income.

You also need to understand the conditions for, and the tax consequences of, investing in the Enterprise Investment Scheme (EIS). Questions could examine the qualifying conditions for the scheme, the tax implications of an investment or the calculation of an investor's tax position.

The EIS was tested in Question 2 of the November 2009 exam.

Step 2 Introduction to the session

In this Study Period the aim is to understand how individuals can make tax efficient investments that can reduce the amount of tax they have to pay.

The investments considered are:

- Tax free investments, including ISAs
- The Enterprise Investment Scheme.

Step 3 Guidance through the Study Text

Please read Chapter 4 of the Study Text after reading the guidance below:

Read quickly through Section 1 so that you can identify the main sources of tax free investments in the exam. The point to note here is that income arising from these investments is tax free.

Read through Section 2 on ISAs, highlighting the key points and terminology.

Concentrate your study during this period on Section 3 on the Enterprise Investment Scheme (EIS). This is another area where you can rely heavily on your legislation in the exam, so take this opportunity to locate the relevant part of the ITA 2007 and highlight the key conditions, rules, rates of relief and limits as you read through the section. Attempt Example 1.

Step 4 Quick Quiz

Please attempt the quiz at the end of Study Text Chapter 4 to reinforce your understanding.

You may find it best to do this after a break, so that you can see what you remember and what you don't.

Step 5 Workbook Questions

Now attempt the ESQs 4.1 and 4.3 which will help to reinforce your knowledge of the topics covered in this study period and give you examples of the types of question you may see in the exam.

The employed earner

High Priority

Step 1 Exam Guidance

You must be able to calculate the amount of income to include in the income tax computation of an employed earner.

Questions can focus on many different aspects of the employed earner, for example:

- The basis of assessment
- Identifying and calculating taxable employment income including the value of benefits received
- Understanding the taxation of termination payments.

Employment income and benefits were tested in:

– Q3 (Sample Paper), Q2 (May 2009), Q1,Q7 & Q12 (Nov 2009) and Q4 (May 2010)

Step 2 Introduction to the session

In this study period we look at the rules for calculating the amount of employment income to include in the income tax computation.

You must be able to identify what is taxable and in which tax year.

A fundamental element of this study period is to learn the rules for calculating the taxable value of benefits. We also need to know how to deal with payments on termination of employment.

Step 3 Guidance through the Study Text

Please read Chapter 5 of the Study Text after reading the guidance below:

Read through Section 1 for background. This is quite a wordy section so highlight key words and terminology only. Attempt Example 1.

Sections 2 and 3 are the core elements of this study period so read through carefully. Section 2 deals with benefits that are taxable on all employees, regardless of their income level, while Section 3 covers those benefits that are only taxable on directors and employees earning £8,500 pa or more. Work through Examples 2 to 10 carefully to ensure you have understood the rules.

You must also be able to identify benefits that are not taxable on any employees so read through the list of tax-free benefits in Section 4 carefully. The most important tax-free benefits are in **bold** so concentrate on learning these.

Read Section 5 to ensure you understand what can be deducted from employment income. There are not many things! Try Example 11.

Read Section 6 which covers the different types of payment that can be received when employment ends ('termination payments'). Do you understand which payments are taxable and which are exempt from tax? Work through Example 12.

Step 4 Quick Quiz

Please attempt the quiz at the end of Study Text Chapter 5 to reinforce your understanding.

You may find it best to do this after a break, so that you can see what you remember and what you don't.

Step 5 Workbook Questions

Now attempt the ESQs 5.1 to 5.9 which will help to reinforce your knowledge of the topics covered in this study period and give you examples of the types of question you may see in the exam.

Share remuneration

Medium Priority

Step 1 Exam Guidance

An employed earner may receive part of his remuneration in the form of shares or may be entitled to join his employer's share scheme(s). This can be a tax efficient way of rewarding employees particularly if the value of the shares increases.

You must understand the conditions that apply for the different share schemes, identify the tax efficiency, or otherwise, of such schemes for the employee and calculate how such remuneration is treated for tax purposes.

Employee share schemes were tested in the following exams:

– Q5 (Sample Paper), Q4 (May 2009) , Q4 (Nov 2009) and Q6 (May 2010)

Step 2 Introduction to the session

Now that we understand how to calculate employment income we can look at how employees can be rewarded in a tax efficient way. Usually this is by taking advantage of an approved share scheme. We need to be able to identify when a share scheme is approved and the conditions for approval.

We also need to be able to understand the tax implications for the employee of both approved and unapproved share schemes.

Step 3 Guidance through the Study Text

Read through Chapter 6 of the Study Text after reading the guidance below:

Read quickly through Section 1 for background.

Sections 2 and 3 deal with employers providing shares and share options to their employees other than through an approved scheme. Read through these sections, highlighting key ideas and terminology (such as 'restricted shares'). Do you understand the difference between an employer giving shares **directly** to employees and granting them share **options**? Attempt Example 1 to check your understanding of the tax treatment of shares received from an unapproved scheme.

Section 4 on the approved share schemes is essential for the exam. Read through the information on the four main approved share schemes and make notes ensuring that you know how each scheme works, the conditions for approval and the tax implications of each scheme. Attempt examples 2 & 3.

Finally, read through Section 5 which deals with the National Insurance Contribution (NIC) implications for the various share schemes.

Step 4 Quick Quiz

Please attempt the quiz at the end of Study Text Chapter 6 to reinforce your understanding.

You may find it best to do this after a break, so that you can see what you remember and what you don't.

Step 5 Workbook Questions

Now attempt the ESQs 6.1 to 6.4 which will help to reinforce your knowledge of the topics covered in this study period and give you examples of the types of question you may see in the exam.

Pensions

Study Period 7

High Priority

Step 1 Exam Guidance

You may be asked to calculate the amount of pension contributions that an individual can make, to either an occupational or a personal pension scheme, on which tax relief is available and to explain how the tax relief is given. You may also be asked about drawing the pension once retirement has taken place.

Tax relief for pension contributions was tested in:

– Q6 (May 2009), Q6 (Nov 2009) and Q8 (May 2010).

Step 2 Introduction to the session

In this study period, we learn how pension contributions made both to occupational schemes run by employers and to personal pension schemes are treated for tax purposes. Tax relief will be given for pension contributions made up to certain limits.

We also need to understand how pension income will be taxed on retirement.

Step 3 Guidance through the Study Text

Read through Chapter 7 of the Study Text after reading the following guidance:

Read through Section 1 for background knowledge. Make sure you can distinguish between occupational and personal pension schemes and understand that one of the main benefits of saving in a pension is that the fund grows free of any tax.

Read through Section 2 on pension contributions. Make sure you can calculate the maximum amount that an individual can contribute to a pension scheme for which tax relief is available. Note that the limit is the same for both occupational and personal pension schemes.

Then read Section 3 which deals with giving tax relief for contributions to occupational and personal pension schemes. Organise your notes so that you can compare the different ways of making of contributions to occupational and to personal pension schemes. Are they made net or gross of tax? Do you understand how both ways of obtaining tax relief fit into the income tax computation you have learnt? Attempt Example 1.

Finally, read through Section 4 to understand how the pension fund can be taken out of the pension on retirement.

Step 4 Quick Quiz

Please attempt the quiz at the end of Study Text Chapter 7 to reinforce your understanding.

You may find it best to do this after a break, so that you can see what you remember and what you don't.

Step 5 Workbook Questions

Now attempt the ESQs 7.1 to 7.4 which will help to reinforce your knowledge of the topics covered in this study period and give you examples of the types of question you may see in the exam.

Study Period 8

Overseas aspects of income tax

Medium Priority

Step 1 Exam Guidance

So far we have considered the income tax position of UK resident individuals. However, you could also be examined on the overseas aspects of income tax, for example, determining the residence status of an individual, to decide if and how they are liable to UK income tax, or how overseas income is taxed.

You should bear in mind that if an individual is taxed both in the UK and another country on the same source of income that double tax relief (DTR) may be available.

The tax position of a non-UK domiciled individual was tested in:

– Q4 (Sample Paper), Q3 (May 2009) and Q3 (May 2010)

Step 2 Introduction to the session

In this study period we learn the definitions of residence, ordinary residence and domicile and how these concepts affect an individual's income tax position.

We also learn how to calculate DTR, which reduces the tax liability where income is taxed in both the UK and overseas.

Finally we look at the provisions that apply to stop individuals attempting to avoid UK income tax by transferring their assets overseas.

Step 3 Guidance through the Study Text

Read through Chapter 8 of the Study Text after reading the following guidance:

Begin by looking back at Section 2.4 of Chapter 1 to refresh your memory on the UK tax implications of residence and domicile status.

Then read Sections 1 and 2 of Chapter 8. Highlight the key issues and terminology used in this area. It is possible that you will see an individual either leaving or coming to the UK in a question, so make sure you understand how residence, ordinary residence and domicile affect individuals in these situations. Work example 1 and see if you can reproduce the summary diagram in Section 2. Section 2.3 covers overseas income. Note the similarity of treatment in many cases to UK income. Also attempt example 2.

Then read Section 3 on the remittance basis whereby individuals who are not domiciled or not ordinarily resident in the UK may only be taxed in the UK on foreign income and gains remitted to the UK. The flowchart in section 3.7 is a useful summary of the rules. Attempt example 3.

Quickly read through Section 4 and note the impact of residency status on the availability of personal allowances.

Then read Section 5 on DTR. Focus on 'unilateral' relief in 5.3 and attempt Examples 4 and 5 to check that you have understood the topic.

Finally read through Section 6 on the anti-avoidance rules that apply when an individual tries to avoid UK tax by transferring their assets abroad to a non-UK resident trust or company. Do not waste time trying to learn the details. Instead locate the provisions in your legislation as you are reading through the section so that you can easily find them in the exam.

Step 4 Quick Quiz

Please attempt the quiz at the end of Study Text Chapter 8 to reinforce your understanding.

You may find it best to do this after a break, so that you can see what you remember and what you don't.

Step 5 Workbook Questions

Now attempt the ESQs 8.1 to 8.3 which will help to reinforce your knowledge of the topics covered in this study period and give you examples of the types of question you may see in the exam.

Study Period 9

National Insurance Contributions and PAYE

Medium Priority

Step 1 Exam Guidance

NICs are payable by employed and self employed earners. In addition, individuals who no longer have earned income can make voluntary NI contributions.

You will **only** be examined on NIC for employees in the Taxation of Individuals Awareness module.

So far we have considered the income tax and national insurance position of employees. You may be examined on the PAYE system which is used to collect income tax and NIC from employees.

NICs for an employee was tested in:

- Q8 (Sample Paper), Q8 (May 2009) and Q12 (May 2010)

Step 2 Introduction to the session

In this Study period we look at National insurance Contributions (NIC). You must be able to identify and calculate the different classes of NIC payable by an employee and his employer.

Look at the Institute's tax tables as you work through this chapter so that you know what information you will be given in the exam.

In this study period we also look at the PAYE system. You could be examined on both the employee and employer aspects of the system.

Step 3 Guidance through the Study Text

Read through Chapter 16 of the Study Text after reading the following guidance:

Read Sections 1 and 2 carefully and work through the example and illustrations. Look at the Institute's tax tables to see what NIC information you will be given in the exam.

Read Section 3 on Class 1A contributions which are **only** payable by employers on benefits provided to employees. Again, locate the information in the tax tables. Then try Example 2. In the exam, you may need to calculate the amount of the benefit and then the Class 1A liability.

Read Section 4 on Class 1B contributions which, again, are only payable by employers, this time on items included in a PAYE Settlement Agreement (PSA). Note the rate and the date the liability is due.

Read through Chapter 17 of the Study Text after reading the following guidance:

Read Section 1 for background information. Read Section 2 noting when PAYE is payable. Read Sections 3 and 4 noting the type of payments on which PAYE is applied. Quickly read Section 5 (especially Section 5.2 on PAYE code numbers. Try Examples 1 and 2). Read Section 6 noting the key forms and submission deadlines. Finally read Sections 7 to 12 (the most important are Sections 11.1 and 11.2 which you will deal with in detail in the next study period).

Step 4 Quick Quiz

Please attempt the quick quizzes at the end of Study Text Chapters 16 and 17 to reinforce your understanding.

You may find it best to do this after a break, so that you can see what you remember and what you don't.

Step 5 Workbook Questions

Now attempt ESQs 16.1 to 17.2 which will help to reinforce your knowledge of the topics covered in this study period and give you examples of the types of question you may see in the exam.

Administration of income tax

Medium Priority

Step 1 Exam Guidance

The administrative provisions are essential knowledge for the exam. They can form part of a question or could be an entire question.

Learning where to find the relevant provisions in your legislation is crucial. Do not waste time learning details that you can easily locate in your open book.

The administration of income tax was tested in:

- Q1 (Sample Paper), Q1 (May 2009), Q10 (Nov 2009) and Q10 (May 2010)

Step 2 Introduction to the session

In this study period our aim is to understand the administrative requirements of the income tax system. Chapter 15 of the Study Text covers the administration rules for both income tax and capital gains tax. You only need to focus on income tax in this period.

We look at the returns of income tax that must be made to HMRC, the due date for submission of these returns and the due date for the payment of tax due and HMRC's powers with regard to returns and payment of tax.

Step 3 Guidance through the Study Text

Read the relevant sections of Chapter 15 of the Study Text, after reading the following guidance:

Chapter 15 considers the administrative aspects of both income tax and capital gains tax (CGT). As you have not learnt CGT yet, only study the income tax aspects of this chapter at this stage. We will come back to CGT administration in a later study period.

Skim read Section 1 for background. Then read Section 2 carefully, noting the deadline for notifying HMRC of chargeability to income tax (and CGT). Locate the rules in your legislation so that you can easily find and refer to them in the exam.

Read Section 3. Note the deadlines for submitting tax returns in the legislation and the new rules for penalties for late filing of returns and the submission of incorrect returns.

Read Section 4 on the time limits for making claims for reliefs, with your legislation, highlighting the key areas.

All of Section 5 (*except* Section 5.5) is essential reading in this period. Highlight key income tax dates and ensure you understand how payments on account are calculated and reduced. Attempt Example 1 (you can leave Example 2 for now).

Read Sections 6 to 8 to understand the powers of HMRC to enquire into returns, the interest and penalty regime and the appeals system. Again, the legislation is your friend here so use it wisely.

Step 4 Quick Quiz

Please attempt questions 1 to 5 of the quiz at the end of Study Text Chapter 15 to reinforce your understanding.

You may find it best to do this after a break, so that you can see what you remember and what you don't.

Step 5 Workbook Questions

Now attempt the ESQs 15.1 to 15.2 and 15.4 and 15.5 which will help to reinforce your knowledge of the topics covered in this study period and give you examples of the types of question you may see in the exam.

Progress Test 1

In order to reinforce what you have learnt so far, answer the following questions. Try to answer them without referring to your Study Text or notes. The test should take you no longer than one hour and covers Study Periods 1-10. Solutions begin on page 29.

1 Ian received dividends of £2,700 in 2010/11. He also had other taxable income of £148,600.

Calculate the tax payable by Ian on his dividend income for 2010/11.

2 Elizabeth has a furnished property. She wants to know what she would have to do to make her property qualify as a furnished holiday let.

State the conditions that must be satisfied for a letting to be classified as a furnished holiday let.

3 Doug let a furnished property in 2010/11. His statement of rental income and expenses was as follows:

	£
Rental income	24,000
Less expenses:	
New kitchen	10,000
Buildings insurance	1,000
Lettings agents fees	1,000
Council tax	1,650

Doug claims the wear and tear allowance.

You are required to calculate Doug's taxable property income for 2010/11.

4 Dorian has the following income in 2010/11:

(a) Bank interest
(b) NS & I Savings Certificates interest
(c) NS & I Savings account interest
(d) Lottery winnings
(e) Employment income
(f) Gross rental income of £2,500 from letting out a room in his house
(g) Dividends from an Enterprise Investment Scheme (EIS) company
(h) Inheritance from great-aunt Maud

You are required to advise Dorian if each item is taxable and, if so, whether it receive net or gross.

5 James was employed by X plc. On 6 June 2010 his employer made available to James for private use a company car. The car has a list price of £30,000 and has a diesel engine and CO_2 emissions of 166g/km. James was also provided with private fuel for the car from 6 June 2010 onwards.

James paid his employer £10 per month towards the private use of the car.

Calculate James' taxable benefit for 2010/11 in respect of the car and car fuel.

6 Ruth received share options in her employer's unapproved share option scheme in 2010/11. The options received were as follows:

5,000 options granted to Ruth on 10 January 2011 at a cost of 50p per option. The market value of one share at 10 January 2011 was £2.

Ruth will exercise the options in March 2011 for a further cost of 50p per option. It is estimated that the market value of each share will have risen to £2.15 by March 2011.

Calculate the amount subject to income tax on the grant and exercise of the share options.

7 Albert is 40 years old and is paid a salary of £50,000 in 2010/11.

What is the maximum pension contribution he can pay into his personal pension scheme, on which tax relief will be available and how will he receive tax relief for these payments?

8 Roscoe is a client of yours and needs some advice. He files a paper self assessment income tax return and wants to know when this should be filed for the 2010/11 tax year. He would also like advice about when he should pay any tax due. In 2009/10 he had income tax payable by self assessment of £10,000. In 2010/11 he expects that once his tax return has been submitted the income tax due under self assessment will be approximately £15,000.

Advise Roscoe:

- **By what date his paper self assessment return for 2010/11 should be submitted to HMRC.**
- **The dates and amounts of tax payable both as payments on account and balancing payments for his 2010/11 self assessment tax liability.**

9 Ernie has the following employment income:

Salary of £50,000 per annum
Bonus of £55,000 paid in March 2011 in respect of the year ended 31 March 2010.
Bonus of £60,000 paid in March 2012 in respect of the year ended 31 March 2011.

Ernie is not a director and has no other sources of income.

You are required to calculate Ernie's income tax liability for 2010/11.

10 An individual is usually either resident or not resident in the UK for income tax purposes for a complete tax year.

You are required to set out the rules for determining an individual's residency position for income tax purposes and explain when it is possible to 'split' the tax year (ie be treated as UK resident for only part of the year) if the individual is leaving the UK.

11 Bertie is aged 55 and is employed by Bask Ltd. Bertie is paid a salary of £900 per week. He also receives annual private medical insurance under a company insurance scheme which costs the company £450 in December each year. On 31 December 2010 Bertie received a performance related bonus of £250.

You are required to calculate the national insurance payable by Bertie and Bask Ltd for 2010/11.

12 Ned earns £36,000 a year. His employer provides him with a company car, which produces a taxable benefit of £2,465. He pays for his own private petrol. His employer also provides private medical insurance which costs his employer £410.

Ned has underpaid tax from 2009/10 of £225.

You are required to calculate Ned's PAYE tax code for 2010/11.

You will find the answers to this test on page 29. If you answer more than 6 questions correctly, your performance is satisfactory; if you answer more than 8 correctly, you are doing well. Once you have reviewed how you have performed, go back over topics where you feel your understanding is poor.

Outline of CGT

Study Period 12

High Priority

Step 1 Exam Guidance

In the exam you must be able to identify transactions that require you to calculate a gain (or loss) for an individual and those that are exempt disposals.

The topics in this study period were not examined in isolation in the Sample Paper or recent exams.

Step 2 Introduction to the session

This study period covers the basic CGT knowledge that underpins any gains question in the exam.

We need to understand who pays CGT and on what?

In addition, we look at the overseas issues affecting the UK CGT liability. We have already considered the meaning of residence, ordinary residence and domicile in Study Period 8.

Step 3 Guidance through the Study Text

Read through Chapter 9 after reading the following guidance:

Read Section 1 for essential CGT background knowledge.

Then read through Section 2, which deals with chargeable and exempt persons, disposals and assets.

Quickly read Section 3 on the administration of CGT, noting the payment date for CGT. This will be dealt with in more detail later, in the 'Administration' Study Period.

Read Sections 4.1 and 4.2 on the impact of residence and domicile status on the chargeability of an individual to UK CGT on the disposal of UK and overseas assets. Read Sections 4.3 to 4.5 quickly and attempt Example 1 on double taxation relief. Finally, learn the rules in Section 4.6 for determining the location of assets for CGT purposes.

Step 4 Quick Quiz

Please attempt the quiz at the end of Study Text Chapter 9 to reinforce your understanding.

You may find it best to do this after a break, so that you can see what you remember and what you don't.

Step 5 Workbook Questions

Now attempt ESQ 9.1 which will help to reinforce your knowledge of the topics covered in this study period.

Study Period 13

High Priority

Computing CGT liability

Step 1 Exam Guidance

The calculation of capital gains tax, on a full or part disposal, is fundamental to your CGT studies.

Ensure that you can set out a basic gain computation quickly and accurately and that you understand which tax rate to use. You must also have a good grip of how capital losses can be used.

Various computational aspects are examinable such as:

- Part disposals
- Assets acquired before 31 March 1982
- Transfers between connected persons or husband and wife.

This topic was tested in Q9 & Q11 (Sample Paper),

Step 2 Introduction to the session

In this study period we learn how to calculate a capital gain and a capital loss in a number of circumstances.

We also learn how to calculate the CGT liability. This is highly examinable as the rules have recently changed.

This session introduces a number of computational aspects. It may take longer than any of your previous study periods, but do not rush as you must have a good grasp of all the topics covered.

Step 3 Guidance through the Study Text

Read through Chapter 10 after reading the following guidance:

Section 1 is fundamental to your study of CGT. Learn the proforma for calculating a capital gain. Attempt Example 1.

Read Sections 2 and 3 on calculating the CGT liability. This is essential knowledge. Attempt Examples 2 to 4 to ensure you have understood this topic.

Read Section 4 on capital losses. Do you understand how current year losses and brought forward losses can be set off differently? Do you understand how to utilise losses in the most tax efficient way? Attempt Examples 5 to 11. Then read through Section 5, which deals with assets acquired before 31 March 1982 and attempt Example 12. You can read through Section 6 on the valuation of assets quickly but make sure you try Examples 13 and 14.

Read Sections 7 and 8, which set out the rules for dealing with disposals between 'connected' persons and married couples or civil partners respectively and attempt Example 15. Then work carefully through Section 9 on part disposals. Can you calculate the cost to use? Try Examples 16 and 17. Finally you should read Section 10 on compensation (ie insurance proceeds) received for damaged and destroyed assets, attempting Examples 18 and 19.

Step 4 Quick Quiz

Please attempt the quiz at the end of Study Text Chapter 10 to reinforce your understanding.

You may find it best to do this after a break, so that you can see what you remember and what you don't.

Step 5 Workbook Questions

Now attempt ESQs 10.1 to 10.7 which will help to reinforce your knowledge of the topics covered in this study period and give you examples of the types of question you may see in the exam.

Study Period 14

Shares and securities

High Priority

Step 1 Exam Guidance

There are special rules for calculating gains on the sale of shares (which includes 'securities' for the purpose of this study guide).

Try and keep the concepts in this study period (such as 'paper for paper' treatment on a takeover of a company) clear in your head. A question can only be worth five marks so a question on shares should not be too complicated at the Awareness level.

Shares and securities were tested in:

– Q12 (Sample Paper), Q10 (May 2009), Q8 (Nov 2009) and Q11 (May 2010).

Step 2 Introduction to the session

In this study period we are now in a position to take the CGT computation further and look at the special rules that apply when there is a disposal of shares.

We need these special 'matching' rules for shares to help us identify which shares are actually being disposed of in a transaction. We build on these basic rules to understand the treatment of shares acquired via bonus issues, rights issues and takeovers. We also consider the implications of a company buying back their own shares.

Step 3 Guidance through the Study Text

Read through Chapter 11 of the Study text after reading the following guidance:

Read Section 1 for background and to understand why we need special rules for dealing with disposals of shares.

Read through Sections 2 and 3 carefully, attempting Examples 1 and 2 to test your understanding. At the end of these two sections you should be able to deal with a basic calculation of a capital gain (or loss) on the sale of shares. This computation forms the basis of all questions involving shares, so make sure you understand it before you move on.

Take your time with Section 4 on 'reorganisations'. The concepts in this section may be completely new to you. First work through Sections 4.1 and 4.2 and try Example 3 on bonus issues. Then read Section 4.3 and try Example 4 on rights issues, and Section 4.4 on capital distributions. Attempt Example 5. Only once you are happy with these sections should you move onto Section 4.5 on the re-organisation of shares and try Examples 6 and 7. Using your knowledge from this section, now read Section 4.6 on takeovers. Try Example 8. Then read Section 4.6.2 on the different ways to receive consideration on a share disposal. Try Example 9.

Only once you are happy with these rules should you move onto Section 5 on transactions involving gilts and QCBs and try Example 10. Now read quickly through Section 6 on the treatment of disposals by close companies and Section 7 on employee shares. Finally read through Section 8 on Purchase of own shares. Make sure you understand the conditions required for capital gains treatment and attempt Example 11.

Step 4 Quick Quiz

Please attempt the quiz at the end of Study Text Chapter 11 to reinforce your understanding.

You may find it best to do this after a break, so that you can see what you remember and what you don't.

Step 5 Workbook Questions

Now attempt ESQs 11.1 to 11.7 which will help to reinforce your knowledge of the topics covered in this study period and give you examples of the types of question you may see in the exam.

Study Period 15

Chattels and wasting assets

Medium Priority

Step 1 Exam Guidance

There are special rules for dealing with the disposal of chattels (broadly personal property) and 'wasting' assets, including leases.

You must understand and be able to use the terminology used in this chapter.

This topic was tested in the following exams:

– Q12 (May 2009) and Q11 (Nov 2009)

Step 2 Introduction to the session

In this study period we again build on our knowledge of the CGT computation and look at the special rules that apply for calculating a gain or loss on the disposal of certain assets.

The terminology can make the topic seem difficult but try to 'translate' what you are reading into language that you can understand (eg when you read the word 'chattel', try and think of the phrase 'personal property', when you see the word 'assignment' think of the word 'sale', and so on).

Step 3 Guidance through the Study Text

Read through Chapter 12 after reading the following guidance:

Read through Section 1 on chattels (personal property) and work through Examples 1 to 3. When dealing with a chattel disposal there is usually some restriction that applies to reduce the loss or the gain. Make sure you are comfortable with the calculations.

Quickly read Section 2.1 on the general treatment of wasting assets and try Example 4. Then carefully work through Section 2.2 on options (a particular type of wasting asset). Make sure you can deal with the grant, exercise (ie the purchase of the underlying asset) and disposal of an option. Attempt Examples 5 to 9.

Take your time working through Section 3 on leases. Do you understand the difference between assigning (ie the sale of) a lease and granting a lease (ie subletting)? Can you define a short and a long lease? Work through the five different scenarios and try Examples 10 to 14. The most effective way of learning the rules for leases is to attempt the questions, noting the different tax treatment in each scenario.

Step 4 Quick Quiz

Please attempt the quiz at the end of Study Text Chapter 12 to reinforce your understanding.

You may find it best to do this after a break, so that you can see what you remember and what you don't.

Step 5 Workbook Questions

Now attempt ESQs 12.1 to 12.8 which will help to reinforce your knowledge of the topics covered in this study period and give you examples of the types of question you may see in the exam.

Study Period 16

Principal private residence relief

Medium Priority

Step 1 Exam Guidance

Reliefs and exemptions are very important in any tax exam.

In the Taxation of Individuals Awareness module the main CGT exemptions and reliefs you may be tested on are Principal Private Residence (PPR) relief (including letting relief) and the Enterprise Investment Scheme (EIS) CGT reliefs. In this study period we focus on PPR relief, which can exempt the gain on the disposal of someone's home.

Questions will rarely focus on a property that is entirely exempt from tax. Instead you will probably need to consider a scenario where a property is only partly exempt because it has not been lived in by the owner throughout the ownership period.

PPR was tested in the following exams: Q10 (Sample paper), Q11 (May 2009) and Q7 (May 2010).

Step 2 Introduction to the session

In the last few study periods we have learnt how to calculate and tax chargeable gains. In this and the next study period we are introduced to some CGT reliefs that can be given to either exempt (or defer) CGT.

In this Study Period we look at PPR relief. The exemption itself is pretty straight forward. Our focus, therefore, is to identify situations when the exemption will only apply to part of the property or part of the period of ownership and how to deal with such a scenario.

Step 3 Guidance through the Study Text

Read through Chapter 13 of the Study Text after reading the following guidance:

Read carefully through Sections 1.1 to 1.3 which establishes the basic principles for when the relief applies. The rest of the Chapter relies on your understanding of these fundamental rules. Find the periods of 'deemed' occupation in your legislation so that you can easily find them in the exam. Attempt Example 1. Then quickly read Section 1.4.

Do not spend too much time on Section 2 which sets out the rules where an individual owns more than one residence. Just highlight key ideas in this section.

When a property is let out the full exemption is not available. This is covered in Section 3. Read this section carefully, making sure that you can identify when letting relief is available (ie when a property is let out and the period is not covered by a period of 'deemed' occupation) and the maximum relief available. Try Example 2 to check your understanding.

The full exemption is also not available is where there is some business use of a home. Attempt Example 3 in Section 4 to ensure you can deal with this scenario.

Step 4 Quick Quiz

Please attempt the quiz at the end of Study Text Chapter 13 to reinforce your understanding.

You may find it best to do this after a break, so that you can see what you remember and what you don't.

Step 5 Workbook Questions

Now attempt the ESQs 13.1 to 13.5 which will help to reinforce your knowledge of the topics covered in this study period and give you examples of the types of question you may see in the exam.

Other CGT reliefs

Study Period 17

High Priority

Step 1 Exam Guidance

The other CGT reliefs that you are examinable on are Entrepreneurs' relief, those connected with the Enterprise Investment Scheme (EIS) and gift relief.

You have already seen the EIS scheme in an earlier study period covering income tax relief on investments in EIS shares.

The CGT aspects of the EIS scheme were tested in Question 6 of the Sample Paper.

Entrepreneurs' relief is a new CGT relief available on certain business disposals after 6 April 2008. It is a valuable relief and is a high priority for your studies.

CGT reliefs were tested as follows:

- Q11 (Sample paper) and Q9 (May 2009).

Step 2 Introduction to the session

In this Study Period we conclude our study of CGT reliefs by looking at Entrepreneurs' relief, gift relief and EIS CGT reliefs.

There are two CGT EIS reliefs: an exemption on the disposal of EIS shares in certain circumstances, and a deferral of a gain arising from the disposal of **any** asset when the taxpayer subscribes for EIS shares.

Entrepreneurs' relief is specifically available for individuals who are withdrawing from a business. Gift relief applies to gifts of business assets or gifts where IHT is chargeable.

Step 3 Guidance through the Study Text

Read through Chapter 14 of the Study Text after reading the following guidance:

Read through Section 4 of Chapter 10 of the '**Taxation of Unincorporated Businesses**' section of the text on Entrepreneurs' relief. Ensure you understand the type of disposals to which the relief applies and how the relief is calculated.

Now turn back to Chapter 14 of the Taxation of Individuals section of the text.

Read through Section 2 carefully. Ensure you understand the implications of selling EIS shares at both a gain and a loss. Attempt Example 1.

Read through Sections 3.1 to 3.3 to understand the deferral relief that is available on the disposal of any asset if the gain is reinvested in EIS shares. Try Example 2 to ensure you understand the amount of relief available. Read through Sections 3.4 and 3.5 and locate the conditions for relief and the events when the deferred gain will crystallise in the relevant legislation.

Finally read through Section 4 on gift relief. Sections 4.2 and 4.3 explain the circumstances in which it is available. Try Example 3 to make sure you follow how gift relief works.

Step 4 Quick Quiz

Please attempt the quiz at the end of Study Text Chapter 14 to reinforce your understanding.

You may find it best to do this after a break, so that you can see what you remember and what you don't.

Step 5 Workbook Questions

Now attempt the ESQs 14.1 to 14.6 which will help to reinforce your knowledge of the topics covered in this study period and give you examples of the types of question you may see in the exam.

Study Period 18

Administration of CGT

Medium Priority

Step 1 Exam Guidance

The administrative provisions are essential knowledge for the exam. The main aspect of CGT administration that differs from income tax is the possibility of paying CGT in instalments.

CGT administration was tested in Question 1 of the May 2009 exam.

Step 2 Introduction to the session

We have already covered the administrative provisions for income tax in an earlier study period. In this study period our aim is to understand the administrative requirements for the capital gains tax system.

This study period is in some ways revision of our earlier study of income tax administration as many of the same rules apply to both income tax and CGT.

Step 3 Guidance through the Study Text

Read the relevant sections of Chapter 15 of the Study Text, after reading the following guidance:

This chapter considers the administration aspects of both income tax and CGT. You have already studied income tax in an earlier study period and, in most cases, the rules are identical. This period is mainly revision with emphasis on areas where the rules for income tax and CGT differ.

Read Sections 1 to 4 quickly. This should be revision for you as you have already read these sections.

Read Section 5 carefully, focusing on the payment date for CGT, contrasting this with the dates for income tax. You must understand how payments on account are calculated where there is both income tax and CGT due for a period. Try Example 2 to test your understanding. Read Section 5.5 carefully so that you can identify the situations when CGT can be paid by instalments.

Revise Sections 6 to 8 on the powers of HMRC to enquire into returns, the interest and penalty regime and the appeals system.

You have now completed your study of the **Taxation of Individuals Awareness** module.

Step 4 Quick Quiz

Please attempt question 6 of the quiz at the end of Study Text Chapter 15 to reinforce your understanding.

You may find it best to do this after a break, so that you can see what you remember and what you don't.

Step 5 Workbook Questions

Now attempt ESQs 15.3, 15.5, 15.6 and 15.7 which will help to reinforce your knowledge of the topics covered in this study period and give you examples of the types of question you may see in the exam.

Progress Test 2

In order to reinforce what you have learnt so far, answer the following questions. Try to answer them without referring to your Study Text or notes. The test should take you no longer than one hour and covers Study Periods 12-18. Solutions begin on page 33.

1 Sophie is UK resident but not UK domiciled.

State the basis on which she will be charged to UK capital gains tax on any capital gains she makes and whether she will be able to use her capital losses against other capital gains.

2 Martin was left a pair of paintings by his uncle. His uncle died in July 2004.

The probate value of the pair of paintings was £100,000.

Martin sold one of the paintings to a dealer in May 2010 for £75,000. The value of the remaining painting at that date was £50,000.

Calculate, showing all your workings, the gain on sale.

3 Brian sold some shares in a quoted company on 1 July 2010, realising a gain of £25,000. He made no other disposals in 2010/11 and had taxable income of £35,000.

Calculate Brian's capital gains tax liability for 2010/11 and state when it is payable.

4 Katy sold an asset for £95,000 on 1 January 2011. She originally bought the asset on 10 October 2000 for £50,000. She sold another asset in December 2010 on which she made a capital loss of £30,000. She had capital losses brought forward from 2009/10 of £20,000.

Calculate Katy's taxable gain for 2010/11.

5 William bought a commercial building to use in his trade on 21 January 1981 for £15,000. By 31 March 1982 the asset was worth £50,000. He spent £7,500 on capital improvements to the building in June 2001.

William ceased to trade in October 2010 and sold the building to his sister on 25 October 2010 for £250,000, when the building was worth £350,000 on the open market.

He made no other disposals during the year and had taxable income of £100,000.

Calculate William's capital gains tax liability for 2010/11 assuming he claims entrepreneurs' relief but not gift relief.

6 Mary bought a plot of land for £30,000 in May 1999. In June 2008 she sold half the land for £50,000, when the remaining half of the land was worth £30,000. In May 2010 she sold the remaining half of the land for £95,000.

Mary has sold no other assets in 2010/11 and has taxable income of £80,000.

Calculate Mary's capital gains tax liability for 2010/11.

7 Amy had the following transactions in the shares of X plc:

Date		*No of shares*	*Cost/Disposal proceeds*
			£
10/1/99	Bought	5,000	5,000
12/6/02	Bonus issue (1 for 2)	2,500	Nil
15/8/10	Sold	4,500	22,500
20/8/10	Bought	1,000	3,000

Calculate Amy's chargeable gain on the sale of X plc shares in 2010/11.

8 Jamie owned 10,000 shares in Twizzler plc. He had bought the shares for £3 each in June 2002.

In January 2011 the board of Twizzler plc agreed to a takeover by Turkey plc. Twizzler plc shareholders were to receive £5 cash and 2 ordinary shares in Turkey plc for every 5 shares in Twizzler plc. Turkey plc shares were worth £10 each immediately after the takeover.

Calculate the amount of capital gain that will be chargeable on Jamie on the takeover and the base cost of the Turkey plc shares for any future share disposal.

9 Gordon sold the following assets in 2010/11:

(a) In January 2011 he sold a racehorse for £35,000. He had bought the racehorse as a foal for £10,000 in July 2005.

(b) In February 2011 he sold a painting for £4,500. He had bought the painting for £9,000 in August 2003.

(c) In March 2011 he sold an antique chest of drawers for £8,500. They had cost him £5,500 in August 2006.

Calculate the amount of capital gain or loss arising from each of the above disposals.

10 Ainsley bought his main residence on 1 March 2003 for £200,000. He lived in the house for the first three years and then on 1 March 2006, Ainsley moved abroad to take up a new job. He came back to the UK in March 2007, but chose to return home to live with his mum rather than re-occupy the house. The property was empty throughout his absence. He never returned to live in the house and sold the house on 1 December 2010 for £500,000.

Calculate Ainsley's gain on the sale of his house, after claiming principal private residence relief.

11 The following individuals subscribed for shares in qualifying EIS companies. They each claimed the maximum available income tax relief:

Gary: Subscribed for £80,000 shares in Kelly Ltd in May 2009. He disposed of the shares in October 2010 for £60,000.

Helen: Subscribed for £50,000 shares in Napier Ltd in May 2006. She disposed of the shares in June 2010 for £70,000.

Mary: Subscribed for £60,000 shares in Collingwood Ltd in April 2009. She disposed of the shares in May 2010 for £90,000.

You are required to set out, with explanations, the capital gains tax position of each of the above disposals.

12 On 1 June 2010 Carl sold a factory for £3,100,000 which he had acquired in May 1983 for £150,000. He had used the factory in his unincorporated business until he ceased to trade on 1 May 2008.

On 1 June 2008 Carl commenced employment with Richmond Ltd. He acquired a 20% shareholding in the company on 1 July 2008 for £80,000. On 1 July 2010 he gave half of his shares to his daughter when they were worth £100,000. A gift relief election will not be made.

Carl has made no other disposals in 2010/11 and has taxable income of £50,000.

You are required to calculate Carl's capital gains tax liability for 2010/11 assuming he makes any beneficial claims (apart from gift relief).

You will find the answers to this test begin on page 33. If you answer more than 6 questions correctly, your performance is satisfactory; if you answer more than 8 correctly, you are doing well. Once you have reviewed how you have performed, go back over topics where you feel your understanding is poor.

Progress Test 1

1 Ian

Tax payable on dividend income 2010/11:

Dividends taxed as the top slice of his income. Tax bands remaining for the dividend income = £ 1,400 of higher rate band (£150,000 - £148,600).

Dividends taxable £2,700 x 100/90 = £3,000

	£
Taxable in higher rate band 1,400 × 32.5%	455
Balance at additional rate 1,600 × 42.5%	680
Total tax due	1,135
Less: tax credit	(300)
Tax payable	835

2 The conditions to be satisfied for a letting to be classified as a furnished holiday let are:

(a) The property must be furnished and situated in the UK or the European Economic Area.

(b) The letting must be on a commercial basis with a view to a profit.

(c) The property must be available for commercial letting to the public for not less than 140 days in a year and actually let for at least 70 days in that period.

(d) Not more than 155 days may fall during periods of longer term occupation. Longer term occupation is a continuous period of more than 31 days during which the accommodation is in the same occupation.

3

	£
Rental income	24,000
Less: expenses	
Buildings insurance	(1,000)
Letting agents fees	(1,000)
Council tax	(1,650)
	20,350
Less: wear & tear allowance	
10% × £(24,000 – 1,650)	(2,235)
Property income 2010/11	18,115

The expenditure on the new kitchen was capital in nature and so not deductible from the property income.

4 Dorian

(a)	Bank interest	Taxable – received net of 20% tax
(b)	NS & I Savings Certificates interest	Exempt
(c)	NS & I Savings account interest	Taxable – received gross
(d)	Lottery winnings	Exempt
(e)	Employment income	Taxable – tax deducted via PAYE system
(f)	Gross rental income of £2,500 from letting out a room in his house	Exempt as gross rental income is less than the rent-a-room limit of £4,250 unless elect to ignore the rent-a-room exemption when income less expenses would be taxable –rental income received gross
(g)	Dividends from an Enterprise Investment Scheme (EIS) company	Taxable – received net of 10% non-refundable tax credit
(h)	Inheritance from great-aunt Maud	Exempt

5 James

Car benefit percentage 15% + (165 – 130/5) = 22% + 3% diesel supplement = 25%.

Note. CO_2 emissions rounded down to 165g/km

	£
Car benefit (30,000 x 25% x 10/12)	6,250
Less Contributions by James (£10 x 10 months)	(100)
	6,150
Fuel benefit (£18,000 x 25% x 10/12)	3,750
	9,900

6 As this is an unapproved share option scheme there will be a charge to tax once the share options are exercised. (There will be no charge to tax on grant of the options).

	£
Market value of shares at exercise (5,000 x £2.15)	10,750
Less: price paid at grant (5,000 x 50p)	(2,500)
Less: price paid at exercise (5,000 x 50p)	(2,500)
Amount liable to income tax	5,750

7 Albert can pay into his personal pension scheme up to 100% of his relevant earnings for 2010/11. This would mean he could make contributions of up to £50,000 in 2010/11. This is below the annual allowance of £255,000.

Contributions to personal pension schemes are made net of basic rate tax and the pension scheme will recover the basic rate tax from HMRC. So, for every £80 contributed to a personal pension scheme a further £20 will be contributed by the Government.

For higher rate taxpayers like Albert, the basic rate tax band is extended by the amount of the gross pension contribution made to ensure that they also receive higher rate relief for their contributions.

8 Roscoe should:

Submit his paper self assessment return by 31 October 2011

The tax due will be as follows:

Payments on account:

(a) 31/1/11 50% x 2009/10 liability £5,000
(b) 31/7/11 50% x 2009/10 liability £5,000

Balancing payment £15,000 – less payments on account = £5,000 due 31 January 2012

9 Ernie

Ernie's employment income is taxed on the receipts basis:

	£
Salary	50,000
Bonus (received in 2010/11)	55,000
Total	105,000
Less: PA (£6,475 – ½ x (£105,000 - £100,000))	(3,975)
Taxable income	101,025
Tax:	
£37,400 @ 20%	7,480
£63,625 @ 40%	25,450
Tax liability	32,930

10 Residency

For an individual to be treated as resident in the UK they must either:

(a) Be present in the UK for at least 183 days (ie more than half the year), or
(b) Make visits totalling more than 91 days on average over a four year period.

However, the number of days that an individual is present in the UK is only one of the factors taken into account when deciding his residence status. If he is present in the UK for less than 91 days, other factors that might also make an individual resident include location of family and property, and business and social ties in the UK.

It is possible to 'split' the tax year if the individual leaves the UK part way through the year and is caught by the above rules, but:

(a) They intend to leave the UK permanently, or
(b) They are leaving to take up full time employment abroad for a period that covers a complete tax year.

11 Bertie – NIC 2010/11

Class 1 earnings: £900 per week for 51 weeks
£1,150 for 1 week

Class 1A benefits: Medical insurance £450

	£
Bertie - Class 1 NIC primary	
(£844 – £110) × 11% × 52	4,198
(£900 – £844) × 1% × 51	29
(£1,150 – £844) × 1% × 1	3
	4,230
Bask Ltd	
Class 1 NIC secondary	
(£900 – £110) × 12.8% × 51	5,157
(£1,150 – £110) × 12.8% × 1	133
	5,290
Class 1A	
£450 × 12.8%	58
	5,348

12 Ned - Tax code 2010/11

	£	£
Basic personal allowance		6,475
Less: deductions for		
Company car	2,465	
PMI	410	
Underpaid tax (W2)	1,125	(4,000)
Available allowances		2,475

Ned's PAYE code is 247L

Working

Underpaid tax

Ned is a basic rate taxpayer so his underpaid tax must be grossed up by 20%

£225 × 100/20 = £1,125

Progress Test 2

1 Sophie

Sophie will be charged to tax on the disposal of assets situated in the UK. In respect of the disposal of assets situated overseas she can claim to only be charged to tax to the extent that the gains are remitted to the UK.

If Sophie does not claim the remittance basis she will get full relief for her capital losses (including losses realised on assets situated overseas). If Sophie claims the remittance basis she will not get relief for losses realised on assets situated overseas unless she irrevocably elects into a regime which allows relief for foreign capital losses in any years where she chooses to be taxed on an arising basis.

2 Martin

	£
Proceeds	75,000
Less: cost	
$\frac{75,000}{75,000 + 50,000} \times £100,000$	(60,000)
Gain	15,000

3 Brian

	£
Gain	25,000
Less: annual exempt amount	(10,100)
	14,900
Capital gains tax payable: Basic rate band remaining £37,400 - £35,000 = £2,400	
Capital gains tax @ 18%: £2,400 x 18%	432
Capital gains tax @ 28%: £14,900 - £2,400 = £12,500 x 28%	3,500
	3,932

Payable: 31 January 2012.

4 Katy

	£
Asset 1:	
Sale proceeds	95,000
Less: cost	(50,000)
Gain	45,000
Current year loss	(30,000)
Losses b/fwd (restricted to preserve AE)	(4,900)
	10,100
Annual exempt amount	(10,100)
Taxable gain	-

5 William

	£
Sale proceeds (deemed = MV)	350,000
Less: MV'82	(50,000)
Less: enhancement expenditure	(7,500)
	292,500
Annual exempt amount	(10,100)
Taxable gain	282,400
CGT @ 10% (qualifies for entrepreneurs' relief) (£282,400 × 10%)	28,240

6 Mary

	£
Sale proceeds	95,000
Less cost (W1)	(11,250)
Gain	83,750
Less: annual exempt amount	(10,100)
Taxable gain	73,650
CGT liability @ 18% (sold pre 23 June 2010)	£13,257

Working

Cost used on first sale in June 2008

£30,000 x 50,000/(30,000 + 50,000) = £18,750

Cost remaining for second sale = £11,250 (£30,000 - £18,750)

7 Amy

(1) Purchase in next 30 days

	£
Sale proceeds 1,000/4,500 × £22,500	5,000
Less: cost	(3,000)
Gain	2,000
Sale proceeds 3,500/4,500 × £22,500	17,500
Less Cost (W)	(2,333)
Gain	15,167
Total gains	17,167

Working

Share pool:

Date	*No*	*Cost* £
10/1/99	5,000	5,000
12/6/02	2,500	Nil
	7,500	5,000
Sale		
15/8/10 3,500/7,500 × 5,000	(3,500)	(2,333)
	4,000	2,667

8 Gain chargeable on takeover:

	£
Consideration for takeover	
Cash £5 × 10,000/5	10,000
Shares £10 × 2 × 10,000/5	40,000
	50,000

Gain chargeable immediately = gain relating to cash

Sale proceeds	10,000
Less cost: 30,000 × 10/50	(6,000)
	4,000
Base cost of Turkey plc shares:	
Cost of Twizzler plc shares	30,000
Less used vs cash consideration	(6,000)
Cost left for shares	24,000

9 Gordon:

(a) Sale of racehorse exempt as wasting chattel.

(b) Sale of painting:

	£
Proceeds – deemed	6,000
Less cost	(9,000)
Restricted capital loss	(3,000)

(c) Sale of antique chest of drawers:

Sale proceeds	8,500
Less cost	(5,500)
	3,000

Restricted to a maximum of 5/3 £8,500 - £6,000 = £4,167

Gain therefore £3,000

10 Ainsley

	£
Sale proceeds	500,000
Less: cost	(200,000)
Gain	300,000
Less PPR (W)	
300,000 × 72/93	(232,258)
	67,742

Working

Period of ownership

1/3/03 – 1/12/10 = 7 years 9 months (93 months)

Period of actual and deemed occupation:

Actual:
1/3/03 – 1/3/06 = 3 years (36 months)

Deemed:
Last 36 months:

1/12/07 – 1/12/10 = 36 months

The period from 1/3/06 to 1/12/07 cannot be treated as deemed occupation, as, although Ainsley went abroad for his employment, he never re-occupied the property, even though he could have done. There is no letting relief as the property was never let.

11 *Gary*

Disposed of shares within 3 years realising a capital loss of £20,000 (£60,000 - £80,000). The loss is an allowable loss for CGT purposes but is reduced by the amount of EIS income tax relief given and not withdrawn.

Income tax relief given 2009/10: £80,000 × 20% = £16,000

Income tax relief withdrawn £60,000 × 20% = £12,000

Allowable loss is therefore:

	£	£
Proceeds		60,000
Cost	80,000	
less IT relief not withdrawn (16,000 – 12,000)	(4,000)	
		(76,000)
Allowable loss		(16,000)

Helen

No income tax relief withdrawn as sold more than 3 years after acquisition.

Gain on disposal is exempt.

Mary

Normal capital gains computation as shares sold within three years. All of the income tax relief is withdrawn.

Capital gain:	£
Proceeds	90,000
Cost	(60,000)
	30,000

12 Carl – Capital gains computation 2010/11

	Pre 23.6.10	Post 22.6.10
	£	£
Factory:		
Proceeds	3,100,000	
Cost	(150,000)	
Gain	2,950,000	
Less Entrepreneurs' relief (Max £2,000,000 × 4/9	(888,889)	
	2,061,111	
Shares:		
Proceeds (Deemed MV)		100,000
Cost (£80,000 × 50%)		(40,000)
Gain (qualifies for entrepreneurs' relief, max £5 million less £2 million above)		60,000
Less: Annual exempt amount (note)	(10,100)	
Taxable gain	2,051,011	60,000
CGT @ 18%/10%	369,182	6,000
Total CGT	375,182	

Note. The annual exempt amount is set off against the gain arising on the factory as this is taxed at 18% whereas the gain on the shares is only taxed at 10%.

Exam style questions

1.1 Roger (aged 69) is married to Vicky (aged 76) and is registered blind.

Roger's net income for 2010/11 was £23,980, made up of rental income (£16,980) and bank interest (£7,000). Vicky's only income is her pension of £4,500.

You are required to calculate Roger and Vicky's allowances and tax reductions for 2010/11. Also give brief advice on how they could improve their joint tax position.

1.2 Charles earned £119,500 from his employment in 2010/11. He paid tax of £36,800 under PAYE.

In 2009 he took out a personal loan of £6,250 to buy a laptop and printer which he uses only for work purposes. He is paying interest at a rate of 6% per annum on this loan.

He paid £12,000 (net) to Oxfam via Gift Aid in the year.

You are required to calculate his income tax payable/repayable for 2010/11.

1.3 George, a 76-year-old retired journalist, received the following income during the year ended 5 April 2011:

	£
Income from writing and lecturing	7,700
Net income distributed from his grandfather's discretionary trust	1,375
Interest on an ISA	800

George entered into a civil partnership with Paul on 1 March 2011. Paul is 63 years old and has net income of £5,000.

You are required to calculate George's income tax payable/repayable for 2010/11.

1.4 Julie had the following income during 2010/11:

	£	
Earnings	34,000	(PAYE deducted £7,200)
Lottery winnings	10,000	
Legacy from late grandfather	15,000	

In July 2007 she had gifted some shares in a UK company to her daughters, Philippa (age 19) and Jessica (age 17). The daughters each received a dividend of £1,800 in 2010/11.

On 8 September 2010, Julie subscribed £20,000 for shares in Brack Ltd, a company qualifying under the Enterprise Investment Scheme.

You are require to calculate Julie's income tax payable/repayable for 2010/11 and explain the income tax treatment of the dividend income received by her daughters.

1.5 **You are required to explain how income tax relief (if at all) is given for the following payments made by an individual in 2010/11:**

(a) **A gift of shares in ICI plc, valued at £10,000, to Oxfam.**

(b) **Interest payable at 4% per annum on a loan taken out in August 2003 to buy printing machinery used within a partnership.**

(c) **Non-trade related patent royalties paid of £1,560.**

(d) **A gift of £2,000 cash to NSPCC, a registered charity.**

(e) **Maintenance payments from a 35 year old man to his ex-wife aged 33.**

2.1 Mr Fairbanks took early retirement in 2005 when he was 55. He now works part-time. In 2010/11 his gross earnings were £6,000 and he paid tax under PAYE of £250. He received £900 in dividends and £800 of building society interest. He received interest on his Midwest Savings Bank account totalling £80.

You are required to calculate his income tax payable/repayable.

2.2 Jonty, aged 38, is a married man whose wife has no income. The following information is relevant for the year ended 5 April 2011:

(1) His salary was £45,000 (PAYE deducted £7,400)

(2) His other income was:

	£
Building society interest received	80
Dividends received	63

(3) In March 2011 Jonty closed down his NS&I investment account which he had kept for many years. Interest of £142 was credited.

(4) He made a donation of £396 to Oxfam in May 2010 under Gift Aid.

(5) Jonty won £100 on the Grand National.

You are required to compute the income tax payable by Jonty for 2010/11.

2.3 Archie (76) is married to Belinda (61). Archie received the following income in 2010/11:

	£
Rental income	23,900
Building society interest	4,400
UK Treasury Stock interest	290

Belinda has no income.

You are required to calculate Archie's income tax payable for 2010/11.

2.4 Fiona, who is 35, lives on her own. She has been running her own business for many years. Her taxable trading profits for 2010/11 are £138,000.

During 2010/11 she received the following investment income:

	£
UK dividends	8,000
Bank interest held with a Jersey bank (gross amount)	4,300
Premium bond winnings	13,000

Fiona borrowed £24,000 in March 2009 to invest in shares in a close company. She pays interest at 4% per annum. She repaid £10,000 of the loan when she received her Premium Bond winnings on 5 December 2010.

She makes an annual donation to charity of £1,600 under the Gift Aid scheme.

You are required to calculate Fiona's income tax payable for 2010/11.

2.5 Mildred, who is aged 76, has the following income for 2010/11:

	£
State pension	11,047
Interest from bank account in Guernsey (gross amount)	13,450

Mildred also owns 1,200 shares in Bassett Ltd. The company paid a dividend of 60p per share on 15 May 2010 in respect of the year ended 31 December 2009. Shareholders were offered the option to take shares in lieu of the dividend, valued at £6.50 per share, at a rate of one share for every 10 held. Mildred chose to take the stock dividend.

Mildred pays £500 each year to the NSPCC (a registered charity) under Gift Aid.

You are required to calculate Mildred's income tax payable/repayable for 2010/11.

2.6 On 15 November 2008, Tennyson Ltd, a close company, made a loan at commercial interest rates of £80,000 to Sylvia who owns 30% of the shares in Tennyson Ltd. The company has a 31 December year end.

On 20 October 2010 the company wrote off the entire loan.

You are required to explain the consequences of the loan and subsequent waiver for the company and Sylvia. You should assume that Sylvia has annual taxable income of £50,000.

2.7 Petra works one day a week at her local internet café. She earned £2,080 during the 2010/11 tax year. No tax was deducted via PAYE.

She can afford to work so little as she has a large investment portfolio that she inherited on the death of her grandmother four years ago.

During 2010/11 she received the following income from the portfolio:

	£
Dividends	49,500
Treasury stock interest (gross)	54,650
Bank interest (net)	1,300
NS&I account interest	600
NS&I Certificate interest	900

Petra donated £10,000 via gift aid to the NSPCC.

You are required to calculate Petra's income tax payable for 2010/11

3.1 Ben owns a house which he lets out furnished to earn extra income. He purchased this with the aid of an interest only mortgage of £60,000 at 7%.

In 2010/11 the property was let for the whole year at a rate of £1,500 per month (although he only received rental income of £16,500 as one month was paid late).

He incurred the following expenses

	£
Agent's fee (6 April 2010 – 5 April 2011)	1,800
Water rates	120
Cost of building new porch	2,500
Insurance	500

You are required to calculate Ben's taxable property income and explain the alternative ways in which tax relief may be obtained for the cost of furnishing the property.

3.2 Lizzie is employed by a firm of accountants, earning a salary of £45,000 per annum. She recently bought a cottage in Devon which she intends to let out to visitors to the area at a rate of £500 a week. Lizzie expects to let the property out through the period from April to October each year, with new tenants in occupation every 2 to 3 weeks. She has spent around £10,000 on furnishing the cottage.

You are required to explain how you would determine whether the cottage will be treated as a 'Furnished Holiday Letting' for income tax purposes.

Assuming that it does satisfy the 'Furnished Holiday Letting' definition, you are required to explain:

(a) How relief for the expenditure on furnishings would be given.
(b) How relief would be given if Lizzie makes a loss on the letting in 2010/11.

3.3 Randall owns three properties which are let on the following terms, all rents being payable quarterly in advance on (31 March, 30 June, 30 September and 31 December). Randall is responsible for repairs on all properties; the rents on properties A, B and C are full rents.

A Let at £620 a year on a 20 year lease which commenced in 1988.

B Let at £348 a year on a lease which expired on 30 September 2010, then empty until 31 December 2010 when let at £440 a year.

C Let at £100 a year throughout the year.

Expenditure by Randall on these properties in the year was as follows:

	A	*B*	*C*
	£	£	£
Agent's commission	20		
Advertising for tenants		76	
Repairs: while let	142		119
while empty		255	

You are required to calculate the property income assessment for Randall for 2010/11.

3.4 Sebastian owns two properties:

A 5 Arnhem Avenue
B 27 Cannae Road.

Both are let out unfurnished.

A This was let until 24 June 2010 at an annual rental of £2,400. On 29 September 2010, it was let out to a new tenant on a 10-year lease agreement. The annual rental is £1,600. The tenant paid a premium of £5,000 on 29 September 2010.

B This was let from 24 June 2010 at an annual rental of £600.

All the rents are payable quarterly in advance on the normal quarter days and are sufficient to cover the landlord's outgoings.

Property A was acquired in 1981; property B was purchased on 15 April 2010.

Expenditure in connection with the properties was as follows:.

	A	*B*
	£	£
Agent's commission: 1 May 2010	25	10
1 November 2010	25	10
Repairs (note)	–	1,800
Advertising for new tenants 10 July 2010	50	–

Note. The repairs in respect of property C are analysed as follows:

	£
Installation of new kitchen equipment	300
Retiling part of the roof after damage in May 2010	1,500
	1,800

You are required to compute Sebastian's property income assessment for 2010/11.

3.5 On 1 October 2000, Adam granted a lease over a building to Brian for a period of 30 years at a premium of £20,000. On 1 October 2010 Brian granted a 5 year sublease to Claire, who paid a premium of £8,000.

You are required to calculate Brian's property income assessment in 2010/11 in respect of the premium received.

3.6 Judy begins to let out a room in her home to a lodger with effect from 1 April 2010, at a rate of £600 per month payable in advance.

She has calculated that in 2010/11 the following expenditure may be attributed to the room which is let out:

	£
Electricity	1,200
Gas	1,400
Cost of new furnishings	2,000

You are required to explain (with supporting calculations):

(a) **The alternative bases under which Judy's property income may be assessed; and**

(b) **The time limit for any election which she should make in order to achieve the more favourable basis in 2010/11, and the impact of this election on future tax years.**

3.7 Seraphina bought a warehouse on 1 June 2010 for £685,000. She took out a loan for 50% of the cost, paying annual interest at 5.25%.

On 1 July 2010 she granted a 15 year lease over the building to Jet Ltd for a one off premium of £50,000, and an annual rent of £42,000, paid monthly in advance.

Although the property could have been rented out immediately, Seraphina spent £7,895 on repairs before Jet Ltd took occupation in July.

Seraphina also paid a management company 15% of the monthly rent. Jet Ltd paid all other expenses in connection with the property.

You are required to calculate Seraphina's property income assessment for 2010/11.

4.1 Patricia Jones had the following income during 2010/11:

	£
Earnings from employment	95,000 (PAYE £27,000)
Interest on NS&I Saving Certificates	3,700
Dividends from Black Ltd (a qualifying EIS company)	3,000 (net)

Patricia subscribed £20,000 for ordinary shares in Blanche Ltd in November 2010 and £30,000 for ordinary shares in Rouge Plc (an AIM listed company) in May 2011. Both companies qualify under the Enterprise Investment Scheme.

You are required to calculate Patricia's 2010/11 income tax payable or repayable assuming that she makes any necessary elections to claim the maximum possible EIS relief in 2010/11.

4.2 Madeleine, aged 45, is interested in investing in an ISA in 2010/11.

You are required to advise on the following:

(a) **The types of investment available and maximum subscriptions;**
(b) **The tax treatments of income and gains within the ISA;**
(c) **Any requirements regarding the individual investor.**

4.3 Maggie is a higher rate taxpayer.

During 2010/11 she invested the maximum possible into an ISA share account.

She also subscribed for 25,000 shares in LiteHead Ltd, an unquoted trading company run by her friend, Lucy, for £25,000. LiteHead Ltd is a very small company with only 10 employees and gross assets of £500,000.

On 1 October 2011 Maggie withdrew half of the funds from her ISA, which had increased in value by £450, and sold half of her shares in LiteHead Ltd to a third party for their market value of £4.50 a share.

You are required to calculate Maggie's total chargeable gains for 2010/11 in respect of these two transactions.

5.1 Penny, a full time employee, was made redundant by her employer in June 2010. She received the following redundancy package:

	£
Statutory redundancy pay	3,800
Non-contractual ex gratia cash payment	45,000
Market value of company car – ownership transferred to Penny	12,000
Outplacement counselling	4,500

Penny spent 10 years out of her 30 years' service with the company working abroad, her last 2 years of service being spent in the UK.

You are required to calculate what amount will be taxable on Penny in 2010/11.

5.2 In 2010/11 Jim, a director of a wine importing company, is paid a salary of £10,000 and is given the use of a new 2-litre car with a list price of £16,000 and an emission rate of 195g/km, plus wine costing £1,000. Jim's 20-year old student daughter, Jane, also works for the company on Saturdays, is paid £15 per day and has the use of a new 1,150cc car with a list price of £12,000 and an emission rate of 158g/km. Jim uses £600 of the wine promoting the company's products. Private petrol is paid for by the company in respect of Jim's car but not his daughter's.

You are required to calculate Jim's taxable earnings for 2010/11.

5.3 Mr Thomas is a director of a private company; his remuneration for 2010/11 was £30,000.

During the year ended 5 April 2011, the following benefits were provided to him:

Accommodation in a four bedroom house, owned by the company.

	£
Original cost 1996	80,000
Cost of extension 2000	25,000
Annual value	750

Mr Thomas moved in on 1 March 2005, at which time the house was valued at £125,000. He pays a nominal rent of £1,200 per annum for use of the house.

Expenses paid directly by company in 2010/11:	£
Council tax	1,400
Electricity	750
Gas	250
Telephone	350
Redecoration (internal)	700
Gardener	1,500

You are required to calculate Mr Thomas's earnings for 2010/11. Assume that the official rate of interest charged throughout 2010/11 was 4%.

5.4 Raymond received the following benefits from his employer as part of his remuneration package in 2010/11:

(1) Interest-free loan for a non-qualifying purpose – first advance 6 June 2010

		£
6.6.10	advance	10,000
6.8.10	advance	5,000
6.12.10	repaid	7,500
6.2.11	advance	4,000
6.3.11	repaid	2,500

(2) Car

- Mercedes, list price £21,500, purchased 1 June 2007. The emission rate is 145g/km.
- 1,600 cc Escort, list price £10,000, purchased 5 August 2010, used by Raymond. The emission rate is 160g/km.

No petrol was provided for either vehicle.

You are required to calculate the benefits assessable on Raymond for 2010/11.

Assume that the official rate of interest charged throughout 2010/11 was 4%.

5.5 You have been consulted by Alf, one of the directors of your company, who has no shareholding in the company, concerning the taxability of emoluments and benefits received. The following information is provided for the tax year 2010/11.

(1) Alf's salary is £32,600 (PAYE £5,755).

(2) An expenses allowance of £2,500 for 2010/11 spent as follows:

	£
Business travelling	1,800
Entertainment:	
Overseas customers	400
Overseas suppliers	100
United Kingdom customers	200

(3) Benefits for the year were as follows:

(i) The company purchased hi-fi equipment for Alf's personal use at a cost of £800. The company retained ownership of the equipment.

(ii) Alf had exclusive use of a new petrol engined car with a list price of £15,000. The emission rate is 100g/km. No petrol was provided for private motoring.

(iii) Medical insurance was provided for £300. Alf would have had to pay £450 to take out the insurance personally.

(iv) Alf visited Saville Row for 5 tailored shirts, which cost the company £400.

You are required to calculate Alf's earnings for 2010/11, giving brief explanatory notes on the treatment of his benefits and expenses.

5.6 Mr Bjork is chairman and chief executive of Peepop Ltd.

He receives a salary of £46,000 per annum and during the income tax year 2010/11 he was provided with the following benefits:

The company provided him with the use of a 2,100 cc petrol Jaguar motor car with a list price of £20,000 from 6 April 2010. The emission rate is 215g/km.

On 31 July 2010 he was involved in a serious road accident and the car was written off.

While he had use of the Jaguar, he contributed 50% of the cost of his private fuel.

When he resumed work on 1 October 2010, he was provided with a Mercedes car with a list price of £30,000 and the use of a chauffeur. This car is used solely for business purposes. The emission rate is 185g/km.

He was given a computer by Peepop Ltd on 6 October 2010, when it had a market value of £200. He had use of that computer since 6 October 2008 when its market value was £6,000.

You are required to compute the total amount of benefits assessable on Mr Bjork for 2010/11.

5.7 Giles has worked for HiTech Computers Plc for many years and he has recently been promoted to sales manager, receiving a £5,000 pay rise from 1 July 2010. His revised salary is £36,000. He has continued to pay contributions into the company's registered occupational pension scheme of 5% of his salary and bonus. He has received sales commission as follows:

Year ended 31 December 2009	£3,000 received 28 February 2010
Year ended 31 December 2010	£4,000 received 28 February 2011

As a result of his promotion, he has been provided with a flat in London, due to being required to spend increasing amounts of time in London. The company pays £5,000 annual rent on the property, which has an annual value of £2,400. He is required to contribute £100 per month towards this.

Giles also receives £100 per month payment towards the provision of crèche facilities for his child who attends a private nursery.

You are required to calculate Giles's taxable earnings for 2010/11.

5.8 Arnold has a salary of £30,000. He drives his own car to work, taking his two year old daughter to crèche on the way. Arnold's employer pays the cost of the crèche which is £200 per week. Arnold is provided with a designated parking space at his employer's premises. This costs his employer £1,000 pa. Sometimes Arnold has to drive to clients and his employer reimburses him for his business mileage at 60p per mile.

In 2010/11 Arnold did 5,000 business miles.

Arnold incurred the following expenses in 2010/11:

- a subscription of £250 to his local golf club, where he sometimes plays with clients.
- a subscription of £800 to a club in London where he stays when his work necessitates an overnight stay in London.

You are required to calculate Arnold's taxable earnings for 2010/11.

5.9 Sally has worked for Generality Ltd for the last three years. Her current annual salary is £52,000.

Due to a downturn in the economy she was made redundant on 6 December 2010. As part of her redundancy package she received the following:

	£
Statutory redundancy	990
Payment in lieu of notice period provided for in her contract	13,000
Non-contractual discretionary payment	28,000

Sally has had her company car, a BMW 320i SE, since she started working for Generality Ltd. It had a list price of £23,000 when it was originally provided to her and CO_2 emissions of 184g/km. Generality Ltd also paid all of her private and business petrol costs. Sally will pay £8,000 to Generality Ltd to keep the car, even though its market value is £10,000.

Sally has decided to take six months to find her ideal replacement job.

You are required to calculate Sally's employment income figure for 2010/11.

6.1 Ray is a director of Sun Ltd, who earned a salary of £60,000 in 2010/11. PAYE of £15,000 was deducted. Ray was granted an Enterprise Management Incentive option in July 2007 to acquire 10,000 shares in Sun Ltd for £1.50 each. The shares were worth £2 each at the date of grant. He exercised the option in July 2010 when the share price was £4.75.

Ray's only other income in 2010/11 was interest received of £1,500 on his NS&I Easy Access Savings Account.

You are required to calculate Ray's 2010/11 income tax payable, explaining the treatment of the option on grant and exercise.

6.2 Sue has been a director of Porchester Ltd, an unquoted company, for three years. In order to reward her performance she was granted 5,000 ordinary share options under an approved Enterprise Management Incentive scheme on 1 January 2011 to buy shares at £4 at any time in the next 10 years. The market value of the shares at January 2011 was £3.96. She is planning to buy the shares in 8 years time when she estimates that the share price will have risen to £10. She plans to sell them shortly afterwards (assume share price at date of sale = £10.40).

You are required to:

(a) Explain the tax consequences of the granting of the share options and the subsequent sale by Sue.

(b) Explain how your answer would change if the scheme did not meet the requirements of an approved Enterprise Management Incentive scheme and the exercise price was £3.

6.3 Sharon is employed by Bruiser Ltd. The company is proposing to offer her some form of share incentive and are considering the following possibilities:

(i) The company could issue her with 10,000 ordinary shares worth £5 per share. Sharon would pay £2 per share.

(ii) The company could grant Sharon an option to buy 10,000 ordinary shares in three years' time at an exercise price equal to £2 per share. It is estimated that in three years the company's shares will be valued at £8 per share.

(iii) The company could issue her with 10,000 preference shares, currently valued at £2 per share, for which Sharon would pay the market value price. The preference shares carry the right to conversion into ordinary shares in 3 years' time on a 1 for 1 basis. The preference shares have limited rights and are not expected to rise in value.

You are required to explain the amounts on which income tax would be payable in each of the above situations. You should assume that Bruiser Ltd will not be willing to set up any form of approved share scheme.

6.4 Janet earns an annual salary of £75,000 and already holds options over the maximum value of shares in her employer's approved Company Share Option Plan.

Her employer granted her options over an additional 10,000 shares at a cost of 12p per option on 1 October 2008. The market value of the shares at that date was £5 per share and the exercise price was set at £2.75.

On 15 March 2011 Janet exercised 5,000 of the October 2008 options when the shares were worth £12.50 per share. She sold the shares one week later, by which time the share price had increased to £13.95.

You are required to calculate Janet's:

(a) Income tax and
(b) Capital gains tax liabilities

in respect of the exercise of the options and sale of the shares. Assume that she made no other disposals of capital assets in 2010/11.

7.1 Jeremy who is finance director of a large public company, has the following earnings in 2010/11:

Salary and bonuses	£380,000
Medical insurance	£1,500
Company car benefit	£12,000

He is also given free parking in a car park next to his office which costs his employer £750. Jeremy pays an annual subscription of £500 to the CIOT.

You are required to advise Jeremy on the maximum contribution he can make to a registered pension scheme in the tax year and obtain tax relief, and the tax consequences of contributing this amount.

7.2 Ed Tommy and Joan Ball are in partnership running a design studio, with profits being shared in the ratio 4:1. They both wish to start saving for their retirement and would like to make maximum contributions to a pension. The partnership's trading profit for 2010/11 is £175,000. Neither Ed or Joan has any other income.

You are required to:

(a) Advise Ed and Joan of the maximum amount they can each contribute to a pension for 2010/11.

(b) Explain the method by which Ed and Joan will be given tax relief for their pension contributions.

(c) Explain how they will be able to continue to contribute to their pensions if the partnership ceases trading on 5 April 2011 and they no longer have any earnings.

7.3 Dwaine is the sales director of a small central heating and plumbing company based in the Midlands. The company draws up accounts to 31 December each year.

Dwaine's salary (paid monthly) for the year ended 31 December 2010 was set at £40,000 per annum. This was raised to £44,000 at the Board meeting on 20 January 2011. PAYE deducted in 2010/11 came to £6,000.

Dwaine also receives half yearly bonuses dependent on the performance of his sales team. These have been as follows:

Bonus period	Bonus	Awarded	Received
6 m/e 31.12.09	£2,000	31.3.10	30.4.10
6 m/e 30.6.10	£6,881	30.9.10	31.10.10
6 m/e 31.12.10	£6,990	31.3.11	30.4.11

The company does not have an occupational pension scheme and therefore agreed to make payments into Dwaine's personal pension. Dwaine pays £150 per month and the company pays £100 per month.

You are required to calculate the income tax payable/(repayable) by Dwaine for the year ended 5 April 2011.

7.4 Alfred earns an annual salary of £200,000. The value of his taxable benefits is a further £44,000.

Alfred owns two investment properties that he rents out. One is let furnished and the taxable rental income (net of expenses) is £18,000 a year. The other qualifies as a furnished holiday let and the net taxable income from this property is £25,000 for 2010/11.

In 2010/11 Alfred also received interest of £112,500 from a bank account that he holds jointly with his wife and dividends of £363,330 from UK companies.

You are required to calculate Alfred's income tax payable assuming he makes the maximum contribution to his personal pension.

8.1 Ricardo Garcia is resident and domiciled in Spain.

He has recently married a British woman and will be coming to live in London when he retires; he has advised you that he would, however return to Spain in the event that his wife should predecease him.

He has a large pension from the Spanish company that he used to work for, which he will need to bring into the UK for living expenses. He will keep his Spanish bank account and his large portfolio of Spanish investments.

You are required to explain the income tax treatment of Mr Garcia's different sources of income. You should also note the basic planning which should be implemented with regard to Mr Garcia's existing funds before he comes to the UK.

8.2 Marco, an Italian client, arrived in the UK on the 5 August 2009 to work for the UK branch of his Italian employer for three years.

In 2010/11 he received the following income:

	£
Salary – Paid in the UK	60,000
– Paid in Italy	15,000
Company car benefit (UK)	5,200
Bank interest – UK (net)	35
– Italy (gross)	500

No element of the income received in Italy was remitted to the UK. 20% of Marco's working time was spent in Italy.

You are required to:

(a) Identify Marco's residence, ordinary residence and domicile for UK income tax purposes in 2010/11.

(b) Comment on the date from which any changes to his residence status as a result of coming to the UK would have taken place.

(c) Calculate Marco's taxable income for 2010/11 assuming he makes all beneficial claims.

8.3 Steffen was born in Germany and spends most of his time living there, but for the last few years has been making regular visits to the UK, as follows:

2006/07	75 days
2007/08	98 days
2008/09	92 days
2009/10	104 days
2010/11	100 days

During 2010/11, Steffen's received interest of £80,000 (net of 45% foreign withholding tax) on his offshore bank account and brought £28,600 of this net interest into the UK. Steffen also received rental income of £57,800 (net of 15% withholding tax) from letting out his villa in Utopia and transferred all of this income to the UK.

You are required to:

(a) Determine, with explanation, at what point (if any) Steffen will be treated as having become UK resident, assuming that he had no previous intention to make this level of visits.

(b) Calculate Steffen's UK income tax payable in 2010/11 assuming he makes all beneficial claims.

9.1 Matilda, who had previously lived in the UK all her life, left the country on 11 January 2006 and moved to France to work at a vineyard in Bordeaux. Having mastered the trade, she then returned to the UK on 22 May 2010 with a view to setting up her own vineyard in East Anglia. During her absence from the UK, Matilda made the following chargeable gains/ allowable losses.

Asset	*Date acquired*	*Date sold*	*Chargeable gain/losses*
Painting	June 2005	August 2009	£55,000
Holiday cottage	September 2006	January 2010	£38,000
Land	June 2003	December 2008	£(15,000)

You are required to:

(a) Explain the basis on which gains made while Matilda was non UK resident may be subject to UK CGT.

(b) Calculate Matilda's total chargeable gains for 2010/11.

10.1 In May 2010 Mark made a gain of £17,900 on the sale of shares in an unquoted trading company (owned for three years). He also made a loss of £7,000 on the sale of a painting at auction and a further loss of £26,000 on the sale of a cottage to his brother. He has losses brought forward of £5,000.

You are required to calculate the losses to carry forward to 2011/12.

10.2 Dorrit has been trading for many years. In 2010/11 he had taxable trading income of £15,000 but in 2011/12 he had a tax adjusted loss of £28,000.

He has UK property income of £3,000 per annum and in 2010/11 realised a chargeable gain of £16,000 on an asset which was originally acquired on 2 May 1998.

You are required to compute Dorrit's revised net income and chargeable gains, before the annual exempt amount for 2010/11 assuming earliest possible relief is sought for the trading loss.

10.3 Ambrose made the following chargeable disposal, of an asset which he had held for investment purposes in 2010/11:

	Asset
Purchase date	31.12.81
Purchase price	£4,500
31.3.82 Market value	£7,500
Enhancement date	1.5.98
Enhancement cost	£1,000
Proceeds	£28,800
Disposal date	1.1.11

Ambrose made no other disposals in 2010/11 and had taxable income of £35,000.

You are required to calculate the capital gains tax payable by Ambrose for 2010/11. State the due date for payment.

10.4 Emily made the following disposals in 2010/11:

(1) *Factory*

Acquired 1 July 2005 for £150,000. Emily let out the factory to Teds R Us Ltd, a soft toy manufacturer. The factory was sold for £225,000 on 10 July 2010.

(2) *Painting*

This had been acquired by Emily's husband Arthur on 1 March 1999 for £50,000. Arthur had given the painting to Emily on 1 July 2001 when it was worth £60,000. Emily sold the painting for £73,000 on 2 May 2010.

Emily made no other disposals in 2010/11 and had taxable income of £50,000.

You are required to calculate the capital gains tax payable by Emily for 2010/11

10.5 Kidson purchased a plot of land on 1 January 1983 for £8,000. On 31 August 2010, he sold part of the land for £45,000 but declined an offer of £50,000 for the rest.

You are required to calculate the capital gains tax arising on the sale assuming this is the only capital transaction Kidson has in 2010/11 and his taxable income is £25,000.

10.6 Cyril buys an asset for £40,000 in June 1999. It is damaged by fire in August 2000. Its unrestored value was £50,000. The asset was restored in September 2000 at a cost of £14,000 and this sum was received from the insurance company in November 2000. Cyril sells the asset on 10 July 2010 for £85,000.

You are required to show Cyril's chargeable gain on the sale in July 2010 if he did not make a claim under s.23(1)(a) in 2000/01.

10.7 Jake buys an asset for £7,500 in February 1986, and it is completely destroyed by fire in February 2011. He received £17,000 from the insurance company in the same month. He bought a replacement asset for £16,000 within six months and made a claim under s.23(4) TCGA 1992.

You are required to show Jake's capital gains tax position for 2010/11 and the base cost of the replacement asset.

11.1 James bought 1,000 shares in G plc for £2,954 in April 1985 and another 1,000 for £6,000 in May 2005. He disposed of 500 shares in August 2010 for £15,000.

You are required to calculate the chargeable gain arising on the disposal in August 2010.

11.2 Mr Smith acquired 5,000 shares in S plc in April 1985 for £5,605. In July 1999 S plc made a bonus issue of one ordinary share for every five held. In December 2010 Mr Smith sold 3,500 of his shares for £6,250.

You are required to calculate the gain arising on the sale of shares in December 2010.

11.3 Peter made the following disposals in 2010/11:

(i) He purchased a building for £50,000 on 1 January 1971 which he let commercially as offices to an unquoted company. On 10 April 2010 he sold the building for £600,000. The value on 31 March 1982 was £200,000.

(ii) He held 20,000 shares in Forum Follies plc which he purchased in May 1986 for £50,000. In March 2011, Exciting Enterprises plc acquired all the share capital of Forum Follies plc. Under the terms of the takeover for every two shares previously held in Forum Follies plc shareholders received three ordinary shares in Exciting Enterprises plc plus £1 cash. Immediately after the take-over the ordinary shares in Exciting Enterprises plc were quoted at £3 each.

You are required to calculate Peter's taxable gain in 2010/11.

11.4 Giles purchased shares in Dassau plc, a quoted company, as follows.

	No of shares	*Cost*
		£
December 1985	1,000	2,000
April 1987 1 for 2 rights issue		£2 per share
15 November 2010	500	£1,500

On 1 November 2010 he sold 1,200 shares for £9,500.

Giles had capital losses brought forward from 2009/10 of £6,400.

You are required to calculate Giles's taxable gain for 2010/11.

11.5 Richard Price works for PB plc, a large UK quoted trading company. He has acquired shares in PB plc via a company share option plan in recent years as follows:

Date	*Shares Acquired*	*Cost*
		£
15.3.1990	2,000	2,000
17.12.1996	4,000	10,000

In May 1999 there was a 1:5 rights issue at £5 per share which Richard took up in full.

On 4 October 2010, Richard sold 1,800 shares at £7.50 each.

He still works for the company and his holding comprises less than 1% of the shares in issue.

You are required to calculate the gain on the disposal.

11.6 Julio has been resident and ordinarily resident in the UK for the last five years but has retained his Spanish domicile.

He makes the following disposals during 2010/11:

Transaction	*Proceeds*	*Cost*
	£	£
Holiday villa in Portugal	319,000	65,000
10,000 shares in CommandN Plc	195,600	see below

CommandN Plc is a quoted UK company. Julio had purchased 7,000 shares in August 2000 for £157,220, a further 8,000 shares for £132,720 in January 2005 and 5,000 shares for £97,050 on 19 April 2011. He sold the shares on 1 April 2011.

The proceeds and cost of the Portuguese villa are shown at their sterling equivalents on the relevant dates. Julio has not brought any of the proceeds from the disposal of the villa to the UK.

You are required to calculate Julio's capital gains tax liability assuming that he makes any beneficial claims and his taxable income in 2010/11 is £50,000.

11.7 George had purchased 10,000 shares in Rover Ltd on 12 August 1981 for £24,000. On 31 March 1982 they were worth £27,200.

On 12 April 2002 there had been a bonus issue of one share for every 4 held. The market value of the shares at that date was £3.25 per share.

On 17 January 2011 Rover Ltd was taken over by Moggie Plc. George received 2 shares and £0.95p for every share held. The Moggie Plc shares were worth £8.95 per share immediately after the takeover.

George sold half of his shares the day after the takeover.

You are required to calculate George's total chargeable gain arising in 2010/11. You should assume that he has never worked for either company and has always held less than 5% of the shares.

12.1 Lionel purchased a Victoria Cross medal in May 1983 for £3,000 and a vintage car in June 1985 for £4,000. He sold them both to a collector in April 2010 for £14,780 and £15,500 respectively.

Lionel also sold a painting for £90 in December 2010 which had cost £6,260 in January 1983.

You are required to calculate Lionel's total chargeable gains for 2010/11.

12.2 In August 2010 Miranda, a trader, disposed of three assets on which capital allowances have been claimed.

	Purchase Price	*Disposal Proceeds*
	£	£
Motor car	8,000	4,000
Machinery: item 1	5,500	7,500
Machinery: item 2	4,000	3,500

All assets were purchased in October 2007.

You are required to calculate Miranda's chargeable gain or allowable loss.

12.3 Adrienne acquired a 90-year lease on 31 March 1981 for £20,000. On 31 March 2011 she granted a sublease of 55 years for £30,000. The reversionary interest is valued at £82,500. The value of the lease at 31 March 1982 was £40,000.

Adrienne also acquired a freehold property for £30,000 in March 1992. In November 2010 she granted an 11-year lease for a premium of £10,000 at which time the reversionary interest was valued at £50,000.

You are required to calculate Adrienne's 2010/11 taxable gain.

12.4 Doug sold the following items on 1 August 2010:

(1) A Leonardo cartoon bought in March 1984 for £7,200 and sold for £5,500.

(2) A lathe bought for use in his business in March 1985 which cost £4,300. The sales proceeds were £10,500. Doug had claimed capital allowances on this asset.

You are required to calculate Doug's chargeable gains for 2010/11 before the annual exempt amount and assuming he made no other disposals in the year.

12.5 (1) Joe acquired an 80 year lease on a property for £28,000 on 29 July 1984. He assigned the lease on 29 July 2010 for £79,000.

(2) As (1) except that it was a 57 year lease when it was acquired.

You are required to calculate the chargeable gain which would arise in situation (1) and (2).

12.6 Harold acquired the freehold of a property for £25,000 on 1 May 1990. On 1 October 2010 he granted a 20 year lease on the premises for a premium of £20,000, the value of the reversion being £17,000.

You are required to calculate Harold's capital gain in 2010/11.

12.7 Evelyn exercised an option over an antique table in August 2010. The option had been granted to her in September 1996 for £2,000 and the option price was £3,500. Evelyn sold the table at auction in February 2011 for £8,000. The auctioneers' costs were 10% of the sale price.

You are required to compute the chargeable gains arising in respect of the above events in 2010/11.

12.8 Seraphina bought a warehouse on 1 June 2010 for £685,000.

On 1 July 2010 she granted a 15 year lease over the building to Jet Ltd for a one off premium of £50,000, and an annual rent of £42,000, paid monthly in advance.

You are required to calculate the chargeable gain or allowable loss arising in 2010/11 assuming that the value of the reversion on 1 July 2010 was £565,000.

13.1 Neil sold a house on 30 June 2010. He realised an £80,000 gain before taking account of any Principal private residence relief. The house was originally purchased on 1 October 1980 and was occupied by Neil until 30 June 1986 at which date he purchased and moved into another residence, letting the original house until the date of sale.

You are required to calculate the chargeable gain arising on the sale of the house.

13.2 Robert owned a property with three storeys of equal value in Sheffield. He bought it on 30 June 1987 for £20,000. He used the top two storeys as his main residence. The ground floor was rented out to students. The ground floor has a separate access door. On 30 November 2010 Robert sold the whole property for £200,000.

You are required to:

(a) Calculate Robert's chargeable gain on the sale of the property.

(b) Give three examples of periods which are deemed occupation for the capital gains tax principal private residence exemption.

13.3 Mr and Mrs Mackay bought their family home for £150,000 in August 1999. It has been occupied by them since purchase and they are now planning to sell the property in May 2010 for £560,000.

The Mackays plan to use the proceeds to purchase two new properties in May 2010.

Country house	– cost £400,000
Flat in town	– cost £175,000

Mr Mackay will live in the flat in town during the week and spend weekends at the country house. Mrs Mackay will live in the country house. Mr Mackay plans to retire in five years and at that stage they will sell the flat and move permanently into the country house.

You are required to explain:

(a) the capital gains tax implications of selling the current family home.

(b) the capital gains tax implication of residing in two homes and any actions the Mackays should consider.

(c) the likely capital gains tax implications of selling the flat in town in five years time, assuming it rises in value.

13.4 On 2 May 1985 Peter Stamp, a retired solicitor, bought a private dwelling-house for £70,000, which he sold for £270,000 under a contract dated 3 July 2010. The house was situated in grounds of one half of a hectare.

He lived in this house as his only residence until 1 February 1988. It was then let for residential purposes until 1 December 1997. From that date until the date of sale the property was unoccupied.

You are required to compute the chargeable gain arising on the sale of the house.

13.5 On 4 April 2011, Mr Sinclair sold his house for £380,200. The house was originally purchased on 6 April 1987 for £110,000 and was used as his principal residence until 5 April 1988. From 6 April 1988 until 5 April 1993 the house was empty while Mr Sinclair was working abroad. Mr Sinclair is an architect and has always been treated as self-employed from when he started to practise in 1974.

On his return to the UK in April 1993 he moved back into the house. In April 1994 the house was converted to a flat upstairs (which Mr Sinclair used as his residence) and offices downstairs from which he ran his practice. He moved out of the flat on 5 October 2008 and the flat was empty until the whole property was sold on 4 April 2011. The flat occupied exactly half of the property. Mr Sinclair continued to use the offices for his practice until shortly before the sale.

You are required to calculate Mr Sinclair' s chargeable gain on the sale of his home.

14.1 Arthur made the following investments in qualifying EIS companies in September 2007 and claimed the maximum available income tax relief:

Company	*Amount subscribed*
Galadriel Ltd	£40,000
Guinevere Ltd	£50,000
Mordred Ltd	£30,000

In 2010/11 Arthur disposes of his shares as follows:

Company	*Date of Disposal*	*Proceeds*
Galadriel Ltd	June 2010	£35,000
Guinevere Ltd	October 2010	£95,000
Mordred Ltd	November 2010	£20,000

You are required to calculate:

(a) The amount of income tax relief withdrawn in 2010/11 (if any) as a result of the disposals, and

(b) The chargeable gains or allowable losses arising on disposal.

14.2 **You are required to identify (with brief explanations) whether EIS income tax relief would be available on the following investments, based on the information given:**

(a) **An employee invests £20,000 in newly issued shares of his employer company, which is an unlisted trading company.**

(b) **Bob subscribes £100,000 for newly issued shares in Brown Plc, an AIM listed company. Three years later the company obtains a full listing on the London Stock Exchange, although this was not envisaged at the time of Bob's investment.**

(c) **Jane subscribes £400,000 for a 55% shareholding in Tarzan Ltd, a UK manufacturing company.**

(d) **Juliet invests £10,000 in Capulet Ltd, a property development company with operations in London and Manchester.**

(e) **Hilda subscribes £600,000 for a 25% shareholding in Wagner Ltd, a London based clothing retail company.**

14.3 Lola sold a holiday cottage for £350,000 in December 2010, having bought it for £180,000 in June 2002. She has capital losses brought forward of £15,000.

You are required to state the minimum investment she must make in qualifying EIS shares in order to reduce her gain to nil and to show her capital gains computation if she makes that investment.

14.4 Alan had been trading as a sole trader for a number of years. On 1 July 2010 he sold his business as a going concern to Bernard for £350,000.

The value of the assets of the business and the capital gains at the date of the transfer were as follows:

	Market value	Cost
	£	£
Freehold land and buildings	250,000	70,000
Goodwill	85,000	–
Machinery and equipment	3,000	4,000
Stock	6,000	6,000
Debtors	7,000	5,000
Creditors	(1,000)	–
	350,000	

The land and buildings were acquired in June 2000.

Alan made no other disposals in 2010/11 and had taxable income of £40,000.

Calculate Alan's capital gains tax liability for 2010/11 assuming he makes any beneficial claims.

14.5 Monty has been a director of a trading company in which he owns 30% of the shares for the last four years. On 1 August 2010 he disposed of his 30% holding in the company for £7,800,000, realising a gain of £5,700,000.

On 1 November 2010 Monty sold a painting for £12,000. He had acquired the painting for £1,000 on 1 May 2001.

Monty had capital losses brought forward of £15,000 and taxable income in 2010/11 of £50,000.

Calculate Monty's capital gains tax liability for 2010/11 assuming he makes any beneficial claims.

14.6 Freda has run her fishing tackle shop since 1988. She sold the whole business as a going concern on 12 May 2010, realising a gain of £2,110,000.

Freda had not previously claimed any entrepreneurs' relief and had losses brought forward of £12,750.

She made one other disposal in August 2010 realising a gain of £24,000 on an investment asset.

Freda's taxable income in 2010/11 is £70,000.

You are required to calculate Freda's capital gains tax liability and state the date by which any claim for entrepreneurs' relief must be made.

15.1 Brandon has bought a flat in Essex with a view to letting it out at a rate of £1,200 per month from November 2010 onwards.

You are required to explain:

(a) **The notification requirements to HMRC for income tax purposes;**

(b) **The penalty which will arise in the event of late notification;**

(c) **Whether Brandon is eligible to submit a simplified return in respect of his rental income and what needs to be recorded on the return.**

15.2 Phyllis was issued with a notice to make a 2010/11 tax return on 15 May 2011. She filed her return electronically on 31 August 2012 and paid the tax payable of £160 on the same date.

Phyllis's 2009/10 income tax payable amounted to £140.

You are required to advise Phyllis on:

(a) **The due dates for submission of her 2010/11 tax return and payment of her 2010/11 income tax.**
(b) **Any penalties and interest which she owes, assuming a rate of interest on overdue tax of 3%.**

15.3 **You are required to explain the two situations where CGT may be paid in instalments, highlighting:**

(a) **The due dates/period of instalments;**
(b) **The deadline for making the claim to pay tax in instalments;**

15.4 Alicia was issued with a notice to make a 2010/11 return on 20 April 2011 and submitted her return on 18 February 2012. In the past she has always filed her tax returns on time.

On 25 February 2013 she received a notice from HMRC advising her that they were opening an enquiry into her 2010/11 return and requesting various documents relating to expenses she has claimed against her self-employment income. Alicia believes it is too late for HMRC to enquire into her return and request documents.

You are required to advise Alicia on:
(a) **Whether HMRC are still within the deadline for opening an enquiry into her 2010/11 return;**
(b) **How long she is expected to retain documents relating to her business;**
(c) **Whether HMRC can re-open previous returns and issue an assessment in respect of earlier tax years.**

15.5 John's income tax and capital gains tax position for 2009/10 was as follows:

	£
Income tax liability	10,250
Tax deducted at source	(5,000)
	5,250
Class 4 NIC	1,000
Capital gains tax liability	8,200
Payments on account made re 2009/10	(5,000)
	9,450

You are required to:

(a) **Calculate John's payments on account for 2010/11 stating the due dates.**

(b) **Explain what action John may take if he knows that his self-employment income will be significantly less in 2010/11 than in 2009/10 and any interest implications involved.**

15.6 Ray's payments on account for 2010/11 based on his income tax liability for 2009/10 were £4,500 each. However when he submitted his 2009/10 income tax return in January 2011 he made a claim to reduce the payments on account for 2010/11 to £3,500 each. The first payment on account was made on 29 January 2011, and the second on 12 August 2011.

Ray filed his 2010/11 tax return in December 2010. The return showed that his tax liabilities for 2010/11 (before deducting payments on account) were income tax £10,000, capital gains tax £2,500. Ray paid the balance of tax due of £5,500 on 19 February 2012.

You are required to identify the time periods and amount(s) of tax on which interest will be charged.

15.7 Tabitha's income tax, NIC and capital gains tax position for 2009/10 was as follows:

	£
Income tax liability	17,895
Class 4 NIC liability	2,808
CGT liability	32,455
Payments on account for 2009/10	15,500
Tax deducted at source	1,275

You are required to calculate the following:

(1) **Tabitha's first payment on account for 2010/11.**

(2) **The interest and any other penalties due assuming Tabitha had paid her first payment on account on 25 May 2011.**

Assume that the interest rate is 3% throughout.

Ignore any balancing payment of tax for 2009/10. Your interest calculation should be to the nearest pound and month.

16.1 Tina commenced employment with Harrison Electrics Ltd on 1 November 2010. She was paid a salary of £1,000 per month and from 1 January 2011, was given the use of a new Ford Escort 1400cc with a list price of £15,000 with all private petrol paid for by the company. The emission rate is 165g/km.

You are required to calculate Tina's earnings for income tax purposes and the NIC payable by Tina and Harrison Electrics Ltd in respect of her 2010/11 remuneration.

16.2 Ruth is an director of Benson Ltd and earns a salary of £45,000 pa. Benson Ltd have loaned her £20,000 so she can redecorate her house. As at 5 April 2010 there was an outstanding balance of £15,000. On 5 January 2011 Ruth repaid a further £5,000. Ruth pays Benson Ltd interest at 3% pa on the loan. Assume that the official rate of interest throughout 2010/11 is 4%.

You are required to calculate the amount of Class 1 secondary and Class 1A contributions payable by Benson Ltd for 2010/11.

16.3 Natalie is a receptionist at Hospitality Hotel. She was provided with the use of a dinner set by the hotel on 6 October 2009. Its market value at that date was £2,000. On 6 October 2010 the hotel agreed to sell the dinner set to Natalie for £1,000, its market value at that date was £1,500.

You are required to calculate the Class 1A payable by Natalie's employer for 2010/11, stating the due date.

16.4 Judy is a director of Markham Ltd. She earns £25,750 pa and is provided with a company owned flat. The flat cost the company £60,000 when it was bought in 1994. Judy moved in 2001 when the flat had a market value of £100,000. The annual value of the flat is £3,000. Markham Ltd also pays for Judy's telephone bills, this costs the company £400 pa. Judy is also provided with furniture for use in her flat. The market value of the furniture was £2,500 in 2001.

Assume that the official rate of interest throughout 2010/11 is 4%.

You are required to calculate the NIC payable by Judy and Markham Ltd in respect of her 2010/11 remuneration.

16.5 The following people work for Dickens Ltd and are paid monthly:

Pip – a salesman who earns a salary of £28,000 pa with a bonus of £4,000 paid in August 2010.

Estella – a secretary who earned £16,000 pa up to 30 September 2010 and had a pay increase to £18,000 from 1 October 2010 onwards.

You are required to calculate the Class 1 primary contributions for 2010/11 payable by the above individuals and state the due date for payment.

16.6 **You are required to advise what types of NIC will be payable by Madison Plc and/or its employees in respect of the following remuneration in 2010/11. You should also state the due dates in each case.**

(a) **Anna (age 67) works part-time for the company and earns a salary of £17,000 pa.**

(b) **Elaine, a manager, receives use of a company car and obtains reimbursement of the cost of her season ticket for Spurs football club.**

(c) **At Christmas the company provides a number of employees with a bottle of Champagne as a gift. Madison Plc has agreed with HMRC to settle the employees' personal tax liabilities in respect of these gifts.**

16.7 Robert earns an annual salary of £65,000.

During 2010/11 his benefits, and expenses paid by his employer, were as follows:

	£
Mileage payments – 8,000 business miles	4,000
Other business related travel expenses	12,500
Interest free loan to purchase season ticket	1,784
Private medical insurance (contracted for by his employer)	450
Professional subscription	220
M&S vouchers	500
Gym membership (reimbursed by his employer)	1,020

You are required to calculate the total NIC due from Robert and his employer for 2010/11.

Your answer should be to the nearest pound.

17.1 Brash Ltd has 75 employees, who all earn in excess of £10,000 per annum. It provides a number of its employees with company cars which they are able to use for private purposes.

You are required to state which year end PAYE returns for 2010/11 Brash Ltd is required to submit and to state their due filing dates..

17.2 In 2010/11 Auster Ltd provided the following to a number of its employees, who all earned in excess of £8,500 p.a.

(1) Emily was made redundant by the company in May 2010. The company paid her statutory redundancy pay of £3,000 and a non-contractual ex-gratia payment of £29,000.

(2) Patrick works in one of the company's restaurants. In 2010/11 he received tips of £1,000 directly from customers which the company allowed him to keep.

(3) Paul was provided with childcare vouchers of £50 per week.

You are required to explain whether Auster Ltd should apply PAYE to the above remuneration.

Solutions to exam style questions

1.1 **Roger**

	£
Allowances:	
Personal allowance (65 or over)	9,490
Restricted : ½ × (23,980 – 22,900)	(540)
PA	8,950
Blind person's allowance	1,890
Tax reductions:	
Married couple's allowance (75 or over, given based on age of older spouse) (relief restricted to 10%)	6,965
Vicky	
PA (>75)	9,640

Some of this is being wasted as Vicky has income of only £4,500.

Roger's allowances have been restricted due to high net income. In order to maximise the benefit of allowances the interest generating bank account and/or the rental property could be held in joint names, leading to a 50:50 split of income for tax purposes. Splitting the rental property would be the most beneficial, as it would lead to £2,440 of the interest being taxed on Roger at the starting rate of 10%.

1.2 **Charles**

INCOME TAX COMPUTATION 2010/11

	Non-savings income
	£
Earnings	119,500
Less: qualifying interest (6% × 6,250)	(375)
Net income	119,125
Less: PA (W1)	(4,413)
Taxable income	114,712
Tax thereon:	
£	£
52,400 (W) @ 20%	10,480
62,312 @ 40%	24,925
Tax liability	35,405
Tax suffered at source (PAYE)	(36,800)
Tax repayable	(1,395)

Workings.

(W1) Personal allowance

	£	£
Personal allowance		6,475
Total net income	119,125	
Less: gross Gift Aid donation (£12,000 x 100/80)	(15,000)	
Adjusted income	104,125	
Less: limit	(100,000)	
	4,125	
Less: ½ × £4,125		(2,062)
Available PA		4,413

(W2) Basic rate band extended by gross donation, ie (£12,000 × 100/80) = £15,000

1.3

	£
Trade profits	7,700
Discretionary trust income (£1,375 × 100/50)	2,750
	10,450
Less PA	(9,640)
Taxable income	810
Tax @ 20%	162
Less MCA (£6,965 × 2/12 × 10%)	(116)
Tax liability	46
Less tax deducted (£2,750 × 50%)	(1,375)
Repayable	(1,329)

Income from a discretionary trust comes with 50% tax credit.

Note: Interest on an ISA is exempt.

1.4

	Non savings income	*Dividend income*
	£	£
Earnings	34,000	
Dividend income (£1,800 × 100/90)		2,000
Lottery winnings (exempt)	–	
	34,000	2,000
Less: PA	(6,475)	
Taxable income	27,525	2,000

Tax thereon:

£	
27,525 @ 20%	5,505
2,000 @ 10%	200
	5,705
Less: EIS IT relief (20,000 × 20%)	(4,000)
Tax liability	1,705
Less: PAYE	(7,200)
tax credit on dividends	(200)
IT repayable	(5,695)

Note: Legacy is capital and therefore excluded from the income tax computation.

Treatment of dividends

Income of a child (<18) arising out of a gift by her parents is treated as the income of the parent for income tax purposes, assuming that the income exceeds £100 gross per annum.

The dividends received by Philippa will not be taxed on Julie as Philippa is aged over 18.

1.5 (a) The value of the shares (£10,000) at the time of the gift may be deducted from the donor's gross total income.

(b) Interest on a loan to buy plant and machinery for use in a partnership is only deductible for three years from the end of the tax year in which the loan is taken out – hence, no deduction is available in this case.

(c) The royalties paid are grossed up by $^{100}/_{80}$ and deducted from the payer's total income. The basic rate tax of £390 must be added back to the payer's income tax liability.

(d) The donation is made net of 20% basic rate tax. Tax relief at higher rates is given by extending the basic and higher rate tax bands by the gross donation of £2,500.

(e) Tax relief is only given for maintenance payments where the payer or recipient was born before 6 April 1935 – therefore, no relief is available here.

2.1 **Mr Fairbanks**

INCOME TAX COMPUTATION 2010/11

		Non-savings income	*Savings income*	*Dividend income*
		£	£	£
Earnings		6,000		
Dividends received	$(£900 \times \frac{100}{90})$			1,000
Building society interest	$(£800 \times \frac{100}{80})$		1,000	
Bank deposit interest	$(£80 \times \frac{100}{80})$		100	
Net income		6,000	1,100	1,000
Less: PA		(6,000)	(475)	
Taxable income		nil	625	1,000

	£
Tax:	
£625 @ 10%	62
£1,000 @ 10%	100
Tax liability	162
Less: Tax suffered at source	
notional credit on dividend	(100)
Interest (£1,100 @ 20%)	(220)
PAYE	(250)
Tax repayable	(408)

2.2 **Jonty**

INCOME TAX COMPUTATION 2010/11

	Non-savings income	*Savings income*	*Dividend Income*
	£	£	£
Earnings	45,000		
Building society interest $£(80 \times \frac{100}{80})$		100	
Dividends $£(63 \times \frac{100}{90})$			70
NS&I interest		142	
Net income	45,000	242	70
Less: PA	(6,475)		
Taxable income	38,525	242	70

Tax:	
£	£
37,400 @ 20%	7,480
495 @ 20% (W)	99
630 @ 40% =	252
242 @ 40% =	97
70 @ 32.5% =	23
Tax liability	7,951
Less: notional credit on dividend	(7)
Less: tax suffered at source £(20 + 7,400)	(7,420)
Tax payable	524

Working

Basic rate threshold extended by gross donation ie (£396 × 100/80) = £495

Note. Betting income is exempt.

2.3 INCOME TAX COMPUTATION 2010/11

	Non-savings income	Savings income	
	£	£	
Property income	23,900		
Interest (£4,400 × 100/80)		5,500	
Gilt interest		290	
Net income	23,900	5,790	Total = £29,690
Less: PAA (W1)	(6,475)		
Taxable income	17,425	5,790	

		£
Tax	£17,425 @ 20%	3,485
	£5,790 @ 20%	1,158
		4,643
Less: Married couples' allowance (W)		(674)
Tax liability		3,969
Less: Tax deducted:		
Interest		(1,100)
Tax payable		2,869

Working

	£
PAA (>75)	9,640
Less: ½ £(29,690 – 22,900) = £3,395	
Max 'restriction' £(9,640 – 6,475)	(3,165)
Allowance given	6,475
Unused restriction (£3,395 – 3,165)	230
MCAA (over 75)	6,965
Less: unused restriction	(230)
	6,735

Tax reducer @ 10% = 674

2.4

	Non-savings income	Savings income	Dividend income
	£	£	£
Trade profits	138,000		
UK dividends (£8,000 × 100/90)			8,889
Jersey bank interest		4,300	
Total income	138,000	4,300	8,889
Less: interest relief (W1)	(827)		
Net income	137,173	4,300	8,889
Less: personal allowance (adjusted net income > £112,950)	(Nil)		
Taxable income	137,173	4,300	8,889

		£
Tax	£37,400 @ 20%	7,480
	£2,000 @ 20%(W2)	400
	£97,773 @ 40%	39,109
	£4,300 @ 40%	1,720
	£8,527 @ 32½ %	2,771
	£362 @ 32½ % (W2)	118
		51,598
Less: tax deducted on dividends		(889)
Tax payable		50,709

Workings

1 *Loan interest relief*

	£
£24,000 × 4% × 8/12	640
£14,000 × 4% × 4/12	187
	827

2 *Basic rate and higher rate threshold extensions:*

Gross gift aid donation £1,600 × 100/80 = £2,000.

Basic rate band is extended to £39,400 and the higher rate threshold is £152,000.

Notes: Premium Bond winnings are tax free.

2.5 **Mildred**

TAX COMPUTATION ON 2010/11

	Non-savings income	*Savings income*	*Dividend income*	
	£	£	£	
State pension	11,047			
Guernsey bank interest		13,450		
Dividends (£720 × 100/90 – see note)			800	
Net income	11,047	13,450	800	Total = £25,297
Less: PAA (W1)	(8,754)			
Taxable income	2,293	13,450	800	

		£
Tax:	£2,293 @ 20%	459
	£147 @ 10%	15
	£13,303 @ 20%	2,661
	£800 @ 10%	80
Tax liability		3,215
Less:	Tax deducted:	
	Dividends	(80)
Tax payable		3,135

Note. Mildred is taxed on the cash alternative to the stock dividend as this differs from the value of shares by less than 15%.

Workings

1 *Personal age allowance*

	£
PAA (>75)	9,640
Less: ½ £(24,672 – 22,900) (W2)	(886)
PAA given	8,754

2 *Adjusted net income*

	£
Actual net income	25,297
Less: gross donation to charity (£500 × 100/80)	(625)
Adjusted net income for age allowance purposes	24,672

Note. Do not need to extend the basic rate band as Mildred is not a higher rate taxpayer.

2.6 *Loan*

The company should have paid tax of £20,000 (i.e. £80,000 × 25%) to HMRC by 1 October 2009 when the loan was made to Sylvia.

The making of the loan has no tax consequences for Sylvia.

Write-off

The company will obtain a refund of the tax of £20,000 previously paid. The write off is not tax deductible for the company.

Sylvia will be treated as having received a gross dividend of £88,889 (i.e. £80,000 × $^{100}/_{90}$). This will be taxable at 32.5%, less a notional tax credit of 10% of £8,889. The dividend should be included in her 2010/11 tax return and the income tax will be payable by 31 January 2012.

2.7

	Non Savings	*Savings*	*Dividends*
	£	£	£
Earnings	2,080		
Dividends: £49,500 × 100/90			55,000
Treasury stock interest		54,650	
Bank interest: £1,300 × 100/80		1,625	
NS&I account interest		600	
Total	2,080	56,875	55,000
Less: PA (W1)	(2,080)	(3,668)	
Taxable income	Nil	53,207	55,000

£2,440 @ 10%	244
£34,960 @ 20%	6,992
£12,500 @ 20% (W2)	2,500
£3,307 @ 40%	1,323
£55,000 @ 32.5%	17,875
Tax liability	28,934
Less: Tax paid/ suffered	
Dividends £55,000 @ 10%	(5,500)
Interest £1,625 @ 20%	(325)
Tax payable	23,109

Note: NS&I certificate is exempt from income tax

Workings

(W1) Personal allowance

	£	£
Personal allowance		6,475
Total net income	113,955	
Less: gross Gift Aid donation (£10,000 x 100/80)	(12,500)	
Adjusted income	101,455	
Less: limit	(100,000)	
	1,455	
Less: ½ × £1,455		(727)
Available PA		5,748

(W2) Extension of basic rate band

Gift aid donation: £10,000 × 100/80 = £12,500

3.1

		£
Gross rents (£1,500 × 12) (accruals basis)		18,000
Less:	Agent's fees	1,800
	Interest (£60,000 × 7%)	4,200
	Water rates	120
	Insurance	500
	Wear and tear allowance ((18,000 – 120) × 10%)	1,788
Property income		9,592

Tax relief may be obtained for the cost of furnishing a rental property in two ways:

(i) an annual 'wear and tear' allowance may be claimed, equal to 10% of rental income (less water rates and council tax if paid by the landlord), or

(ii) under the 'renewals basis', the cost of replacing items of furniture may be deducted.

Note: The cost of the new porch is capital and therefore not allowable.

3.2 The letting will meet the 'Furnished Holiday Letting' definition provided it is let furnished on a commercial basis and:

(i) It is available for letting at least 140 days in the year and actually let for at least 70 days, and
(ii) Not more than 155 days may fall during periods of longer term occupation. Longer term occupation is a continuous period of more than 31 days during which the accommodation is in the same occupation.

Based on the facts given, it appears likely that Lizzie's cottage will qualify.

Capital allowances may be claimed on the cost of furnishings. In the year of expenditure, an annual investment allowance at 100% of £10,000 may be claimed.

Lizzie may claim the same losses as a trader – she may offset a 2010/11 loss against her other general income in 2010/11 and/or 2009/10. She may alternatively carry back the loss against her general income of 2007/08, 2008/09 and 2009/10. Finally, the loss may be carried forward against future profits from the letting business.

3.3

		Property	
	A	*B*	*C*
	£	£	£
Rent	620	284 (W)	100
Agent's commission	(20)		
Advertising for tenants		(76)	
Repairs	(142)	(255)	(119)
Profit/(loss)	458	(47)	(19)

	£
Profit on A	458
Less loss on B and C	(66)
Property income assessment	392

Working

	£
April – Sept ($\frac{6}{12}$ × £348)	174
Dec – March ($\frac{3}{12}$ × £440)	110
	284

3.4 Property income:

		A	B
		£	£
Income	(3/12 × £2,400 + 6/12 × £1,600)	1,400	
	(9/12 × £600)		450
Expenditure:			
Agent's commission:			
1.5.10		(25)	(10)
1.11.10		(25)	(10)
Repairs		–	(1,500)
Advertising		(50)	–
		1,300	(1,070)
Net rents			£230

Note. Installation of new kitchen equipment is a capital *not* a revenue expense.

Lease premium:

£5,000 x $\frac{50 - 9}{50}$ = £4,100 assessable as property income

Total property income assessment £230 + £4,100 = £4,330

3.5 *October 2000 premium*

£20,000 x $\frac{50 - 29}{50}$ = £8,400 assessable as property income

Therefore, Brian's annual deductions amount to: £8,400 ÷ 30 years = £280 p.a.

October 2010 premium

	£
Premium assessable as property income	
£8,000 x $\frac{50 - 4}{50}$	7,360
Less allowable deductions:	
£280 × 5 years	(1,400)
	5,960

3.6 (a) The normal basis would be to assess Judy on her rental income less allowable expenses as follows:

	£
Rent (£600 × 12)	7,200
Less allowable expenses:	
Electricity	(1,200)
Gas	(1,400)
Wear & tear allowance (10% × 7,200)	(720)
	3,880

The alternative basis, for which Judy may elect would be to assess her on rental income less the 'rent a room' exemption (ignoring actual expenses):

	£
Rent	7,200
Less rent-a-room exemption	(4,250)
	2,950

(b) It will be more beneficial for Judy to elect for the alternative basis in 2010/11.

The deadline for the election for 2010/11 is 31 January 2013. The election will remain in force for future tax years unless it is withdrawn.

3.7 Seraphina is assessable on the net rental income for the period 1 June 2010 – 5 April 2011 as well as the income proportion of the lease premium.

	£
Rental income (W1)	3,896
Lease premium (W2)	36,000
2010/11 property income	39,896

Workings

(1) Rental income

	£
Rent (1.7.10 – 5.4.11): 9/12 × £42,000	31,500
Less: management fee: 15% × £31,500	(4,725)
Less: interest 5.25% × £685,000 × 50% × 10/12	(14,984)
Less: repairs	(7,895)
Net rental income	3,896

(2) Lease premium

$£50{,}000 \times \frac{50 - 14}{50}$ = £36,000 assessable as property income

4.1

	Non savings Income £	Dividends £
Income :		
Employment income	95,000	
Dividends ($3{,}000 \times \frac{100}{90}$)		3,333
Personal allowance	(6,475)	
Taxable income	88,525	3,333
Tax thereon:		
£37,400 @ 20%	7,480	
£51,125 @ 40%	20,450	
3,333 @ 32.5	1,083	
	29,013	
Less: EIS relief [Notes]		
(50,000 × 20%)	(10,000)	
Tax liability	19,013	
Less tax credits:		
Dividends	(333)	
PAYE	(27,000)	
IT repayable	(8,320)	

Notes:

(1) Patricia can claim to treat her 2011/12 EIS investment of £30,000 as if it were made in 2010/11.

(2) Interest on NS&I Certificates is exempt.

4.2 (a) An ISA may contain investments in cash and in stocks and shares (also including life insurance). The maximum subscription in 2010/11 is £10,200 pa overall, with no more than £5,100 pa in cash.

(b) Income and gains are both tax free within the ISA.

(c) The investor must be aged at least 18 (or 16 for a cash only ISA) and UK resident and ordinarily resident.

4.3 Any gain arising as a result of withdrawing funds from an ISA account is exempt from CGT.

LiteHead Ltd appears to be an EIS company. As a result, Maggie would have obtained income tax relief (at 20%) on making the investment, which will be withdrawn on the disposal (at the same rate) as sale takes place within three years of acquisition.

As the shares are sold at a gain, albeit within 3 years of their acquisition, the gain is calculated as normal ie ignoring any remaining EIS relief

	£
Proceeds £4.50 × 12,500	56,250
Less: cost	(12,500)
Gain	43,750

5.1

	£
Statutory redundancy pay	3,800
Ex-gratia cash payment	45,000
MV of car	12,000
Outplacement counselling (exempt)	–
	60,800
Less exempt amount	(30,000)
	30,800
Less foreign service exemption	
(30,800 × $^{10}/_{30}$)	(10,267)
Taxable	£20,533

5.2 Earnings:

	£
Salary	10,000
Car (£16,000 × 28%)	4,480
Second car (£12,000 × 20%)**	2,400
Fuel (18,000 × 28%)	5,040
Cost of wine	1,000
Earnings	22,920
Less: expenses	(600)
	22,320

The second car is assessed on Jim because his daughter receives it by virtue of *his* employment, not hers (would you expect a company car if you just worked on Saturdays?)

* $\frac{195-130}{5} = 13\%$. 15% + 13% = 28%

** $\frac{155-130}{5} = 5\%$. 15% + 5% = 20% (*Note.* Round down the emissions to 155)

5.3 Earnings – 2010/11

	£
Salary	30,000
Accommodation (W1)	1,550
Related expenses (W1)	4,950
	36,500

Workings

1 *Accommodation*

	£
Annual value	750
Additional charge: 4% × £(125,000 – 75,000)	2,000
less employee contribution	(1,200)
	1,550

Mr Thomas occupied the property for the first time more than 6 years after it was purchased in 1996, therefore the additional charge is based on the market value of the property when first occupied, not on cost plus alterations carried out prior to occupation.

Related expenses

	£
Household bills – light, heat, telephone £(750 + 250 + 350)	1,350
Council tax	1,400
Redecoration	700
Gardener	1,500
	4,950

5.4 (1) *Cheap taxable loan*

Average basis: $\frac{(10{,}000 + 9{,}000)}{2} \times \frac{10}{12} \times 4\% = £317$

Strict basis:		£
	£10,000 × 2/12 × 4%	67
	£15,000 × 4/12 × 4%	200
	£7,500 × 2/12 × 4%	50
	£11,500 × 1/12 × 4%	38
	£9,000 × 1/12 × 4%	30
		385

HMRC may insist on the strict basis, although in practice the difference might be considered insignificant.

(2) *Cars*

Mercedes: £21,500 × 18% = £3,870 $\left(\frac{145-130}{5}\right)$ = 3 + 15 = 18%

Escort: £10,000 × 21% × 8/12 = £1,400 $\left(\frac{160-130}{5}\right)$ = 6 + 15 = 21%

5.5 Earnings

	£	£
Salary		32,600
Expenses allowance:		
Gross allowance (N1)	2,500	
Less business travel	(1,800)	
		700
		33,300
Benefits:		
Hi-fi equipment £(800 × 20%) (N2)	160	
Car £(15,000 × 10%) (N3)	1,500	
Medical insurance (N4)	300	
Clothing (N4)	400	
		2,360
Amount chargeable as earnings		35,660

Notes

(1) The expenses allowance is taxable, but Alf can claim the cost of business travel as an allowable deduction. Entertainment of clients is not deductible as this would not have been deductible for his employer.

(2) The annual value of the hi-fi equipment subject to tax is 20% of its cost.

(3) The emission rate is 100g/km and the appropriate percentage is 10%.

(4) The taxable value of the medical insurance and clothing is the cost to the company of providing the benefits.

5.6 **Mr Bjork's benefits**

	£	£	£
Jaguar: car (£20,000 × 32% × $^4/_{12}$) (W1)			2,133
petrol (£18,000 × 32% × $^4/_{12}$) (W1)			1,920
Mercedes: no private use (all business use)			–
Use of computer £6,000 × 20% × 6/12			600
Gift of compute			
Market value at acquisition		200	
Original market value	6,000		
Less assessed in respect of use:			
- 2008/09: £6,000 x 20% x 6/12	(600)		
- 2009/10: £6,000 x 20%	(1,200)		
- 2010/11: as above	(600)		
		3,600	3,600
Total benefits			8,253

Working

$$\left(\frac{215-130}{5}\right) = 17 + 15 = 32\%$$

5.7 EARNINGS INCOME FOR 2010/11

	£	£
Salary:		
April – June ($^3/_{12}$ × £31,000)	7,750	
July – March ($^9/_{12}$ × £36,000)	27,000	
		34,750
Bonus – paid in year		4,000
		38,750
Accommodation:		
Higher of (i) Rent paid £5,000 × $^9/_{12}$ = £3,750	3,750	
(ii) Annual value 2,400 × $^9/_{12}$ = £1,800		
Less contribution (£100 × 9 months)	(900)	
		2,850
		41,600
Less: pension contribution (covered in Chapter 7) (5% × £38,750)		(1,938)
Earnings		39,662

Note. Employers' contributions of up to £55 per week towards childcare provision are tax free therefore the £100 monthly payment is not taxable.

5.8

	£	£
Salary		30,000
Crèche [(200 – 55) × 52]		7,540
Parking space (exempt)		–
Mileage:		
Amount received (5,000 × 60p)	3,000	
Less authorised amount (5,000 × 40p)	(2,000)	
		1,000
		38,540
Less allowable deduction (club subscription)		(800)
Earnings		37,740

Note: Golf subscription is not allowable deduction.

5.9 *Employment income:*

	£
Salary: £52,000 × 8/12	34,667
Company car (W1) 25% × £23,000 × 8/12	3,833
Fuel 25% × £18,000 × 8/12	3,000
Termination package (W2)	13,990
Employment income:	55,490

Workings

(1) *Company car*

(180-130)/5 + 15% = 25%

(2) *Redundancy package*

	£	£	£
PILON			13,000
Discretionary payment		28,000	
Statutory redundancy		990	
Car	10,000		
Less: payment	(8,000)		
		2,000	
		30,990	
Less: exemption		(30,000)	
			990
Taxable			13,990

6.1

	Non savings income £	Savings £
Salary	60,000	
Exercise of EMI option (note)	5,000	
NS&I a/c interest		1,500
Net income	65,000	1,500
Personal allowance	(6,475)	
Taxable income	58,525	1,500
Tax thereon:		
£37,400 @ 20%	7,480	
£21,125 @ 40%	8,450	
£1,500 @ 40%	600	
	16,530	
Less PAYE	(15,000)	
IT payable	1,530	

Note: There are no income tax consequences at the time of grant of the option.

However, as the option was granted at a discount, there will be an income tax charge at the date of exercise on the amount of the discount i.e. 10,000 × (£2 – £1.50) = £5,000.

6.2 (a) If the scheme meets the qualifying conditions of an approved EMI scheme then as the options price is not less than the market value of the shares at the date the options were granted there are no tax consequences on the grant or exercise of the options.

When Sue comes to sell the shares she will have a chargeable gain as follows:

	£
Sale proceeds = 5,000 × £10.40	52,000
Cost = 5,000 × £4.00	(20,000)
Gain	32,000

(b) If the scheme did not meet the qualifying conditions of an EMI scheme, an employment income charge will arise on the exercise of the option as follows:

	£
Market value at date of exercise	10.00
Less exercise price	(3.00)
	7.00 per share

£7.00 × 5,000 shares = £35,000

There is no national insurance charge as the shares are not readily convertible assets (ie not quoted shares).

Sale of shares

	£
Sale proceeds	52,000
Cost = MV at date of exercise	(50,000)
Chargeable gain	2,000

6.3 (i) As income tax charge would arise on the date of acquisition of the shares on the difference between the market value of the shares and the price paid.

i.e. 10,000 × (£5 – £2) = £30,000

(ii) There would be no income tax charge on grant of the option.

On exercise, there would be an income tax charge on the difference between the market value of the shares and the exercise price:

i.e. 10,000 × (£8 – £2) = £60,000

(iii) There would be no income tax charge on acquisition of the preference shares, as Sharon is paying market value for them.

On conversion of the preference shares, there would be an income tax charge on the difference between the market value of the preference shares and the ordinary shares.

i.e. 10,000 × (£8 – £2) = £60,000

6.4 These are unapproved share options, as Janet already holds options over shares worth £30,000 (the maximum in a CSOP scheme).

The difference between the exercise price (plus the cost of the options) and the market value at the exercise date is subject to income tax. The market value at the date of exercise is the base cost for CGT purposes.

Grant – no tax consequences

Exercise

	£
Market value at exercise: 5,000 × £12.50	62,500
Less: Exercise price: 5,000 × £2.75	(13,750)
Less: cost of options: 5,000 × 0.12p	(600)
Specific employment income	48,150
Tax @ 40%	19,260

Sale

	£
Proceeds: 5,000 × £13.95	69,750
Less cost (MV at exercise)	(62,500)
Chargeable gain	7,250
Less: Annual exempt amount	(10,100)
Taxable gain	Nil

7.1

	£
Earnings:	
Salary/bonuses	380,000
Medical insurance	1,500
Company car	12,000
Free parking (exempt)	–
Less: subscription	(500)
Relevant earnings	393,000

Jeremy can pay up to 100% of his earnings (i.e. £393,000) and obtain tax relief. He would pay 80% (i.e. £314,400) to the pension fund and the fund would reclaim 20% (£78,600) from HMRC.

However, as Jeremy would by paying more than the annual allowance of £255,000 into his pension, he will have to pay 40% on the excess:

40% × £138,000 = £55,200

7.2 (a) **Maximum contributions**

Ed and Joan can contribute any amount to their pension regardless of the level of their earnings. However tax relief will only be given for contributions up to the level of their earnings for the tax year.

The partnership profits for 2010/11 of £175,000 split 4:1 gives Ed earnings of £140,000 and Joan £35,000. Therefore Ed could contribute a maximum of £140,000 and Joan £35,000 and receive tax relief on their contributions.

(b) **Tax relief**

Basic rate tax relief is given through the pension holder paying contributions net of 20%. This means that they pay only 80% of the gross payment into the pension. HMRC pays the extra 20% on their behalf to the pension provider.

Ed will pay £112,000 (£140,000 × 80%) and Joan will pay £28,000 (£35,000 × 80%).

In addition Ed will be entitled to higher rate tax relief. This is given by extending the basic rate band for the tax year by the amount of the gross contribution ie £37,400 + £140,000 = £177,400.

(c) **No earnings**

There is no need for the individual to have earnings. Tax relief is available for a contribution of up to £3,600 per tax year into a pension regardless of the level of earnings.

7.3 INCOME TAX COMPUTATION 2010/11

	Non-savings income £
Earnings (W1)	54,871
Less: Personal allowance	(6,475)
Taxable income	48,396
Tax thereon:	
£39,650 @ 20% (W1)	7,930
£8,746 @ 40%	3,498
Tax liability	11,428
Less: tax deducted:	
PAYE	(6,000)
Tax due	5,428

Workings

1 *Earnings*

	£
Salary	
(£40,000 × $^{9}/_{12}$)	30,000
(£44,000 × $^{3}/_{12}$)	11,000
	41,000
Bonuses (note 1)	
Awarded 30.9.10	6,881
Awarded 31.3.11	6,990
Pension contributions by employer	Exempt
Total	54,871

2. *Personal pension contributions*

Dwaine pays £150 × 12	£1,800
$\times \frac{100}{80}$	£2,250

Basic rate threshold: £37,400 + £2,250 = £39,650

Note: Bonus becomes taxable in the year in which a director is *entitled* to the payment (even if this is before actual receipt).

7.4 Alfred's earned income includes his salary, benefits and the FHL rental income. He can make contributions to his pension up to this amount. However, as this exceeds the annual allowance he will suffer an income tax clawback charge at 40%.

	Non Savings	*Savings*	*Dividends*
	£	£	£
Earnings	244,000		
Rental income (incl FHL)	43,000		
Bank interest: £112,500 × 100/80 ÷ 2		70,312	
Dividends: £363,330 × 100/90			403,700
Total	287,000	70,312	403,700
Less: PA (adjusted net income > £112,950)	(Nil)		
Taxable income	287,000	70,312	403,700
£37,400 @ 20%	7,480		
£269,000 @ 20% (W1)	53,800		
£50,912 @ 40%	20,365		
£61,688 @ 32.5%	20,049		
£342,012 @ 42.5%	145,355		
Tax liability	247,049		
Less: Tax paid/ suffered			
Dividends £403,700 @ 10%	(40,370)		
Interest £70,312 @ 20%	(14,062)		
	192,617		
Add: pension charge (W2)	5,600		
Tax payable	198,217		

Workings

(1) *Extension of basic rate and higher rate bands*

Pension contribution:

Maximum contribution (gross) = relevant earnings ie £244,000 + £25,000 (FHL) = £269,000.

(2) *Pension tax charge*

	£
Contribution (above)	269,000
Less: annual allowance	(255,000)
Excess	14,000
Tax @ 40%	5,600

8.1 Mr Garcia will be resident and ordinarily resident but non-domiciled in the UK. Therefore, any UK income will be taxed on an arising basis, but he may claim the remittance basis for his overseas income. If he claims the remittance basis he will not be subject to the £30,000 remittance basis charge until he has been resident in the UK for at least 7 of the 9 preceding tax years. He will lose entitlement to the personal allowance.

(1) **The pension**

If Mr Garcia claims for the remittance basis to apply, the pension income will be taxable only when remitted to the UK. However, if he does not make a claim only 90% of the income from his Spanish pension will be taxable in the UK.

As it appears that he is planning to bring all of the pension income into the UK, he may decide not to make the claim for the remittance basis so that he is only taxed on 90% of the income. In this case, the income will be taxed at 20% and 40%.

(2) **Investment income**

If Mr Garcia makes a claim for the remittance basis to apply, his Spanish bank account interest and dividends will only be taxable when he brings the funds into the UK. It will be taxed as non-savings income, so even the dividends will be taxed at 20%, 40% or 50%, depending on the level of his income.

Remittance planning

Assuming that Mr Garcia makes a claim for the remittance basis to apply to his overseas income, he should have any overseas income arising after he comes to the UK paid into a bank account in Spain separate from his existing savings. He can then bring his previous savings into the UK without giving rise to income tax, as this does not represent income arising while resident in the UK.

8.2 (a) Marco has become resident and ordinarily resident in the UK as he has come for at least three years. However, he remains domiciled in Italy as he has not severed ties with his country of origin.

(b) As Marco came to the UK to take up an employment which is expected to last at least two years, he may by concession split the tax year of his arrival and be treated as a resident in the UK from the date of his arrival – i.e. from 5 August 2009.

(c) *Taxable income*

	£
Total employment earnings	80,200
Amount relating to the UK duties (80%)	64,160
Amounted enjoyed in the UK (£60,000 + £5,200)	65,200
Income from employment	65,200
Interest (£35 × $^{100}/_{80}$)	44
	65,244
Less PA	-
Taxable income	65,244

Marco is non-domiciled in the UK and can claim to be taxed on the remittance basis on his foreign income. He will not be subject to the £30,000 remittance basis charge as he has not been resident in the UK for 7 years of the preceding 9 tax years.

Individuals who claim the remittance basis are not entitled to a personal allowance.

8.3 (a) After four years of making regular visits to the UK which average 91 days or more per tax year, Steffen is then treated as resident from the start of the fifth tax year.

By the end of 2009/10 average visits from the last four tax years amount to:

(75 + 98 + 92 + 104) / 4 = 92.25

Hence, Steffen will be treated as a UK resident from 6 April 2010.

(b) Income tax 2010/11

	£
Offshore interest (£28,600 × $^{100}/_{55}$)	52,000
Rent (£57,800 × $^{100}/_{85}$)	68,000
	120,000
Tax thereon:	
£37,400 @ 20%	7,480
£82,600@ 40%	33,040
	40,520
Less DTR on	
Rent: 68,000 × 15% (foreign tax clearly lower)	(10,200)
Interest: 52,000 × 40% (UK tax clearly lower)	(20,800)
Income tax payable	9,520

Steffen is non-domiciled in the UK and can claim to be taxed on the remittance basis on his foreign income. He will not be subject to the £30,000 remittance basis charge as he has not been resident in the UK for 7 out of the preceding 9 tax years. As he is claiming the remittance basis his foreign source bank interest is taxed as non-savings income.

Individuals who claim the remittance basis are not entitled to a personal allowance, but as Steffen's income exceeds £112,950 no personal allowance would be available if the remittance basis was not claimed.

9.1 (a) Matilda is a 'temporary non-resident' as her period of absence from the UK covers less than five complete tax years. As a result, gains made on assets which she owned before she left the UK and sold during her period of absence are taxable in the tax year of her return – i.e. 2010/11.

(b)

	£
Painting	55,000
Less CY loss (land)	(15,000)
Total chargeable gains	40,000

Note: The gain on the cottage is not chargeable because Matilda acquired it after she became non UK resident.

10.1

	£
Gain: sales of shares	17,900
CY Loss (painting)	(7,000)
	10,900
Losses b/f (10,900 – 10,100)	(800)
	10,100
Less: annual exempt amount	(10,100)
Taxable gain	Nil

Losses c/f (5,000 – 800) = £4,200

The loss on the sale of a cottage to Mark's brother is a connected party loss. Therefore, it must be carried forward separately and can only be offset against future gains on disposal to Mark's brother.

10.2

	2010/11
	£
Trade profits	15,000
Property income	3,000
Original net income	18,000
s.64 loss relief	(18,000)
Revised net income	nil
Chargeable gains	16,000
s.261B TCGA 1992 loss relief (W)	(10,000)
Revised gains (covered by AE)	6,000
Loss memo	
Loss incurred in 2011/12	28,000
s.64 against net income of 2010/11	(18,000)
	10,000
Relief against chargeable gain of 2010/11	(10,000)
	–

Working

Maximum offset of trading loss against chargeable gains:

Lower of:	£
(i) trading loss remaining after s.64	10,000
and	
(ii) net gains less any capital losses b/f	16,000
	∴ £10,000

10.3

Asset – Post 22.6.10 disposal	£
Proceeds	28,800
31.3.82 MV	(7,500)
Enhancement expenditure	(1,000)
Gain	20,300
Less Annual exempt amount	(10,100)
Taxable gain	10,200

CGT payable: Basic rate band remaining = £2,400 (£37,400 - £35,000)

CGT @ 18%: £2,400 x 18%	432
CGT @ 28%: £7,800 x 28%	2,184
	2,616

CGT due 31 January 2012

10.4 *Computation of capital gains tax*

	Pre 23.6.10	*Post 22.6.10*
	£	£
Factory		75,000
Painting	23,000	
Less: Annual exempt amount	(Nil)	(10,100)
Taxable gains	23,000	64,900
CGT @ 18%/28%	4,140	18,172
Total CGT	22,312	

Note. The annual exempt amount is set off against the gain arising on the factory as this is taxed at 28% (as Emily is a higher rate taxpayer) whereas the gain on the painting is only taxed at 18%.

Workings

1 *Factory*

	£	Gains £
Proceeds	225,000	
Less: cost	(150,000)	
Gain	75,000	75,000

2 *Painting*

Transfer to Emily on 1.7.01 on no gain/no loss basis

	£
Cost to Arthur	50,000
Becomes base cost for Emily	

Sale by Emily

	£	
Proceeds	73,000	
Less: cost	(50,000)	
Gain	23,000	23,000

10.5

	£
Proceeds	45,000
Cost £8,000 × $\frac{45,000}{45,000+50,000}$	(3,789)
Gain	41,211
Less: Annual exempt amount	(10,100)
Taxable gain	31,111
CGT payable: Basic rate band remaining = £12,400 (£37,400 - £25,000)	
CGT @ 18%: £12,400 x 18%	2,232
CGT @ 28%: £18,711 x 28%	5,239
	7,471

Note. No claim is available for a 'small part' disposal as proceeds > £20,000 and > 20% of MV of land.

10.6 (1) No s.23 claim made – part disposal

2000/01

	£	£
Proceeds		14,000
Less: cost: £40,000 × $\frac{14,000}{14,000+50,000}$		(8,750)
Gain		5,250

The cost remaining for future disposals is £31,250 (ie £40,000 – £8,750)

2010/11

Proceeds		85,000
Less: Cost £(40,000 – 8,750)	31,250	
Restoration (enhancement) costs	14,000	(45,250)
Gain		39,750

10.7 Chargeable gain in 2010/11

	£
Insurance proceeds	17,000
Less: cost	(7,500)
Gain	9,500
Less gain deferred (balancing figure)	(8,500)
Gain restricted to proceeds not spent on replacement £(17,000 – 16,000)	£1,000

Allowable expenditure of replacement asset is:

	£
Actual cost	16,000
Less: deferred (above)	(8,500)
Allowable expenditure	7,500

11.1

Share pool

	No of shares	*Cost* £
April 1985 acquisition	1,000	2,954
May 2005 acquisition	1,000	6,000
	2,000	8,954
August 2010 disposal		
$\frac{500}{2,000} \times £8,954$	(500)	(2,239)
	1,500	6,715

August 2010 disposal	£
Proceeds	15,000
Less Cost	(2,239)
Chargeable gain	12,761

11.2

Share pool

	No of shares	*Cost* £
April 1985 acquisition	5,000	5,605
July 1999 bonus issue 1:5	1,000	–
	6,000	5,605
December 2010 disposal	(3,500)	(3,270)
Pool c/f	2,500	2,335

	£
Proceeds	6,250
Less cost	(3,270)
Gain	2,980

11.3 *Summary of gains:*

	£
Building (W1)	400,000
Forum Follies plc (W2)	5,000
Total chargeable gains	405,000
Less: Annual exempt amount	(10,100)
Taxable gain	394,900

Workings

1 *Building*

	£
Proceeds	600,000
Less 31.3.82 value	(200,000)
Gain	400,000

2 *The takeover of Forum Follies plc*

The elements in the takeover consideration have the following values:	£
Ordinary shares (30,000 × £3.00)	90,000
Cash	10,000
Total consideration received	100,000

A gain only arises on the date of the takeover in respect of the cash element.

	£
Cash received (above)	10,000
Cost $50,000 \times \frac{10,000}{100,000}$	(5,000)
Gain	5,000

11.4 *Dassau plc shares*

(i) Acquisition 15 November 2010 (Acquired in following 30 days)

	£
Proceeds 500/1200 × £9,500	3,958
Cost	(1,500)
Gain	2,458

(ii) *Share pool (s.104 holding)*

	Shares	*Cost* £
December 1985	1,000	2,000
Rights issue April 1987 1:2 @ £2	500	1,000
	1,500	3,000
Disposal November 2010	(700)	(1,400)
	800	1,600

	£
Proceeds 700/1200 × £9,500	5,542
Less cost	(1,400)
Gain	4,142

Summary	£
Total gains (£2,458 + £4,142)	6,600
less capital losses b/f (restricted)	–
	6,600
Less annual exempt amount	(10,100)
Taxable gain	–

11.5 *Gain*

	£
Proceeds	13,500
Less: Cost	(4,500)
Gain	9,000

Working

Share pool

	Shares	*Cost*
		£
March 1990	2,000	2,000
December 1996	4,000	10,000
	6,000	12,000
May 1999 rights issue 1: 5 @ £5	1,200	6,000
	7,200	18,000
October 2010 sale	(1,800)	(4,500)
C/f	5,400	13,500

11.6 Julio is taxable on his worldwide gains as he is UK resident. However, if he makes a claim to use the remittance basis he will only be taxed when he brings the overseas gain to the UK, although he will lose his annual exempt amount (and income tax personal allowances).

Since he has not yet remitted any of the gain he should make the claim. He will not be subject to the remittance basis charge of £30,000 as he has not been resident for seven years out of the last nine tax years.

CommandN Plc

The matching rules apply.

(i) Next 30 days

	£
Proceeds 5,000/10,000 × £195,600	97,800
Less: cost	(97,050)
Chargeable gain	750

(ii) Share pool

	£
Proceeds 5,000/10,000 × £195,600	97,800
Less: cost (W)	(96,647)
Chargeable gain	1,153

	£
Total gain £(750 + 1,153)	1,903
No Annual exempt amount as makes remittance basis claim	
Tax @ 28%	533

Working

Share pool

		Cost
		£
Purchase	7,000	157,220
Purchase	8,000	132,720
Total	15,000	289,940
Disposal	(5,000)	(96,647)
c/f	10,000	193,293

11.7 On the takeover there is an immediate charge to CGT in respect of the cash received:

	£
Cash proceeds (W1)	11,875
Less: cost (W1)	(1,371)
Chargeable gain	10,504

Disposal of ½ the shares

	£
Cash proceeds £8.95 × 12,500 (W2)	111,875
Less: cost (W2)	(12,915)
Chargeable gain	98,960
Total gains	109,464

Workings

(1) *Takeover package*

	Market value	*Cost*
	£	£
Cash received: 95p × 12,500	11,875	1,371
Shares received: 12,500 × 2 × £8.95	223,750	25,829
Total	235,625	27,200

(2) *Rover Ltd share pool*

Detail	*Number*	*Cost*
		£
Purchase (use MV82)	10,000	27,200
Bonus issue 1:4	2,500	-
Total	12,500	27,200
Takeover 2:1	25,000	(1,371)
	25,000	25,829
Disposal (½)	(12,500)	(12,915)
c/f	12,500	12,914

12.1

		£
Victoria Cross:		
Proceeds		14,780
Less cost		(3,000)
		11,780

Chargeable gain not to exceed 5/3 × £(14,780 – 6,000) = £14,633

Note. Medals are only exempt if awarded for bravery or inherited.

Vintage car: Exempt

		£
Painting:		
	Gross proceeds (deemed)	6,000
	Cost	(6,260)
		(260)

	£
Gain	11,780
Less CY loss	(260)
Chargeable gains	11,520

12.2

Motor car: exempt

Machinery item 1:	£
Proceeds	7,500
Less cost	(5,500)
	2,000

Restrict to 5/3 £(7,500 – 6,000) = £2,500

Therefore gain = £2,000

Machinery item 2. There is never a capital loss on an item on which capital allowances have been claimed as a balancing allowance would be given instead through the capital allowances computation.

12.3

Grant of long lease:

	£
Proceeds	30,000
Less 31.3.82 MV	
$£40,000 \times \frac{30,000}{30,000 + 82,500}$	(10,667)
Chargeable gain	19,333

Grant of short lease:	£
Proceeds (capital element of premium)*	2,000
Cost $£30,000 \times \frac{2,000}{10,000 + 50,000}$	(1,000)
	1,000

* Premium	10,000
Less: Amount assessed as property income	
$£10,000 \times \frac{50 - 10}{50}$	(8,000)
Capital element of premium	2,000

Total chargeable gains (19,333 + 1,000)	20,333
Less: Annual exempt amount	(10,100)
	10,233

12.4

Summary

	£
Gain	6,200
Less: loss	(1,200)
Net gains	5,000

Workings

1 Leonardo cartoon:

	£
Proceeds (deemed)	6,000
Allowable cost	(7,200)
Allowable loss	(1,200)

2 Lathe

	£
Proceeds	10,500
Allowable cost	(4,300)
Gain	6,200
Restrict to $\frac{5}{3} \times$ £(10,500 – 6,000) = £7,500 ∴ gain	£6,200

12.5 (1) Assignment of long lease

	£
Proceeds	79,000
Cost	(28,000)
Chargeable gain	51,000

(2) Assignment of short lease

			Cost £
Proceeds			79,000
Cost: £28,000 ×	$\frac{88.371}{100.000}$	(31yrs) / (57yrs)	(24,744)
Chargeable gain			54,256

12.6 Grant of short lease out of freehold

	£
Proceeds: capital element of premium =	
£20,000 – (£20,000 x $\frac{50-19}{50}$)	7,600
Cost: £25,000 × $\frac{7,600}{20,000+17,000}$	(5,135)
Gain	2,465

12.7 *Sale of table*

		£	£
Proceeds			8,000
Less: cost of disposal			(800)
			7,200
Less: cost	– option	2,000	
	– asset	3,500	(5,500)
Gain			1,700

Chattels rules ($^5/_3$ × £(8,000 – 6,000) = £3,333) give a higher gain so do not apply.

12.8 The grant of a lease for a premium is a disposal for CGT purposes.

This is the grant of a short lease (≤ 50 years) from a freehold so we need to use a modified part disposal formula:

	£
Capital element of premium (W)	14,000
Less: cost: $\frac{14,000}{50,000+565,000} \times$ £685,000	(15,593)
Allowable loss	(1,593)

(W) Lease premium

	£
Premium	50,000
Less: income element: £50,000 x $\frac{50-14}{50}$	(36,000)
Capital element	14,000

13.1

		£
Gain		80,000
Exempt:		
1.4.82 – 30.6.86	51 months	
1.7.07 – 30.6.10	36 months	
	87 months	
Total period		
1.4.82 – 30.6.10	339 months	
$\therefore \frac{87}{339} \times$ £80,000		(20,531)
Letting gain		59,469
Less: letting relief		
Lowest of (i)	£40,000	
(ii)	PPR relief: £20,531	
(iii)	letting gain (1.7.86 – 30.6.07 = 252m): £59,469	(20,531)
Chargeable gain		38,938

Note: Occupation and ownership prior to 1 April 1982 is ignored

13.2 (a)

	£
Proceeds	200,000
Less: cost	(20,000)
Gain	180,000
Less PPR exemption	
£180,000 × 2/3	(120,000)
Chargeable gain	60,000

Note. As the students occupy separate self-contained accommodation, the ground floor is treated as a separate residence, the gain on which is fully chargeable to CGT.

(b) Any **three** of:

(i) Any period employed outside the UK

(ii) Periods of up to four years working (employed or self-employed) elsewhere

(iii) Up to three years for any reason

(iv) The last three years of ownership where the property has been the principal private residence at some time.

(v) Any period whilst living in job related accommodation

(vi) First 12 months if not occupied due to building work or because unable to sell old home..

Note. (i) – (iii) must be preceded and followed by a period of actual occupation.

13.3 (a) On the sale of the current family home there will be no capital gains tax implications due to principal private residence (PPR) relief which ensures that the sale of a property which has been the taxpayer's only or main residence is exempt from capital gains tax.

(b) However, where a taxpayer owns two properties, even if he actually resides in both, PPR relief can only apply to one property. A husband and wife living together such as Mr and Mrs Mackay can only have one PPR between them ie it is not possible for the flat to be Mr Mackay's PPR and for the house to be Mrs Mackay's.

Instead, Mr and Mrs Mackay should elect which of the house and flat they wish to have treated as their main residence for the purposes of PPR relief. The election should be made within two years of residing in the two properties, in this case by May 2012 – otherwise the main residence will be determined as a question of fact.

Mr and Mrs Mackay do have a right to vary the election by a further written notice which can take effect for any period starting not more than two years before the date of the second notice.

(c) As Mr & Mrs Mackay are likely to sell the flat at a profit in five years time they should elect for the flat to be treated as the main residence. They should vary the election so that the house is treated as the main residence not more than three years before sale. The gain on the flat will then be exempt at the expense of a loss of approximately two years exemption on the house.

13.4 Computation of chargeable gain on sale of house

Period	*Explanation*	*Occupation or deemed occupation (months)*	*Non occupation (months)*
2.5.85 – 1.2.88	Actual occupation	33	
2.2.88 – 1.12.97	Letting		118
2.12.97 – 3.7.07	Absence		115
4.7.07 – 3.7.10	Last three years deemed occupation	36	
		69	233

Total ownership period = 302 months

		£
Proceeds (3.7.10)		270,000
Less: Cost		(70,000)
Gain		200,000
Less:	Exemption for main residence $\frac{69}{302} \times £200,000$	(45,695)
		154,305
Less:	letting exemption: lowest of £45,695 (gain exempted by private residence relief) £78,146 (chargeable gain attributable to letting) (W) £40,000 (maximum relief available for lettings)	(40,000)
Chargeable gain		114,305

Working

Gain in let period: $\frac{118}{302} \times £200,000 = £78,146$

13.5 *Calculation of chargeable gain*

	£
Proceeds	380,200
Less: Cost	(110,000)
Gain before PPR	270,200

	Flat	*Office*
	£	£
Gain $\frac{17}{24} : \frac{7}{24}$	191,392	78,808
PPR	(191,392)	
Chargeable gain	Nil	78,808

PPR exemption

	Occupation	*Non occupation*	*Total*
6.4.87 – 5.4.88 (occupation)	1	–	1
6.4.88 – 5.4.92 (deemed 4 years)	4	–	4
6.4.92 – 5.4.93 (part of 3 years for any reason)	1	–	1
6.4.93 – 5.4.94 (occupation)	1	–	1
6.4.94 – 5.4.08 (14 years joint use)	7	7	14
6.4.08 – 4.4.11 (final 3 years deemed occupation)	3	–	3
	17	7	24

14.1 *Galadriel Ltd*

Income tax relief given 2007/08: 40,000 × 20% = £8,000

Income tax relief withdrawn in 2010/11: £8,000 × $\frac{35,000}{40,000}$ = £7,000

Capital loss:	£	£
Proceeds		35,000
Cost	40,000	
less IT relief not withdrawn	(1,000)	
		(39,000)
Allowable loss		(4,000)

Guinevere Ltd

No income tax relief withdrawn as sold more than 3 years after acquisition.

Gain on disposal is exempt.

Mordred Ltd

No income tax relief withdrawn as more than 3 years after acquisition.

Capital loss:	£	£
Proceeds		20,000
Cost	30,000	
less IT relief (30,000 × 20%)	(6,000)	
		(24,000)
Allowable loss		(4,000)

14.2 (a) EIS income tax relief will *not* be available, as the employee is 'connected' with the company.

(b) EIS income tax relief of £20,000 should be available as the company is unlisted (AIM listings being regarded as unlisted for this purpose) at the time of issue and there was no intention to obtain a full listing at that time.

(c) EIS relief will *not* be available as Jane is connected with the company since she has a shareholding of over 30%.

(d) EIS relief will *not* be available as property development is not a qualifying activity.

(e) EIS income tax relief of £100,000 (i.e. £500,000 × 20%) will be available – this is the maximum relief available.

14.3 To reduce her taxable gains to nil she must make a minimum investment of:

£(350,000 – 180,000 - 15,000 – 10,100) = £144,900.

Her gains computation would be as follows:

	£
Proceeds	350,000
Cost	(180,000)
	170,000
Less EIS deferral relief	(144,900)
Less capital losses	(15,000)
	10,100
Annual exempt amount	(10,100)
	Nil

14.4 Alan – Capital gains computation 2010/11

	£	£
1. *Land and buildings*		
Proceeds	250,000	
Less cost	(70,000)	
Chargeable gain		180,000
2. *Goodwill*		
Proceeds	85,000	
Less cost	-	
Chargeable gain		85,000
Total gains (qualifying for entrepreneurs' relief)		265,000
Annual exempt amount		(10,100)
Taxable gain		254,900
CGT @ 10%		25,490

14.5 Monty – Capital gains computation 2010/11

			Qualifying for ER £	Not qualifying for ER £
1.	*Shares*			
	Gain (max ER £5 million)		5,000,000	700,000
2.	*Painting*			
	Proceeds	12,000		
	Less cost	(1,000)		
	Gain	11,000		
	Restricted to 5/3 x (12,000 – 6,000)	10,000		10,000
	Total gains			710,000
	Less capital losses bfwd			(15,000)
	Total chargeable gains			695,000
	Annual exempt amount			(10,100)
	Taxable gain		5,000,000	684,900
	CGT @10%/28%		500,000	191,772
	Total CGT		691,772	

Note. The capital losses and annual exempt amount are set off against the gains not qualifying for entrepreneurs' relief as they are taxed at 28% (as Monty is a higher rate taxpayer) whereas the gains qualifying for entrepreneurs' relief are only taxed at 10%.

14.6 This is a material disposal of whole or part of a business, so entrepreneurs' relief is available. Claim must be made by 31 January 2013. As the business was sold prior to 23 June 2010 the maximum entrepreneurs' relief available is £2 million.

	Pre 23.6.10 £	Post 22.6.10 £
Gain	2,110,000	24,000
Less: entrepreneurs' relief 4/9 × £2,000,000	(888,889)	
Chargeable gain	1,221,111	
Less loss b/f		(12,750)
Chargeable gain		11,250
Less: Annual exempt amount		(10,100)
Taxable gain		1,150
CGT @ 18%/28%	219,800	322
Total CGT	220,122	

Note. The capital losses and annual exempt amount are set off against the gain arising after 22 June 2010 as it is taxed at 28% (as Freda is a higher rate taxpayer) whereas the remaining chargeable gain on the business is taxed at 18% as it arose before 23 June 2010.

15.1 (a) Brandon must notify HMRC of his new source of income by 5 October 2011.

(b) The penalty for failure to notify is a percentage of the tax lost, depending on the behaviour of the taxpayer. The maximum percentage is 100% if Brandon deliberately fails to notify HMRC and conceals the need to notify. If the failure by Brandon is not deliberate the percentage is reduced to 30%. The maximum penalties can be reduced by the extent of disclosure to HMRC.

(c) Brandon may submit a simplified return for his rental income as the gross income is less than £70,000 for the year.

He is required to record three lines:

- Gross property income
- Total allowable expenses
- Net income

15.2 (a) As the notice was issued before 31 October 2011, Phyllis's 2010/11 tax return was due on 31 January 2012.

Her income tax payment for 2010/11 was also due on 31 January 2012. There were no payments on account required for 2010/11, as her 2009/10 income tax was below £1,000.

(b) *Penalty for late return*

Late filing: Immediate penalty of £100. The return is more than 6 months late, but less than 12 months late. A daily penalty of £10 may be charged up to a maximum of 90 days. A tax geared penalty of 5% of the tax due will be charged. The tax geared penalty is subject to a minimum of £300, which will apply in this case.

Late payment penalty: As the return is more than 6 months late a penalty of 10% of the tax unpaid will be charged ie £16.

Interest on late tax payment:

Interest runs from 31 January 2012 to 30 August 2012:

i.e. $£160 \times 3\% \times \frac{7}{12} = \underline{£3}$

15.3 Proceeds received in instalments

If proceeds are received in instalments over a period exceeding 18 months, the tax may be spread over the shorter of:

- the period of instalments, and
- eight years.

Gifts

The CGT on gifts which do not qualify for gift relief may be paid in instalments, provided the asset gifted is:

- land
- shares or securities out of a controlling holding, or
- unquoted shares or securities.

CGT is payable in ten yearly instalments, commencing on the normal due date of 31 January following the tax year.

The deadline for these elections is four years from the end of the tax year of disposal.

15.4 (a) As Alicia submitted her 2010/11 return late, HMRC have until 12 months following the next quarter day after submission to open an enquiry – i.e. until 30 April 2013.

(b) Alicia must keep records relating to her business for 5 years after 31 January following the tax year i.e. until 31 January 2017 for 2010/11.

(c) HMRC may raise a discovery assessment in respect of earlier years if:

- Alicia or her agent have carelessly or deliberately omitted information, or
- HMRC were not given sufficient information in the return to be able to identify the loss of tax.

The time limits for raising a discovery assessment are as follows:

• Ordinary time limit	4 years from the end of the tax year
• Where the omission is careless	6 years from the end of the tax year
• Where the omission is deliberate	20 years from the end of the tax year.

15.5 (a) POA

	£
Income tax liability	10,250
Class 4 NIC	1,000
Less: tax deducted at source	(5,000)
	6,250

POAs of £3,125 are due 31 January 2011 and 31 July 2011. Any balancing payment is due 31 January 2012.

(b) John may make a claim to reduce his payments on account for 2010/11.

He must state the reason for the reduction in his claim.

If John reduces the payments on account too far, so that there is a balancing payment for 2010/11, interest will be charged on the difference between the amount of POA as calculated in (a) and the amount actually paid.

15.6 Ray has made an excessive claim to reduce his payments on account, and will therefore be charged interest on the reduction. The payments on account should have been £4,500 each based on the previous year's liability (not £5,000 each based on the current year's liability). He will be liable to interest as follows:

- 1st POA
  - on £3,500 – nil – paid on time
  - on £1,000 from due date of 31 January 2011 until the date of payment, 19 February 2012
- 2nd POA
  - on £3,500 from due date of 31 July 2011 until the date of part-payment of £3,500, 12 August 2011
  - on £1,000 from due date of 31 July 2011 until the date of payment, 19 February 2012
- Balancing payment of income tax and CGT
  - on £3,500 from due date of 31 January 2012 until the date of payment, 19 February 2012

15.7 *(1)* *Payment on account*

Payments on account are based on the previous year's income tax and Class 4 NIC only. The previous year's POAs are irrelevant here. CGT is never included.

	£
Income tax liability	17,895
Class 4 NIC liability	2,808
Less: tax deducted at source	(1,275)
	19,428
POA due 31 January (and July) 2011	9,714

(2) *Interest*

Interest is due from the due date until the date of payment, 31 January 2011 until 25 May 2011, 4 months:

3% × 4/12 × £9,714 = £97

There are no penalties on late paid payments on account.

16.1

	£
Salary (5 × £1,000)	5,000
Car benefit (£15,000 × 22% × 3/12)*	825
Fuel benefit (£18,000 × 22% × 3/12)*	990
Earnings for income tax	6,815

* $\frac{(165-130)}{5}$ = 7%

Percentage: 15% + 7% = 22%

Class 1 NIC primary (payable by Tina)

(1,000 –476) × 11% × 5 = £288

Class 1 NIC secondary (payable by Harrison Electrics Ltd)

(1,000 – 476) × 12.8% × 5 = £335

Class 1A NIC (payable by Harrison Electrics Ltd)

(825 + 990) × 12.8% = £232

16.2 *Class 1 secondary NIC*

(45,000 – 5,715) × 12.8% = £5,028

Class 1A

Loan benefit

	£
Average method: $\frac{15,000 + 10,000}{2} \times 4\%$	500
Less: interest paid 5/4/10 – 5/1/11: £15,000 × 3% × 9/12	(338)
6/1/11 – 5/4/10: £10,000 × 3% × 3/12	(75)
	87
Strict basis:	
5/4/10 – 5/1/11: £15,000 × (4% – 3%) × 9/12	112
6/1/11 – 5/4/11: £10,000 × (4% – 3%) × 3/12	25
	137

HMRC have the option to assess Ruth using the strict basis, giving a benefit of £137.

Class 1A: £137 × 12.8% = £17

[Credit also given if Class 1A calculated using benefit from 'average' method.]

16.3 Assessable benefit is the greater of

		£
(a)		
	Market value at acquisition	1,500
	less price paid	(1,000)
		500
(b)	Original market value	2,000
	less assessed in respect of use (09/10)	
	$^{6}/_{12}$ × 20% × £2,000	(200)
	less assessed in respect of use (10/11) $^{6}/_{12}$× 20% × £2,000	(200)
	less price paid	(1,000)
		600

∴ Benefit is £600 + £200 (use in 10/11) = £800

Class 1A = £800 × 12.8% = £102

Due date is 19 July 2011.

16.4

Earnings	£
Salary	25,750
Telephone bills	400
	26,150

Class 1 primary NIC (payable by Judy)

(26,150 – 5,715) × 11%= £2,248

Class 1 secondary NIC (payable by Markham Ltd)

(26,150 – 5,715) × 12.8% = £2,616

Class 1A (payable by Markham Ltd)

Benefits:	£
Flat (annual value)	3,000
Furniture (20% × £2,500)	500
	3,500

Class 1A = £3,500 × 12.8% = £448

Note: There is no additional charge for the accommodation as the original cost was less than £75,000.

16.5 *Pip: Class 1 primary contributions*

Normal months:

Earnings = £28,000 ÷ 12 = £2,333

Bonus month

Earnings = £4,000 + £2,333 = £6,333

Class 1 primary

		£
Normal month:	(2,333 – 476) × 11% × 11	2,247
Bonus month:	(3,656 – 476) × 11%	350
	(6,333 × 3,656) × 1%	27
		2,624

Estella: Class 1 primary contributions

		£
1st 6 months:	(1,333 – 476) × 11% × 6	566
Last 6 months:	(1,500 – 476) × 11% × 6	676
		1,242

Due dates : 19th following each tax month (22nd if paid electronically).

16.6 (a) Anna is not liable to Class 1 primary NIC as she is over the pensionable age.

Madison Plc will be liable to Class 1 secondary NIC - due on 19th following each tax month (22nd if paid electronically).

(b) The reimbursement of the season ticket will be subject to Class 1 primary contributions payable to Elaine and Class 1 secondary contributions payable by Madison Plc. Both are payable by 19th (22nd if electronic payment) following each tax month.

The company car benefit will be subject to Class 1A NIC payable by Madison Plc. This is due by 19th July 2011 (22nd if paid electronically).

(c) The benefits within the PAYE Settlement Agreement will be subject to Class 1B payable by Madison Plc. This is due by 19th October 2011.

16.7 Class 1 is due on salary and expense payments, unless the expense payment is contracted for by the employer, in which case Class 1A is due instead, from the employer only.

Class 1 is due on:	£
Salary	65,000
Mileage payments (W)	800
M&S vouchers	500
Gym membership (as reimbursed)	1,020
Total	67,320

Class 1A is due on:	£
Private medical insurance (as contracted for by employer)	450
Total	450

NIC due:

Employee	£	£
£(43,875 – 5,715) = 38,160 @ 11%	4,198	
£(67,320 – 43,875) = 23,445 @ 1%	234	
Total		4,432
Employer		
£(67,320 – 5,715) = 61,605 @ 12.8%		7,885
Class 1A		
Employer only: £450 @ 12.8%		58
Total NICs due		12,375

Other business related travel expenses and the professional subscription are exempt from NIC as they are deductible for Robert.

The beneficial loan is below the £5,000 threshold, so no (tax or) NICs are due.

Workings

Mileage payments

	£
Employer reimburses	4,000
Allowable under the HMRC scheme:	
8,000 × 40p	(3,200)
Excess	800

17.1 Year end returns:

- P35 – End of year summary return – due 19 May 2011
- P14 (P60 employee copy) – End of year return – due 19 May 2011
- P11D – Return of benefits for employees earning £8,500 or more) – due 6 July 2011
- P11Db – Class 1A return – due 6 July 2011

17.2 (1) The statutory redundancy pay and the ex-gratia payment are subject to income tax but the first £30,000 is exempt. PAYE should therefore be applied to £2,000 (3,000 + 29,000 – 30,000) of the ex-gratia payment.

(2) The company is not required to deduct PAYE from the tips as they are paid directly to Patrick by the customer and the company is not involved in any sharing out of the tips.

(3) The vouchers are tax free and therefore PAYE Is not required to be operated.

Awareness Paper

IHT, trusts and estates

Study Period Planner
Inheritance Tax, Trusts and Estates

Use this schedule and your exam timetable to plan the dates on which you will complete each Study Period. The letters 'H' and 'M' tell you whether the topic is high or medium priority.

Study Period	Topic		Due Date
1	Inheritance tax – basic principles	H	
2	Calculation of IHT on lifetime transfers	H	
3	IHT valuation/ BPR/APR	H	
4	Death estate	H	
5	Reliefs for falls in value on death	H	
6	IHT – additional aspects	M	
7	**Progress Test 1**	**H**	

Study Period	Topic		Due Date
8	Capital gains tax – basic principles	H	
9	IHT for trusts	H	
10	CGT for trusts	H	
11	Income tax for trusts	H	
12	Estates in administration	H	
13	**Progress Test 2**	**H**	

COURSE EXAM 1

A practice exam covering Study Periods 1 to 6

COURSE EXAM 2

A Practice exam covering all Study Periods

REVISION PHASE

Your revision phase will begin when **Course Exam 2** is complete. This should ideally be four months before the final exam.

TQT Note: The Course Exams contain questions for all FIVE of the awareness paper modules. In your exam you must answer questions from THREE modules. We suggest that you identify the THREE modules you will study and then work through the Study Period Planners for each of those modules until the point where you are told to take Course Exam 1. When you have completed all THREE modules to that point, sit Course Exam 1. Similarly, you should complete all THREE modules before you sit course exam 2. Course Exam 2 covers all of the Study Periods, although it is weighted towards the second half of your studies.

Study Period 1

High Priority

Inheritance tax – basic principles

Step 1 Exam Guidance

The contents of this study period are fundamental to any inheritance tax (IHT) question in the exam.

It introduces concepts and terminology that you must grasp and be able to use confidently to perform well in the exam.

These basic principles were tested in:

- Q12 (May 2009) & Q1 (Nov 2009), Q5 (May 2010).

Step 2 Introduction to the session

In this period we begin our study of inheritance tax (IHT). This study period provides the background information, so that you can understand the rationale behind the charging of inheritance tax and identify situations when an inheritance tax liability will arise.

Step 3 Guidance through the Study Text

Read through Chapter 1 of the Inheritance Tax, Trusts and Estates Awareness Study Text after reading the following guidance:

In this chapter we learn the basics for calculating inheritance tax.

Read through Section 1. This should be fairly quick to read but is an **essential** section as it explains when a charge to IHT arises on a 'transfer of value' and sets out the types of property that are excluded from the IHT charge. Make sure you understand these basic principles before continuing. Attempt Example 1.

Read through Section 2 which lists the exemptions available for lifetime transfers and those available for both lifetime and death transfers. Attempt Examples 2 and 3.

Finally, read through Sections 3 and 4. These sections are very brief, but very important. They explain the difference between the two types of lifetime transfers: chargeable transfers and potentially exempt transfers. You must be able to identify the types of transfer that fall into each category. Consolidate your understanding of the basics of IHT by ensuring that you understand the flow chart at the end of the chapter.

Step 4 Quick Quiz

Please attempt the quick quiz at the end of Study Text Chapter 1 to reinforce your understanding.

You may find it best to do this after a break, so that you can see what you remember and what you don't.

Step 5 Workbook Questions

Now attempt exam style questions (ESQs) 1.1 to 1.6 which will help to reinforce your knowledge of the topics covered in this study period and give you examples of the types of question you may see in the exam.

Study Period 2

Calculation of IHT on lifetime transfers

High Priority

Step 1 Exam Guidance

The calculation of inheritance tax on lifetime transfers of value is one of the key areas of IHT. Computations could cover lifetime tax or the IHT due as a result of a death.

You must be able to complete these calculations quickly and accurately. Remember, you only have one minute per mark in the exam.

This topic has been tested as follows:

– Q1 (Sample Paper), Q5 (Nov 2009) and Q3 (May 2010)

Step 2 Introduction to the session

In this study period we continue to look at transfers of value and in particular at the tax on transfers of value made during lifetime.

By the end of this Study Period you will be able to calculate the IHT due in lifetime and on death on both chargeable lifetime transfers and on potentially exempt transfers.

Step 3 Guidance through the Study Text

Read through Chapter 2 of the Study text, after reading the following guidance:

This chapter is very structured. In the last period we learnt to identify chargeable lifetime transfers (CLTs) and potentially exempt transfers (PETs). In this study session we learn to compute the IHT arising as a result of making both CLT's and PETs.

CLTs		PETs	
Tax in lifetime (Section 1)	Further tax on death (Section 2)	No tax in lifetime	Tax on death (Section 3)
Attempt Examples 1 to 5	Attempt Examples 6 and 7	(no examples)	Attempt Examples 8 and 9

These calculations are very examinable – take your time to work through the chapter and examples slowly to make sure you understand them fully.

Step 4 Quick Quiz

Please attempt the quick quiz at the end of Study Text Chapter 2 to reinforce your understanding.

You may find it best to do this after a break, so that you can see what you remember and what you don't.

Step 5 Workbook Questions

Now attempt ESQs 2.1 to 2.6 which will help to reinforce your knowledge of the topics covered in this study period and give you examples of the types of question you may see in the exam.

IHT valuation/BPR/APR

High Priority

Step 1 Exam Guidance

The topics covered in this Study Period are essential for the exam. You must be able to value assets for IHT purposes and identify the circumstances where agricultural property relief (APR) and/ or business property relief (BPR) are available.

These topics were tested in:

- Q4, Q8 & Q12 (Sample paper), Q7 (May 2009), Q4 & Q8 (Nov 2009), Q8, Q9 & Q12 (May 2010)

Step 2 Introduction to the session

Now that we know how to calculate IHT on lifetime transfers, in this Study Period we learn how to:

- Value a transfer for IHT purposes, with special rules for specific types of assets.
- Identify situations when APR and/ or BPR may be available and at what rate. These can reduce the value of a transfer to nil and apply before any other exemption (eg the annual exemption).

Step 3 Guidance through the Study Text

Read through Chapters 3 and 4 of the Study text after reading the following guidance:

Having learnt the loss to donor rule for valuing transfers, in this study period we learn more detailed valuation rules in Chapter 3:

Read Section 1 and attempt Example 1 to reinforce the 'loss to donor' principle of valuation.

Section 2: Related property rules – where the value of a transfer is determined by reference to the total value of related property and not just the property owned by the transferor. Try Example 2 to test your understanding of this principle.

Section 3: Special valuation rules for certain assets – there are special rules for a number of assets, most importantly quoted shares and securities (Section 3.2). Try Examples 3 and 4.

Chapter 4 considers business property relief (BPR) and agricultural property relief (APR). You must be aware of the conditions that need to be satisfied for the relief to be available (Sections 2 and 3). Locate them in the relevant part of your legislation. Then attempt Examples 2 and 3. Attempt Example 4 to test your understanding of the implications of the relief being withdrawn (Section 4).

This study period may take longer than the usual 3 hours.

Step 4 Quick Quiz

Please attempt the quick quizzes at the end of Study Text Chapters 3 and 4 to reinforce your understanding.

You may find it best to do this after a break, so that you can see what you remember and what you don't.

Step 5 Workbook Questions

Now attempt ESQs 3.1 to 3.6 and 4.1 to 4.7, which will help to reinforce your knowledge of the topics covered in this study period and give you examples of the types of question you may see in the exam.

Death estate

Step 1 Exam Guidance

The calculation of IHT on the death estate is a key IHT computation that can be examined in the same question with some other aspect (or aspects) of the syllabus, such as lifetime gifts, valuation rules or reliefs.

This topic has been tested as follows:

- Q4 (Sample paper), Q1 & Q10 (May 2009), Q3, Q6 & Q7 (Nov 2009), Q7 (May 2010)

Step 2 Introduction to the session

In previous study periods we looked at the calculation of IHT on lifetime gifts, both during lifetime and as a result of death.

In this study period we learn how to value an individual's death estate and calculate any IHT due on their estate at death.

Step 3 Guidance through the Study Text

Read through Chapter 5 of the Study Text after reading the following guidance:

Section 1.2 sets out the different elements that could make up an individual's death estate. Note that all assets are valued at 'probate value' (ie the market value at the date of death) using the valuation rules we learnt in the previous study period.

At this point, refer to the death estate proforma in Section 1.4 so that you can see how all the possible components of the death estate fit together. Learn this proforma so that you know how and where to include each item. Also look at Sections 1.5 and 1.6 and note the treatement of debts, funeral expenses and proceeds from life assurance policies.

Go back to Section 1.3 where we learn how to calculate the tax due on the death estate. Attempt Examples 1 and 2 to reinforce your understanding of the calculation.

Section 2 covers the transfer of an unused nil rate band between spouses/civil partners on the second death where the nil rate band was not used on the first death.

Section 3 explains how 'quick succession relief' (QSR) is available where two deaths occur within a short time of each other and IHT is charged on both. The percentages you need for the formula are in your tax tables. Locate them now and try Example 4.

Step 4 Quick Quiz

Please attempt the quick quiz at the end of Study Text Chapter 5 to reinforce your understanding.

You may find it best to do this after a break, so that you can see what you remember and what you don't.

Step 5 Workbook Questions

Now attempt ESQs 5.1 to 5.9, which will help to reinforce your knowledge of the topics covered in this study period and give you examples of the types of question you may see in the exam.

Study Period 5

Relief for falls in value on death

High Priority

Step 1 Exam Guidance

Reliefs and exemptions are essential knowledge for the exam. You will be covering a further two reliefs in this period. Your challenge is to ensure that you learn how to spot when each relief applies.

This topic was tested in Q11 (May 2010).

Step 2 Introduction to the session

Earlier we saw APR and BPR, which apply to both lifetime gifts and the death estate, and QSR which reduces death tax.

We now focus on two further reliefs that may apply when calculating death tax:

- Fall in value relief – where the value of an asset gifted during lifetime is lower at the date of death, and
- 'Post mortem relief' – where assets are sold from the death estate at a loss

Step 3 Guidance through the Study Text

Read through Chapter 6 of the Study Text after reading the following guidance:

In Section 1 we consider the relief available when an asset gifted during lifetime has *fallen in value* by the date of death. This can reduce the IHT due where the donor has died within seven years of making that gift. Attempt Example 1 to reinforce your understanding of the calculation.

Then read through Section 2, which covers relief for sales at a loss from the death estate of:

- Quoted shares
- Land and buildings
- Property valued using the related property rules.

There is no relief for any other assets.

Work through Examples 2 to 4 carefully, making sure you understand the slight difference in the rules depending on the asset being sold from the estate.

Step 4 Quick Quiz

Please attempt the quick quiz at the end of Study Text Chapter 6 to reinforce your understanding.

You may find it best to do this after a break, so that you can see what you remember and what you don't.

Step 5 Workbook Questions

Now attempt ESQs 6.1 to 6.6, which will help to reinforce your knowledge of the topics covered in this study period and give you examples of the types of question you may see in the exam.

Study Period 6

Medium Priority

IHT – additional aspects

Step 1 Exam Guidance

There are four topics within this Study period. They broadly modify the basic IHT computation that we have already learnt in earlier study periods.

The following questions were set on these areas:

- Domicile: Q2 (Sample Paper), Q2 & Q4 (May 2009), Q6 (May 2010)
- Pre-owned asset tax: Q3 (Sample Paper)
- Gift with reservation: Q9 (Sample Paper), Q8 (May 2009), Q2 (Nov 2009), Q4 (May 2010)

Step 2 Introduction to the session

In this study period we look at additional elements of the IHT computation:

1. The overseas aspects of IHT
2. Gifts with reservation of benefit
3. Conditional exemption for national heritage property
4. Jointly owned property

These topics are also important for IHT planning.

Step 3 Guidance through the Study Text

Read through Chapter 7 of the Study Text after reading the following guidance:

This chapter contains four different topics: Read through Section 1 – the overseas aspects of IHT to understand how overseas issues can affect who pays IHT and on what assets.

Then read carefully through Section 2 – gifts with reservation of benefit to understand the impact and consequences of retaining use of, or an interest in, an asset after it has been gifted. You should be able to identify when an income tax charge might apply instead of an IHT charge and how any tax liability is calculated. Attempt Examples 1 to 3.

Quickly read through Section 3 to understand the implications of making gifts of heritage property.

Finally read through Section 4 identifying how property can be held jointly, how such ownership affects the value entered into an individual's estate.

Step 4 Quick Quiz

Please attempt the quick quizzes at the end of Study Text Chapter 7 to reinforce your understanding.

You may find it best to do this after a break, so that you can see what you remember and what you don't.

Step 5 Workbook Questions

Now attempt ESQs 7.1 to 7.7, which will help to reinforce your knowledge of the topics covered in this study period and give you examples of the types of question you may see in the exam.

Progress Test 1

In order to reinforce what you have learnt so far, answer the following questions. Try to answer them without referring to your Study Text or notes. The test should take you no longer than one hour and covers Study Periods 1-6. Solutions start on page 117.

1 Jennifer makes the following lifetime transfers of value:

January 2006	£4,000 to her sister.
January 2010	£15,000 to her husband.
August 2010	£25,000 to her son on his wedding day.
February 2011	£5,000 to a discretionary trust.

You are required to state how each of these transfers will be treated for IHT purposes and how Jennifer's annual exemptions will be allocated to the above gifts.

2 A lifetime gift can be categorised for IHT purposes as either exempt, a potentially exempt transfer or a chargeable lifetime transfer.

You are required to define a potentially exempt transfer (PET) and to state the lifetime and death consequences of making a potentially exempt transfer.

3 Callum gifts £30,000 in cash to his daughter, on the occasion of her marriage in September 2007. Callum dies on 1 October 2010 leaving a death estate totalling £450,000.

You are required to calculate the IHT due during lifetime and on Callum's death.

4 Steven made the following gifts during his lifetime:

1 August 2005	cash gift to a cousin of £343,000
1 January 2006	cash gift to a discretionary trust of £100,000

Steven dies on 10 February 2011.

You are required to calculate the IHT due in respect of the above gifts both in lifetime and on death.

5 Russell died owning 1,000 shares in Brand plc. These shares were quoted at 210p-230p on the date of Russell's death and there were marked bargains on that day of 200p, 210p and 220p.

Calculate the value of Russell's shares in Brand plc for the purposes of inclusion in his death estate.

6 **State the four main conditions that must be satisfied for business property relief (BPR) to be available.**

7 **Explain when an individual is deemed to be domiciled in the UK for IHT purposes.**

8 Jean set up an investment company with her husband, Lewis, her brother, Eric and an unrelated person, Roy. The shareholdings were:

Jean 20% (valued at £80,000)
Lewis 10% (valued at £25,000)
Eric 40% (valued at £260,000)
Roy 30% (valued at £150,000)

Jean wants to give half of her shares to her son, William.

You are required to explain how the transfer will be valued for inheritance tax purposes and calculate the value of the transfer which may be chargeable to inheritance tax.

9 Sylvia died on 29 June 2010 leaving an estate valued at £432,000 to her daughter. Sylvia had received £30,000 (a tax free gift) on the death of her uncle Peter in May 2007. Uncle Peter's estate had settled the tax of £4,500.

You are required to calculate the IHT payable on Sylvia's death, assuming she had made no lifetime transfers.

10 Edna gifted a painting to her son, Albert, on 12 April 2005 when it was worth £75,000.

Edna had made gross chargeable transfers totalling £320,000 in 2002.

She died on 22 September 2010, leaving her estate worth £1.2 million to Albert. The painting was found to be a copy worth only £12,500 at the date of Edna's death.

You are required to calculate the IHT payable in respect of the gift and on Edna's death.

11 Wayne, who is now in poor health and has had to stop work, plans to transfer ownership of his house to his son James. He wishes to continue to live in the house.

You are required to set out the implications of Wayne's intentions for inheritance tax purposes and explain how can any potential problems be mitigated.

12 Jon who is resident, ordinarily resident and domiciled in the UK died on 3 December 2010. The following assets were included in his estate:

- His sole trader business, owned for the past 3 years and valued at £300,000
- Farm in Canada tenanted throughout the last 9 years with an open market value of £200,000 and an agricultural value of £70,000:
- 4,000 shares in Tin Ltd, an unquoted investment company, which he has owned for three years and are worth £120,000.

You are required to calculate the values of these assets to be included in the estate, after any available reliefs have been claimed.

You will find the answers to this test starting on page 117. If you answer more than 6 questions correctly, your performance is satisfactory; if you answer more than 8 correctly, you are doing well. Once you have reviewed how you have performed, go back over topics where you feel your understanding is poor.

Study Period 8

Capital gains tax – basic principles

High Priority

Step 1 Exam Guidance

The principles in this Study Period will not be examined in isolation. This chapter provides the fundamental information you need to be able to calculate capital gains tax (CGT) liabilities for trusts and their beneficiaries.

The topics in this chapter are likely to be examined as part of a trusts CGT question, as they were in Question 10 of the sample paper.

Step 2 Introduction to the session

To be in a position to deal with many tax issues relating to trusts, we must have some basic CGT knowledge. If you have already studied CGT for another paper of the CTA syllabus you may only need to review this Chapter, revising the basic principles.

The instructions given in Step 3 below presume you are studying this chapter **without** any previous knowledge and are based on Chapters 9 and 10 of the Taxation of Individuals module.

Step 3 Guidance through the Study Text

Read through Chapter 8 of the Study Text after reading the following guidance. After reading Section 1 for introduction turn to Chapters 9 and 10 of the **'Taxation of Individuals Awareness'** section of the text.

Sections 1 and 2 of Chapter 9 provide essential CGT background knowledge. Read through quickly but carefully.

Now turn to Chapter 10. Learn the proforma for calculating a capital gain in Section 1. Attempt Example 1. Read Sections 2 and 3 on how to calculate a CGT liability. This is a very important section. Attempt examples 2 to 4 to consolidate your knowledge. Read Sections 4.1 to 4.3 only on capital losses. Attempt Examples 5 to 9. You do not need to read the rest of this section. Then read through Section 5 which deals with assets acquired before 31 March 1982 and attempt Example 12. Read Section 6 on valuation and try Examples 13 and 14. Quickly read through Section 7 on connected persons. Then cover Section 9 on part disposals and attempt Examples 16 and 17. Then read Section 10 on compensation and work through Examples 18 and 19.

Next you need to study entrepreneurs' relief which is covered in detail in Section 4 of Chapter 10 of the Taxation of Unincorporated Businesses section of the text. Turn to this section and, after ensuring you understand when the relief applies, attempt Examples 7 to 10.

Finally, turn back to Section 2.2 of Chapter 8 of the IHT, Trusts and Estates text. Gift relief is an **essential** topic for trusts and is considered again in a later study period. Attempt Examples 1 & 2.

Step 4 Quick Quiz

Please attempt the quick quiz at the end of Study Text Chapter 8 to reinforce your understanding.

You may find it best to do this after a break, so that you can see what you remember and what you don't.

Step 5 Workbook Questions

Now attempt ESQs 8.1 to 8.4 which will help to reinforce your knowledge of the topics covered in this study period and give you examples of the types of question you may see in the exam.

Study Period 9

IHT for trusts

High Priority

Step 1 Exam Guidance

Trusts are a vital part of the IHT, Trusts and Estates Awareness syllabus. You cannot pass this module without a good knowledge of the different types of trusts that an individual may set up and how they are treated for inheritance tax, capital gains tax and income tax purposes.

This study period focuses on the IHT aspects of trusts. It is essential that you can differentiate between the different types of trust from the beginning of your study of trusts.

The topic was tested in:

– Q5 (Sample paper), Q5 & Q11 (May 2009), Q9 (Nov 2009) and Q1 (May 2010)

Step 2 Introduction to the session

In this Study period we consider the IHT treatment of trusts set up during lifetime and those set up on death. This can be very different depending on the type of trust.

We also look at the special IHT rules for certain trusts set up for children on the death of a parent.

Step 3 Guidance through the Study Text

Read through Chapter 9 of the Study Text, after reading the following guidance:

Read through Section 1 which covers the IHT rules for lifetime trusts. Make sure that you can distinguish between the different IHT charges (the 'exit' and 'principal' charges) and can calculate them accordingly using the proformas provided. Attempt Examples 1 to 5.

Section 1.7 is lower priority, so read through quickly and try the two examples, following through with the solution on this occasion.

Then read Sections 2.1 to 2.2 which deal with immediate post death interest trusts (IPDI trusts): special 'interest in possession' (IIP) trusts set up on death. Could you spot an IPDI trust in the exam? Work through Examples 8 and 9.

Section 2.3 covers trusts for children that have favourable IHT treatment. Again, make sure that you can distinguish between the different types as the IHT treatment for each differs. Attempt Example 10.

Read through Sections 3 to 6 quickly as these are lower priority. Do however read Section 7 carefully as this sets out the rules that applied to trusts before 22 March 2006 and are still potentially examinable, although the new rules are more important.

Step 4 Quick Quiz

Please attempt the quick quiz at the end of Study Text Chapter 9 to reinforce your understanding.

You may find it best to do this after a break, so that you can see what you remember and what you don't.

Step 5 Workbook Questions

Now attempt ESQs 9.1 to 9.7 which will help to reinforce your knowledge of the topics covered in this study period and give you examples of the types of question you may see in the exam.

Study Period 10

CGT for trusts

High Priority

Step 1 Exam Guidance

CGT for trusts is very examinable.

It is possible that you will see trustees actually disposing of an asset. However, more likely is seeing the trustees passing out a trust asset to a beneficiary (a 'deemed' disposal). This will require the calculation of a gain and almost always the consideration of gift relief.

CGT for trusts was tested in:

- Q10 (Sample paper), Q3 & Q6 (May 2009), Q11 (Nov 2009), Q10 (May 2010)

Step 2 Introduction to the session

In this Study period we consider the CGT treatment of trusts.

The CGT position for all trusts is the same in terms of the calculations required and rules that apply (contrast this with the IHT treatment). However, the gift relief position differs depending on what type of trust it is and entrepreneurs' relief is only available to trustees of IIP trusts.

This is a relatively short session, so spend any extra time you may have recapping the IHT and CGT treatment of trusts.

Step 3 Guidance through the Study Text

Read through Chapter 10 of the Study Text, which deals with the CGT consequences during the life of a trust, after reading the following guidance:

Read Section 1 which looks at the CGT consequences of setting up a trust from the settlor's perspective. Bear in mind the gift relief position as you are reading through.

Then read Section 2 which looks at actual disposals. Note the similarities between the computation for trustees and individuals and ensure you understand when entrepreneurs' relief is available. No gift relief to consider here as there is no gift.

Section 3 is extremely important as it deals with 'deemed disposals' by trustees (ie usually where the trustees give the assets to the beneficiaries) and capital losses. Note the different gift relief position depending on the type of trust. Attempt Example 1.

Quickly read through Sections 4 to 6 which are lower priority. Do however spend some time working through the summary table in Section 7. Try to see if you can reproduce this table without looking!

Step 4 Quick Quiz

Please attempt the quick quiz at the end of Study Text Chapter 10 to reinforce your understanding.

You may find it best to do this after a break, so that you can see what you remember and what you don't.

Step 5 Workbook Questions

Now attempt ESQs 10.1 to 10.7 which will help to reinforce your knowledge of the topics covered in this study period and give you examples of the types of question you may see in the exam.

Income tax for trusts

Step 1 Exam Guidance

The final area of trusts that could be examined in the IHT, trusts and estates Awareness module is income tax for trusts.

Income tax for trusts was tested as follows:

- Q6 & Q7 (Sample paper), Q8 (May 2009), Q10 (Nov 2009) and Q2 (May 2010)

Step 2 Introduction to the session

We now complete our study of trusts by considering the income tax treatment of trustees and beneficiaries.

The treatment depends on the type of trust, so you must be able to distinguish between a discretionary trust and an interest in possession (IIP) trust.

Step 3 Guidance through the Study Text

Read through Chapter 11 of the Study Text after reading the following guidance:

Skim read Section 1 on bare trusts.

Carefully read through Section 2 covering the income tax position of IIP trusts and their beneficiaries. Try Examples 1 and 2. You should find the trust's tax calculation even easier to deal with than one for an individual.

Then read Sections 3.1 to 3.4 which set out the rules for discretionary trusts and their beneficiaries. Work through Examples 3 and 4.

A very important section is Section 3.5 which deals with the 'tax pool' that exists for discretionary trusts. Read it through carefully and then attempt Example 5.

Quickly read Section 4. You may wish to look back at your CGT notes on vulnerable beneficiary trusts so that you have a complete picture of the income tax and CGT treatment of them.

Finally read Section 5 on settlor interested trusts. Again you may wish to refer to your notes on the CGT implications for settlor interested trusts at this point.

Step 4 Quick Quiz

Please attempt the quick quiz at the end of Study Text Chapter 11 to reinforce your understanding.

You may find it best to do this after a break, so that you can see what you remember and what you don't.

Step 5 Workbook Questions

Now attempt ESQs 11.1 to 11.6 which will help to reinforce your knowledge of the topics covered in this study period and give you examples of the types of question you may see in the exam.

Study Period 12

Estates in administration

High Priority

Step 1 Exam Guidance

It is likely that at least one question will be set on some aspect of the taxation of a deceased person's estate whilst it is in 'administration'. A question could have an income tax or capital gains tax slant.

This topic was tested in:

– Q11 (Sample Paper), Q12 (Nov 2009)

Step 2 Introduction to the session

In this study period we consider the tax position of estates in administration. An estate is 'in administration' from the date the deceased dies after the value of the estate is worked out, all IHT is paid and the assets are distributed to beneficiaries of the estate.

You must understand the income tax and capital gains tax implications for both the personal representatives of the estate and any beneficiaries of the estate.

Step 3 Guidance through the Study Text

Read Chapter 12 of the Study Text after reading the following guidance:

Quickly read Section 1 for background.

Read Section 2 covering the PRs' income tax liability. Which type of trust is taxed in a very similar way? Discretionary or IIP? Attempt Example 1.

Then read Section 3 which sets out the income tax rules for the beneficiaries of an estate and work through Examples 2 to 4.

We then turn to the CGT aspects of estates in administration. Section 4 deals with the PRs' position and Section 5 with the beneficiaries. Try Example 5.

You have now completed your study of the **Inheritance Tax, Trusts and Estates Awareness** module.

Step 4 Quick Quiz

Please attempt the quick quiz at the end of Study Text Chapter 12 to reinforce your understanding.

You may find it best to do this after a break, so that you can see what you remember and what you don't.

Step 5 Workbook Questions

Now attempt ESQs 12.1 to 12.6 which will help to reinforce your knowledge of the topics covered in this study period and give you examples of the types of question you may see in the exam.

Progress Test 2

In order to reinforce what you have learnt so far, answer the following questions. Try to answer them without referring to your Study Text or notes. The test should take you no longer than one hour and covers Study Periods 8-12. Solutions start on page 121.

1 Mr Roberts died on 5 April 2009.

Calculate the income tax payable by his estate for 2010/11 assuming the estate received the following income:

	£
Rents received from a furnished letting	9,000
Bank interest received	948
Dividends received	1,170

2 The Hick interest in possession trust received the following income in 2010/11:

	£
Bank interest	828
Dividends	1,215
Gross rental income	27,000

And incurred the following expenses:

Expenses re: rental property	2,700
Trust administration expenses	1,350

Calculate the trust's income tax liability for 2010/11.

3 The Danston discretionary trust received the following income in the tax year 2010/11.

	£
Dividends	3,240
Gross rental income	32,400

And, incurred the following expenses:

Expenses re: rental property	2,700
Trust administration expenses	1,701

No distributions were made during 2010/11.

Calculate the trust's income tax liability for the tax year 2010/11.

4 Orinocho transferred an investment property worth £200,000 to a discretionary trust on 1 October 2005. The property had cost Orinocho £150,000 on 1 August 2005. Orinocho claimed gift relief on the transfer of the property into trust.

The trustees sold the property on 1 February 2011 for £500,000. The property has never been occupied by a beneficiary of the trust.

Calculate the trustee's chargeable gain on this disposal.

5 Petra created a discretionary trust on 1 September 2004, placing £380,000 of cash into the trust. Her cumulative total of gross chargeable lifetime transfers up to that point was £245,000 (relating to a transfer on 1 August 2001). Petra paid the IHT due on creation of the trust. On 31 March 2011, the trustees made an absolute appointment of trust capital to one of the beneficiaries of £100,000. The trustees bear the IHT payable.

Calculate the inheritance tax payable by the trustees on the exit from the trust.

6 Jimmy died on 12 September 2000 and under his will he set up a discretionary trust with £250,000 of cash with any IHT due being paid by his estate. The trust used the cash to buy shares in an unquoted trading company worth £150,000.

In the 7 years before his death he had made gross chargeable transfers totalling £208,000.

Calculate the first principal charge on the trust assuming that on 11 September 2010 the shares were worth £200,000 and the rest of the trust assets consisted of £140,000 in cash.

7 In 1990 Henry had set up a life interest trust for his niece Amy. A 5% holding of shares in Bramble Ltd (an unquoted company) had been settled and Henry had made a claim to hold over the gain of £20,000 on those shares. Holdings of quoted shares had also been settled at the same time.

Amy died in June 2010. At that time the trust assets consisted of:

Holding	Value at death	Cost	Date of acquisition
	£	£	
5% holding in Bramble Ltd	80,000	55,000	1989
1,000 Orange plc shares	15,000	6,000	1996
2,000 Apricot plc shares	25,000	9,000	1990

You are required to explain the CGT position of the trustees on Amy's death.

8 On 1 March 2001, Lisa transferred quoted shares valued at £709,000 into a discretionary trust, with Lisa paying any inheritance tax due.

On 1 August 2010, the trustees distributed half of the shares, worth £482,000, to Paul, a beneficiary. Paul paid any tax due. The remaining shares were worth £495,000 on 1 March 2011.

Lisa had made no other lifetime gifts.

You are required to calculate the inheritance tax payable:

(a) When the trustees distribute the shares to Paul, and

(b) On 1 March 2011.

9 From 22 March 2006 interest in possession (IIP) trusts set up during lifetime are relevant property trusts.

You are required to state the IHT position both before *and* after 22 March 2006:

(a) When an individual set up an IIP trust during lifetime.

(b) When assets leave an IIP trust either during the lifetime of the life tenant or on the death of the life tenant.

10 Stanley died on 15 August 2009. He left his entire estate worth £1,575,000, including an investment property with a probate value of £625,000, to his daughter Emily.

Emily requested the executors of her father's estate to sell the property on 12 May 2011. The executors received proceeds of £679,900 but had incurred £2,000 of legal fees in obtaining title to the property.

You are required to calculate the executors' gain on the sale of the property.

11 On 6 May 2010 all of the assets comprised in a discretionary settlement were advanced to Sally, one of the beneficiaries. The trustees made a capital loss on the advance of £5,000.

The trustees had made substantial capital gains in 2007/08 and 2008/09 but had made a capital loss in 2009/10 of £10,000.

You are required to explain what relief is available for the capital losses.

12 Beryl died on 1 April 2010 leaving her entire estate to her daughter, Janice.

During 2010/11 the personal representatives (PRs) of Beryl's estate received the following income:

	£
Rental income	30,000
Interest income (net)	9,600
Dividend income (net)	18,900

The PR's made a payment to Janice of £45,000 on 31 March 2011.

You are required to calculate the PR's income tax payable for 2010/11 and to explain how the payment to Janice will be treated.

You will find the answers to this test starting on page 121. If you answer more than 6 questions correctly, your performance is satisfactory; if you answer more than 8 correctly, you are doing well. Once you have reviewed how you have performed, go back over topics where you feel your understanding is poor.

Solutions

Progress Test 1

1 January 2006 – PET

January 2006 – PET	£4,000	
Less: AE 2005/06	(3,000)	
Less: AE 2004/05 (b/fwd)	(1,000)	Remaining £2,000 of AE lost
	Nil	

January 2010 – exempt transfer to husband does not use AE of 2009/10

August 2010 – PET	£25,000
Less: Marriage exemption	(5,000)
AE 2010/11	(3,000)
AE 2009/10 (b/fwd)	(3,000)
	14,000

February 2011 – CLT	£5,000
2010/11 AE already used against PET	(Nil)
	£5,000

2 A potentially exempt transfer (PET) is a transfer of value made during lifetime either from one individual to another or from one individual to a bare trust or a disabled person's trust.

During the lifetime of the transferor, a PET is treated as exempt from IHT.

It does, however, use the available annual exemption(s).

If the transferor dies more than seven years after making the PET, it becomes completely exempt.

If he dies within seven years of making the PET, it becomes chargeable.

3 In lifetime, the gift is a potentially exempt transfer (PET) and so no IHT is payable.

The value of the gift is:

		£
Gift		30,000
Less: marriage exemption (parent)		(5,000)
Less: annual exemption	2007/08	(3,000)
	2006/07	(3,000)
		19,000

As Callum dies within 7 years of the gift, there is tax to pay on death.

However, as Callum has made no other transfers of value, the gift of £19,000 is fully covered by his nil rate band and no tax is payable.

Tax on Death Estate

	£
Death estate value	450,000
Less: nil rate band remaining (£325,000 – £19,000)	(306,000)
	144,000
Tax due £144,000 × 40%	57,600

4 *Lifetime tax:*

Gift to cousin = PET, no tax due

Gift to discretionary trust – CLT, therefore tax due:

	£
Value of gift	100,000
No AE as used by PET	
Covered by nil rate band of £275,000, therefore no tax to pay	

Death tax:

	£	£
Gift to cousin:		343,000
Less AE 2005/06		(3,000)
2004/05		(3,000)
		337,000
Nil rate band at death	325,000	
Chargeable transfers in last 7 years	(Nil)	
NRB remaining		(325,000)
Taxable transfer		12,000
Tax @ 40%		4,800
Taper relief (5 – 6 years)		
60% × £4,800		(2,880)
Tax payable		1,920
Gift to discretionary trust:		
Value of gift		100,000
No nil band remaining		
£100,000 × 40%		40,000
Taper relief (5 – 6 years)		
60% × £40,000		(24,000)
Tax payable (no lifetime tax to deduct)		16,000

5 Share valuation

Lower of:

(a) Quarter-up valuation:

210p + (230p-210p/4) = 215p

(b) Average of highest and lowest marked bargains:

(220p + 200p)/2 = 210p

Therefore 210p × 1,000 shares = £2,100

6 The conditions that need to be satisfied for BPR to be available are (ROSE):

(a) *Relevant business property*: the property gifted must be relevant business property (eg a business, qualifying shares etc).

(b) *Ownership*: The property must have been owned for two years or be replacement business property.

(c) *Sale contract*: there must be no contract in place for the onward sale of the gifted asset

(d) *Excepted assets*: when shares are gifted, relief is restricted where the company holds 'excepted' assets (ie investment assets such as rental property, shares, etc.)

7 An individual is deemed to be domiciled in the UK for IHT purposes:

(a) If he has been resident in the UK for at least 17 out of the past 20 tax years.
(b) For 36 months after ceasing to be domiciled in the UK for all other purposes.

These rules only apply for IHT purposes and have no effect for income tax or capital gains tax purposes.

8 The transfer will be subject to the related property rules.

The value of the transfer is:

	£
Before: 20/30 × £150,000	100,000
After: 10/20 × £80,000	(40,000)
Related value	60,000

The related value will be used as it is higher than the isolated value which would be:

	£
Before: 20%	80,000
After: 10%	(25,000)
Unrelated value	55,000

9

	£	£
Sylvia's estate		432,000
Less: nil rate band	325,000	
Less: GCTs in last 7 years	(nil)	
		(325,000)
Chargeable estate		107,000
Tax @ 40%		42,800
Less QSR (W)		(1,565)
IHT payable		41,235

Working

QSR

1st tax × net/gross × % (for 3-4 yrs)

£4,500 × 30,000/34,500 × 40%	1,565

10 The gift to Albert was a PET so no tax was due during Edna's lifetime. It did however use the annual exemptions of 2005/06 and 2004/05.

As Edna dies within seven years of making the gift the PET becomes chargeable.

The painting has fallen in value since the date of the gift so 'fall in value' relief is available to reduce the IHT due. The original value, however, remains in Edna's cumulative total.

	£	£
Transfer of value		75,000
Less: AE × 2		(6,000)
PET		69,000
Less: fall in value £(75,000 – 12,500)		(62,500)
		6,500
Less: nil rate band	325,000	
Less: GCTs in last 7 years	(320,000)	(5,000)
Chargeable		1,500
Tax @ 40%		600
Less: taper relief (5 – 6 yrs) 60%		(360)
IHT payable		240
Death estate		
Estate		1,200,000
Less: nil rate band	325,000	
Less: GCTs in seven years before death (the 2002 GCT is before this)	(69,000)	(256,000)
		944,000
Tax @ 40%		377,600

11 As Wayne plans to give the house away but continue to enjoy the benefit of the house this would be a gift with reservation of benefit. Consequently:

(a) The transfer of ownership is a PET, which will become chargeable if Wayne dies within seven years of the gift.

(b) The house will also be counted as part of Wayne's estate on death.

Whichever calculation produces the higher tax is chargeable.

The reservation of benefit rules can be avoided if Wayne pays a full commercial rent to James.

12 Jon's Estate

	£	£
Sole trader business	300,000	
less: 100% BPR	(300,000)	
		NIL
Canadian farm (no APR – not in UK or EEA)		200,000
Tin Ltd shares (no BPR – investment company)		120,000

Solutions

Progress Test 2

1

	£		£
Rents from furnished let	9,000		
Less: 10% furnished letting wear and tear allowance	(900)		
	8,100	× 20%	1,620
Bank interest			
Gross up (£948 × 100/80)	1,185	× 20%	237
Dividends (£1,170 × 100/90)	1,300	× 10%	130
IT liability			1,987
Less taxed at source			
Bank			(237)
Dividends			(130)
IT payable			1,620

2 The Hick interest in possession trust

	£
Bank interest (£828 × 100/80) £1,035 @ 20% =	207
Dividends (£1,215) × 100/90) £1,350 @ 10% =	135
Rental income (£27,000 – £2,700) £24,300 @ 20% =	4,860
Liability	5,202

Note the trustees' expenses are not deductible

3 The Danston discretionary trust

	£
Rental income (£32,400 – £2,700)	29,700
Dividends (£3,240 × 10/90)	3,600
Gross income	33,300
Gross income	33,300
Less: expenses of trust (£1,701 × 100/90)	(1,890)
	31,410
£1,000 @ 20% =	200
£28,700 @ 50% =	14,350
£1,710 (£3,600 - £1,890) @ 42.5% =	727
£1,890 @ 10% =	189
	15,466

4

	£	£
Proceeds		500,000
Less: Cost	200,000	
Less: gain held over £(200,000 – 150,000)	(50,000)	
		(150,000)
Trustees gain		350,000

5 Petra Discretionary Trust

	£
Initial value	380,000
Nil rate band	325,000
Less: GCT of settlor in 7 years before trust was set up	(245,000)
Available	80,000

£380,000 – £80,000 = £300,000 × 20% = £60,000

Effective rate on £380,000 is $\frac{60,000}{380,000} \times 100\% = 15.789\%$

Number of quarter years from 1 September 2004 to 31 March 2011 = 26

Rate of IHT is therefore 30% × 26/40 × 15.789% = 3.0789%

Tax payable by the trustees is therefore £100,000 x $\frac{3.0789}{100 - 3.0789}$ = £3,177

6

	£	£
Shares (100% BPR)		Nil
Cash		140,000
Current value of trust		140,000
Nil band at PC date	325,000	
Settlor's transfers in 7 years before trust was set up	(208,000)	
		(117,000)
		23,000
Tax at 20%		4,600

Effective rate of tax 4,600/140,000 × 100% =	3.2857%
IHT payable 3.2857% × 30% × £140,000	£1,380

7 When Amy's qualifying life interest terminates on death there is a tax free uplift to market value at the date of death. However, if gains were held over when an asset was settled, the gain on that asset will be chargeable, but is limited to the amount of the gain held over.

The maximum chargeable gain accruing to the trustees on Amy's death is £20,000, ie the gain held over when the Bramble Ltd shares were settled. It may be possible to make a further claim to hold over the gain against the base cost of the shares in the beneficiary's hands if there is also an inheritance charge when the assets are included in Amy's death estate.

8

(a) *Exit charge*

	£
Notional gift (initial value)	709,000
Less: nil rate band (no GCTs in 7 years before trust was set up)	(325,000)
	384,000
Tax @ 20%	76,800
Effective rate	
76,800/709,000 × 100% = 10.83216%	
*Actual rate (*complete quarters: 1.3.01– 1.8.10 = 37)	
10.83216% × 37/40 × 30% = 3.00592%	318,000
Exit charge	
3.00592% × £482,000	£14,488

(b) *Principal charge 1.3.11*

	£	£
Notional gift (current value of remaining shares)		495,000
Less: nil rate band (no GCTs in 7 years before trust was set up)	325,000	
Less: amount subject to exit charge in previous 10 years	(482,000)	
		Nil
		495,000
Tax @ 20%		99,000
Effective rate		
99,000/495,000 × 100% = 20%		
Actual rate		
20% × 30% = 6%		
Principal charge		
6% × £495,000		£29,700

9 *Before 22 March 2006*

If an interest in possession (IIP) trust was set up before 22 March 2006, the transfer to the trust was treated as a potentially exempt transfer (PET) by the settlor.

If the trust ended during the life tenant's lifetime (ie the assets were distributed from the trust) the life tenant was (usually) treated as making a PET (if the assets went to another individual who was not the life tenant's spouse/ civil partner).

If the trust ended on the life tenant's death, the value of the assets in the trust would enter the life tenant's death estate as their 'settled property'.

After 22 March 2006

If an interest in possession (IIP) trust is set up after 22 March 2006, the transfer to the trust is treated as a chargeable lifetime transfer (CLT) by the settlor.

If the trust ends during the life tenant's lifetime or on their death there is an exit charge for IHT purposes as the trust is a relevant property trust.

10

	£
Proceeds	679,900
Less: cost (probate value)	(625,000)
Less: legal fees (actual fees higher than scale charge allowed (W))	(2,000)
Chargeable gain	52,900

Working – scale charge

Probate value of assets sold/ PV of the total estate × £4,000 (SP 2/04)

£625,000/ £1,575,000 × £4,000	1,587

11 Where a loss accrues on the advance of property, that loss may be transferred to the beneficiary. The loss of £5,000 may be transferred to Sally, but it may only be set off against any gain arising on a disposal of the same property by Sally.

It is not possible for the trustees to carry the losses back against earlier gains. The loss in 2009/10 of £10,000 is unrelieved.

12

Income tax payable by PRs	*Non savings*	*Savings*	*Dividends*
	£	£	£
Rental income	30,000		
Interest: £9,600 × 100/80		12,000	
Dividends £18,900 × 100/90			21,000
Taxable income	30,000	12,000	21,000

	£
Non-savings income: £30,000 @ 20%	6,000
Savings income: £12,000 @ 20%	2,400
Dividend income: £21,000 @ 10%	2,100
	10,500
Less: tax credits on	
Interest @ 20%	(2,400)
Dividends @ 10%	(2,100)
Income tax due	6,000

Janice will be treated as having received income of £45,000 net, which will be taxable on her in 2010/11. This is made up as follows:

	Net	*Tax*
	£	£
Rental income	24,000	6,000
Interest	9,600	2,400
Dividends (balance)	11,400	1,267
	45,000	9,667

TQT
Tax Qualification Training

Exam style questions

1.1 John has the following transactions in 2010/11:

(1) On 1 May 2010 he sells a painting to an antique dealer for £8,000. He later discovers that the painting was actually worth £50,000 at the time of the sale.

(2) He gifts cash of £50,000 to his spouse on 25 June 2010.

(3) He donates £150,000 cash to Mencap on 18 August 2010.

(4) He transfers his own main residence valued at £110,000 to a discretionary trust on 12 November 2010.

(5) He gifts £5,000 to his father on the occasion of his second marriage on 1 February 2011.

He has not made any other gifts during his lifetime.

You are required to explain the inheritance tax treatment of these transactions.

1.2 Raymond and Sally married in December 2010.

The following gifts were made:

	£
By Raymond's father	
To Raymond, cash of	20,000
To Sally, cash of	20,000
By Raymond (before marriage)	
To Sally, an engagement ring valued at	10,000
By Sally's sister	
To Sally, cash of	5,000

You are required to explain the inheritance tax treatment of these gifts assuming the donors have already used their annual exemptions for 2010/11 and 2009/10.

1.3 Explain what is meant by the following terms for inheritance tax purposes and give an example of a common gift which falls into each category.

(1) Chargeable lifetime transfer.
(2) Potentially exempt transfer.
(3) Exempt transfer.

1.4 Charles is domiciled in the UK. He made the following transfers to his wife Tamara:

31 January 2004	House in South Africa	£200,000
1 January 2011	Cash	£320,000.

Charles dies on 12 February 2011. He had made no other lifetime transfers.

You are required to explain the inheritance tax implications on the above transfers as a result of Charles's death ignoring annual exemptions and assuming:
(i) Tamara is domiciled in South Africa.
(ii) Tamara is domiciled in the UK.

You are not required to calculate any IHT due.

1.5 In 2010/11 Spencer receives an annual salary of £150,000 and has the following transactions:

(1) He pays his two nieces' school fees which total £1,500. He has paid the fees for the last three years.

(2) He gifts cash of £50,000 to his civil partner, Simon, who is domiciled in Canada.

(3) He gives £100 to his three nephews for their birthdays and a further £100 at Christmas.

(4) He transfers his holiday home in Hawaii, valued at £120,000, to an interest in possession trust of which his sister is the life tenant.

(5) He makes a donation of £50,000 to the Labour Party.

He has not made any other gifts during his lifetime.

You are required to explain the inheritance tax treatment of these transactions.

1.6 Liam makes a number of dispositions during 2010/11.

You are required to state which two of the following dispositions are not transfers of value for Liam for IHT purposes, rather than falling within a specific IHT exemption.

For the purpose of the statements below you should assume that Liam is UK domiciled and is the life tenant of a qualifying interest in possession trust.

A Liam sells a painting for £5,000. He later finds out that it was an original worth ten times what he sold it for.

B Liam gives his three nieces £20 each for their birthdays and £25 each for Christmas.

C The trustees of the life interest trust pass out half of the trust assets to Liam.

D The trustees of the life interest trust pass out half of the trust assets to Liam's wife.

E Liam gifts £5,000 to his god-daughter each year at Christmas. He has sufficient after-tax income to cover the payments.

2.1 Thomas made a gift of £295,000 to a discretionary trust in May 2005 and paid any tax due.

He made a further gift of £106,000 to the trust in July 2010, the trustees agreeing to pay any tax due.

You are required to calculate the inheritance tax due in respect of these lifetime transfers.

2.2 William gifted £361,000 to a discretionary trust on 1 June 2007, when the nil rate band was £300,000. William had made no earlier transfers of value.

On 15 August 2010 William died.

You are required to calculate the tax payable as a result of William's death if:

(i) The trustees agreed to pay the inheritance tax.
(ii) William paid the inheritance tax.

2.3 Andy put £363,000 into a relevant property trust on 3 April 2011 paying any tax due.
He dies on 17 September 2015.

His only other lifetime gift was a gross chargeable transfer of £139,500 on 14 June 2007.

You are required to calculate the IHT due on his death assuming that the nil rate band for 2010/11 continues to apply to all future years.

2.4 Walter gifted a painting he had owned for ten years to a discretionary trust in June 2010 when its value was £313,000. The trustees agreed to pay any tax arising.

His only other lifetime transfers had been a gift of £200,000 to the same discretionary trust when he set it up in March 2007 and a gift of £16,000 cash to his son in December 2009.

You are required to calculate the IHT due in respect of the gift of the painting.

2.5 Jake gave his daughter £84,000 on the event of her marriage in August 2007.

His only other lifetime transfer was the transfer of £265,000 into a discretionary trust, the beneficiaries of which were Jake's wife and their children, in May 2006.

Jake died on 25 November 2010.

You are required to calculate the inheritance tax due in respect of these lifetime transfers.

2.6 Sherry dies on 6 November 2010.

On 1 July 2005 she had given a car worth £32,000 to her daughter, Frances, and on 14 January 2006 she had set up a discretionary trust with cash of £428,000. Frances was one of the class of beneficiaries.
She had made no other lifetime gifts.

You are required to calculate the IHT due on Sherry's death.

3.1 Hazel owns 51% of the issued share capital of Oxford Ltd, an unquoted investment company. There are 10,000 £1 ordinary shares in the company.

The shares in the company are valued as follows:

51% holding	£150 per share
49% holding	£120 per share
2% holding	£ 50 per share

On 20 April 2010 Hazel gave 200 of her shares to a discretionary trust. She had set up the trust with cash of £163,000 on 15 May 2007.

You are required to calculate the IHT due in respect of the gift of shares.

3.2 The 10,000 issued shares in Brown Plc, an investment company, are held as follows:

	% holding	*No of shares*
Mr Brown	40	4,000
Mrs Brown (wife)	20	2,000
Jim Brown (son)	30	3,000
David Brown (nephew)	10	1,000

On 1 June 2007 Mrs Brown gave 1,500 shares to Jim. On that date the values of Brown Plc shares are agreed to be:

	£
0 – 25%	300
26 – 50%	600
51 – 75%	900
76 – 100%	1,200

Mrs Brown dies on 24 September 2010. She had made no other lifetime gifts.

You are required to calculate the IHT due in respect of the shares.

3.3 Shares in Finance Ltd, an investment company, with an issued share capital of 100 ordinary shares of £1 each, are held as follows:

Michael	45
Adrianne (his wife)	25
Unrelated third parties	30
	100

Current values for the shares are:

Shareholding	£
5%	20,000
40%	380,000
45%	420,000
65%	680,000
70%	740,000

Michael gifts a 5% holding to an interest in possession trust for his three children on 6 May 2010.

His only other lifetime gift was a gross chargeable transfer of £290,000 in June 2004.

You are required to calculate the IHT due in respect of the shares.

3.4 Conrad made a gift on 14 March 2011 of 10,000 shares in Minitip plc and 10,000 shares in Maxipack plc to a discretionary trust. The trustees agreed to pay the tax.
At the date of the gift the shares were valued as follows:

Minitip plc

Quoted at £21.80 – £22.25. Recorded bargains of £21.20, £21.75, £22.20 and £22.25.

Maxipack plc

Quoted at £12.00 – £12.80. There was only one recorded bargain of £12.25.

Conrad had made an earlier gross chargeable transfer of £175,000 in June 2009.

You are required to calculate the IHT due in respect of the shares.

3.5 Anya owns 12,000 Dale plc shares.
On 1 February 2011 the shares were quoted at 331.75 – 334.25, with bargains at 330, 333.25 and 334.

The shares had gone ex-dividend on 19 January 2011 and the dividend of 12.2p per share was paid on 5 February 2011.

You are required to explain and calculate the IHT value of the Dale plc shares if:

(i) Anya gifts the shares to a discretionary trust on 1 February 2011.

(ii) Anya dies on 1 February 2011 still owning the shares.

3.6 Sebastian made the following lifetime gifts:

(i) Villa in Spain to his brother, Richard on 12 August 2004.

At the date of the gift the villa is worth €468,000. The buying exchange rate on that day was €1.39 and the selling rate was €1.20.

(ii) 10,000 units in the Cosby Unit Trust to an interest in possession trust on 4 May 2009.

The bid price of units on that date was £3.58 and the offer price was £3.62.

Sebastian dies on 12 October 2010.

You are required to calculate the IHT due on his death in respect of his lifetime gifts.

4.1 Luke acquired 30% of Horace Ltd, a trading company, in July 2006. In February 2010 he gave the shares to his son, Marc, when they were worth £750,000. The value of the assets owned by Horace Ltd at the date of transfer were as follows:

	£
Office building	2,225,000
Goodwill	525,000
Net current assets	75,000
Cash (for day to day transactions)	20,000
Listed shares (<1% investments)	45,000
	2,890,000

Luke's only other transfer was a gross chargeable lifetime transfer of £500,000 in 2005.

Luke died on 12 March 2011. Marc still held the shares at the date of Luke's death which were then worth £795,000.

You are required to explain and calculate the IHT liability on Luke's death.

4.2 Jack has owned a newsagent since 1983. He sold it in February 2010, and reinvested the proceeds three months later in a health food store. He gave away the health food business in June 2011.
Olga inherited her husband's business when he died in June 2010. He had run the business since 2000. Olga gave the business away in December 2010, to her son.

Simon set up a trading business in January 2008. In July 2009 he gifted the business to his civil partner, John. John died in August 2010, leaving his estate to his niece, Amy.

You are required to explain on which of the above transfers business property relief be available and why.

4.3 Joan gave her entire 20% holding in ABC Ltd to her son on 4 June 2007. She had acquired these in 1999 for £40,000. Her husband, Alex owns 10% of the shares.
The assets of ABC Ltd at the date of the gift comprised:

	£
Land and buildings	300,000
Plant and machinery (exempt from CGT)	50,000
Investments	80,000
Net current assets	70,000
Total market value	500,000

The values of various shareholdings on 4 June 2007 are:

10% : £30,000
20% : £90,000
30% : £147,000

Joan dies on 21 March 2011. She had made one gross chargeable transfer of £427,500 in April 2002.

You are required to calculate the inheritance tax liability on Joan's death.

4.4 Arthur owned a factory for many years which was used for business purposes by Daley Ltd, an unquoted company wholly owned by Arthur.

In August 2010 Arthur gave the factory to his son when its value was £650,000. He had made no other gifts during his lifetime.

His son sold the factory in November 2010.

The factory was used throughout by Daley Ltd.

Arthur died on 25 December 2010.

You are required to calculate the inheritance tax liability on Arthur's death.

4.5 Arthur owned a factory for many years which was used for business purposes by Daley Ltd, an unquoted company wholly owned by Arthur.

In August 2010 Arthur gave the factory to an interest in possession trust for his son when its value was £676,000. He had made no other gifts during his lifetime.

The trustees sold the factory in November 2010.

The factory was used throughout by Daley Ltd.

Arthur died on 25 December 2010.

You are required to calculate the inheritance tax liability on Arthur's death.

4.6 Barney has had a 10% stake in his family's partnership for many years. His assets include:

(i) Partnership capital account valued at £60,000.

(ii) Land which he owns but which is occupied and farmed by the partnership under a 30 year agricultural tenancy dated October 1990. It is valued at £800,000, of which £600,000 is agricultural value. There is a mortgage of £200,000 on the property.

You are required to explain and calculate the APR and BPR available if Barney gifts both assets on 15 January 2011.

4.7 Barry died on 18 July 2010 leaving his entire estate to his wife, Melody.

During his lifetime he had made the following gifts:

14 May 2001 he made a cash gift of £91,000 to his nephew, Keith.

12 April 2005 he made a gross chargeable transfer of £238,000 to a discretionary trust.

25 June 2006 he gave £50,000 to his daughter, Francesca, in consideration of her marriage, which took place on that date.

3 October 2009 he transferred a 3% holding of unquoted trading company shares, valued at £750,000, to the discretionary trust created in April 2005 with his grandchildren as beneficiaries. The trustees had sold the shares by the date of Barry's death.

You are required to calculate the IHT due as a result of Barry's death.

5.1 Raoul, who is UK domiciled, dies in September 2010 leaving a house in France worth £125,000, personal property situated in France worth £30,000, a house in Scotland worth £180,000 and personal property situated in the UK worth £100,000.

His debts are a loan secured against the French house of £110,000, a loan secured against the Scottish house of £200,000 and a British Gas bill of £120.

Funeral expenses were £1,500.

You are required to calculate Raoul's death estate for IHT purposes.

5.2 Joe died on 10 August 2010.

His free estate was worth £293,000 which passed to his children. He was also the life tenant of a trust set up on his brother's death. The assets in the trust were worth £350,000 and passed to his son on his death.

Joe's only lifetime gift had been a gift to a discretionary trust of £380,000 in June 2001.

You are required to calculate the IHT liability arising as a result of Joe's death and state by whom it is payable.

5.3 Nicholas died in December 2005 leaving his whole estate of £130,000 to his brother David. IHT payable on Nicholas' death was £38,250.

David died on 1 December 2010 and his estate comprised:

Villa abroad	€260,000
Personal chattels (in UK)	£400,000

At the date of David's death the buying exchange rate was €1.5286 and the selling rate was €1.4086.

His personal representatives incurred additional costs in administering the foreign property of €15,750.

David had made no lifetime transfers .

You are required to calculate the IHT liability arising as a result of David's death.

5.4 Roberta died on 12 January 2007 leaving a UK property worth £250,000 to her brother Ronald. The IHT payable in respect of the property was £12,750. She left the rest of her estate to her daughter, Pearl.

Ronald died on 16 March 2011. He left his entire estate worth £500,000 to his niece, Pearl. He had made a gross chargeable transfer of £350,000 in October 2006.

You are required to calculate the IHT payable in respect of Ronald's estate.

5.5 Lionel was left a cottage in France on his uncle's death in August 2006. The cottage was worth £100,000 and the tax paid on it was £19,000.

Lionel sold the cottage in July 2008 for £263,000 and immediately gifted the entire proceeds to a discretionary trust. The trustees agreed to pay the tax.

Lionel dies in October 2010, leaving a free estate worth £500,000.

He also had a qualifying interest in possession in a trust, the capital assets of which are worth £105,000.

You are required to show the IHT payable in respect of Lionel's estate by the executors and the trustees.

5.6 Samantha died on 17 March 2011. She was UK resident, ordinarily resident and domiciled at the time of her death.

On that date her estate contained the following assets:

- The family home valued at £675,000. This was owned as joint tenants with her husband, Neil, who is also UK resident, ordinarily resident and domiciled.

- 15,000 shares in QuickTab Plc. On the date of death the shares were quoted at 562 – 568 with bargains at 562.5, 563, 565 and 567.5.
- A holiday home in Tuscany valued at €727,000. The selling rate €1.15 at the date of death was and the buying rate was €1.19. Expenses incurred in connection with administering the property came to €40,000.
- Personal chattels totalling £100,000.

There was an outstanding repayment mortgage of £175,000 on the UK property. Samantha's funeral costs were £15,675.

Samantha's will left everything to her three children equally.

You are required to calculate the value of Samantha's death estate.

5.7 Bart died on 7 August 2010 leaving a free estate valued at £800,000.

Bart was the life tenant of an IIP trust set up by his wife, Lily, on her death three years ago. Lily had left her entire estate to the trust and had never made any lifetime gifts except within her annual exemptions.

The capital value of the assets in the trust at the date of Bart's death was £400,000. The remaindermen of the trust are Bart's two daughters.

Included in Bart's free estate was a holiday cottage in Cornwall that he had inherited on his grandfather's death on 12 September 2008. On that date the cottage was worth £215,000 and his grandfather's executors had paid inheritance tax of £42,000.

Bart left his estate to his two daughters.

Bart had made one gross chargeable transfer of £171,000 in May 2006.

You are required to calculate the Inheritance Tax due from:

(1) Bart's PRs and
(2) The trustees of the IIP trust

as a result of Bart's death, assuming all relevant claims are made.

5.8 Stuart Rumsfeld died on 14 November 2010 leaving his entire estate to his children. In his estate were the following assets:

(i) 25,000 shares in Aspen Ltd

Aspen Ltd is an unquoted trading company with 100,000 issued shares. Stuart has owned the shares since 1997.

The current values of the shares are as follows:

100% holding	£1,000,000
75% holding	£600,000
50% holding	£375,000
25% holding	£150,000

Stuart's second wife, Miranda, also owns 25% of the shares.

(ii) Rumsfeld farm

The farm is located in the UK and includes a farmhouse, workers cottages and farm buildings. It is worth £2.6 million. Stuart inherited the farm on the death of his first wife, Doreen, on 1 May 1996. The farm is still rented to the same farmer on the 25 year lease that began on 1 January 1993.

(iii) Cash and personal assets valued at £300,000.

Doreen had left most of her estate, including the farm, to Stuart in May 1996 but had left gifts that used up two thirds of the nil rate band at the time to her two children.

You are required to calculate the Inheritance Tax due on Stuart's death assuming all available reliefs are claimed and that Stuart had made no previous lifetime gifts.

5.9 Tasha has been UK resident and ordinarily resident since 1997. She is legally domiciled in Estonia.

In her estate she currently has the following assets:

Property in Estonia	£45,000
Shares in HB Plc, a UK incorporated company	£12,000
House in UK	£354,000
Deposits with HSBS Bank	
Estonian branch	£10,000
UK branch	£50,000
Jewellery and other personal assets in the UK	£7,500
Cash ISA accounts	£30,000
Car in the UK	£23,000

Tasha has never made any gifts during her lifetime, except to use her annual exemptions.

You are required to advise Tasha on her potential Inheritance Tax liability if she were to die during 2010/11 leaving her entire estate to her brother who lives in Estonia.

6.1 Andrew died on 10 May 2010.

His estate included a property in London worth £705,000, a car worth £35,000 and a villa in Portugal worth £120,000.

He also held a number of quoted shares at his death which were valued for probate purposes as follows:

	£
Lue Plc	15,000
Range plc	22,000
Reen plc	32,000

His personal representatives sold the shares as follows:

	Date of Sale	*Gross Sale Proceeds* £
Lue plc	14 November 2010	9,000
Range plc	15 January 2011	20,000
Reen plc	15 June 2011	30,000

The PRs acquired shares in Rown plc for £15,000 on 11 March 2011.

Andrew's only lifetime gift had been a gross chargeable transfer of £213,000 to a discretionary trust on 12 June 2005.

You are required to calculate the inheritance tax due assuming all available reliefs are claimed.

6.2 Tom died on 12 February 2011 owning personal assets worth £350,000.

The only transfers that he had made during his lifetime were as follows:

(i) 18 November 2003 – Gift of £155,000 cash to a discretionary trust.
(ii) 14 February 2008 – Gift of quoted investments worth £235,000 to his brother.

The investments transferred to his brother in 2008 were still owned by him at the date of Tom's death when they were worth £197,500.

You are required to calculate the inheritance tax due on Tom's death and state who is responsible for payment.

6.3 Keith died on 24 May 2010. His estate included 120,000 shares in Madden Ltd, an unquoted investment company. Keith's civil partner, Martin, owned the remaining 80,000 shares in the company.

HMRC Shares Valuation Division agreed the following values for the shares:

100% holding	£2,500,000
60% holding	£1,000,000
40% holding	£480,000

On 28 February 2013 the PRs sold the shares to an unconnected third party for £1,200,000.

Keith had made a gross chargeable lifetime transfer of £400,000 on 12 October 2005. The other assets in Keith's estate were valued at £325,000. He left his entire estate to his niece, Louise.

You are required to calculate:

(i) **The original IHT liability on the estate, and**

(ii) **The tax repayment obtained as a result of the sale of the shares.**

6.4 Maureen transfers land worth £700,000 into a discretionary trust. This is her only lifetime transfer and she paid the tax.

Almost four years later, Maureen dies.

Due to a fall in property values, the land is worth only £550,000 at the date of her death.

You are required to discuss briefly the IHT implications of the gift to the trust during Maureen's lifetime and on her death.

6.5 Serena died on 12 June 2010.

Her estate included the following:

(i) 10,000 shares in Regedit Ltd, an unquoted trading company, worth £540,000, that she had owned for six years.

(ii) Personal property worth £65,000.

(iii) A house in Lancashire worth £250,000.

(iv) A flat in London worth £750,000.

Serena's executors sold the flat on 18 July 2012 for £775,000. They paid legal fees of £15,000. They bought another flat for £565,000 on 28 September 2012.

On 24 November 2013 they sold the house in Lancashire for £195,000 (legal fees of £2,500).

Serena's only lifetime gift had been £450,000 to a discretionary trust in May 2003.

You are required to calculate the inheritance tax due on Serena's death assuming all available reliefs are claimed.

6.6 Charlotte died on 28 April 2010 leaving her entire estate, worth £1,895,000, to her only daughter, Emily. Her husband, Spencer, had died in 2001, leaving his assets to a nil band discretionary trust.

Included in the value of the estate were two properties, Moore Manor, valued at £750,000 and Crompton Hall, valued at £925,000.

On 16 June 2012 Charlotte's executors sold Crompton Hall for £888,000 and immediately purchased a much smaller property, Marston Mews, for £475,000.

Charlotte's only lifetime gift had been a gross chargeable transfer of £113,000 to a discretionary trust on 4 May 2005.

You are required to calculate the IHT due on Charlotte's death, assuming all available reliefs are claimed.

7.1 Mike and Sue have been married for many years. Mike is UK domiciled, but Sue is non-UK domiciled.

In January 2008, Mike gives Sue £40,000. He has previously used up his annual exemptions for 2007/08 and 2006/07. His only other lifetime transfer was a gross chargeable transfer of £120,000 in May 2004.

In July 2010 Mike dies leaving his estate, worth £320,000 to Sue.

You are required to explain, with calculations, the IHT position for Mike's estate.

7.2 Nikki is considering making a lifetime gift. She is deciding which of the following gifts she should make:

(i) Creation of a discretionary trust with herself as one of the beneficiaries.

(ii) Gift of an antique painting to her daughter. The painting will need to be kept in Nikki's house for insurance purposes.

(iii) Gift of her house to her son. Nikki will continue to live in it but will pay her son a market rent unless it is tax effective to live in it without any payment.

You are required to comment on the inheritance tax implications of each of the gifts.

7.3 For the whole of 2010/11 Lisa has the use of a vase that is within the Pre Owned Asset Tax (POAT) rules.

The current market value of the vase is £150,000.

Assume that the official rate of interest for 2010/11 is 4%

You are required to calculate Lisa's income tax liability for 2010/11 in respect of the vase and to advise her how she can avoid paying this income tax charge.

7.4 Serge dies on 17 April 2010. He came to England in 1984 and had been resident there ever since. His intention had always been to retire to his home country of Latvia.

Serge's estate included the following:

(i) Personal property in the UK worth £25,000.

(ii) A house in Surrey worth £650,000.

(iii) A property in Latvia worth £55,000.

(iv) 10,000 shares in BigTime Plc, a UK registered company, worth £15,000.

(v) An outstanding loan of £10,000 that he made to his brother, Dimitri, who still lives in Latvia.

There is a mortgage on the house in Surrey of £400,000.

Serge had made one lifetime gift of £58,000 cash to his brother on 6 June 2007.

You are required to calculate the IHT liability arising as a result of Serge's death.

7.5 **You are required to show how your calculation of the IHT liability would differ if Serge (example 7.4 above) had come to England in 1995 instead of 1984.**

7.6 Celia has owned a painting that HMRC has agreed qualifies as heritage property, important for its artistic interest. She has owned it for the last ten years and its current market value is £1,500,000.

Celia is considering placing the painting into a discretionary trust. She has made no other lifetime gifts.

You are required to advise Celia of the inheritance tax implications of the transfer assuming all beneficial claims are made.

7.7 Shamus gifted a painting, a Rembrandt original, to his daughter, Marian, on 7 May 2007. The painting was worth £2 million.

Shamus agreed with Marian that he would continue to hang the painting in his drawing room for the foreseeable future.

Shamus died on 21 October 2010 leaving his entire estate, worth £4.5 million, equally to Marian and his son, Bruce.

Shamus's only other chargeable lifetime transfer had been a gift of £500,000 to a discretionary trust in June 2001.

The Rembrandt painting had a value of £2.5 million by the date of Shamus's death.

You are required to calculate the IHT due as a result of Shamus's death.

8.1 Mary gifted an investment property worth £250,000 to a discretionary trust on 25 June 2010. It had cost her £157,500 in July 2001.

You are required to explain whether gift relief is available and, if so, how much. You should also state the base cost of the investment property for the trustees.

8.2 Bill, a higher rate taxpayer, bought 20 acres of land in 1996 as an investment for £20,000. He sold 5 acres in July 2010 for £30,000 when the remaining 15 acres were valued at £120,000. He has capital losses brought forward from 2009/10 of £12,000.

You are required to calculate the capital gains tax payable.

8.3 June buys a statue in July 1986 for £100,000.

It is destroyed in December 2009 and she immediately receives compensation of £230,000. It has no scrap value. She buys another statue for £180,000 in January 2011.

You are required to explain her CGT position, assuming she makes all relevant claims for relief.

8.4 Sam had been trading as a sole trader for a number of years. On 1 June 2010 he sold his business as a going concern to Angela for £1,500,000.

The value of the assets of the business and the capital gains at the date of the transfer were as follows:

	Market value	Cost
	£	£
Freehold land and buildings	950,000	80,000
Goodwill	500,000	–
Machinery and equipment	6,000	4,000
Stock	50,000	50,000
Debtors	5,000	5,000
Creditors	(11,000)	–
	1,500,000	

The land and buildings were acquired in June 2003.

Calculate Sam's capital gains tax liability for 2010/11 assuming he makes any beneficial claims and had taxable income of £35,000 in the year.

9.1 Linda created a discretionary trust on 1 November 2005, placing £200,000 of cash into the trust. Her cumulative total of chargeable lifetime transfers prior to that point was £208,000 (relating to a transfer on 16 September 2002) and she paid the tax due on the creation of the trust. On 21 March 2011 the trustees made an absolute appointment of capital of £50,000 to one of the beneficiaries.

You are required to calculate the inheritance tax on the exit from the trust assuming it is paid by the beneficiary.

9.2 On 18 November 2000 Anne, who had already used all available exemptions, settled £375,000 on a discretionary trust. She had made no previous chargeable transfers.

On 18 November 2008 the trustees distributed £125,000 to a beneficiary, who agreed to pay any tax. The trust fund had grown in value to £500,000 by that date.

By 18 November 2010 the discretionary settlement was valued at £650,000.

You are required to compute the exit and principal charges.

9.3 On 5 November 2010 Deanna set up a discretionary trust with cash of £650,000. She had made a previous gross chargeable lifetime transfer of £200,000 in August 2007.

On 7 January 2011 the trustees gave £25,000 from the trust to one of the beneficiaries, Lucy, Deanna's daughter.

You are required to explain the IHT consequences of both the gift to the trust and the distribution of cash to the beneficiary, assuming that the trustees pay any IHT liability.

9.4 Colin is the life tenant of an immediate post death interest trust. His daughter, Karen is the remainderman of the trust. The trust assets are currently worth £600,000.

Colin has made no lifetime transfers.

You are required to explain the IHT consequences if the trustees distribute all the trust assets to Karen:

(i) During Colin's lifetime, or
(ii) On Colin's death.

9.5 Fiona dies on 17 April 2009. Her will provides for a trust to be set up with £450,000 for her children Paul (date of birth 19 January 1994) and Stephanie (date of birth 14 June 1997). Fiona made no lifetime gifts.

The trust provides that the beneficiaries will become entitled to their share of the trust capital and income at age 25.

The trustees exercise their discretion on 19 January 2015 and distribute £35,000 to Paul for a deposit on a flat.

You are required to calculate the exit charge in January 2015 assuming 2010/11 tax rates and allowances continue to apply for later years.

9.6 Roger is considering a number of different trusts that he can possibly set up in his will for his three young children. On his shortlist are:

(i) A bereaved minor trust.
(ii) Age 18-25 trust.
(iii) Immediate post death interest trust.
(iv) Discretionary trust.

You are required to comment on the inheritance tax implications of each of the trusts.

9.7 Elizabeth set up a discretionary trust with £400,000 on 1 May 2002, the trustees agreeing to pay the tax. She had made one other gross chargeable transfer of £135,000 in June 1999.

On 15 August 2010 the trustees appointed £50,000 cash out of the trust capital to one of the beneficiaries.

You are required to calculate the Inheritance due:

(1) When the trust was set up, and
(2) When the trustees make the distribution in August 2010.

10.1 The Dibble Interest in Possession Trust was set up in May 2002 when unquoted shares worth £40,000 were transferred into the trust. The gain of £15,000 was deferred by gift relief (under s.165 TCGA 1992). The trust was to benefit Annie during her lifetime, with Jeremy becoming absolutely entitled on her death. Annie died in July 2010 when the shares were worth £65,000.

You are required to explain the capital gain tax consequences arising as a result of Annie's death.

10.2 Philippa bought an investment property for £100,000 in February 2002.

In April 2008 she settled the property into a discretionary trust for the benefit of her son, Angus, when it was valued at £150,000.

On 15 June 2009 Angus celebrated his thirtieth birthday. On that day he became absolutely entitled to the trust capital. Its value at that date was £575,000. Angus sold the property on 30 June 2010 for £650,000.

Angus is a higher rate taxpayer in all relevant years.

You are required to:

(1) Calculate Angus's CGT on the disposal, assuming that all relevant reliefs have been claimed where available.

(2) State whether it would it have been better, had the trust allowed it, for the trustees to retain the property until sale giving reasons for your decision.

10.3 Jane sets up a discretionary trust in March 1997 with an asset she acquired in July 1984. Her deferred gain was £12,000 and the value of the asset was £30,000.

The trustees sell the asset in January 2011 for £50,000.

You are required to calculate the trustees' capital gains tax liability for 2010/11.

10.4 In 1990 David had set up a life interest trust for his nephew Darren. A 5% holding of shares in Alpha Ltd (an unquoted company) had been settled and David had made a gift relief claim to defer the gain of £10,000 on those shares. Holdings of quoted shares had also been settled at the same time.

Darren died in August 2010. At that time the trust assets consisted of:

Holding	*Value at death*	*Cost*	*Date of acquisition*
	£	£	
5% holding in Alpha Ltd	60,000	45,000	1990
1,000 Beta plc shares	10,000	8,000	1996
2,000 Gamma plc shares	15,000	5,000	1990

You are required to explain the chargeable gains accruing to the trustees on Darren's death.

10.5 On 6 October 2010 all of the assets in the Jones Discretionary Trust were advanced to Cedric, one of the beneficiaries.

At that date the trustees had capital losses brought forward from the previous year of £2,000 and they made further capital losses on the advance of £3,000. The trustees had made substantial capital gains in 2007/08 and 2008/09.

You are required to briefly explain the reliefs available for the capital losses.

10.6 On 1 May 2002 Samuel gifted his entire 15% holding (1,500 shares) in Dockside Ltd, an unquoted trading company, to a discretionary trust for his son.

The other shares in the company are owned by his two brothers. The company was set up in July 1981 by all three brothers, when each subscribed £5,000 for his shares.

The 15% holding was worth £15,000 in March 1982 and £90,000 at the date it was transferred to the trust. A 100% holding would have been worth £1m.

On 2 November 2010 the trustees of the discretionary trust appoint the Dockside shares to Samuel's son, when they were worth £105,000. The son agrees to pay any IHT due.

You are required to show the CGT consequences of the gift and appointment of the Dockside shares, assuming any available reliefs are claimed.

10.7 The trustees of the Jameson life interest trust are considering distributing 150,000 shares in Jameson Ltd, an unquoted trading company, to the life tenant, Jeremy Jameson.

The shares were first subscribed for at par by Joyce Jameson, the settlor of the trust and Jeremy's aunt, in 1994 when the company was set up. The shares represent a 25% holding.

When Joyce put the shares into the trust in September 2001 they were worth £4.50 per share and a gain of £275,000 arose. She made a gift relief claim. At the time, 12% of the company's chargeable assets were investments.

The trustees would like to know their potential capital gains tax exposure if they distribute the shares to Jeremy in January 2011 when the estimated value will be £9.25 per share. The company's investments have increased to 17% of the total chargeable assets.

Jeremy has never worked for Jameson Ltd.

You are required to calculate the potential capital gains tax liability for the trustees. You should assume that all beneficial claims are made.

11.1 The Pritchard interest in possession trust received the following income in 2010/11:

	£
Bank interest (net)	460
Dividends (net)	675
Gross rents	15,000

The trustees incurred the following expenses:

	£
Expenses in respect of the rental property	1,500
Trust administration	450

You are required to calculate the income tax payable by the trustees and show the statement of income that the life tenant will receive.

11.2 The Young Discretionary Trust received the following income in 2010/11:

	£
Dividends	1,800
Gross rents	18,000

It incurred the following expenses:

	£
Expenses in respect of the rental property	1,500
Trust administration	945

A £500 distribution of income was made to a beneficiary during the year.

You are required to calculate the income tax payable by the trustees and show the statement of income that the beneficiary will receive.

11.3 You are preparing the Trust tax return for 2010/11 for the Elvin Discretionary Trust.

The trust's only income is net rental income of £8,500. Trust administration expenses of £882 were incurred.

In 2009/10, the year the trust was set up, tax of £650 was paid at 20% and 40%.

The first distribution was made in 2010/11 of £6,000.

You are required to calculate the income tax payable by the trustees in 2010/11.

11.4 Frazer is the trustee of an interest in possession trust. The income of the trust is paid to Miranda during her life. For the tax year 2010/11 the trust has the following income and expenses:

Rental income (gross)	£2,500
Dividends (net)	£1,800
Bank interest (net)	£960
Legal fees relating to income	£500
Letting expenses	£275

You are required to calculate the trust's total tax liability, how much tax the trust will have to pay under self-assessment and to show Miranda's statement of income from the trust.

11.5 The Foster Trust is a trust for Joey, a bereaved minor, who has no other sources of income. In the 2010/11 tax year the trustee has the following income and expenses:

Bank interest (net)	£1,800
Dividends	£6,655
Rental income (net of allowable expenses)	£1,100
Expenses relating to income generally	£630

No income was distributed to Joey during the year.

You are required to calculate the total tax liability of the trustee.

11.6 The trustees of the Percy Smythe discretionary trust received the following income during 2010/11:

Rental income	£16,800
Interest	£2,880
Dividends	£103,500

The trustees incurred revenue expenses of £520 relating to the letting of the trust's unfurnished rental property.

They made income payments of £5,000 to each of the five beneficiaries of the trust on 31 March 2011.

The trust pool carried forward at 6 April 2010 was £1,675.

You are required to:

(1) Calculate the income tax payable by the trustees, and
(2) Show the balance on the tax pool at 5 April 2011.

12.1 Bernard dies on 16 June 2010. Following his death his PRs had the following income and expenses for the rest of 2010/11:

Rental income (gross)	£2,500
Dividends (net)	£1,800
Bank interest (net)	£960
Letting expenses	£275
Administration expenses in relation to income	£500

You are required to calculate the PRs' income tax payable for 2010/11.

12.2 Bernard's estate (question 12.1) above is left equally to his two children, Jayne and Jack.

The administration of the estate is completed on 4 April 2011.

You are required to show the net income due to Jayne and Jack and the tax deduction certificate that each will receive from the PRs.

12.3 Mr Carr died on 30 June 2009. His estate had the following income and expenses during the period 6 April 2010 to 5 November 2010:

	£	
Rental income		
Tax adjusted property income	13,775	
Bank interest		
Credited 1 November 2010 (when account to be closed)	2,240	(net)
Dividends		
15 July 2010 (for the period ended 30.6.10)	2,812	
Professional expenses paid		
Interest on loan taken out to pay IHT (loan taken out 1 October 2009, ceased 1 November 2010)	95	per month
Accountancy fees	1,200	
Agents' fees re rental property	1,650	

You are required to calculate the income tax liability in respect of Mr Carr's estate for 2010/11.

12.4 Tanya dies on 12 December 2009 leaving her entire estate to her son, Jamie.

On 7 January 2011, the estate is still in administration and her executors sell 10,000 shares in Splendid Ltd, an unquoted trading company, from the estate for £156,000. The shares had cost Tanya £116,000 in April 2001 and had a probate value of £127,500.

You are required to calculate the executors' capital gains tax liability.

12.5 Tanya dies on 12 December 2009 leaving an estate worth £565,000.

On 7 January 2011, the estate is still in administration and her executors pass 10,000 shares in Splendid Ltd, an unquoted trading company, to Jamie. At that date they were worth £156,000. Jamie, a higher rate taxpayer, immediately sells the shares.

The shares had cost Tanya £116,000 in April 2001 and had a probate value of £127,500.

You are required to explain the capital gains tax consequences of the appointment of the shares to Jamie and calculate the CGT liability on the sale of the shares.

12.6 The personal representatives of Colin Holden's estate are preparing the tax deduction certificate (R185 (Estate income)) for his wife, Caroline Holden, the sole beneficiary of the estate.

Colin Holden died on 1 July 2010. Since that date the PRs have received the following income

Rental income	£9,900
Interest	£1,200
Dividends	£33,345

The PRs have incurred expenses of £575 so far in connection with the administration of the estate, which is still ongoing. They made an interim payment of £25,000 to Caroline on 12 December 2010.

You are required to calculate:

(1) The income tax payable by the PRs, and
(2) The net figures to be included on the R185 to be given to Caroline.

Solutions to exam style questions

1.1 The IHT treatment of the transactions are as follows:

(1) A sale of an asset at less than market value is not a transfer of value for inheritance tax purposes if there is no intention to confer a gratuitous benefit on the purchaser. Hence, this sale will not have any inheritance tax consequences.

(2) The gift to his spouse is exempt.

(3) The donation to the UK charity is exempt.

(4) The transfer of the main residence is a chargeable lifetime transfer (CLT):

	£
Gift	110,000
Less: AE 2010/11	(3,000)
AE 2009/10 b/f	(3,000)
Chargeable	104,000

(5) The gift to John's father is covered partly by the marriage exemption. There is no annual exemption left as it has been allocated to the CLT. The balance of the gift is a potentially exempt transfer, which means that it is exempt during John's life time and will only become chargeable if he dies within seven years of making the gift.

	£
Gift	5,000
Less: ME (child to parent)	(1,000)
PET	4,000

1.2 When a gift is made on the occasion of a marriage/ civil partnership ceremony at least £1,000 of the gift is always exempt regardless of who makes the gift and to whom it is made.

Higher exemptions apply depending on the relationship of the donor to the done.

Parent's gift on their child's wedding

A maximum of £5,000 is exempt. So, Raymond's father will be treated as making two potentially exempt transfers (PETs) as follows:

	£
To Raymond	20,000
Less: marriage exemption (ME)	(5,000)
PET	15,000
To Sally – PET	20,000

One party to the marriage making a gift to the other before the marriage

A maximum of £2,500 is exempt. As the couple are not yet married the spouse exemption cannot apply. So, Raymond will be treated as making a PET as follows:

	£
To Sally	10,000
Less: ME	(2,500)
PET	7,500

Any other individual making a wedding gift

A maximum of £1,000 is exempt. So, Sally's sister will be treated as making a PET as follows:

	£
To Sally	5,000
Less: ME	(1,000)
PET	4,000

1.3 IHT definitions:

(1) *Chargeable lifetime transfer.*

A chargeable lifetime transfer is a gift made during lifetime which gives rise to an immediate charge to IHT.

A gift to a relevant property trust during lifetime (ie any trust except a bare trust or a trust for a disabled person) is a CLT.

(2) *Potentially exempt transfer.*

A potentially exempt transfer is a gift made during lifetime which does not give rise to an immediate charge to IHT. There is only an IHT charge if the donor dies within seven years of making the gift.

A gift from one individual to another is a PET.

(3) *Exempt transfer.*

An exempt transfer is a gift made during lifetime or on death which is ignored for IHT purposes.

An example of a gift that is only exempt during lifetime is one that is within the annual exemption.

An example of a gift that is exempt both during lifetime and on death is a gift to a spouse or civil partner.

Note. Candidates may also have mentioned the following examples under (3):

Lifetime exemptions

- Small gifts under £250
- Normal expenditure out of income
- Marriage exemption

Exemptions during lifetime and on death

- Donations to UK charities
- Donations to certain political parties
- Gifts for national purposes (eg National Trust)

1.4

(i) *Tamara domiciled in South Africa*

Gifts from UK domiciled spouses to non-UK domiciled spouses are only exempt up to £55,000. This is a lifetime limit.

	£
Gift 31.1.04	200,000
Less: spouse exemption	(55,000)
PET	145,000

Charles survives more than seven years from making this gift so the PET is completely exempt and no IHT is due.

	£
Gift 1.1.11	320,000
Less: spouse exemption (used)	(nil)
PET	320,000

Charles dies within seven years of making this gift so the PET becomes chargeable and IHT will be due on £320,000.

(ii) *Tamara UK domiciled*

Gifts between UK domiciled spouses are completely exempt with no limit.

There is therefore no IHT due on either of the gifts.

1.5 The IHT treatment of the transactions are as follows:

(1) IHT is a tax on gifts out of capital, so if Spencer can show that the payments of his nieces' school fees come within the exemption for 'normal expenditure out of income' they could be completely exempt. To prove this he must show:

(i) The gifts are made out of his normal expenditure (ie are part of a pattern of giving)
(ii) They are made out of his income, and
(iii) They leave him with sufficient income to maintain his usual standard of living.

Based on the facts it is likely that the exemption will apply.

(2) The transfer to his civil partner is completely exempt as it is within the £55,000 limit for gifts from UK to non-UK domiciled spouses/ civil partners.

(3) The gifts to his nephews are exempt as they come within the small gift exemption. This allows gifts up to £250 each year to the same recipient to be completely exempt.

(4) The transfer of the Hawaii holiday home to the interest in possession trust is a chargeable lifetime transfer (CLT) because the trust is a relevant property trust:

	£
Gift	120,000
Less: AE 2010/11	(3,000)
AE 2009/10 b/f	(3,000)
Chargeable	114,000

(5) The gift to the Labour Party is exempt as it is a gift to a political party.

1.6 A Liam sells a painting for £5,000. He later finds out that it was an original worth ten times what he sold it for.

C The trustees of the life interest trust pass out half of the trust assets to Liam.

Certain dispositions are exempt from an Inheritance Tax (IHT) charge, while others are not even transfers of value, so fall outside the scope of IHT.

When Liam sells the painting for less than it was worth, even though his estate has gone down in value considerably, Liam did not mean to make a 'gift' of the painting, ie he had no gratuitous intent. This is a bad bargain and is not caught by the IHT provisions.

When the trustees of the life interest trust pass out half of the trust assets to Liam, there is no transfer of value as before the 'gift' Liam was deemed to own the trust assets and after, he actually owns them, so his estate has not gone down in value.

The other dispositions fall within specific exemptions:

The gifts to his nieces fall within the small gifts exemption of £250 per recipient per tax year

When the trustees of the life interest trust pass out half of the trust assets to Liam's wife, it is treated as Liam making the gift directly, in which case it is exempt (by virtue of the spouse exemption).

The gift to his god-daughter is covered by the 'normal expenditure out of income' exemption.

2.1 When the donor pays the tax the rate must be grossed up.

May 2005

	£	£
Gift		295,000
AEs 2005/06 and 2004/05 b/f		(6,000)
		289,000
Nil rate band	275,000	
GCTs in the 7 years before the gift	–	
		(275,000)
		14,000
IHT @ 20/80		3,500
GCT = £(289,000 + 3,500) =		292,500

July 2010

	£	£
Gift		106,000
AEs 2010/11 and 2010/11 b/f		(6,000)
		100,000
Nil rate band	325,000	
GCTs in the 7 years before the gift	(292,500)	
		(32,500)
		67,500
IHT @ 20%		13,500

2.2 (i) *Trustees pay the tax*

	£
CLT	361,000
AE 2007/08	(3,000)
2006/07	(3,000)
Gross chargeable transfer	355,000
Tax payable on death	
40% £(355,000 – 325,000)	12,000
Less: taper relief (3-4 years) @ 20%	(2,400)
Less lifetime tax £(355,000 – 300,000) × 20%	(11,000)
Death tax payable	–

Note that lifetime tax is not repayable.

(ii) *William pays the tax*

	£
Lifetime tax:	
Gift less annual exemptions (see (i)) £(361,000 – 6,000)	355,000
Lifetime tax (355,000 – 300,000) × 20/80	13,750
Gross chargeable transfer	368,500
Additional tax on death:	
GCT	368,500
Nil rate band on death	(325,000)
	43,750
Tax payable at 40%	17,500
Less taper relief (3 – 4 years) @ 20%	(3,500)
Less lifetime tax	(13,750)
Death tax payable	250

2.3 The lifetime tax is:

	£	£
Transfer of value	363,000	
Less: AE 2010/11		(3,000)
AE 2009/10 b/f		(3,000)
CLT		357,000
Less: nil rate band	325,000	
Less: GCTs in last 7 yrs	(139,500)	(185,500)
Chargeable		171,500
Tax @ 20/80 or 25%		42,875

The GCT is the total amount that leaves Andy's estate as a result of the gift (ie the gift PLUS the tax): £357,000 + £42,875 = £399,875.

TQT

Tax Qualification Training

The GCT in 2007 took place more than 7 years before death, so no further tax is due. The tax on the 2011 GCT is:

	£	£
GCT		399,875
Less: nil rate band	325,000	
Less: GCTs in the 7 yrs before the gift	(139,500)	(185,500)
Chargeable		214,375
Tax @ 40%		85,750
Less: taper relief		
(3.4.11 – 17.9.15) = 4 – 5 yrs: 40%		(34,300)
		51,450
Less: lifetime tax		(42,875)
IHT due		8,575

2.4

	£	£
Gift		313,000
AE 2010/11		(3,000)
2009/10 (used against PET)		nil
CLT		310,000
Less: nil rate band	325,000	
Less: GCTs in 7 yrs before gift		
£(200,000 – 6,000) (AEs 2006/07 and 2005/06)	(194,000)	(131,000)
		179,000
IHT @ 20%		35,800

Notes.

(i) The gift to the son is a PET and does not therefore use up any of the nil rate band whilst Walter is alive although it does use the available annual exemption(s).

(ii) The original transfer to the trust was covered by the nil rate band in that year.

2.5 Jake's gift into the relevant property trust is a chargeable lifetime transfer (regardless of who might benefit from the trust).

Lifetime tax

	£
CLT May 2006	
Transfer	265,000
Less: AE 2006/07 & 2005/06 bf	(6,000)
	259,000

Covered by nil rate band

PET August 2007

Transfer	84,000
Less: marriage exemption	(5,000)
AE 2007/08	(3,000)
	76,000

Death tax

CLT – nil as covered by nil rate band

PET	76,000
Nil rate band available £(325,000 – 259,000)	(66,000)
	10,000
Tax @ 40%	4,000
Less: taper relief (3 – 4 years) 20%	(800)
Death tax chargeable	3,200

2.6 (i) The gift to Frances is a PET, so no tax during lifetime. It does, however, use the available annual exemptions. A car is not an exempt asset for IHT purposes.

(ii) The gift to the discretionary trust is a chargeable lifetime transfer:

14.1.06

	£	£
Gift		428,000
AEs (used against PET)		(nil)
CLT		428,000
Nil rate band	275,000	
GCTs in the 7 years before the gift (PET does not use nil band during lifetime)	–	
		(275,000)
		153,000
IHT @ 20/80 (if the question is silent regarding who pays the tax assume the donor pays it)		38,250
GCT = £(428,000 + 38,250) =		466,250

Death tax: November 2010

(i) The PET becomes chargeable.

	£
Gift	32,000
AEs 2005/06 & 2004/05 b/f	(6,000)
PET	26,000

This is within the nil rate band so no tax is due.

(ii) There is additional tax due on the CLT:

	£	£
GCT		466,250
Less: nil rate band	325,000	
Less: GCTs in the 7 years before the gift (now includes the PET as it became chargeable)	(26,000)	(299,000)
		167,250
IHT @ 40%		66,900
Less: taper relief: 1.06 – 11.10 = 4-5 yrs: 40%		(26,760)
		40,140
Less: lifetime tax		(38,250)
IHT due		1,890

3.1 The loss to donor principle is used when valuing unquoted shares:

		£	£	£
Before the transfer	5,100 × £150			765,000
After the transfer	4,900 × £120			(588,000)
Transfer of value				177,000
Less: AE 2010/11				(3,000)
AE 2009/10 b/f				(3,000)
CLT				171,000
Less: nil rate band			325,000	
Less: GCTs in the 7 yrs before the gift		163,000		
Less: AEs 2007/08 & 2006/07 b/f		(6,000)	(157,000) (N)	
				(168,000)
Chargeable				3,000
IHT @ $^{20}/_{80}$ / 25% (assume donor pays the tax as question is silent)				750

Note. The original gift to the trust was within the nil rate band at the time.

TQT
Tax Qualification Training

3.2 The gift to Jim is a PET, so there is no tax during Mrs Brown's lifetime, although the annual exemptions of 2007/08 and 2006/07 are allocated to it.

When Mrs Brown dies within seven years of making the gift, the PET becomes chargeable. The loss to donor principle is used when valuing unquoted shares. Where there is related property we must also take this into account.

		£
Before the transfer	2,000 × £900 (W1)	1,800,000
After the transfer	500 × £600 (W2)	(300,000)
Transfer of value		1,500,000
Less: AE × 2		(6,000)
PET		1,494,000
Less: nil rate band		(325,000)
Chargeable		1,169,000
IHT @ 40%		467,600
Less: taper relief 1.6.07 – 24.9.10 = 3 – 4 yrs: 20%		(93,520)
IHT due		374,080

Workings

(1) Mr B 40%
Mrs B 20%
60% ie value at £900 per share

(2) Mr B 40%
Mrs B 5%
45% ie value at £600 per share

Note The value of the transfer ignoring related property is £450,000 (1,500 × £300). As the value using the related property rules is higher (£1,500,000) this higher value is used.

3.3 The gift to the interest in possession trust is a chargeable lifetime transfer as all lifetime trusts (except to bare trusts and trusts for disabled persons) are relevant property trusts.

When valuing the shares we use the loss to donor and related property rules.

We are given the gross chargeable transfer amount for the earlier transfer which is the amount *after* annual exemptions.

		£
Before the transfer	$\frac{45}{45+25} \times £740,000$	475,714
After the transfer	$\frac{40}{40+25} \times £680,000$	(418,462)
Transfer of value		57,252
Less: AE 2010/11		(3,000)
AE 2009/10 b/f		(3,000)
CLT		51,252
Less: nil rate band £(325,000 – 290,000)		(35,000)
Chargeable		16,252
IHT @ 25% (assume Michael pays the tax as the question is silent)		4,063

Note. The value of the transfer ignoring related property (£20,000 (5% holding)) is lower than the value using the related property rules so the related property valuation is used.

3.4

	£
Shares (W)	339,250
Less: AE 2010/11	(3,000)
AE 2009/10 (used against June 2009 transfer)	(Nil)
CLT	336,250
Less: nil rate band £(325,000 – 175,000)	(150,000)
Chargeable	186,250
IHT @ 20%	37,250

Working

Minitip: Lower of: ¼-up: £(22.25 – 21.80) ÷ 4 + 21.80 = £21.9125	
and average: $£\frac{21.20+22.25}{2}$ = £21.725 × 10,000	217,250
Maxipack: Lower of: ¼-up: £(12.80 – 12.00) ÷ 4 + 12.00 = £12.20 × 10,000	122,000
and £12.25	
Total	339,250

3.5 (i) *Lifetime gift to discretionary trust*

The value of the shares is the lower of the ¼-up rule and the average.

¼-up: (334.25 – 331.75) ÷ 4 + 331.75 = 332.375p

average: $£\frac{330+334}{2}$ = 332p

ie 12,000 × 332p = £39,840

The price on the date of the gift reflects the fact that the shares have gone ex-div.

(ii) *Shares held on death*

The value of the shares at the date of death is the lower of the ¼-up rule and the average.

However, because the dividend has gone ex-div and the dividend was paid after the date of death the net dividend must be added to the value.

	£
12,000 × 332p	39,840
Add net dividend: 12,000 × 12.2p	1,464
Total value	41,304

3.6 *Lifetime tax*

(i) The gift to Richard is a PET, so no tax during lifetime. It does, however, use the available annual exemptions.

(ii) The gift to the interest in possession trust is a chargeable lifetime transfer as the trust is a relevant property trust (lifetime trust set up after 21 March 2006):

4.5.09

	£	£
Gift: 10,000 × £3.58 (the bid price)		35,800
AEs 2009/10 and 2008/09 b/f		(6,000)
CLT		29,800
Nil rate band	325,000	
GCTs in the 7 years before the gift (PET does not use nil band during lifetime)	–	
		(325,000)
		Nil

Death tax: October 2010

(i) The PET becomes chargeable.

	£
Gift: €468,000 ÷ €1.39 (buying rate)	336,691
Less: AEs 2004/05 and 2003/04 b/f	(6,000)
PET	330,691
Less: nil rate band	(325,000)
	5,691
IHT @ 40%	2,276
Less: taper relief (12.8.04 – 12.10.10) 6 – 7 yrs: 80%	(1,821)
IHT due	455

(ii) There is additional tax due on the CLT:

	£	£
GCT		29,800
Less: nil rate band	325,000	
Less: GCTs in the 7 years before the gift (now includes the PET as it became chargeable)	(330,691)	(Nil)
		29,800
IHT @ 40%		11,920
Less: taper relief: <3yrs		(nil)
		11,920
Less: lifetime tax		(nil)
IHT due		11,920

4.1 The gift to Marc is a PET, so no tax during lifetime. BPR is potentially available at 100% for any level of shareholding in an unquoted trading company. The BPR is restricted by any 'excepted assets' held by the company (eg investments and surplus cash).

When Luke dies within seven years of gifting the shares the PET becomes chargeable.

BPR is available as Marc still holds the shares. It is, however, restricted by the investments held by the company (the cash is required for day-to-day transactions and is therefore not an excepted asset).

	£
Transfer	750,000
Less: BPR $\frac{2,845,000}{2,890,000} \times £750,000 \times 100\%$	(738,322)
	11,678
Less: AE 2009/10 and 2008/09 b/f	(6,000)
	5,678
IHT @ 40% (nil rate band fully used by other lifetime gifts)	2,271
Less: taper relief (< 3 yrs)	(nil)
IHT due	2,271

4.2 Business property relief (BPR) will be available on Jack's transfer. This is because the property that Jack is gifting replaced other relevant business property and the combined period of ownership is more than two years.

BPR will also be available on Olga's transfer. Olga inherited the business on the death of her husband and therefore the combined ownership period by her and her husband is taken into account.

Even though Simon has not run the business for more than two years, BPR is not relevant for the transfer from him to John as this is covered by the spouse/ civil partner exemption. When John dies BPR is not available for the business in his estate as he has not held the asset for long enough. Simon and John's periods of ownership cannot be combined as the asset was acquired on a lifetime gift and not inherited on death.

4.3 When Joan makes the gift to her son in 2007 it is a PET, so no tax due during her lifetime. BPR is potentially available. When she dies within seven years of making the gift the PET becomes chargeable.

When valuing the shares we must use the loss to donor and related property rules. The value of the shares is therefore based on Joan and Alex's combined shareholding of 30%.

BPR is available for any number of unquoted trading company shares, with a restriction for excepted assets.

		£
Value of holding before the transfer: 20/(20 + 10) × £147,000 (30% holding)		98,000
Less: value after the transfer (no shares left)		(nil)
Transfer of value		98,000
Less: BPR: 100% × £98,000 × $\frac{(500-80)}{500}$		(82,320)
		15,680
Less: AE 2007/08 and 2006/07 b/f		(6,000)
PET	£	9,680
Less: nil rate band	325,000	
Less: GCTs in 7 years before gift	(427,500)	(nil)
Chargeable		9,680
IHT @ 40%		3,872
Less: taper relief (4.6.07 – 21.3.11) = 3 – 4 yrs: 20%		(774)
IHT due		3,098

4.4 When Arthur makes the gift to his son in August 2010 it is a PET, so no tax due during his lifetime. BPR is potentially available.

When Arthur dies within seven years of making the gift the PET becomes chargeable. However, BPR is not available at the date of his death because his son no longer owns the factory (or replacement relevant business property).

The IHT due is therefore:

		£
Gift		650,000
BPR (not available as son no longer owns factory)		–
AE	2010/11	(3,000)
	2009/10	(3,000)
PET		644,000
Less: nil rate band (available in full)		(325,000)
		319,000
IHT @ 40% (no taper as owned for < 3yrs)		127,600

4.5 When Arthur makes the gift to the interest in possession trust for his son in August 2010 it is a CLT as the trust is a relevant property trust (not a bare trust or trust for disabled person(s)).

BPR is available at 50% as this is an asset used in a business.

The lifetime tax is therefore:

		£
Gift		676,000
Less: BPR @ 50%		(338,000)
		338,000
Less: AE	2010/11	(3,000)
	2009/10	(3,000)
		332,000
Less: nil rate band (available in full)		(325,000)
		7,000
IHT @ 25% (assume Arthur pays the tax as the question is silent)		1,750

The gross chargeable transfer is: £(332,000 + 1,750 =) £333,750

When Arthur dies within seven years of making the CLT there may be additional tax due. However, BPR is no longer available at the date of his death because the trustees no longer own the factory (or replacement relevant business property).

The IHT due is therefore:

	£
GCT	333,750
Add: BPR withdrawn	338,000
Total chargeable	671,750
Less: nil rate band (available in full)	(325,000)
	346,750
IHT @ 40% (no taper as owned for < 3yrs)	138,700
Less: lifetime tax	(1,750)
IHT due	136,950

4.6 The capital account is relevant business property for BPR purposes. BPR is available at 100%.

The mortgage on the land will reduce the IHT value of the land, which has agricultural value (AV) so APR will be available. The rate of APR is 50% because this is a pre-1.9.95 lease that has more than 24 months left to run.

Because the land is run as a business, BPR will be available on the remaining value. The farm is occupied and farmed by the partnership. The transfer of the farm will therefore reduce the net value of the partnership business and therefore the transfer should qualify for 100% BPR (Nelson Dance Family Settlement v HMRC (2009)).

APR is given before BPR.

The IHT values are therefore:

	Capital account	*Land (AV)*	*Land (balance)*
	£	£	£
Assets	60,000	600,000	200,000
Less: mortgage (60:20)		(150,000)	(50,000)
	60,000	450,000	150,000
Less: APR @ 50%		(225,000)	
BPR @ 100%			(150,000)
BPR @ 100%	(60,000)		
IHT values	Nil	225,000	Nil

4.7 It is essential to calculate any lifetime tax on the gifts first, then any death tax on them.

Lifetime tax

14.5.01 – PET
12.4.05 – GCT within nil rate band, so no IHT
25.6.06 – PET – marriage exemption £5,000 available and annual exemption of 2006/07 (2005/06 used against GCT)
3.10.09 – CLT but BPR available at 100% so no lifetime tax

Death tax

14.5.01 – >7 yrs before death so no IHT implications
12.4.05 – Additional IHT but within nil rate band so no IHT due
25.6.06 – PET becomes chargeable

	£	£
Gift 25.6.06		50,000
Less: ME		(5,000)
Less: AE		(3,000)
PET		42,000
Less: nil rate band	325,000	
Less: GCTs in 7 yrs before gift	(238,000)	(87,000)
Taxable		Nil

3.10.09 – CLT – BPR withdrawn as trustees no longer hold the shares

	£	£
GCT	Nil	
Add: BPR withdrawn	750,000	750,000
Less: AE 2009/10		(3,000)
Less: AE 2008/09 b/f		(3,000)
		744,000
Less: nil rate band	325,000	
Less: GCTs in 7 yrs before gift £(238,000 + 42,000)	(280,000)	(45,000)
Taxable		699,000
IHT @ 40%		279,600

No taper relief as < 3 years + no lifetime tax

5.1

		£	£
UK assets			
House in Scotland		180,000	
Less:	Secured loan	(180,000)	nil
Other UK assets		100,000	
Less:	Balance of secured loan £(200,000 – 180,000)	(20,000)	
	Unsecured UK debt	(120)	
	Funeral expenses	(1,500)	78,380
Non-UK assets			
House in France		125,000	
Less:	Secured loan	(110,000)	15,000
Other Non-UK assets			30,000
Net estate for IHT			123,380

5.2 The gift to the discretionary trust took place more than seven years before Joe's death. There is therefore no additional IHT due on Joe's death and it can be ignored when considering the available nil rate band at the date of death.

			£
Free estate			293,000
Settled property (life tenant of qualifying interest in possession trust)			350,000
			643,000
Less: nil rate band remaining at death			(325,000)
			318,000
IHT @ 40%			127,200
Payable by:	Executors	293,000/643,000 × £127,200	57,962
	Trustees	350,000/643,000 × £127,200	69,238

5.3 David died within five years of inheriting the assets on his brother's death so quick succession relief (QSR) is available to reduce the IHT on his estate.

Because David was left the entire estate he had to pay the tax on it.

His death estate is:

	£	£
Free estate		
Personal chattels		400,000
Foreign property (€260,000 ÷ €1.5286 (buying rate))	170,090	
Less: costs: lower of: (i) €15,750 ÷ €1.5286 = £10,304		
(ii) 5% × £170,090 = £8,505	(8,505)	161,585
Value of estate		561,585
Less: nil rate band		(325,000)
		236,585
Tax @ 40%		94,634
Less: QSR $£38,250 \times \frac{£91,750^{*}}{£130,000} \times 20\%$ (4 to 5 years)		(5,399)
IHT payable		89,235

* increase in David's estate (he paid the original IHT): £(130,000 – 38,250) = £91,750.

5.4 As Roberta and Ronald's deaths are within 5 years of each other, QSR applies to reduce the IHT payable on Ronald's death estate.

Because the asset left to Ronald was a specific gift of UK property it was tax-free (ie Ronald did not have to pay the tax on it, Roberta's residuary legatee, ie Pearl, did).

Consequently, the full value of the property is the 'net' amount in the QSR fraction.

	£
IHT on death estate:	
£500,000 × 40% (all nil band used)	200,000
Less: QSR(W)	(2,426)
IHT due	197,574

Working

QSR: 1st tax × net gift/ gross gift @ % for 4 – 5 years

$$£12,750 \times \frac{250,000}{250,000 + 12,750} \times 20\% = £2,426$$

5.5 Lionel's gift to the discretionary trust was a CLT. However there is no tax to pay as a result of Lionel's death as it is below the nil rate band.

Lionel's death estate

	£	£
Free estate		500,000
Settled property		105,000
Total estate		605,000
Less: nil rate band	325,000	
Less: GCTs in seven years before death		
(263,000 – 6,000 (2 × AEs))	(257,000)	(68,000)
		537,000
IHT @ 40%		214,800
Less: QSR (W)		(3,078)
Net tax due		211,722

Payable by executors

$$\frac{500,000}{605,000} \times £211,722 = £174,977$$

Payable by trustees

$$\frac{£105{,}000}{£605{,}000} \times £211{,}722 = £36{,}745$$

Working

As the period between the uncle's and Lionel's deaths was less than five years (it was between 4 and 5 years) QSR is available (at 20%).

The cottage left to Lionel was a specific gift of non-UK property so it was tax-bearing, ie Lionel had to pay the tax on it. The net amount (ie the top figure) in the QSR fraction is therefore the value of the cottage *less* the tax.

QSR is therefore:

$$\frac{100{,}000 - 19{,}000}{100{,}000} \times £19{,}000 \times 20\% = £3{,}078$$

5.6 The value of assets in the death estate is the probate value, ie the market value at the date of death.

Special rules apply for calculating the value of certain assets such as shares and overseas assets.

Total estate

	£
Family home (W1)	Nil
Shares (W2)	84,525
Tuscany property (W3)	580,378
Personal property	100,000
Total	764,903
Less: funeral costs	(15,675)
Death estate	749,228

Workings

(1) *Family home*

The family home is held as joint tenants with Samantha's husband. Her share of the property will pass automatically to Neil by operation of law, regardless of what it says in her will. Assets passing to a spouse are exempt from IHT. The value is therefore £Nil.

(2) *Shares*

Lower of:	
(i) Quarter-up rule:	
(568-562)/4 = 1.5 + 562	563.5p
(ii) Average	
(562.5 + 567.5)/ 2	565p
ie 563.5p × 15,000	£84,525

(3) *Tuscany villa*

	£	£
€727,000 / 1.19 (buying rate)		610,924
Less: admin expenses		
Lower of:		
(i) €40,000 / 1.19	33,613	
(ii) 5% × £610,924	30,546	
		(30,546)
Probate value		580,378

5.7 The capital value of the IIP trust will be included in Bart's estate as his settled property as it is a qualifying IIP trust (an IPDI), having been set up on Lily's death.

Bart had made one lifetime gift in the seven years before his death, which was well within the nil rate band. No IHT is due but the gift does use up the nil rate band for the death estate.

Also, Lily had died having not used her nil rate band, so it is assumed that Bart's PRs will claim the unused amount (100%) to use against his death estate.

	£	£
Death estate		
Free estate		800,000
Settled property		400,000
Total estate		1,200,000
Less: own nil rate band	325,000	
Lily's unused nil rate band	325,000	
Less: GCT in 7 years before death	(171,000)	
		(479,000)
		721,000
Tax @ 40%		288,400
Less QSR (W)		(28,109)
IHT due		260,291

Split:

PRs $\frac{800,000}{1,200,000} \times$ £260,291	173,527
Trustees of IIP trust $\frac{400,000}{1,200,000} \times$ £260,291	86,764

Working - QSR

Relief is available

1st tax × net/ gross × % 1-2 years

£42,000 × 215,000/(215,000 + 42,000) × 80% = £28,109

5.8

	£	£
Estate		
Cash etc...		300,000
Shares (W)	187,500	
Less: BPR @ 100%	(187,500)	Nil
Farm (Note)	2,600,000	
Less: APR @ 50%	(1,300,000)	1,300,000
Total		1,600,000
Less: own nil rate band	325,000	
Add: spouse's unused nil rate band	108,333	
1/3 × £325,000		
		(433,333)
		1,166,667
Tax @ 40%		466,667

Note: The farm is eligible for APR on the full value @ 50% (pre 9.95 lease with more than 2 years left to run). There is no indication that there is any non-agricultural value from the facts.

Working - shares

The shares must be valued using the related property rules.

25,000/ 50,000 × £375,000 = £187,500

5.9 Tasha is not legally domiciled in the UK, and has only been resident for 13 years, so she is not deemed domicile. As a result she is only chargeable to IHT on her UK located assets.

Note. ISA accounts and cars, although exempt for CGT, are chargeable for IHT.

	£
HB Plc shares	12,000
House in UK	354,000
Deposits with HSBS Bank UK	50,000
Jewellery and other personal assets	7,500
Cash ISA accounts	30,000
Car in the UK	23,000
Total	476,500
Less: nil rate band	(325,000)
	151,500
Tax @ 40%	60,600

6.1 As the PRs sold quoted shares from the death estate within one year of death at a loss, loss on sale relief (post mortem relief) is available. It is restricted by the purchase of replacement quoted shares within 2 months of the last sale.

	£	£
London house		705,000
Car		35,000
Portuguese villa		120,000
Quoted shares (W)		65,138
Total estate		925,138
Less: nil rate band	325,000	
Less: GCTs in 7 yrs before death	(213,000)	(112,000)
		813,138
IHT @ 40%		325,255

Working

Original probate value of shares		69,000
Less: loss on sale relief		
Probate value of shares sold within 12 months £(15,000 + 22,000)	37,000	
Less: gross sale proceeds £(9,000 + 20,000)	(29,000)	
Loss	8,000	
Less: restriction $\frac{15,000}{29,000} \times £8,000$	(4,138)	(3,862)
Revised probate value		65,138

6.2

CLT 18.11.03	£
Gift	155,000
AE 2003/04	(3,000)
2002/03	(3,000)
CLT	149,000

Below nil rate band so no IHT due.

PET 14.02.08

No lifetime tax, uses 2007/08 & 2006/07 annual exemptions

Death tax

CLT 18.11.03 > 7 yrs so no additional tax to pay

	£	£
PET 14.02.08: Gift		235,000
AE 2007/08		(3,000)
2006/07 b/f		(3,000)
GCT for cumulation purposes		229,000
Fall in value relief £(235,000 – 197,500)		(37,500)
		191,500
Nil rate band	325,000	
Less: CGTs in 7 yrs to gift	(149,000)	
		(176,000)
		15,500
Tax @ 40% (payable by brother)		6,200
No taper relief as < 3yrs		
Death estate		350,000
Nil rate band at death	325,000	
Less: GCTs in 7 yrs to death	(229,000)	
		(96,000)
		254,000
Tax @ 40% (Payable by PRs)		101,600

6.3 The shares are related property as Keith's civil partner also holds some of the shares.

The original value in the death estate would have been:

£2,500,000 × 120,000/200,000 = £1,500,000

No BPR is available as the shares are not qualifying business assets (shares in an investment company).

The spouse/civil partner exemption does not apply as the shares are not left to Martin – they are left to Keith's niece.

(i) *IHT liability*

The original IHT liability would therefore have been:

	£
Other assets	325,000
Madden Ltd shares	1,500,000
Total	1,825,000
Less: nil rate band (none remaining)	(nil)
Chargeable estate	1,825,000
IHT @ 40%	730,000

(ii) *Repayment*

As the shares are sold for less than £1,500,000 within three years of death, the original 'stand alone' value of the shares replaces the related property value in the death estate.

The revised value is therefore £1,000,000. We ignore the sales proceeds.

The tax repayment is:

(£1,500,000 - £1,000,000 =) £500,000 @ 40% = £200,000.

6.4 When Maureen made the gift to the discretionary trust it was a chargeable lifetime transfer (CLT). The annual exemption of £3,000 for the year of the transfer and the previous year (as she has made no other transfers) would have been available to reduce the value of the transfer.

The amount of the transfer within the nil rate band would have been chargeable at 0% and the balance taxable at lifetime rates (25% as Maureen paid the tax herself).

When Maureen dies four years after the gift, there is additional IHT due on the CLT.

The starting point for the death tax calculation is the gross chargeable transfer (the gift after annual exemptions plus the tax Maureen paid). However, relief is available for the fall in value of the land by reducing the GCT by the amount that the it has fallen in value, ie £150,000.

Tax is then charged at 40% (the death rate) and taper relief is available, based on the period between the gift and death. Maureen survived almost four years from making the gift so relief will be given at 20% (3 – 4 years).

Finally, a deduction is given for the lifetime tax paid.

It should be noted that fall in value relief applies only for the purposes of calculating the death tax payable on the lifetime transfer, it does not affect the cumulative total (ie the amount that uses up the nil rate band).

6.5 As the executors sold property from the death estate within three years of death, loss on sale relief (post mortem relief) is available. The loss in the 4th year can be netted off against the gain on the flat. The loss is restricted by the purchase in the period ending 4 months after the last sale in the three year period.

	£	£
Regedit Ltd shares	540,000	
Less: BPR @ 100%	(540,000)	Nil
Personal property		65,000
Property (W) £(1,000,000 – 12,526)		987,474
Total estate		1,052,474
Less: nil rate band	325,000	
Less: GCTs in 7 yrs before death (May 2003 gift outside period)	(nil)	(325,000)
		727,474
IHT @ 40%		290,990

Working	Probate value	Gross sale proceeds	(Loss)/ profit
	£	£	£
Lancashire house	250,000	195,000	(55,000)
London flat	750,000	775,000	25,000
	1,000,000	970,000	(30,000)
Less: restriction for purchases			
£30,000 × 565,000/970,000			17,474
Allowable loss			(12,526)

6.6 The GCT on 4 May 2005 is below the nil rate band at the date of death so there is no IHT due.

As Crompton Hall was sold at a loss within 3 years of Charlotte's death, post mortem relief is available (as restricted for the purchase of Marston Mews).

There is no transferable nil rate band available from Spencer's death as his remaining nil rate band at the date of his death would have been fully used by the nil rate band discretionary trust.

Estate	£	£
Chargeable estate	1,895,000	
Less: post mortem relief (W)	(17,208)	
Total		1,877,792
Less: nil rate band	325,000	
Less: GCTs in 7 yrs before death	(113,000)	
		(212,000)
		1,665,792
Tax @ 40%		666,317

Working – post mortem relief

	Probate value	*Sale proceeds*	*Gain/ (loss)*
	£	£	£
Crompton Hall	925,000	888,000	(37,000)
Net loss			(37,000)
Less: restriction for purchases:			
$\frac{475,000}{888,000} \times £(37,000)$			19,792
Allowable loss			(17,208)

7.1 Gifts between spouses (and civil partners) are usually exempt from IHT. However, only the first £55,000 of transfers from a UK domiciled spouse to a non-UK domiciled spouse are exempt. This exemption applies to the total of all transfers between spouse throughout lifetime and on death.

As Sue is not UK domiciled the lifetime gift of £40,000 will be covered by this spouse exemption.

Part of the death estate will be chargeable as only £15,000 (£55,000 – £40,000) of the exemption remains.

The GCT in May 2004 has no tax liability as it falls within the nil rate band.

The liability on the estate will be:

	£	£
Estate		320,000
Less: remaining spouse exemption (£55,000 – 40,000)		(15,000)
Chargeable estate		305,000
Less: Nil rate band	325,000	
Less: GCTs in seven years before death	(120,000)	(205,000)
		100,000
IHT @ 40%		40,000

7.2 (i) If Nikki sets up a discretionary trust this will be a chargeable lifetime transfer. Depending on the amount put into the trust and the level of Nikki's other lifetime gifts, if any, there may be IHT due. If she dies within seven years of making the gift there may be additional IHT due.

In addition, because Nikki will herself be a beneficiary of the trust this will be a gift with reservation of benefit (GWR). This means that the assets she places into the trust will continue to form part of her estate for IHT purposes, so when she dies they will be part of her death estate. There could therefore potentially be two charges to IHT on her death (the additional tax on the CLT and the death tax on the asset in the death estate). If this does happen, double charges relief should be available so that HMRC will only collect the higher of the two amounts.

(ii) If Nikki gifts the painting to her daughter this will be a potentially exempt transfer (PET) for IHT purposes. There is no tax during her lifetime but the annual exemption will be allocated to it. The PET will become chargeable if she dies within seven years of making the gift.

In addition, because Nikki will continue to keep the painting in her house this will also be a gift with reservation of benefit, so the painting will continue to form part of her estate for IHT purposes.

If she dies within seven years of making the gift there will be two IHT charges (the PET becoming chargeable and death tax on the painting in her death estate) in which case relief will be available so that HMRC will only collect the higher of the two amounts.

(iii) If Nikki gifts her house to her son this will again be a potentially exempt transfer (PET) for IHT purposes, with the same IHT consequences as outlines above.

In addition, if Nikki continues to live in the property and not pay a market rent this will also be a gift with reservation of benefit, so the house will continue to form part of her estate for IHT purposes, with the same IHT consequences as above if she dies within seven years of making the gift.

It is not therefore tax effective to live in the house and not pay rent. However, she can avoid the GWR rules by paying her son the market rent as suggested.

7.3 Where a chattel (ie a moveable tangible asset) is subject to the POAT rules, there is a tax charge based on the market value of the asset multiplied by the official rate of interest.

The taxable amount in respect the vase is:

4% × £150,000 = £6,000

To avoid an income tax charge Lisa can notify HMRC that the asset should come within the gift with reservation rules, usually by the self assessment return filing deadline (ie by 31 January 2012 for 2010/11).

Lisa should be aware that this does not avoid tax entirely as making the election brings the asset into her estate for IHT purposes.

7.4 Serge probably has not acquired a domicile of choice in the UK as he always intended to return to Latvia. However he is deemed domiciled in the UK for IHT purposes as he has been resident in the UK for at least 17 out of the last 20 years. Consequently he is chargeable on his worldwide assets.

The potentially exempt transfer to his brother becomes chargeable as he dies within seven years of making the gift.

	£	£
Personal property		25,000
Surrey house	650,000	
Less: mortgage	(400,000)	250,000
Latvia property		55,000
UK shares		15,000
Debt		10,000
Total estate		355,000
Less: nil rate band	325,000	
Less: GCTs in 7 yrs before death (£58,000 – £6,000 (2 × AEs))	(52,000)	(273,000)
		82,000
IHT @ 40%		32,800

7.5 Serge probably has not acquired a domicile of choice in the UK as he always intended to return to Latvia. He is not deemed domiciled in the UK for IHT purposes as he has not been resident in the UK for at least 17 out of the last 20 years. Consequently he is only chargeable to IHT on his UK assets. His non-UK assets are 'excluded property' and are outside the scope of IHT.

The potentially exempt transfer to his brother becomes chargeable as he dies within seven years of making the gift.

	£	£
UK personal property (UK assets)		25,000
Surrey house (UK asset)	650,000	
Less: mortgage	(400,000)	250,000
Latvia property (non-UK asset)		Nil
UK shares (UK asset)		15,000
Debt (non-UK asset)		Nil
Total estate		290,000
Less: nil rate band	325,000	
Less: GCTs in 7 yrs before death (£58,000 – £6,000 (2 × AEs))	(52,000)	(273,000)
		17,000
IHT @ 40%		6,800

7.6 Usually when an asset is placed into a discretionary trust there is a chargeable lifetime transfer. The annual exemption of £3,000 is available if no other gifts have been made in the current tax year and the previous year's exemption is also available if not used in that year. The amount of the gift that comes within the nil rate band is chargeable at 0% and the balance at 20% (or 25% if the donor pays the tax).

However, when the asset is classed as heritage property the transfer is 'conditionally exempt' for IHT purposes. A claim must be made within 2 years of the transfer.

This means that no IHT is due so long as certain conditions ('undertakings') are fulfilled by the donee (ie the trustees) regarding the property.

For example the trustees may be forbidden from taking the painting out of the UK and may have to make the painting available for public access.

IHT will be due if the undertakings are broken or the asset is sold or otherwise transferred without the undertakings being renewed by the new owner.

7.7 The June 2001 gift is more than 7 years before Shamus's death so there is no IHT due.

The gift to Marian in 2007 is a gift with reservation of benefit, ie it is a PET but the value of the asset also stays in Shamus's death estate.

On Shamus's death two calculations are required to ensure that there is no double taxation. The first taxes the PET and ignores the value in the death estate:

	£	£
PET becomes chargeable		
Gift		2,000,000
Less: AE × 2		(6,000)
PET		1,994,000
Less: nil rate band	325,000	
Less: GCTs in 7 years before gift	(500,000)	(Nil)
		1,994,000
Tax @ 40%		797,600
Less: taper relief (3 – 4 yrs): @ 20%		(159,520)
IHT due from Marian		638,080
Death estate		
Estate		4,500,000
Less: nil rate band	325,000	
Less: GCTs in 7 years before death	(1,994,000)	(Nil)
		4,500,000
Tax @ 40%		1,800,000
Total IHT		2,438,080

The second calculation ignores the PET and charges the current market value in the death estate:

	£	£
Death estate		
Estate	4,500,000	
Add: painting	2,500,000	7,000,000
Less: nil rate band	325,000	
Less: GCTs in 7 years before death	(Nil)	(325,000)
		6,675,000
Tax @ 40%		2,670,000

HMRC will collect the higher tax ie £2,670,000

8.1 As the gift is a chargeable lifetime transfer (CLT) for IHT purposes, gift relief is available for any asset.

	£
Deemed proceeds (MV)	250,000
Less: cost	(157,500)
Gain	92,500
The full gain can be deferred	£92,500
The base cost of the property for the trustees is:	
Cost (MV)	250,000
Less: gift relief claimed (ie gain deferred)	(92,500)
Cost c/f	157,500

Note. Effectively the trustees have taken over the donor's base cost.

8.2 *Part disposal:*

	£
Proceeds	30,000
Less: cost $\frac{30,000}{30,000+120,000} \times £20,000$	(4,000)
Gain	26,000
Capital losses bfwd	(12,000)
Total chargeable gains	14,000
Less: annual exempt amount	(10,100)
Taxable gain	3,900
CGT liability @ 28%	1,092

8.3 Gain on receipt of compensation:

	£
Proceeds	230,000
Less: Cost	(100,000)
Gain	130,000
Proceeds not reinvested and chargeable £(230,000 – 180,000)	50,000
Available for deferral £(130,000– 50,000)	80,000
Base cost of new asset £(180,000 – 80,000)	100,000

8.4 Sam – Capital gains computation 2010/11

	£	£
1. *Land and buildings*		
Proceeds	950,000	
Less cost	(80,000)	
Chargeable gain		870,000
2. *Goodwill*		
Proceeds	500,000	
Less cost	-	
Chargeable gain		500,000
Total gains		1,370,000
Entrepreneur's relief £1,370,000 × 4/9		(608,889)
Chargeable gains		761,111
Annual exempt amount		(10,100)
Taxable gain		751,011
CGT @ 18%		135,182

Notes

(1) The machinery and equipment are exempt as their cost and market value is less than £6,000.

(2) Entrepreneurs' relief is given as a reduction of the gain as the disposal took place before 23 June 2010. The lifetime limit is £2 million as the disposal took place after 5 April 2010 and before 23 June 2010.

(3) Sam's level of income does not affect his CGT rate (18%) as the disposal took place before 23 June 2010.

9.1

	£	£
Initial value		200,000
Nil rate band	325,000	
Less: b/f	(208,000)	
Available		(117,000)
		83,000
IHT @ 20%		16,600
Effective rate of tax $\frac{16,600}{200,000} \times 100$		8.3%

Actual rate of tax

8.3% × 30% × 21/40 = 1.30725%

IHT payable £50,000 × 1.30725% = £654

9.2 (i) *Exit charge*

	£
Pretend 'gift' 18.11.08	
Initial value of property on 18.11.00	375,000
Less: Nil rate band left 2008/09 (no previous transfers)	(312,000)
	63,000
Tax @ 20%	12,600

Effective rate $\frac{12,600}{375,000}$ = 3.36%

Actual rate: 30% × 3.36% × $\frac{32}{40}$ = 0.8064%

Exit charge £125,000 × 0.8064% = £1,008

(ii) *Principal charge*

	£
Pretend 'gift' 18.11.10	
Current value of relevant property on 18.11.10	650,000
Less: Nil rate band left 2010/11 £(325,000 – 125,000)	(200,000)
	450,000
Tax @ 20%	90,000

Effective rate $\frac{90,000}{650,000}$ = 13.84615%

Ten year charge rate 30% × 13.84615% = 4.153845%

Ten year anniversary charge £650,000 × 4.153845% = £27,000

9.3 When Deanna sets up the discretionary trust it is a chargeable lifetime transfer (CLT). The annual exemption of £3,000 for the year of the transfer and the previous year (as she made no other transfers in that year) will be available to reduce the value of the transfer.

The amount of the transfer within the remaining nil rate band (ie £325,000 – 200,000) will be chargeable at 0% and the balance taxable at lifetime rates (20% as the trustees agreed to pay the tax).

When the trustees distribute assets from the trust to beneficiaries this is usually a chargeable event for IHT purposes, an 'exit' charge. The charge is based on the value of what leaves the trust multiplied by a percentage calculated by reference to the settlor's lifetime transfers in the seven years before setting up the trust, adjusted for the number of complete quarters that have elapsed since the trust was set up.

However, as this 'exit' occurs within the first three months (ie full quarter) of the trust being set up, there is no exit charge.

9.4 The trust is a qualifying interest in possession trust. The IHT consequences are as follows:

(i) If the trustees distribute the trust assets to the remainderman (ie the capital beneficiary) during the life tenant's lifetime, this is treated as a transfer by the life tenant himself.

Consequently, Colin is treated as making a transfer of £600,000 to his daughter, which is a potentially exempt transfer (PET) for IHT purposes as this is a gift between individuals. There is no tax due during Colin's lifetime but the PET will become chargeable if he dies within seven years of making the gift.

Colin can request that his annual exemptions of the current and previous years are set against the transfer.

(ii) If the trustees distribute the trust assets as a result of the life tenant's death, the value of the trust assets enters the life tenant's death estate.

As a result, Colin's death estate will include settled property of £600,000. His nil rate band will cover part of this, and the balance will be taxable at 40%. The trustees will pay the tax.

9.5 The trust is an age 18-25 trust as it has been created on Paul and Stephanie's parent's death after 21 March 2006 and provides for them to receive the capital and income by age 25.

On 19 January 2015 (when Paul turns 21) there will be an exit charge.

Exit charge

	£
Pretend 'gift' 19.1.15	
Initial value of property on 17.4.09	450,000
Less: Nil rate band left 2014/15 (no previous transfers)	(325,000)
	125,000
Tax @ 20%	25,000

Effective rate $\frac{25,000}{450,000} = 5.55556\%$

The complete number of quarters from Paul's 18th birthday to the exit is: 19.1.12 – 19.1.15 = 12

Actual rate: $30\% \times 5.55556\% \times \frac{12}{40} = 0.5\%$

Exit charge (gross up as trustees pay the tax):

$£35,000 \times \frac{0.5\%}{100 - 0.5}\%$ = £176

9.6 (i) If Roger provides for a trust for bereaved minors (TBM) to be set up on his death, the assets that enter the trust will be chargeable in Roger's estate on his death.

The trustees will be able to exercise their discretion over the income and capital until the beneficiaries reach age 18.

When the beneficiaries receive the capital up to age 18 there will be no IHT consequences.

(ii) If Roger provides for an age 18-25 trust to be set up on his death, the assets that enter the trust will be chargeable in Roger's estate on his death.

The trustees can exercise their discretion over the income and capital until the beneficiaries reach age 25, at which time they must receive the capital and the income outright.

If they receive the capital up to age 18 there will be no IHT consequences (as for a TBM). If they receive the capital after 18 and up to age 25 there will be an IHT exit charge.

(iii) If Roger provides for an immediate post death interest trust to be set up on his death, again the assets that enter the trust will be chargeable in Roger's estate on his death.

The trustees can exercise their discretion over the capital of the trust but the beneficiaries will be entitled to an interest in possession, ie they will be entitled to receive the trust income (after expenses).

If assets leave the trust the transfer will be treated as a transfer by the life tenant(s).

(iv) If Roger provides for a plain discretionary trust to be set up on his death, again the assets that enter the trust will be chargeable in Roger's estate on his death.

The trustees can exercise their discretion over the capital and income of the trust until whatever age is specified in the trust deed, but there will be an exit charge every time assets leave the trust and a principal charge on every ten year anniversary of the trust being set up (ie Roger's death).

9.7 Setting up the trust is a chargeable lifetime transfer and the appointment out of trust capital is an exit charge.

CLT

	£	£
Gift		400,000
Less: AE 2002/03		(3,000)
Less: AE 2001/02 b/f		(3,000)
CLT		394,000
Less: nil rate band (2002/03)	250,000	
Less: GCT	(135,000)	(115,000)
		279,000
Tax @ 20%		55,800

Exit charge – the question is silent so assume the trustees pay the tax

	£	£
'Gift'		
Initial value of trust	400,000	
Less: tax paid by trustees	(55,800)	
		344,200
Less: nil rate band (2010/11)	325,000	
Less: GCTs in 7 years before trust set up	(135,000)	(190,000)
		154,200
Tax @ 20%		30,840
Effective rate		
30,840/344,200 × 100 =	8.9599%	
No of quarters since set up:		
1.5.02 – 15.8.10 = 33		
Actual rate		
8.9599% × 30% × 33/40 =	2.217577%	
Exit charge		
$\frac{2.217577\%}{100-2.217577\%} \times £50,000$	£1,134	

10.1 Ordinarily there is no CGT when a qualifying interest in possession trust comes to an end.

However, as gift relief was claimed when the trust was created, a chargeable gain will arise on the death of the life tenant.

The gain will be the lower of the gain arising using market value for proceeds and the original deferred gain ie the lower of:

(i) £(65,000 – 25,000 =) £40,000, and

(ii) £15,000

ie £15,000.

The gain may itself be deferred using gift relief as the assets are charged in the life tenant's death estate (settled property).

10.2 (1) The gain on settlement into the trust, and the gain on the property passing to Angus, would both have been held over under s.260 as both would have resulted in an IHT charge (CLT and exit charge respectively).

Angus's gain will be:

	£
Proceeds	650,000
Less: cost	(100,000)
Gain	550,000
Less Annual exempt amount	(10,100)
	539,900
Tax at 28%	151,172

(2) The trustees would have been taxable on the gain at the same rate as Angus, ie 28% although they would only be entitled to half the annual exempt amount. The tax due would have been:

	£
Proceeds	650,000
Less: cost	(100,000)
Gain	550,000
Less Annual exempt amount	(5,050)
	544,950
Tax at 28%	152,586

Therefore the tax will have increased by £1,414 if the trustees had sold it before distributing the cash proceeds. It therefore would not have been better for the trustees to have sold the property.

10.3 The deferred gain reduces the base cost of the asset in the hands of the trustees.

	£	£
Proceeds of sale		50,000
Less: Cost	30,000	
Less: Held over gain	(12,000)	(18,000)
Gain		32,000
Less: annual exempt amount		(5,050)
Taxable gain		26,950
CGT @ 28%		£7,456

10.4 When a qualifying life interest terminates on death there is no CGT for the trustees who obtain a tax free uplift to market value for the assets as at the date of death.

The exception to this is if gains were held over when an asset was put into the trust, the gain on that asset will be chargeable, but will be limited to the amount of the gain held over.

The chargeable gain accruing to the trustees on Darren's death is therefore a maximum of £10,000, the gain held over when the Alpha Ltd shares were settled.

It may be possible to make a further claim to hold over the gain against the base cost of the shares in the beneficiary's hands as death tax will be charged on the assets in Darren's estate as his settled property.

10.5 Trustees' capital losses can be used in the same way as an individual's, ie they can be used in the current year or carried forward against future gains.

Additionally, where a loss arises when an asset is advanced to a beneficiary, that loss may be transferred to the beneficiary.

So, the loss of £3,000 may be transferred to Cedric, but it may only be set off against any gain arising when Cedric comes to dispose of that same asset. He cannot use the losses against gains arising from any other asset.

It is not possible to carry losses back against earlier years' gains.

The brought forward losses of £2,000 are unrelieved and will be wasted as all the trust assets have been advanced.

10.6 *Gain on gift to trust (May 2002)*

	£
MV of shares	90,000
Less: 31.3.82 MV	(15,000)
Gain	75,000

A claim for gift relief can be made to defer the gain under s.260 TCGA 1992. The base cost of the shares for the trustees is £(90,000 – 75,000) = £15,000.

Gain on appointment to son

	£
MV of shares	105,000
Less: cost	(15,000)
Gain	90,000

This gain can be deferred using gift relief under s.260 TCGA 1992. The claim is made by the trustees and the son. The base cost of the shares for the son is £(105,000 – 90,000) = £15,000.

10.7 When the trustees distribute the shares there will be a deemed disposal at market value. The cost will be affected by the original gift relief claim made when the shares were put into the trust.

Gift relief will be available to defer the gain again (unquoted trading company shares)

	£
Proceeds £9.25 × 150,000	1,387,500
Less: cost (W)	(433,000)
Chargeable gain	954,500
Gift relief claim	
£954,500 × (100% – 17%)	(792,235)
Chargeable gain	162,265
Less: Annual exempt amount	(5,050)
Taxable gain	157,215
Tax @ 28%	44,020

Working

	£
Original gain	275,000
Less: gift relief	
£275,000 × (100% – 12%) (Note)	(242,000)
Chargeable gain	33,000

Base cost for trustees	
Market value: £4.50 × 150,000	675,000
Less: gift relief claimed	(242,000)
Cost c/f	433,000

Note The gift relief is restricted as 12% of the company's chargeable assets were non business assets (investments).

11.1

			£
Bank interest (£460 × 100/80)	£575	@ 20% =	115
Dividends (£675 × 100/90)	£750	@ 10% =	75
Rental Income £(15,000 – 1,500)	£13,500	@ 20% =	2,700
Tax liability			2,890
Less: tax credits			
Interest: 20% × £575			(115)
Dividends: 10% × £750			(75)
Tax due			2,700

R185 Statement of income	*Net*	*Tax*
	£	£
Non savings income	10,800	2,700
Savings Income	460	115
Dividend Income	225 (W)	25

Working

Net dividend income £(675 – 450) = £225

11.2

	£	£
Rental income (£18,000 –1,500)	16,500	
Dividends (£1,800 × 100/90)		2,000
Gross income	16,500	2,000
Less: trust expenses (£945 × 100/90)		(1,050)
Amount chargeable at trust rates	16,500	950

£ 1,000 @ 20% =	200
£16,500 – 1,000 = £15,500 @ 50% =	7,750
£ 950 @ 42.5% =	404
£ 1,050 @ 10% =	105
Tax liability	8,459
Less: tax credits on dividends: £2,000 @ 10%	(200)
Tax due	8,259

R185 Statement of income	*Net*	*Tax*
	£	£
Non savings income	500	500

11.3 The trustees will pay tax at the basic rate on their first £1,000 of income and also on any income used to pay expenses. The balance of income is taxable at the trust rate.

	£
Net rental income	8,500
Less: trust expenses (£882 × 100/80)	(1,103)
	7,397
Tax at 20% on £1,000	200
Tax at 50% on £6,397	3,198
Tax at 20% on £1,103	221
Tax due	3,619
Tax pool b/f	650
Add: current year tax paid @ 20%	421
@ 50%	3,198
	4,269
Less: tax credit needed to cover £6,000 distribution to beneficiary	(6,000)
Additional tax payable	(1,731)
Total tax due (£3,619 + £1,731)	5,350

11.4 *Trust's income tax liability 2010/11*

	Non Savings Income	Savings Income	Dividend Income
	£	£	£
Rental income £(2,500 – 275)	2,225		
Bank interest £960 × $^{100}/_{80}$		1,200	
Dividends £1,800 × $^{100}/_{90}$			2,000
Taxable income	2,225	1,200	2,000

Total tax liability of trustee

	£
£2,225 × 20%	445
£1,200 × 20%	240
£2,000 × 10%	200
Total tax liability	885
Less: tax credits	
£1,200 × 20%	(240)
£2,000 × 10%	(200)
Tax to pay by self assessment (ie the tax on rental income)	445

R185 Statement of income	Net	Tax
	£	£
Non savings income	1,780	445
Savings income	960	240
Dividend income	1,300 (W)	144

Working

Net dividend income £(1,800 – 500) = £1,300

11.5 As the trust is a Bereaved Minor Trust, it is also a vulnerable beneficiary trust. We therefore need to calculate the income tax as if the income was received directly by the beneficiary. The difference between the trustees' liability and the beneficiary's liability is then available as a deduction for the trustees.

	£
Trustees' liability (W1)	4,290
Less relief (W3)	(3,863)
Trustees' revised liability	427

Workings

(1) Trustees' IT liability	Non Savings income	Savings Income	Dividend Income	Income used for expenses
	£	£	£	£
Property income	1,100			
Bank interest £1,800 × $^{100}/_{80}$		2,250		
Dividends £(6,655 – 630) × $^{100}/_{90}$			6,694	
Dividends used for expenses £630 × $^{100}/_{90}$				700
Taxable income	1,100	2,250	6,694	700

Tax on distributable income:

	£	£
NS: £1,000 × 20% (basic rate band)	200	
£ 100 × 50%	50	
NS: £1,100		
S: £2,250 × 50%	1,125	
D: £6,694 × 42.5%	2,845	
	4,220	
Basic rate tax on income used to meet expenses:		
£700 × 10%		70
Total tax liability	4,220	70

(2) Beneficiary's IT liability	*Non Savings income*	*Savings Income*	*Dividend Income*
	£	£	£
Property income	1,100		
Bank interest £1,800 × $^{100}/_{80}$		2,250	
Dividends £6,655 × $^{100}/_{90}$			7,394
Less: PA	(1,100)	(2,250)	(3,125)
Taxable income	Nil	Nil	4,269
Tax liability @ 10%			427

(3) *Vulnerable beneficiary relief*	£
Trustees' liability (W1)	4,290
Vulnerable beneficiary's liability (W2)	(427)
Relief for trustees	3,863

11.6

	Non savings	*Savings*	*Dividends*
	£	£	£
Property income £(16,800 – 520)	16,280		
Interest £2,880 × 100/80		3,600	
Dividends £103,500 × 100/90			115,000
Total	16,280	3,600	115,000
£1,000 @ 20%	200		
£(15,280 + 3,600) @ 50%	9,440		
£115,000 @ 42.5%	48,875		
Tax liability	58,515		
Less: non-refundable tax credits on dividends	(11,500)		
Tax for tax pool	47,015		
Less: real tax credits	(720)		
IT payable	46,295		

Tax pool

	£
Tax pool c/f	1,675
Add: 2010/11 tax	47,015
Tax available to cover distributions	48,690
Less: required for distributions	(25,000)
5 × £5,000 × 50/(100 – 50)	
c/f	23,690

12.1 *PRs' income tax payable 2010/11*

	Non savings Income	Savings Income	Dividend Income
	£	£	£
Rental income £(2,500 – 275)	2,225		
Bank interest £960 × $^{100}/_{80}$		1,200	
Dividends £1,800 × $^{100}/_{90}$			2,000
Taxable income	2,225	1,200	2,000

PRs' total tax liability

	£
£2,225 × 20%	445
£1,200 × 20%	240
£2,000 × 10%	200
Total tax liability	885
Less: tax credits	
£1,200 × 20%	(240)
£2,000 × 10%	(200)
Tax due (ie the tax on rental income)	445

12.2 Jayne and Jack are the residuary beneficiaries of the estate. As the administration of the estate has been finalised, they are treated as receiving the income on the completion date.

The trust expenses are deductible when calculating the income due to the residuary beneficiaries and are deducted from dividend income in priority to other income.

The available net income is:

- Non-savings: £(2,225 – 445) = £1,780, ie £890 each
- Savings: £960 ie £480 each
- Dividends: £(1,800 – 500) = £1,300, ie £650 each.

The total income receivable by Jayne and Jack is £2,020 each.

R185 Statement of income (Estate)	*Net*	*Tax*
	£	£
Non savings income	890	223
Savings income	480	120
Dividend income	650	72

12.3 *Calculation of income tax liability*

	Non-savings	Savings	Dividends	
	£	£	£	£
Property income (note)	13,775			
Bank interest (£2,240 × 100/80)		2,800		
Dividends (£2,812 × 100/90)			3,124	
	13,775	2,800	3,124	
Less:				
Interest on loan to pay IHT (W)	(570)			
Net income	13,205	2,800	3,124	
Tax liability (@20%/20%/10%)	2,641	560	312	3,513

Working

Relief is only available for the loan interest paid in the 12 months from the date the loan was taken out. The first six months of interest would have been deductible in the previous year. No relief is available for the payment made on 1 November 2010:

6 × £95 = £570

Note. The property income has already been adjusted for tax so the agent's fees will have already been deducted.

12.4 The base cost of the shares is the probate value (ie value at the date of death).

PRs are entitled to the full annual exempt amount for the year of death and the two following years.

They pay CGT at 28%

The executors' gain will be:

	£
Proceeds	156,000
Less: cost (probate value)	(127,500)
Gain	28,500
Less Annual exempt amount	(10,100)
	18,400
Tax at 28%	5,152

12.5 The base cost of the shares for the executors is the probate value (ie value at the date of death).

When they pass the shares to Jamie, he effectively takes over the executors' CGT position, ie their base cost. There is no disposal for CGT purposes.

Jamie's gain will be:

	£
Proceeds	156,000
Less: cost (probate value)	(127,500)
Gain	28,500
Less Annual exempt amount	(10,100)
	18,400
Tax at 28%	5,152

12.6 (1) PRs

The PRs are taxable on the income received after the date of death, but receive no relief for any expenses of administration.

	Non savings	*Savings*	*Dividends*
	£	£	£
Property income	9,900		
Interest £1,200 × 100/80		1,500	
Dividends £33,345 × 100/90			37,050
Total	9,900	1,500	37,050
Tax @ 20%/20%/10%	1,980	300	3,705
Less: tax credit		(300)	(3,705)
IT payable	1,980	Nil	Nil

Note: that this is simply the tax due on the non savings income as the rest of the tax liability is covered by the tax credits.

(2) Caroline

Until the administration is finalised, Caroline is taxable on a receipts basis. The income is matched with non-savings, then savings and finally dividend income.

	Non savings	*Savings*	*Dividends*
	£	£	£
Gross income	9,900	1,500	37,050
Less: tax paid/ suffered	(1,980)	(300)	(3,705)
Net income	7,920	1,200	33,345
Less: expenses			(575)
Available for distribution	7,920	1,200	32,770
Matched with interim payment	(7,920)	(1,200)	(15,880)
c/f	Nil	Nil	16,890

R185 (Estate income)

	Net	*Tax*
	£	£
Non savings	7,920	1,980
Savings income	1,200	300
Dividends	15,880	1,764

Awareness Paper
Unincorporated businesses

Study Period Planner
Taxation of Unincorporated Businesses

Use this schedule and your exam timetable to plan the dates on which you will complete each Study Period. The letters 'H' and 'M' tell you whether the topic is high or medium priority.

Study Period	Topic		Due Date
1	Taxable income	H	
2	Taxable trade profits	H	
3	Capital allowances on plant and machinery	H	
4	Basis periods	H	
5	Trading losses	M	
6	**Progress Test 1**	**H**	

Study Period	Topic		Due Date
7	Partnerships	M	
8	National Insurance Contributions	M	
9	Outline of CGT/ Computing CGT liability	H	
10	Reliefs	H	
11	Partnerships and CGT	H	
12	Administration	H	
13	**Progress Test 2**	**H**	

COURSE EXAM 1

A Practice exam covering Study Periods 1 – 5

COURSE EXAM 2

A practice exam covering all Study Periods

REVISION PHASE

Your revision phase will begin when **Course Exam 2** is complete. This should ideally be four months before the final exam.

TQT Note: The Course Exams contain questions for all FIVE of the awareness paper modules. In your exam you must answer questions from THREE modules. We suggest that you identify the THREE modules you will study and then work through the Study Period Planners for each of those modules until the point where you are told to take Course Exam 1. When you have completed all THREE modules to that point, sit Course Exam 1. Similarly, you should complete all THREE modules before you sit course exam 2. Course Exam 2 covers all of the Study Periods, although it is weighted towards the second half of your studies.

Study Period 1

Taxable income

High Priority

Step 1 Exam Guidance

This study period introduces the topic of taxable income, which may or may not already be familiar to you.

It is unlikely that this topic will form the subject of an exam question in its own right but it is essential knowledge for the Taxation of Unincorporated Businesses Awareness Module.

Step 2 Introduction to the session

To understand how the topics in the remaining study periods of this Awareness module fit together, we require some background knowledge.

Although the topics studied in this chapter may not be examined in their own right, they underpin the rest of the syllabus and so are essential to your understanding of the module.

Step 3 Guidance through the Study Text

Read through Chapter 1 of the Taxation of Unincorporated Businesses Awareness Study Text after reading the following guidance:

In this chapter we learn the basics of income tax which are fundamental to our understanding of the Taxation of Unincorporated Businesses module.

Read quickly through Sections 1 and 2 for background. Then read carefully through Section 3, learning the proforma income tax computation in Illustration 1 and, noting, in particular, the position of trading income. The tax rates and allowances are in the Institute Tax Tables provided in the exam. Make sure you know where to find the relevant information. Work through Illustration 2 to check your understanding of the basic income tax computation.

Read quickly through Section 4 which covers the taxation of spouses (which includes civil partners) and introduces some simple planning issues.

Step 4 Quick Quiz

Please attempt the quick quiz at the end of Study Text Chapter 1 to reinforce your understanding.

You may find it best to do this after a break, so that you can see what you remember and what you don't.

Step 5 Workbook Questions

As this chapter is mainly background reading there is only one exam style question (ESQ) to attempt: Q 1.1.

Study Period 2

Taxable trade profits

High Priority

Step 1 Exam Guidance

In this study period we cover a number of topics that can form the basis of a whole question:

- The badges of trade.
- Adjusting accounting profit to reach taxable profit.

This area is very examinable and has been tested in:

- Q1, Q2 & Q10 (Sample Paper), Q2 & Q3 (May 2009), Q6, Q7 & Q11 (Nov 2009), Q1, Q3, Q6 (May 2010)

Step 2 Introduction to the session

In the previous study period we looked at how individuals are taxed on their income. In this period we cover how to turn a business's accounting profit into the self employed trader's taxable profit.

To complete the picture we will need to understand the calculation of capital allowances, covered in the next study period.

Step 3 Guidance through the Study Text

Read through Chapter 2 of the Study Text after reading the following guidance:

Read Section 1 quickly for background. Then read through Sections 2 and 3 on the badges of trade and self employment versus employment. Make notes on the key points as these are important areas.

Read through the rules in Section 4 for calculating the taxable profit of a self employed person, starting with the accounting profit. Follow through Illustration 1 and note the adjustments that are made to the accounting profit to arrive at the taxable profit. Attempt Examples 1 and 2 to check your understanding of the steps you need to go through to arrive at the taxable profit.

Section 5 gives you the opportunity to practise a comprehensive example of a profit adjustment calculation in Example 3. Work through this example carefully. This is an important area of the syllabus.

Finally, read quickly through Sections 6, 7 and 8 which are all quite brief.

Step 4 Quick Quiz

Please attempt the quick quiz at the end of Study Text Chapter 2 to reinforce your understanding.

You may find it best to do this after a break, so that you can see what you remember and what you don't.

Step 5 Workbook Questions

Now attempt ESQs 2.1 to 2.6 which will help to reinforce your knowledge of the topics covered in this study period and give you examples of the types of question you may see in the exam.

Study Period 3

Capital allowances on plant and machinery

High Priority

Step 1 Exam Guidance

In this study period we look at the capital allowances available for expenditure on plant and machinery.

Look at the Institute's tax rates and allowances, which will be provided in the exam, to see how much information is given on capital allowances rates.

Capital allowances have been tested in:

- Q3, Q4 & Q11 (Sample Paper), Q10 (May 2009), Q10 (Nov 2009), Q5 & Q11 (May 2010)

Step 2 Introduction to the session

In the previous study period we learnt how to calculate the taxable profits of the self employed. In arriving at taxable profits we saw an entry in the proforma for the deduction of 'capital allowances'.

You can think of these as a form of tax depreciation.

Step 3 Guidance through the Study Text

Read through Chapter 3 of the Study text after reading the following guidance:

Read through Section 1 for background. Then read Section 2 which sets out the type of assets that qualify as plant. This is also background knowledge, so do not get bogged down in the detail. Instead, locate the rules in the legislation so that you can refer to them easily in the exam.

Read carefully through Sections 3 to 5 of the Chapter. These set out how to calculate capital allowances. Attempt Examples 1 to 3, making sure you know how to set out a capital allowances computation proforma. Section 5 is a useful summary of how to approach capital allowances computational questions.

The rest of the chapter deals with the calculation of plant and machinery capital allowances in special circumstances. Read these sections quickly. If you are short of time instead of working through the examples you could follow through with the solutions.

Step 4 Quick Quiz

Please attempt the quick quiz at the end of Study Text Chapter 3 to reinforce your understanding.

You may find it best to do this after a break, so that you can see what you remember and what you don't.

Step 5 Workbook Questions

Now attempt the ESQs 3.1 to 3.8 which will help to reinforce your knowledge of the topics covered in this study period and give you examples of the types of question you may see in the exam.

Study Period 4

High Priority

Basis periods

Examined: Sample Paper

Step 1 Exam Guidance

The allocation of taxable trading profits to the correct tax year's income tax computation is very examinable.

You will be expected to deal with three main situations:

- What happens in the opening years of a new trade? (Q2 & Q11 (Sample Paper), Q2 (May 2010)
- What happens if an existing business changes its accounting date? (May 2009 Question 6)
- What happens when a business ceases? (Q4, (Sample Paper), Q1 (Nov 2009)).

Step 2 Introduction to the session

In the first study period we learnt that income tax is calculated for tax years. However, we then saw in study periods 2 and 3 that taxable trading profit is calculated for accounting periods, which may or may not coincide with the tax year.

In this study period we learn how to allocate taxable trading profits for accounting periods to the appropriate tax year(s).

Step 3 Guidance through the Study Text

Read through Chapter 4 of the Study Text after reading the following guidance:

You must learn the rules for allocating taxable profits to tax years (ie identifying the correct basis period for a tax year) for:

- Continuing businesses – Section 1.1.
- Opening years of a business, including the identification of overlap profits – Sections 1.2 to 1.5.
- Closing years of a business, including the use of overlap profits – Section 1.6. Attempt Examples 1, 2 and 3.

Before attempting Examples 4 and 5 ensure you understand the order of approach required for examples where capital allowances need to be calculated.

Then read Section 2 which deals with existing businesses that change their accounting date. Can you identify the year of change and determine whether the change of accounting date leads to the creation or relief of overlap profits? Attempt Examples 6 to 8.

Step 4 Quick Quiz

Please attempt the quick quiz at the end of Study Text Chapter 4 to reinforce your understanding.

You may find it best to do this after a break, so that you can see what you remember and what you don't.

Step 5 Workbook Questions

Now attempt the ESQs 4.1 to 4.9 which will help to reinforce your knowledge of the topics covered in this study period and give you examples of the types of question you may see in the exam.

Trading losses

Medium Priority

Examined: Sample Paper

Step 1 Exam Guidance

You must be able to identify the amount of a trading loss and know how such losses can be used (ie when and against what the loss can be set off).

For the purpose of your exam, there are only eight ways in which an individual can use their trading losses: carry forward, current year, previous year, special extended carry back relief, against gains, special opening year relief, special final year relief and incorporation relief. Try and bear this in mind when deciding what loss relief is most appropriate.

Trading losses have been tested in:

– Q5 (Sample Paper), Q5 & Q9 (May 2009), Q9 (Nov 2009), Q10 (May 2010)

Step 2 Introduction to the session

We use the same 'adjustment of profit' rules that we have already seen to calculate the tax adjusted loss. The trading profit figure in the income tax computation for a loss-making year is always nil. We then have to consider how any loss can be used to reduce other tax liabilities and the tax years in which any relief can be claimed.

Step 3 Guidance through the Study Text

Read through Chapter 5 of the Study Text, after reading the following guidance:

Read through Section 1 paying particular attention to section 1.3 and the Illustration. The loss relief rules are in the Income Taxes Act 2007. Locate this and refer to it as you work through.

Sections 2 and 3 are **essential** for your understanding of the rest of the loss reliefs covered so concentrate on these in this session.

Read Section 2 on carrying forward losses (s.83). This happens automatically if no other claims are made. Try Example 1.

Carefully read Sections 3.1 and 3.2 which deal with setting losses off against general income (s.64). This claim can be made for the current loss-making year and/ or the previous year only and can lead to the individual wasting their personal allowance. Attempt Examples 2 and 3. Read quickly through Sections 3.3 and 3.4. However, do note (in Section 3.4) that if there is any loss left after a current or prior year claim it can be set against chargeable gains (which we deal with in a later study period).

Read Section 4 and try Example 4 to consolidate your knowledge. Read Section 5 for the special loss relief rules that apply in the early years of a trade (s.72) and attempt Example 5. Then read Section 6 for the special 'terminal loss relief' rules that apply on the cessation of a trade (s.89) and attempt Examples 6 and 7. Read Section 7 which deals with the loss relief rules when an unincorporated business becomes a company (s.86) and, finally, Section 8 on restrictions on loss relief.

Step 4 Quick Quiz

Please attempt the quick quiz at the end of Study Text Chapter 5 to reinforce your understanding.

You may find it best to do this after a break, so that you can see what you remember and what you don't.

Step 5 Workbook Questions

Now attempt the ESQs 5.1 to 5.7 which will help to reinforce your knowledge of the topics covered in this study period and give you examples of the types of question you may see in the exam.

Progress Test 1

In order to reinforce what you have learnt so far, answer the following questions. Try to answer them without referring to your Study Text or notes. The test should take you no longer than one hour and covers Study Periods 1-5. Solutions start on page 197.

1 Mr Matthews' accounts for his butchers shop for the year to 31 October 2010 show the following:

	£	£
Sales		50,000
Less cost of goods sold		(20,000)
Gross profit		30,0000
Less expenses:		
Depreciation	5,500	
Salary (note)	3,900	
Gift of 40 'Matthew Butchers' diaries	200	
Bank overdraft interest	500	
Utility bills	2,500	
		(12,600)
Net profit		17,400

Note. Salary was paid to Mr Matthews' daughter for working in the shop on a Saturday morning. Mr Matthews' previous Saturday girl would have been paid £1,500 for the same hours.

Calculate Mr Matthews' adjusted taxable trading profit before capital allowances for the year ended 31 October 2010.

2 For the year ended 31 December 2010, Mr Smith had the following transactions in capital assets in respect of his butchers shop business

		Cost/Proceeds
		£
1 May 2010	Purchase of equipment	45,000
28 June 2010	Sale of van	3,000
1 July 2010	Purchase of van	12,000
1 December 2010	Purchase of car for Mr Smith	10,000

The van sold on 28 June 2010 had originally cost Mr Smith £8,000. The car has CO_2 emissions of 172g/km and is used 20% for business and 80% privately.

The balance brought forward on the main pool at 1 January 2010 was £5,000.

Calculate the capital allowances in respect of Mr Smith's business for the year ended 31 December 2010.

3 Mr Harrowven started a new sole trader business on 1 October 2010. He made up his first set of accounts to 31 May 2011 and annually thereafter, until 1 December 2013 when he ceased to trade.

His adjusted taxable trading profits, after capital allowances, for all accounting periods have been as follows:

	£
Period ended 31 May 2011	16,000
Year ended 31 May 2012	36,000
Year ended 31 May 2013	48,000
Period ended 30 November 2013	10,000

Calculate the amount of taxable trading profit assessable to tax for all tax years affected by the profits above. You are required to identify and utilise overlap profits as part of your answer.

4 Mr Faragher had been trading for many years as a Fast Food Retailer. Due to trends in healthier eating he has had a difficult time trading in recent accounting periods and has made a trading loss.

Details of his adjusted trading profits and losses for recent accounting periods are as follows:

Year ended 31 March 2009	Profit	£50,000
Year ended 31 March 2010	Loss	£(20,000)
Year ended 31 March 2011	Profit	£20,000

Mr Faragher has no other taxable income or deductible expenses.

You are required to state how the adjusted trading loss for the year ended 31 March 2010 can be used for income tax purposes.

5 Carol produces the following profit and loss account for her hairdressing business for the year ended 31 March 2011:

	£	£
Gross operating profit		30,000
Taxed interest received		860
		30,860
Wages and salary	7,000	
Rent and rates	2,000	
Depreciation	1,500	
Impairment of trade receivables	150	
Entertainment expenses	750	
Patent royalties	1,200	
Bank interest	300	
Legal expenses on acquisition of new factory	250	
		(13,150)
Net profit		17,710

(a) Salaries include £500 paid to Bob, Carol's husband, who works full time in the business

(b) No staff were entertained

(c) Taxed interest and patent royalties (trade related) are shown gross

You are required to calculate Carol's adjusted taxable trading profit before capital allowances for the year ended 31 March 2011.

6 Spencer, a sole trader, incurred the following expenditure in his year ended 31 March 2011.

	£
Donation to the Labour Party	2,000
Patent royalty (paid for trade purposes)	780
Legal expenses relating to the creation of a 40 year lease	1,500
Lease payment on a BMW car (CO_2 emissions 175g/km, purchase price £23,000)	6,440
Client entertaining	2,500

The lease agreement in respect of the BMW car was signed on 1 June 2010.

You are required to state, with reasons, the amount that will be disallowed in arriving at trade profits.

7 **You are required to state five of the badges of trade and give a brief explanation of the application of each.**

8 Ralph began trading on 1 June 2010 and prepared accounts for the 14 month period to 31 July 2011. In the period to 31 July 2011 he made the following additions and disposals:

1 July 2010	Spent £95,000 on a new heating system for his offices.
12 August 2010	Purchased a new car for the production manager for £18,000. The car has CO_2 emissions of 100g/km.
10 June 2011	Purchased a second hand lorry for £24,000.
1 July 2011	Sold furniture for £5,000 which had cost £4,500 in May 2010.

You are required to calculate the capital allowances computation for the period to 31 July 2011 assuming that Ralph claims the maximum allowances available and that rates and allowances for 2010/11 continue into the future.

9 David began trading on 1 October 2007 and prepared accounts to 30 September until he changed his accounting date by preparing accounts for the fifteen months to 31 December 2010.

His results for the period were as follows:

	£
Year to 30 September 2008	24,000
Year to 30 September 2009	48,000
Fifteen months to 31 December 2010	75,000

You are required to calculate David's taxable trade profits for his first four years of trade, stating any overlap profit carried forward.

10 Penelope began trading on 1 January 2011. In her first year of trading to 31 December 2011 she made trading losses of £52,000. Her projected loss for her second year is £36,000.

You are required to show Penelope's allowable trading loss for her first two years of trade and to state how she can use the losses.

11 Ray commenced trading in 2002 making up accounts to 31 January each year. He has unused overlap profits of £20,000.

Ray ceased to trade on 31 July 2010. His trading results in recent years have been:

	Profit/(Loss)
	£
Year to 31 January 2007	40,000
Year to 31 January 2008	30,000
Year to 31 January 2009	20,000
Year to 31 January 2010	8,000
6 months to 31 July 2010	(31,000)

Ray has taxable property income of £5,000 each year.

You are required to show Ray's net income for all periods affected by the above results assuming terminal loss relief is claimed.

12 Jane commenced trading on 1 January 2011 preparing her first set of accounts to 30 April 2011. In this period she generated £37,800 of profits before deducting capital allowances. On 1 January 2011 she bought a van for the business costing £30,000, a laptop and printer costing £3,000 and some office furniture costing £10,300. A month later she bought a car (CO_2 emissions 155g/km) for £18,000 which she would drive 80% of the time for business purposes.

You are required to calculate her trading income assessment for 2010/11. Assume that rates and allowances for 2010/11 continue into the future.

You will find the answers to this test starting on page 197. If you answer more than 6 questions correctly, your performance is satisfactory; if you answer more than 8 correctly, you are doing well. Once you have reviewed how you have performed, go back over topics where you feel your understanding is poor.

Study Period 7

Partnerships

Medium Priority

Step 1 Exam Guidance

Partners in a partnership are effectively a group of self employed individuals working together. So, the rules that you have already learned in earlier study periods apply equally to partners.

Partnership income was examined in:

- Q8 (Sample Paper), Q1 (May 2009), Q2 (Nov 2009), Q4 (May 2010).

Step 2 Introduction to the session

In this study period you will use your knowledge of adjusted taxable profits and basis periods and apply it to the profits of a partnership business. You will learn how to split this profit between partners for income tax purposes, both in continuing partnerships and in situations where the composition of the partnership changes.

Step 3 Guidance through the Study Text

Read through Chapter 6 of the Study Text, after reading the following guidance:

Read Section 1 on how to split the profits of a partnership between the partners in a continuing partnership for income tax purposes, Follow through the Illustration and note the order of steps to follow. Then attempt Example 1.

Read Section 2, which deals with the profit split when there is a change in the membership of the partnership (eg new partner joins, partner retires), and work through Illustrations 2.2 and 2.3. Do not move on until you are confident with the calculations in these illustrations.

Section 3 deals with losses. No new rules to learn here as those we learnt in the last study period apply equally to partners. However, we need to know how much of the partnership's total loss should be allocated to each partner. Attempt Example 2.

Quickly read through the brief section on 'notional' profits and losses in Section 4, concentrating on working through Examples 3 and 4.

Finally read through Section 5 on Limited Liability Partnerships and attempt Example 5.

Step 4 Quick Quiz

Please attempt the quick quiz at the end of Study Text Chapter 6 to reinforce your understanding.

You may find it best to do this after a break, so that you can see what you remember and what you don't.

Step 5 Workbook Questions

Now attempt the ESQs 6.1 to 6.7 which will help to reinforce your knowledge of the topics covered in this study period and give you examples of the types of question you may see in the exam.

National Insurance Contributions

Study Period 8

Medium Priority

Step 1 Exam Guidance

NICs are payable by the employed and the self employed. In addition, individuals who no longer have self employment income can make voluntary NI contributions.

You will **not** be examined on NIC for employees in the Taxation of Unincorporated Businesses Awareness module.

This topic has been examined in:

– Q9 (Sample Paper), Q7 (May 2009), Q3 (Nov 2009), Q9 (May 2010).

Step 2 Introduction to the session

In this Study period we look at National Insurance Contributions (NIC). You must be able to identify and calculate the different classes of NIC payable by the self employed.

Look at the Institute's tax tables as you work through this chapter so that you know what information you will be given in the exam.

This is a very short study period so use any additional time to review any earlier period(s) that you may have struggled with.

Step 3 Guidance through the Study Text

Read through Chapter 7 of the Study Text after reading the following guidance:

Read quickly through Section 1 for background. Remember you are only examinable on NIC for self employed individuals and **not** employees.

Read Sections 2.1 and 2.2 carefully and follow through the Illustration. These are the essential NIC rules for the self employed and apply equally to partners, so once you are happy with them read Section 2.3 and attempt Example 1.

Read quickly through Section 3 which is not as important for the exam.

Step 4 Quick Quiz

Please attempt the quick quiz at the end of Study Text Chapter 7 to reinforce your understanding.

You may find it best to do this after a break, so that you can see what you remember and what you don't.

Step 5 Workbook Questions

Now attempt ESQs 7.1 to 7.7 which will help to reinforce your knowledge of the topics covered in this study period and give you examples of the types of question you may see in the exam.

Study Period 9

Outline of CGT/Computing CGT liability

High Priority

Step 1 Exam Guidance

The areas covered in the 'Outline of capital gains tax' (CGT) section of this study period are unlikely to be examined in their own right, but they are fundamental to any question involving CGT. The rules for calculating a CGT liability have recently changed and are therefore highly examinable.

A likely exam scenario is a sole trader or partnership disposing of an asset and you will need to calculate the gain on disposal dealing with any reliefs that may be available.

The calculation of gains was examined in the Sample Paper as part of Question 6 on CGT reliefs.

Step 2 Introduction to the session

This study period covers the basic CGT knowledge that underpins any gains question in the exam.

If you have already studied CGT for another paper of the CTA syllabus you may only need to review this chapter, revising the basic principles.

The instructions given in Step 3 below presume you are studying this chapter **without** any previous knowledge.

Step 3 Guidance through the Study Text

Chapters 8 and 9 of the Study Text direct to you Chapters 9 and 10 of the '**Taxation of Individuals**' section of the text. You should read those chapters after reading the following guidance:

Chapter 9 provides essential CGT background knowledge. Read Sections 1 to 3 to understand the scope of CGT and how it is assessed and the tax paid. Then read Section 4 on the overseas aspects and attempt Example 1.

Sections 1 to 3 of Chapter 10 are fundamental to your study of CGT. Learn the proforma for calculating a capital gain and make sure you understand which rate of CGT to apply. Attempt Examples 1 to 4.

Read all of Section 4 on capital losses except Section 4.4 (year of death). Attempt Examples 5 to 9 and 11. Read through Sections 5, 6 and 7 which deals with assets acquired before 31 March 1982, valuations and connected persons.

Read through Section 9 on part disposals. It is important that you understand how to calculate the cost element of the CGT computation in this situation. Attempt Examples 16 and 17.

Finally read through Section 10 on compensation and insurance monies. This is less important than the other sections in this chapter.

Step 4 Quick Quiz

Please attempt the quick quizzes at the end of Chapters 8 and 9 of the Unincorporated Businesses text to reinforce your understanding.

You may find it best to do this after a break, so that you can see what you remember and what you don't.

Step 5 Workbook Questions

Now attempt ESQs 8.1 and 8.2 and 9.1 to 9.4 which will help to reinforce your knowledge of the topics covered in this study period and give you examples of the types of question you may see in the exam.

Study Period 10

Reliefs

High Priority

Examined: Sample paper

Step 1 Exam Guidance

Reliefs and exemptions are very important in any tax exam.

In the CGT part of the syllabus, you may be examined on how the payment of CGT on the disposal of an asset can be deferred (ie delayed) or reduced. This section covers a number of important reliefs, such as incorporation relief and rollover relief.

Reliefs have been examined in:

- Rollover relief: Q6 (Sample Paper), Q4 (May 2009), Q12 (Nov 2009), Q12 (May 2010)
- Incorporation relief: Q11 (May 2009), Q4 (Nov 2009)
- Gift relief: Q8 (Nov 2009)
- Entrepreneurs' relief: Q8 (May 2010)

Step 2 Introduction to the session

In this study period we learn about the CGT business reliefs that are available. We consider the situations in which gains can be deferred when the trader incorporates his business and when new business assets are bought to replace assets that have been sold (rollover relief)

In addition CGT gift relief is available when a trader gifts certain business assets or sells them at below their market value and entrepreneurs' relief also applies to reduce CGT payable on certain business disposals.

Step 3 Guidance through the Study Text

Read through Chapter 10 of the Study Text after reading the following guidance:

Section 1 gives the background to this chapter, so read it quickly. Note that in all cases the gain on disposal is calculated as normal and then CGT reliefs are applied to reduce the tax payable /defer the gain.

Then read Section 2 on rollover relief for replacement of certain business assets. Attempt Examples 1 and 2. The relief for 'depreciating' assets in Section 2.4 is a form of rollover but contrast the way in which the gain is deferred (it is 'frozen') with the way normal rollover applies (it is 'rolled over' into the base cost of the replacement asset).

Read Section 3 on gift relief, noting the types of assets for which the relief is available. In particular note the CGT position when some cash is received (sale at an undervalue) in Section 3.5. Attempt Examples 3 to 6.

Read Section 4 on entrepreneurs' relief noting to which type of disposals the relief applies. Attempt Examples 7 to 10.

Read carefully through Section 5 which covers the basic principles of incorporation relief. Attempt Example 11

Finally, read quickly through Section 6 which deals with the CGT consequences of an asset becoming part of trading stock.

Step 4 Quick Quiz

Please attempt the quick quiz at the end of Study Text Chapter 10 to reinforce your understanding.

You may find it best to do this after a break, so that you can see what you remember and what you don't.

Step 5 Workbook Questions

Now attempt ESQs 10.1 to 10.9 which will help to reinforce your knowledge of the topics covered in this study period and give you examples of the types of question you may see in the exam.

Study Period 11

Partnerships and CGT

High Priority

Examined: Sample Paper

Step 1 Exam Guidance

So far we have dealt with how partnerships are treated for income tax purposes. We now consider how CGT applies to partnerships.

You may be examined on the disposal of partnership assets, the distribution of assets to individual partners or the CGT implications of changes in partnership profit sharing arrangements.

The CGT aspects of partnership income was examined in:

– Q7 (Sample Paper), Q12 (May 2009), Q7 (May 2010)

Step 2 Introduction to the session

In this study period you will use your knowledge of capital gains tax and apply it to capital transactions carried out by partnerships.

You will learn how to deal with the disposal of partnership assets and the effects of changes in profit sharing ratios.

Step 3 Guidance through the Study Text

Read through Chapter 11 of the Study Text, after reading the following guidance:

Read Section 1 on how disposals of partnership assets are dealt with for CGT purposes. Note that on the sale of an asset to an outside party the partners are treated as disposing of their share of the asset. Attempt Example 1. Now read Section 1.4 which deals with the division of assets among partners. Try Example 2.

Read Section 2, which deals with changes in partnership sharing ratios, including when partners join and leave the partnership. Make sure you understand how the CGT treatment differs depending on whether partnership assets are revalued in the accounts. Try Examples 3 to 5.

Step 4 Quick Quiz

Please attempt the quick quiz at the end of Study Text Chapter 11 to reinforce your understanding.

You may find it best to do this after a break, so that you can see what you remember and what you don't.

Step 5 Workbook Questions

Now attempt the ESQs 11.1 to 11.3 which will help to reinforce your knowledge of the topics covered in this study period and give you examples of the types of question you may see in the exam.

Study Period 12

Administration

High Priority

Examined: Sample Paper

Step 1 Exam Guidance

The administrative provisions are essential knowledge for the exam. They can form part of a question or could be an entire question.

Learning where to find the relevant provisions in your legislation is crucial. Do not waste time learning details that you can easily locate in your open book.

Administration was tested in:

– Q12 (Sample Paper), Q8 (May 2009), Q5 (Nov 2009).

Step 2 Introduction to the session

This study period deals with the administrative requirements of the tax system for individuals. If you have already studied the Taxation of Individuals Awareness module some of this chapter will be familiar to you.

Here we concentrate on self assessment for individuals, ie the rules for income tax returns and paying tax.

Step 3 Guidance through the Study Text

Chapter 12 of the Study Text directs you to Chapter 15 of the Taxation of Individuals Awareness Study Text. Read that chapter through after reading the following guidance:

Section 1 is background knowledge only.

Read Section 2 carefully, noting the deadline for notifying HMRC of chargeability to income tax/capital gains tax (CGT). You should try to locate the rules in your legislation so that you can easily find and refer to them in the exam.

Read Sections 3 to 5 again locating the deadlines for submission of paper and electronic self assessment tax returns in the legislation. Whilst you are there, highlight any penalties and time limits/ periods mentioned in the section. Attempt Examples 1 and 2.

Read Section 6 and, then read Sections 7 and 8, noting HMRC powers, identifying the situations when penalties and interest are charged and noting the appeals procedure.

You have now completed your study of the **Taxation of Unincorporated Businesses Awareness** module.

Step 4 Quick Quiz

Please attempt the quick quiz at the end of Study Text Chapter 12 to reinforce your understanding.

You may find it best to do this after a break, so that you can see what you remember and what you don't.

Step 5 Workbook Questions

Now attempt the ESQs 12.1 to 12.6 which will help to reinforce your knowledge of the topics covered in this study period and give you examples of the types of question you may see in the exam.

Progress Test 2

In order to reinforce what you have learnt so far, answer the following questions. Try to answer them without referring to your Study Text or notes. The test should take you no longer than one hour and covers Study Periods 7-12. Solutions start on page 203.

1 Mr Buxton disposed of the following assets in 2010/11:

(a) A vintage motor car, which had cost him £2,500 in 1997 was sold for £35,000 on 12 May 2010.

(b) 1,000 shares in Matlock Ltd, an unquoted trading company, were gifted to his daughter on 11 August 2010. They were then worth £20,000 and had cost £3,000 in June 1985.

(c) A piece of land was sold for £25,000 on 3 September 2010. This was part of a parcel of land which had been purchased in 1992 for £7,000. The land retained was valued at £55,000 in September 2010.

Mr Buxton has capital losses brought forward of £1,000.

Mr Buxton made no other disposals in 2010/11 and has taxable income of £30,000.

You are required to calculate the capital gains tax payable by Mr Buxton for 2010/11 assuming all available reliefs are claimed.

2 Mr Paxton has a manufacturing business. He wants to sell one of his factories and buy a new one. He has heard there is a relief available to reduce the tax payable on the factory sale.

You are required to explain the conditions that must be met in order for Mr Paxton to defer any chargeable gain arising on the disposal of the old factory.

3 Mrs Octagon has asked for your help in understanding how much income tax she must pay as payments on account of her 2010/11 self assessment tax liability.

In 2009/10 she agreed her self assessment tax liability to be:

	£
Income tax due	5,500
Class 4 NIC due	500
Capital gains tax due	2,500

She has not yet calculated her actual tax liability for 2010/11.

You are required to calculate the payments on account due by Mrs Octagon for the 2010/11 tax year and state the due dates of payment for the payments on account and the final balancing payment for 2010/11.

4 Maurice runs a consultancy business. His taxable profits for the year ended 30 June 2010 are £95,400.

You are required to calculate his NIC liability for 2010/11 and state when it is due.

5 Miss Johnson has been in partnership with Mr Smith for many years, sharing profits and losses equally, after deduction of a salary of £10,000 p.a. each. The partnership makes up accounts to 31 December each year. On 1 July 2010 the partners agreed to change the profit sharing agreement to reflect recent changes in the time each partner can dedicate to the business. From 1 July 2010 onwards the profit sharing agreement allowed for a salary of £20,000 p.a. to Miss Johnson and no salary for Mr Smith and the profits would be split 60:40 in favour of Miss Johnson.

Adjusted trading profits for the year ended 31 December 2010 were £150,000.

You are required to show how this profit would be allocated to the partners for this accounting period and state the tax year these profits would be taxed in.

6 Oliver started receiving rental income in 2010/11. He was not aware that it was necessary to notify HMRC of this source of income but did so on 1 December 2011 as soon as he became aware of the need. His previous income had been employment income and taxed bank interest.

HMRC issued a self assessment return on 15 January 2012.

Oliver submitted his return, and paid the tax due of £10,000, on 25 June 2012.

You are required to advise Oliver of any penalties and interest due. Assume a rate of interest of 3%.

7 Reuben incorporated his sole trade business in August 2010. The gains arising on incorporation were:

Warehouse	£74,500
Goodwill	£12,000

In exchange for the transfer of the business he received shares worth £225,000 from the company and cash of £75,000.

He made no other disposals in 2010/11 and had taxable income of £85,000.

You are required to calculate Reuben's capital gains tax liability after incorporation relief and entrepreneurs' relief and to state the base cost of the shares for any future disposal.

8 On 1 July 2010 Craig sold all of the assets of his business as a going concern for £8,200,000. He realised gains, before any reliefs, on a building and goodwill of £4,700,000 and £800,000 respectively.

On 1 August 2010 Craig gave his 500 shares in Lambert plc (a quoted trading company) to his sister. He had acquired the shares for £1,000 in May 2000. They were worth £5,000 on 1 August 2010.

He made no other disposals in 2010/11 and had taxable income of £45,000.

You are required to calculate the capital gains tax payable by Craig for 2010/11 assuming he makes all beneficial elections.

9 Brianna has been trading for many years, preparing accounts to 31 March each year. She ceased trading on 30 June 2011. Her last set of accounts were for the three months to 30 June 2011.

The main pool's written down value at 1 April 2010 was £25,260. Brianna's car, which she used 40% of the time for private use, was acquired for £27,225 in April 2008 and had a written down value at 1 April 2010 of £21,225.

Brianna's capital transactions since 1 April 2010 were as follows:

Bought machinery	31 May 2010	£1,620
Bought machinery	14 April 2011	£1,740
Sold all pool items (below original cost)	30 June 2011	£25,295
Sold car	30 June 2011	£16,500

You are required to calculate the balancing adjustment arising on cessation.

10 Tracey started trading on 1 November 2010, preparing accounts to 30 April each year. Her results are as follows:

	£
Period to 30 April 2011	36,000
Year ended 30 April 2012	96,000

You are required to show Tracey's taxable profits for the tax years 2010/11 to 2012/13 inclusive, identifying any overlap profits.

11 Jake bought a freehold property in 1970 for £80,000. In March 1982 it was worth £100,000. Throughout ownership he used the property 90% of the time for his business. He sold it in September 2010 for £400,000 replacing it with a slightly smaller property that he moved into in December 2010 for £370,000. He planned to use this new property 100% of the time for business use.

You are required to calculate Jake's chargeable gain on the sale of the property, and state the base cost of the replacement property, assuming he claims all available reliefs?

12 Basil and Sybil have been in partnership, preparing accounts to 31 December each year and sharing profits and losses equally. On 1 January 2010 Polly is admitted to the partnership and from that date profits are to be shared equally.

The agreed profits are as follows:

Year to 31 December 2009	£72,000
Year to 31 December 2010	£84,000

You are required to calculate each partner's trading income assessment for 2009/10 and 2010/11 and identify any overlap profits.

You will find the answers to this test starting on page 203. If you answer more than 6 questions correctly, your performance is satisfactory; if you answer more than 8 correctly, you are doing well. Once you have reviewed how you have performed, go back over topics where you feel your understanding is poor.

Progress Test 1

1 Mr Matthews

Adjusted trading profit for the year ended 31 October 2010

	£
Net profit per accounts	17,400
Add:	
Depreciation	5,500
Salary (£3,900 – £1,500)	2,400
Taxable trading profit before capital allowances	25,300

Note that the gifts of diaries were tax deductible as they carried and advert for his business, were not food, alcohol, tobacco or vouchers exchangeable for goods and cost less than £50 per donee.

2 Mr Smith

Capital allowance computation

Year ended 31 December 2010

	Main pool	*Special rate car (PU 20%)*		*Allowances*
	£	£		£
TWDV Bfwd	5,000			
Additions qualifying for AIA:				
Equipment	45,000			
Van	12,000			
AIA (Max £87,500 (W))	(57,000)			57,000
Other additions:				
Car (special rate)		10,000		
Disposal	(3,000)			
	2,000	10,000		
WDA at 20%	(400)			400
WDA at 10%		(1,000)	× 20%	200
TWDV c/f	1,600	9,000		
Total allowances				57,600

Working.

The maximum AIA is calculated as follows:

	£
1.1.10 – 5.4.10 = 3/12 × £50,000	12,500
6.4.10 – 31.12.10 = 9/12 × £100,000	75,000
Total AIA	87,500

3 Mr Harrowven: Taxable profits

Starts to trade on 1 October 2010 – 'in' the 2010/11 tax year:

2010/11

Actual basis 1/10/10 to 5/4/11 = 6 months

6/8 × £16,000 =	£12,000

2011/12

Accounting period ending in tax year = 8 months to 31 May 2011. As < 12 months long, tax the profits of the first 12 months of trade:

	£
p/e 31 May 2011	16,000
Add: 4/12 x y/e 31 May 2012	
4/12 x 36,000	12,000
	28,000

2012/13

Accounting period ending in tax year = y/e 31 May 2012

CYB	£36,000

2013/14

	£
CYB y/e 31 May 2013	48,000
Period to cessation	
p/e 30 November 2013	10,000
	58,000
Less: overlap profits (W)	(24,000)
	34,000

Working

Overlap profits		£
10/11 and 11/12	1.10.10-5.4.11	12,000
11/12 and 12/13	1.6.11-30.9.11	12,000
Total		24,000

Check:

Taxed:		*Profits used*
£		£
12,000		16,000
28,000		36,000
36,000		
76,000		52,000
	Difference £24,000	

4 Mr Faragher

Use of the loss for the year ended 31 March 2010.

The loss could be carried forward to use against the first available trading profits from the same trade, under S.83. This would mean that the loss of £20,000 would be deducted in full from the £20,000 of adjusted trading profit taxable in 2010/11, from the year ended 31 March 2011.

The loss could be relieved against general income in the accounting period of loss and/or the previous tax year. As the loss making period (the y/e 31 March 2010), ends in 2009/10, this loss relief could be used in 2009/10 and/or 2008/09. As he has no income in 2009/10, the loss could only be used in 2008/09, when there are adjusted trading profits of £50,000 to absorb the loss of £20,000.

5 Carol

Adjusted trading profit for the year ended 31 March 2011

	£	£
Net profit per accounts		17,710
Add:		
Depreciation	1,500	
Client entertaining	750	
Legal expenses	250	
		2,500
		20,210
Less: interest received (taxed as savings income not trading income)		(860)
Taxable trade profits		19,350

6 £6,966

Explanations:

	£
Political donations are never deductible	2,000
Legal expenses incurred in connection with the creation of a short lease are not allowable (expenses incurred in *renewing* the lease are allowable)	1,500
Expenditure on entertaining customers is never allowable	2,500
Car lease payment restricted as CO_2 emissions exceed 160g/km: Disallowable: £6,440 x 15%	966
	6,966

The patent royalty is allowed as a trade expense on the accruals basis

7 Any five of the following badges of trade:

(a) Subject matter
Is the asset the type of item that is usually held as an investment, eg works of art compared to one million toilet rolls! The former would usually indicate an investment and the latter would indicate trading.

(b) Frequency of transactions
The more frequent the transaction the more likely it is going to be treated as a trading activity.

(c) Length of ownership
The longer an item is held the more likely it is to be treated as a capital investment rather than trading stock.

(d) Supplementary work
If work is done to an asset to make it more 'marketable' (ie attractive to a purchaser) it is more likely to be treated as trading stock and not an investment.

(e) Profit motive
If the seller's motive is to make a profit it is likely he will be treated as trading.

(f) Way in which asset acquired
If the asset has been inherited or received by way of gift there is a strong possibility any sale will be treated as a capital transaction rather than a trading activity.

8 Ralph - Capital allowances computation for the 14 months ending 31 July 2011

	FYA	*Main pool*	*Special rate pool*	*Allowances*
	£	£	£	£
Additions qualifying for 100% FYA:				
Low emission car	18,000			
FYA at 100%	(18,000)			18,000
Additions qualifying for AIA:				
Furniture (May 2010)		4,500		
Heating system			95,000	
Lorry		24,000		
AIA (Max £100,000 × 14/12) (Note)		(21,667)	(95,000)	116,667
Less disposal proceeds				
Furniture		(4,500)		
		2,333		
WDA at 20% × 14/12		(544)		544
TWDV c/f		1,789		
Total allowances				135,211

Note: The AIA is allocated to the additions in the special rate pool (WDA 10%) in priority to the additions in the main pool (WDA 20%).

9 David

David's first year of trade is 2007/08.

His 'year of change' is 2010/11 where there is one long period ending in that tax year.

2007/08 (1.10.07 – 5.4.08)	
6/12 × £24,000	£12,000
2008/09 (1.10.07 – 30.9.08)	£24,000
2009/10 (1.10.08 – 30.9.09)	£48,000
Overlap profits = £12,000 (from 6 months to 5.4.08).	
2010/11 – 15 months (1.10.09 – 31.12.10)	£75,000
Less: 3 months' overlap (so only 12 months taxed)	
3/6 × £12,000	(6,000)
Taxable profit	£69,000
Overlap profits carried forward: £(12,000 – 6,000)	£6,000

10 Penelope

Penelope's first year of trade is 2010/11 (1.1.11 to 5.4.11).

2010/11	
3/12 × £(52,000)	£(13,000)
2011/12	
Year ended 31.12.11 (do not double count losses) £(52,000 – 13,000)	£(39,000)

Penelope can use the loss of 2010/11 as follows:

(a) Against her other current year income (before the personal allowance), and then against gains of that year.

(b) Against her income in the previous tax year (before personal allowance), and then against gains of that year.

(c) Against her income in the three tax years before the loss on a FIFO basis (ie 2007/08, 2008/09, 2009/10 in that order)

Penelope can use the loss of 2011/12 as follows:

(a) Against her other current year income (before the personal allowance), and then against gains of that year.

(b) Against her income in the previous tax year (before personal allowance), and then against gains of that year.

(c) Against her income in the three tax years before the loss on a FIFO basis (ie 2008/09, 2009/10, 2010/11 in that order)

11 Ray - Taxable income computations

	2006/07	2007/08	2008/09	2009/10	2010/11
	£	£	£	£	£
Trading income (Note)	40,000	30,000	20,000	8,000	-
Less: terminal loss relief (W1)		(19,000)	(20,000)	(8,000)	-
Property income	5,000	5,000	5,000	5,000	5,000
Net income	45,000	16,000	5,000	5,000	5,000

Note: 2010/11 trading income assessment: 6 months to 31 July 2010 - £31,000 loss thus assessment is £nil

(W1) Terminal loss

	£
2010/11	
6.4.10 – 31.7.10	
4 months to 31.7.10: 4/6 × (31,000)	20,667
Plus overlap profits	20,000
2009/10	
1.8.09 – 5.4.10	
6/12 x 8,000 + 2/6 × (31,000)	6,333
	47,000
Use of loss:	
Terminal loss	47,000
2009/10	(8,000)
2008/09	(20,000)
2007/08 – balance	(19,000)
	-

12 Jane – Taxable trading profit 2010/11

	£
Profit for 4 months to 30 April 2011	37,800
Less capital allowances	
Additions qualifying for 100% AIA: (30,000 + 3,000 + 10,300) = 43,300	
AIA, restricted to 4/12 × £100,000	(33,333)
Balance qualifies for 20% WDA restricted to 4/12 (43,300 – 33,333) x 20% x 4/12	(664)
Addition not qualifying for AIA:	
Main rate car (80% business use) £18,000 x 20% × 4/12 × 80%	(960)
Tax adjusted trading profit	2,843
2010/11 Trading income assessment	
1 Jan 2011 to 5 April 2011 ¾ × £2,843	2,132

Progress Test 2

1 Mr Buxton

Gains:

(a) The sale of a motor car is an exempt disposal.

(b) Gift of shares in Matlock Ltd:

	£
Deemed proceeds (MV)	20,000
Less: Cost	3,000
	17,000
Less: Gift relief	(17,000)
Chargeable gain	–

(c) Land

	£
Sale proceeds	25,000
Less Cost £7,000 × £25,000/(25,000 + 55,000)	(2,188)
Chargeable gain	22,812

CGT liability 2010/11:	
Current year gain (post 22.6.10)	22,812
Less brought forward losses	(1,000)
	21,812
Less: annual exempt amount	(10,100)
	11,712

CGT payable: Basic rate band remaining £37,400 - £30,000 = £7,400

£7,400 @ 18%	1,332
£4,312 @ 28%	1,207
	2,539

2 Mr Paxton:

The relief that can be used to defer capital gains tax payable in these circumstances is rollover relief. The conditions that Mr Paxton must meet are as follows:

- Mr Paxton must sell a qualifying asset (freehold land and buildings are qualifying assets).
- The asset must have been used in Mr Paxton's trade.
- Mr Paxton must reinvest the proceeds for the sale of the qualifying asset in another qualifying asset to be used in his trade.
- The reinvestment must take place within the 12 months before and up to 36 months after the original qualifying asset was sold.

3 Mrs Octagon

Payments on account are based on the self assessment tax liability of the previous tax year. In this case, Mrs Octagon will pay two payments on account, each calculated as 50% of her 2009/10 self assessment tax liability. For these purposes her liability to income tax and Class 4 NIC is taken into account, but not her liability to capital gains tax.

The payments on account are therefore:

		£
31 January 2011	[(£5,500 +£500)/2]	3,000
31 July 2011		3,000

Any additional tax due for the year will then be due in a final payment on 31 January 2012.

4 Maurice

As Maurice is self employed he must pay both Class 2 and Class 4 NI contributions as follows:

Class 2 – it is reasonable to assume that as his taxable profits are £95,400 that his accounting profits will exceed the small earnings exemption.

52 × £2.40 = £125

This is due monthly, usually via direct debit.

Class 4	£
£(43,875 – 5,715) @ 8%	3,053
£(95,400 – 43,875) @ 1%	515
Total Class 4 NIC due	3,568

This is due with the income tax liability, ie two payments on account of 50% × the previous year's Class 4 liability, on 31 January in the tax year and 31 July after the tax year, with any balancing payment on 31 January following the tax year.

5 The profits of the 31 December 2010 accounting period would be taxed in the tax year 2010/11, under the CYB rules.

Allocation of profit between the partners:

Year ended 31 December 2010:

	Total	*Miss J*	*Mr S*
Period 1/1/10 to 30/6/10	£	£	£
Salary £10,000 each × 6/12	10,000	5,000	5,000
Profit share (50:50)	65,000	32,500	32,500
Total £150,000 × 6/12	75,000	37,500	37,500
Period 1/7/10 to 31/12/10			
Salary £20,000 × 6/12/nil	10,000	10,000	Nil
Profit share (60:40)	65,000	39,000	26,000
Total £150,000 × 6/12	75,000	49,000	26,000
Total taxable in 2010/11		86,500	63,500

6 Oliver

(a) Late notification of chargeability

Oliver should have notified HMRC by 5 October 2011. He did not do so until 1 December 2011. As it would appear that Oliver was not deliberately trying to mislead HMRC the maximum penalty for late notification is 30%. As the disclosure was unprompted by HMRC and occurred within 12 months of the date the tax was payable (31 January 2012) HMRC are likely to reduce the penalty to nil.

(b) Late tax return

The tax return was due the later of 31 January 2012 and three months after issue, ie 15 April 2012.

Oliver did not submit the return until 25 June 2012 As the return is less than 3 months late the only penalty will be an immediate £100 charge.

(c) Interest

The tax was due on 31 January 2012. Late payment interest applies for the period 31 January 2012 to 24 June 2012 ie 5 months

£10,000 × 5/12 × 3% = £125

(d) Late payment penalty

As the payment is more than 30 days but less than 6 months late the penalty 5% of the outstanding tax:

5% × £10,000 = £500

7 Reuben

Gain on incorporation – post 22.6.10 disposal

	£	£
Total gains – warehouse	74,500	
– goodwill	12,000	86,500
Less: incorporation relief (automatic)		
£86,500 × £225,000/£300,000		(64,875)
Gain (qualifying for entrepreneurs' relief)		21,625
Less: Annual exempt amount		(10,100)
Taxable gain		11,525
CGT @ 10%		1,152
Market value of shares		225,000
Less: Incorporation relief		(64,875)
Base cost c/f		160,125

8 Craig – Capital gains computation 2010/11

			Qualifying for ER	Not qualifying for ER
		£	£	£
1	Sale of business			
	Building	4,700,000		
	Goodwill	800,000		
	Total gains	5,500,000		
	Entrepreneurs' relief (Max £5 million)		5,000,000	500,000
2	Shares			
	Proceeds (Deemed MV)	5,000		
	Cost	(1,000)		
				4,000
Total chargeable gains				504,000
Less annual exempt amount				(10,100)
Taxable gain			5,000,000	493,900
CGT @ 10%/28%			500,000	138,292
Total CGT				638,292

9 Brianna

	FYAs	Main pool	Old expensive car (60%)		Allowances
1.4.10 – 31.3.11	£	£	£		£
TWDV b/f		25,260	21,225		
Addition qualifying for AIA/40% FYA:	1,620				
AIA	(1,620)				1,620
WDA @ 20%		(5,052)			5,052
WDA @ £3,000 restricted			(3,000)	× 60%	1,800
TWDV c/f		20,208	18,225		
Total allowances					8,472
1.4.11 – 30.6.11					
Addition		1,740			
Disposals		(25,295)	(16,500)		
No allowances in year of cessation					
		(3,347)	1,725		
Balancing charge		3,347			(3,347)
Balancing allowance			(1,725)	× 60%	1,035
Total balancing charge (additional profit)					(2,312)

10

	£	£
2010/11		
01.11.10 – 05.04.11 (Actual)		
£36,000 × 5/6		30,000
2011/12		
01.11.10 – 31.10.11 (first 12 months)		
£36,000 + 6/12 × £96,000		84,000
2012/13		
01.05.11 – 30.04.12 (CYB)		96,000
Overlap		
01.11.10 – 05.04.11	30,000	
01.05.11 – 31.10.11	48,000	
	78,000	

11 Jake – Capital gains 2010/11

	BA	*NBA*
	£	£
Proceeds (90:10)	360,000	40,000
Less: 1982 MV (90:10)	(90,000)	(10,000)
	270,000	30,000
Less rollover relief (Note)	(270,000)	
Chargeable gain	-	30,000
Base cost of new property		
Cost	370,000	
Less: rolled over gain	(270,000)	
	100,000	

Note: Business proceeds (£360,000) were fully reinvested (£370,000). Therefore gain can be deferred in full.

12 Basil, Sybil and Polly

	Total	*Basil*	*Sybil*	*Polly*
	£	£	£	£
Y/e 31.12.09				
Profits (1:1)	72,000	36,000	36,000	
Y/e 31.12.10				
Profits (1:1:1)	84,000	28,000	28,000	28,000

Trading income assessments

Basil & Sybil - continue to be assessed on CYB
2009/10 £36,000 each
2010/11 £28,000 each

Polly - apply opening year rules
2009/10: 1.1 10 – 5.4 10 3/12 × 28,000 = £7,000

2010/11: CYB year to 31 December 2010 = £28,000

Overlap profits of £7,000 (1.1.10 to 5.4.10)

Exam style questions

1.1 During 2010/11 Edward, a married man aged 47, had trading income of £96,600 and property income of £5,000. On 1 June 2010 he took out a loan in order to contribute capital to the partnership in which he is a partner. On 1 December he paid interest on the loan of £600. Interest payable on the loan at 5 April 2011 was £400.

His wife, Pat's only income during 2010/11 was trading income of £10,000.

You are required to calculate Edward and Pat's income tax liability for 2010/11.

2.1 Albert's accounts for the year ended 31 March 2011 show a trading profit of £291,000. This is after deducting legal expenses of £2,816 and repairs of £26,600.

These comprised:

1. Legal expenses	£
Renewal of an existing short lease	424
Unsuccessful application for planning permission	1,720
Debt collection	672
	2,816
2. Repairs	£
Replacing the old slate roof on the office buildings with a new slate roof	8,900
Overhauling a second-hand printing press purchased during the year but requiring repair before it could be used	5,200
Demolishing an out-house and building new ladies' toilets	12,500
	26,600

You are required to calculate the adjustment to the trading profit which is required in respect of the above expenses for tax purposes.

2.2 The sundries account of Harry, a food wholesaler who employs 10 people, is as follows:

	£
Gifts to customers	2,700
Entertaining staff at Christmas party	300
Entertaining local customers at trade shows	140
Harry's annual subscription to food wholesaler's trade association	250
Charitable donation to fundraising event by local hospice for which the business received publicity	500
	3,890

The gifts were leather wallets, purchased wholesale at £45.00 each (retail value £55.00); all had an advertisement for Harry's business on the side.

You are required to state, with reasons, the amount which will be allowed in the computation of trading profits.

2.3 Paula, who has been trading for many years, makes up her accounts to 31 December.

She took goods for her own use costing £560 during the year ended 31 December 2010. Her normal mark-up is 40%. No adjustment had been made to the accounts for the goods.

In addition, she provided for impairments as follows:

	£
Debtors in liquidation	600
Specific debtors outstanding for more than six months	200
50% provision on other balances outstanding for between three and six months	350
Loan to John Williams, a former employee	125
	1,275

You are required to show the adjustments required to Paula's accounts for the year to 31 December 2010 in respect of the above items.

2.4 Mary's accounts for the year ending 30 June 2010 show the following:

	£	£
Fees (note 1)		90,000
Bank interest received		2,500
Total income		92,500
Less:		
Salaries (note 2)	30,000	
National Insurance (note 3)	4,800	
Utilities and telephone	2,700	
Case of wine to employee at Christmas	150	
Loan to former employee written off	500	
Bank overdraft interest	300	
		(38,450)
Net profit		54,050

Notes

(1) During the year Mary provided interior design consultancy services to her sister for free. She would normally charge £700 for such services.

(2) Salary costs for two employees.

(3) National Insurance costs represent Mary's Class 4 liability of £4,800.

You are required to calculate the tax adjusted trading profit before capital allowances for the year to 30 June 2010.

2.5 Richard commenced trading on 1 May 2010 and prepared his first accounts for 15 months ended 31 July 2011.

He incurred advertising costs of £500 on 1 April 2010.

On 1 May 2010 he leased a car, with a list price of £14,000 and CO_2 emissions of 163g/km, for use by one of his employees at a monthly rental of £300. The car is used 75% for business purposes and the employee makes no reimbursement for private use.

You are required to:

(a) State how (if at all) Richard can obtain income tax relief for the advertising costs.

(b) Calculate the deduction for car leasing costs that will be allowed in calculating his taxable trading profits for the period to 31 July 2011.

2.6 Olive is in business running a health food shop. Her accounts for the year to 30 June 2010 show a trading profit of £45,000, this is after deducting the following:

(1) Legal fees of £400 in connection with terminating an onerous trading contract.

(2) Gift of ten food hampers to local, loyal customers at Christmas, worth £30 each

(3) Cost of £500 for Olive to attend an IT course at the local college in order for Olive to acquire some basic IT skills. She had never used a computer prior to the course.

(4) Parking fine of £50 incurred by Olive's assistant while delivering food boxes to customers.

(5) Costs of running Olive's car of £8,000. She travels 10,000 miles a year of which 2,000 relate to travel from home to the shop each day, 5,000 relate to business journeys and the balance to private journeys.

You are required to calculate Olive's taxable trading profit for the year to 30 June 2010.

3.1 Wainwright, who owns a garage, incurred the following expenditure on plant and equipment:

	£
New light fittings for the offices	1,000
Canopy over the petrol filling station	10,500
Car ramp for the car repair workshop	3,800
Moveable partitions for the accounts offices moved from time to time	8,400
New display cabinets for the shop	2,000
	25,700

You are required to state, with reasons, how much is eligible for inclusion in the main plant and machinery capital allowance pool.

3.2 Fielding commenced trading on 1 May 2005 and prepares accounts to 30 April.

The tax written-down value of his plant and equipment on 1 May 2010 was £8,300.

On 4 September 2010, he sold a machine for £3,600 which had cost him £2,000 in August 2005.

On 4 April 2011, he purchased office equipment for £750 and a van for £8,000. He uses the van 20% of the time for private purposes.

You are required to calculate the total capital allowances available for the year to 30 April 2011. Assume that rates and allowances for 2010/11 continue into the future

3.3 John has been trading for many years, preparing accounts to 31 March. In the year ended 31 March 2011, his capital transactions were as follows:

1 May 2010	Purchased Volvo (CO_2 emissions 167g/km, for employee)	£16,000
4 May 2010	Purchased Ford Fiesta (CO_2 emissions 135g/km, used by John)	£6,500
10 May 2010	Sold Ford Cortina for (CO_2 emissions 145g/km, used by John)	£3,700

The tax written down value brought forward of the Cortina was £4,200. There was no balance on the main pool or special rate pool as at 1 April 2010.

All of the cars have 10% private use.

You are required to calculate the capital allowances available for the year ended 31 March 2011.

3.4 Maggie operates a chocolate-making business as an unincorporated trader. The following capital transactions took place in the year to 31 March 2011:

		£
Acquisitions		*Cost*
1 April 2010	Delivery van	13,000
1 September 2010	Vauxhall car (CO_2 emissions 105g/km, 25% private use)	11,000
1 March 2011	Volvo car (CO_2 emissions 159g/km, 30% private use)	22,000
Disposals		*Proceeds*
1 August 2010	Audi - Old expensive car (CO_2 emissions 145g/km, 30% private use)	13,000

The Volvo car acquired and the Audi car disposed of during the year were used by Maggie. The Vauxhall car was used by the production manager.

The original cost of the Audi car was £24,000.

The value of the capital allowance pools as at 1 April 2010 were:

Main pool	£40,000
Expensive car (Audi)	£18,000

You are required to calculate the capital allowances available to Maggie for the year to 31 March 2011.

3.5 On 1 June 2010 Robert commenced trading as a self-employed baker. His first set of accounts showed a tax adjusted trading profit, before capital allowances and hire purchase payments, of £105,000 for the nine month period to 28 February 2011.

The following assets were acquired in the period to 28 February 2011:

		£
1 June 2010	Car (CO_2 emissions 172g/km, 25% private use)	11,000
3 June 2010	Equipment	44,240
1 July 2010	New electrical system for bakery	40,000

The car was used exclusively by Robert.

In addition on 1 July 2010 Robert acquired a photocopier on hire purchase. Robert agreed to pay 36 monthly instalments of £180, which included finance charges of £20. The hire purchase payments have not yet been reflected in Robert's accounts for the nine month period.

You are required to calculate Robert's taxable trading profits for the period to 28 February 2011.

3.6 Tintin had been trading for many years preparing accounts to 30 November when he decided to cease trading on 31 July 2010.

On 1 May 2010 he acquired machinery for £1,500 and a car (CO_2 emissions 145g/km) for £6,000. He used the car 20% of the time for private purposes.

All items of plant and machinery were sold on 31 July 2010 for £3,000 (no item was sold for more than cost). The car acquired during the period was retained by Tintin. The market value of the car at 31 July 2010 was £5,000.

The tax written down value of the main pool at 1 December 2009 was £9,498.

You are required to calculate the capital allowances available to Tintin in the period to 31 July 2010.

3.7 Cameron is a self employed vet. His accounts for the year to 31 December 2010 show a trading profit of £125,000. He has recently moved into new premises.

He is unsure of the tax treatment of the following items that he has deducted in calculating his trading profit:

(1) Golf club membership of £2,500. Cameron has joined the club purely for business networking purposes.
(2) Legal fees of £750 in respect of a three year lease on the new premises.
(3) Lease payment of £4,520 on a Mercedes (CO_2 emissions 170g/km, purchase price £25,000)
(4) Parking fine of £60 incurred by one of Cameron's staff whilst picking up a delivery from a supplier.
(5) £24,000 on the purchase of new equipment on 1 August 2010.

The lease of the Mercedes car was taken out on 1 May 2010.

You are required to calculate Cameron's taxable trading profit for the year to 31 December 2010.

3.8 Anne has run her pony trail business for many years, drawing up accounts to 28 February each year.

In the year to 28 February 2011 she had the following capital transactions:

14 April 2010	£95,000 on an air conditioning system for the indoor paddock, which qualifies as an integral feature.
1 June 2010	Sold equipment for £13,500 which had originally been purchased for £12,000 in May 2009.
22 September 2010	Purchased a second hand van for £6,500. The van will be used by one of her employees and will have 20% private use.
1 November 2010	£24,000 on a Jeep 4 wheel drive vehicle (CO_2 emissions 180g/km) which she will use 40% of the time for private purposes.

The tax written down value of her main pool at 1 March 2010 was £136,733.

You are required to calculate the capital allowances that Anne can claim for her year ended 28 February 2011.

4.1 Stephen started trading as a landscape gardener on 1 July 2007. He prepared accounts to 30 April 2008 and annually thereafter.

You are required to state Stephen's basis periods for the first four tax years, identifying any overlap profits.

4.2 Avril has traded as a self-employed painter and decorator for a number of years. On 30 November 2010 she ceased to trade.

Avril's taxable trading profits had been as follows:

Year to 30 June 2009	£42,000
Year to 30 June 2010	£38,000

Her final accounts for the five months to 30 November 2010, show a tax adjusted trading profit before capital allowances of £16,000

The only assets used in the business were a van, which she retained for her personal use, and items of plant and machinery which she sold for £2,000. None of the individual items of plant and machinery were sold for more than their original cost.

Avril had only ever used the van for business purposes which had cost £13,000 in April 2002. It had a market value of £1,500 at 30 November 2010.

The tax written down value of the main capital allowances pool as at 1 July 2010 was £3,000.

Avril had overlap profits in respect of her opening tax years' of £2,500

You are required to calculate Avril's trading income assessment for 2010/11.

4.3 Wayne commenced trading on 1 May 2006. On 31 December 2010 he ceased trading. His trading results had been as follows:

Y/e 30 April 2007	£15,000
Y/e 30 April 2008	£21,000
Y/e 30 April 2009	£23,000
Y/e 30 April 2010	£24,000
P/e 31 December 2010	£14,000

You are required to calculate Wayne's trading income assessment for all tax years in which he was in business.

4.4 Martina commenced in business as a sports consultant on 1 August 2006. She made up accounts to 31 January 2007 and annually thereafter. Recent profits are as follows:

Y/e 31 January 2010	£21,000

In order to change her accounting date to 30 June, Martina prepares accounts for the period to 30 June 2011, giving the appropriate notice to HMRC. The accounts show taxable profits of £34,000. She has two months worth of opening years overlap profits of £2,000.

You are required to calculate her trading income assessments for 2010/11 and 2011/12.

4.5 Cecil commenced trading on 1 September 2009. He prepared accounts to 30 June 2010 and annually thereafter.

His tax adjusted trading profits for the first two periods were as follows:

	£
10 months ending 30 June 2010	52,500
Year ending 30 June 2011	71,500

On 1 September 2009 he acquired a machine for £5,000.

You are required to calculate Cecil's trading income assessments for the first three tax years.

4.6 Doug commenced trading 1 January 2010 and makes his first set of accounts up to 31 December 2010 and annually thereafter.

Results have been as follows:

Year ended	£
31 December 2010	18,000
31 December 2011	20,000
31 December 2012	28,000

You are required to:

(a) Calculate his trading income assessment for the first three tax years.

(b) Calculate his overlap profits and state how these can be used.

4.7 Olivia commenced business as a self-employed acupuncturist on 1 January 2010. Her results for her first set of accounts for the eighteen month period to 30 June 2011 are as follows:

		£	£
Gross operating profit			95,000
Less:	Wages (Note 1)	45,750	
	Rent and rates (Note 2)	12,000	
	Depreciation	250	
	Telephone and utilities	1,800	
	Sundry expenses (all allowable)	425	
			(60,225)
Net profit			34,775

Notes:

(1) Olivia paid herself a salary of £30,000. She also employed a receptionist for £15,000 and her husband, Jake, to do the business's accounts for £750.

(2) Rent and rates relate to the whole of the practice building. The two rooms on the ground floor are used for the business. Olivia and her husband live above. Olivia uses one of the rooms as her office; the other two upstairs rooms are used for private purposes.

(3) In addition, she spends £950 on equipment during the period.

You are required to:

(1) Calculate Olivia's taxable trading profit for the eighteen month period to 30 June 2011.

(2) State the amount that will be taxed in 2010/11.

(3) State the amount of any overlap profits created in respect of the eighteen month period to 30 June 2011.

4.8 Carrie has run her own 'personal shopper' business since 1 January 2002, when she prepared her first accounts to 30 September 2002 and then 30 September thereafter. Her overlap profits on commencement were £17,490.

In 2010 she decides to change her accounting date to 31 December.

Her recent taxable trade profits have been as follows:

	£
1.10.07 – 30.9.08	24,500
1.10.08 – 30.9.09	47,000
1.10.09 – 31.12.10	84,000

You are required to calculate Carrie's assessments for 2008/09, 2009/10 and 2010/11 and state the overlap profits carried forward.

4.9 Chandler starts to trade on 1 January 2009, making up his first account to 30 June 2009.

His results, before capital allowances, are as follows:

	£
1.1.09 – 30.6.09	12,000
1.7.09 – 30.6.10	45,000

Capital allowances are calculated and claimed as follows:

	£
1.1.09 – 30.6.09	16,000
1.7.09 – 30.6.10	22,000

You are required to calculate the taxable trade profits and/ or losses for all relevant tax years and to state the overlap profits created, if any.

5.1 Sophie has been trading for many years making up accounts to 30 June. Her recent results were as follows:

		£
Year ended 30 June 2010	Profit	12,000
Year ended 30 June 2011	Loss	(14,000)

In addition she had a trading loss brought forward at 6 April 2010 of £3,000. In 2010/11 she also had property income of £1,000, and bank interest income of £500 (gross).

You are required to calculate the loss that will be carried forward to 2011/12, assuming maximum relief is taken in 2010/11. Show your workings.

5.2 Brenda commenced trading as a self-employed beautician on 1 January 2010. Her recent tax adjusted trading results have been as follows:

Six months to 30 June 2010	£(5,000) loss
Year to 30 June 2011	£12,000

You are required to calculate the trading income assessments for the first two tax years of trading.

5.3 Darren has run a hardware shop as a sole trader for a number of years.

He makes up his accounts to 30 September and his trading results for the last two years have been:

		£
Year ended 30 September 2009	Profit	5,000
Year ended 30 September 2010	Loss	(18,000)

Darren receives rental interest of £7,000 annually. In May 2010 he sold an investment property on which he realised a chargeable gain of £40,000.

You are required to state the ways in which Darren may utilise the trading loss.

5.4 Parker, who had traded since 2001, ceased to trade on 30 September 2010. His recent results have been:

		£
Year ended 31 December 2008	Profit	6,800
Year ended 31 December 2009	Profit	7,200
Period ended 30 September 2010	Loss	4,500

His overlap profits on commencement were £600.

Parker has no other income.

You are required to calculate Parker's terminal loss.

5.5 Keith incurs a loss of £9,000 in 2010/11, having commenced trading that year. His general income has been as follows:

	£
2006/07	5,000
2007/08	6,000
2008/09	2,000
2009/10	8,000

He wishes to claim relief available for losses in the opening years of a business against total income of earlier years.

You are required to state how much of the loss will be relieved and in which years and which order.

5.6 Pipchin commenced trading on 1 October 2005, making up his accounts to 30 September 2006 and annually thereafter. His recent results have been:

Year ended	£
30 September 2007	12,000
30 September 2008	(45,000)
30 September 2009	8,000
30 September 2010	14,000

He has received property income as follows:

	£
2007/08	10,400
2008/09	11,000
2009/10	11,000
2010/11	11,000

You are required to compute Pipchin's net income for 2007/08 to 2010/11, assuming maximum s.64 ITA 2007 claims are made to offset the loss against general income.

5.7 Alex has traded for many years making up accounts to 30 June each year. He has overlap profits brought forward from the beginning of the business of £24,000.

He ceased trading on 31 December 2010.

His recent trading results have been as follows:

	£
1.7.07 – 31.6.08	45,000
1.7.08 – 31.6.09	22,000
1.7.09 – 30.6.10	12,000
Period ending 31.12.10	(27,000)

You are required to calculate the terminal loss available for offset on the cessation of the trade and to state which years it can be set against, in the order in which they can be offset.

6.1 George is an employee of a partnership of solicitors and on 1 January 2011 will become an equity partner. It is envisaged that he will have a 10% share of income and capital profits. The firm's forecast trading profits are as follows:

Year ending 30 June 2011	£330,000
Year ending 30 June 2012	£420,000

You are required to calculate George's assessable income from the partnership for each of the tax years 2010/11, 2011/12 and 2012/13 and any overlap profits.

6.2 Peter and Paul have been in partnership for many years, sharing profits equally.

From 1 July 2010 it was agreed that Peter and Paul would receive a salary of £30,000 and £35,000 per annum respectively. From this date Peter and Paul would share profits in the ratio 3:4.

The tax adjusted trading profits for the year to 31 December 2010 were £220,000.

You are required to calculate the trading income assessments for each of the partners for 2010/11.

6.3 Kenneth and Gail commenced trading on 1 January 2009, sharing profits and losses equally, until 1 January 2011 when they started sharing profits and losses 3:1 respectively.

Their results since they started trading have been:

	£
Year ended 31 December 2009	15,000 profit
Year ended 31 December 2010	28,000 loss
Year ended 31 December 2011	20,000 profit

You are required to:

(a) Calculate Kenneth's trading income assessments for the first four years of trading.

(b) State how the loss can be offset under s.72 ITA 2007 relief for losses in early years of trading.

6.4 A and B had been in partnership for many years sharing profits equally before C joined them on 1 June 2010. They agreed to continue sharing profits equally.

The profits were as follows:

Year ended	31.12.09	£60,000
Year ended	31.12.10	£72,000
Year ended	31.12.11	£84,000

You are required to calculate the trading income assessment for 2010/11 for all three partners.

6.5 Victor, Ann and Joan have been in partnership for a number of years sharing profits 20:30:50 after allowing for annual salaries of £35,000 for Victor and £25,000 for Ann.

Tax adjusted trading profits of the partnership for the year ended 31 December 2010 were £45,000.

You are required to calculate the trading income assessments for each of the partners for 2010/11.

6.6 Neil became a partner in a trading limited liability partnership on 1 January 2009.

He contributed capital to the partnership of £15,000 and £18,000 on 1 January 2009 and 1 January 2011 respectively.

Neil's share of the partnership's losses is as follows:

Year ended 5 April 2009	£10,000
Year ended 5 April 2010	£20,000
Year ended 5 April 2011	£11,000

You are required to state the amount of loss relief that Neil is entitled to in respect of the tax years 2008/09 to 2010/11 inclusive assuming he wishes to claim relief against other income under s.64 Income Tax Act 2007. State the amount of any unrelieved losses as at 5 April 2011.

6.7 Bill and Steve have been in partnership for many years, drawing up accounts to 31 March. They share profits equally after taking a salary of £36,000 each.

On 1 May 2010 Molly joined the partnership, from which time the profits were split 40:40:20 between Bill, Steve and Molly. None of the partners took a salary from this date.

The tax adjusted trading profit, before capital allowances, for the year ended 31 March 2011 was £275,000.

The tax written down value of the partnership's capital allowances main pool on 1 April 2010 was £116,500. On 15 April 2010 the partnership invested £45,000 in new plant and machinery.

You are required to calculate how much is taxed on each partner for 2010/11.

7.1 Steven has the following details for 2010/11:

	£
Taxable trade profits	49,000
Loss brought forward	3,000

In 2009/10 £2,000 of the trading loss had been offset against non-trading income.

You are required to calculate Steven's class 4 national insurance liability for 2010/11.

7.2 Charlie has been trading for many years. His profits per the accounts for the years to 30 June 2010 and 30 June 2011 were £4,000 and £6,500 respectively. These figures are after charging depreciation of £20,000 each year.

You are required to calculate Charlie's national insurance liability for 2010/11.

7.3 On 1 September 2010 Simon commenced trading as a self-employed decorator. His first set of accounts showed a tax adjusted trading profit before capital allowances of £70,000 for the 9 month period to 31 May 2011.

On 1 September 2010 Simon purchased equipment for £12,000 and on 1 October 2010 he purchased a car for £16,000. His mileage in the car was 70% for business purposes and 30% for private purposes and the CO_2 emissions of the car were 166g/km.

You are required to calculate Simon's trading income assessment and Class 4 National Insurance liability for 2010/11. Assume rates and allowances for 2010/11 continue into the future.

7.4 John and Fred have been in partnership for many years.

John and Fred receive an annual salary from the partnership of £35,000 and £20,000 respectively. Profits are shared in the ratio 2:3.

The tax adjusted trading profits for the year to 31 December 2010 were £90,000.

You are required to calculate the Class 4 National Insurance liability for each of the partners for 2010/11.

7.5 Lynne commenced trading as a sole trader on 1 March 2010. Her first set of accounts for the 15 months to 31 May 2011 showed a tax adjusted trading profit of £57,000.

You are required to calculate Lynne's Class 4 National insurance liability for 2010/11 and state when it is payable.

7.6 Malcolm, Pat and Rose have been in partnership for a number of years, sharing profits equally. Overlap profits on the commencement of trade were £20,000, £8,000 and £12,000 for Malcolm, Pat and Rose respectively.

On 1 December 2010 Rose retired from the partnership.

Recent tax adjusted profits of the partnership have been:

Year ended 30 April 2010	£240,000
Year ended 30 April 2011	£250,000

You are required to calculate the trading income assessment and the Class 4 National insurance liability for Rose for 2010/11.

7.7 Miranda is a self employed nail technician, drawing up accounts to 31 March.

Her accounting profits for the year ended 31 March 2011 show a profit before tax of £4,685. This is after drawing a salary of £5,435.

This accounting profit includes £150 for the cost of goods taken for her own use. The market value of the goods is £350.

The figure is also before making adjustments for depreciation of £280 and customer entertaining of £150.

The tax written down value on Miranda's capital allowances main pool was £900 at 1 April 2010.

You are required to calculate Miranda's total NIC liability for 2010/11.

8.1 **You are required to state which of the following assets are exempt for capital gains tax purposes.**

- a diamond brooch
- a thoroughbred racehorse
- a lease with an unexpired term of 25 years
- a micro-computer used in a business
- a limousine used by a car hire company

8.2 **You are required to state, with reasons, which of the following transactions are liable to UK capital gains tax:**

(1) Carl is resident in Germany but ordinarily resident in the UK. During 2010/11 he sold a house which is situated in Germany.

(2) Tracey is resident and ordinarily resident in Australia, During 2010/11 she sold her UK holiday home.

(3) Brad is resident and ordinarily resident in the UK. During 2010/11 he gave a part share in a greyhound to his daughter.

9.1 In August 1990, Jeremy bought a warehouse for £120,000 for use in his trade. He sold it for £220,000 in May 2010.

In August 2010 he sold an investment property for £500,000, that he had acquired in May 1981 for £50,000. He extended the property at a cost of £20,000 in May 1990. The property was valued on 31 March 1982 at £60,000.

Jeremy made no other disposals during 2010/11 and had taxable income of £40,000.

You are required to calculate Jeremy's capital gains tax liability for 2010/11.

9.2 Julie owned a field which she purchased on 13 August 1987 for £8,000. On 10 September 2010, she sold a quarter of the field for development for £30,000. The remainder of the field was then worth £10,000.

Julie had made no other disposals in 2010/11. She had capital losses brought forward from 2009/10 of £15,000 and taxable income in 2010/11 of £20,000.

You are required to calculate Julie's capital gains tax liability for 2010/11 and state the amount of any losses carried forward.

9.3 Felicity invited the following people to dinner:

(1) Her husband
(2) Her mother-in-law
(3) Her business partner
(4) The civil partner of her business partner
(5) Her uncle
(6) Her step-father
(7) Her brother-in-law
(8) Her sister

You are required to state, with reasons, who is connected with Felicity for capital gains tax purposes.

9.4 Amber had the following transactions in the shares of Zingo Ltd:

		£
19.2.83	Purchased 2,000 shares, cost	10,000
20.9.90	Purchased 1,000 shares, cost	8,000
15.11.10	Sold 1,500 shares, proceeds	22,000

What is Amber's chargeable gain for 2010/11?

10.1 Luther sold a factory on 10 November 2010. He purchased the following assets for use in his business:

Date of purchase	*Asset*
21 September 2009	Freehold factory
4 June 2010	Fork lift truck
8 October 2012	Hovercraft
5 July 2014	Office block

You are required to explain, giving reasons, against which purchase(s) he may claim rollover relief.

10.2 Henry has run his own business for many years. In May 2010 he sold a factory for £100,000, which had cost £40,000 in May 1993. He bought another factory in January 2010 for £80,000.

You are required to calculate the chargeable gain arising on the sale of the factory and the base cost of the new factory assuming rollover relief is claimed.

10.3 Steven sold all of the assets of his unincorporated business, as a going concern to Carts Ltd on 1 January 2011. Details of the assets sold are as follows:

	Market value 1.1.11	*Gain*
	£	£
Goodwill	50,000	40,000
Freehold building	200,000	90,000
Stock	30,000	
Debtors	8,000	
	288,000	

Steven had purchased the building on 1 April 2009. He had acquired the goodwill when he purchased the trade and assets of a sole trader on 1 April 2002.

Steven received shares in Carts Ltd, with a value of £288,000, in consideration for the sale of the business.

You are required to:

(a) **Explain why the gains arising on the sale of the business will be rolled over into the base cost of the shares in Carts Ltd**

(b) **Calculate the base cost of the shares in Carts Ltd acquired by Steven in consideration for the sale of the business.**

10.4 Mr Terry transferred his sole trader business to a quoted company on 1 August 2010 realising gains of £46,000. The consideration comprised cash of £16,000 and shares with a nominal value of £50,000 and a market value of £60,000.

You are required to:

(a) **Calculate the chargeable gain on transfer and the base cost of the new shares for Mr Terry**

(b) **State the date by which Mr Terry must submit an election if he wishes to disapply incorporation relief.**

10.5 Jeremy Brett, who had run a manufacturing business for many years, decided to reduce the size of the operation in 2010/11. He therefore gave one of the factories (which had always been used for his business) to his son John although John persuaded his father to accept £50,000 in return.

The factory had been acquired on 2 January 1970 for £31,000. The market value in March 1982 was £42,000. It was worth £152,000 and was standing at a gain of £110,000 when it was passed to John in August 2010.

You are required to:

(a) **Calculate Jeremy's chargeable gain, if any, for 2010/11 and state the base cost for John, on the assumption that all possible claims for relief are made**

(b) **State who needs to make the appropriate claim and the deadline for the claim.**

10.6 Robert bought an 80% holding in an unquoted trading company on 10 July 2005 for £160,000. He gave the holding to his daughter, Lauren, on 13 December 2010, when it was worth £300,000. At that date, the assets of the company were:

	£
Factory	300,000
Quoted investments	50,000
Net current assets	25,000
	375,000

Robert has never worked for the company.

You are required to:

(a) **Calculate the gain chargeable on Robert, after all available reliefs, but before the annual exempt amount.**

(b) **State the date that Robert's capital gains tax liability in respect of the above is payable.**

10.7 In 2010/11 Arthur made the following disposals:

(1) On 1 July 2010 he sold a freehold warehouse for £3,850,000 which he had acquired in 1992 for £80,000. He had always used the building for the purposes of his unincorporated business until he ceased to trade in May 2009. The building has not been in use since May 2009.

(2) On 1 February 2011 he sold an unincorporated business, which he had established in May 2009, as a going concern. The following gains arose on the business's chargeable assets:

	Chargeable gain £
Goodwill	600,000
Business premises	800,000
Building held as an investment	180,000

Arthur made no other disposals in 2010/11 and had taxable income of £50,000.

Calculate Arthur's capital gains tax liability for 2010/11 assuming he makes any beneficial claims.

10.8 Jen, a very successful hairdresser, sold her business as a going concern on 1 June 2010, realising a gain of £950,000.

On 1 September 2010 she sold 20,000 shares in Matted Ltd, an unquoted trading company with 400,000 shares in issue, to her sister for £190,000. The market value of the shares on the date of disposal was £800,000. Jen has been a non-executive director of Matted Ltd since she acquired her shares for £10,000 in July 2003.

Jen made no other disposals in 2010/11 and had taxable income of £80,000.

You are required to calculate Jen's capital gains tax liability for 2010/11 assuming that she makes any beneficial claims.

10.9 Daryl had run his business as a sole trade since October 2000, at which date he purchased premises for £250,000 and goodwill for £100,000.

On 14 July 2010 he incorporated the business. The market value of the premises had increased to £790,000 and the value of the goodwill was now £500,000.

He received the following consideration from the company:

Cash	£200,000
Shares	£1,800,000

Daryl made no other disposals in 2010/11 and had taxable income of £60,000.

You are required to calculate Daryl's capital gains tax liability for 2010/11, after all available reliefs, and to state the base cost of the shares for any future disposal.

11.1 Paul and Jason have been in partnership sharing all profits equally for a number of years. In May 1999 the partnership acquired a freehold building for £500,000. In June 2010 Susan was admitted as a partner and thereafter profits were shared in the ratio 5:3:2. No adjustment for asset values have been made through the accounts.

In March 2011 the building was sold for £800,000.

You are required to explain the capital gains tax implications of the above and to calculate the chargeable gain arising for each partner in 2010/11.

11.2 Millie, Whisper and Brooke, have been in partnership for a number of years, sharing all profits equally.

On 1 March 2011 the partners ceased trading. A building, with a market value of £300,000 was transferred to Millie at the date of cessation. The building had been acquired for £90,000 on 1 June 1999.

You are required to set out the capital gains tax implications of the transfer of the building on each of the partners.

11.3 Gary and Kevin have been in partnership for many years sharing all profits equally. The only chargeable partnership asset is goodwill, which they purchased for £240,000 when they took over the partnership in September 2001.

On 7 August 2010 Veronica joined the partnership, from which time the profits were split 40:40:20 between Gary, Kevin and Veronica. The goodwill was revalued in the balance sheet at £585,000 on that date.

You are required to calculate the gain chargeable on each partner as a result of Veronica joining the partnership for 2010/11 and to show each partner's base cost carried forward. You should also explain the effect of any available reliefs.

12.1 Jones, who has never received a tax return, commenced his first business on 5 May 2011.

You are required to:

(a) **State by what date he must give notice that he is chargeable to income tax**

(b) **State the penalty for not notifying HMRC by this date.**

(c) **Give two situations where notification to HMRC of a new source of income is not required.**

12.2 Percy has a final income tax liability for 2010/11 of £12,500 of which £3,000 has been deducted at source. He also has a capital gains tax liability of £2,000. In 2009/10 his final income tax liability was £10,500 of which £3,500 was paid at source.

You are required to show how Percy's 2010/11 tax liability will be settled.

12.3 Jamie is in business as a sole trader. His 2010/11 tax return showed a balancing payment due of £2,000. He submitted his 2010/11 return and paid the tax due 7 months after the due filing date.

You are required to state:

(a) **The date by which Jamie should have submitted his tax return for 2010/11.**

(b) **The penalties that will be payable by Jamie in respect of the late submission and payment of tax**

12.4 Donald is in business as a sole trader. His tax position for the last two tax years is as follows:

	2009/10	*2010/11*
	£	£
Income tax liability	22,000	25,000
Tax deducted at source	500	900
Capital gains tax liability	3,000	4,000
Class 4 NIC liability	5,000	5,500
Class 2 NIC liability	125	125
Payments on account	11,000	

You are required to state the amount of tax Donald should pay on 31 January 2011 to avoid any interest or penalties accruing.

12.5 Dan had an income tax and Class 4 NIC liability less tax deducted at source of £23,000 for 2009/10.

He made payments on account of his 2010/11 liability of £11,500 on 1 March 2011 and 1 October 2011. His 2010/11 income tax and Class 4 liability less tax deducted at source is £25,000. He paid the additional tax due on 31 January 2012.

You are required to show the interest and penalties due in respect of the payment of the 2010/11 income tax and Class 4 NIC liability. Assume a rate of interest of 3%. Ignore leap years.

12.6 You act for Roger who is concerned about the penalty which may be charged for errors in tax returns.

You are required to state the range of penalties (in percentage terms) for Scenarios 1 to 3 below and to state what HMRC is likely to do in Scenario 4:

1. Roger submits his return and it is processed by HMRC. He had innocently forgotten to provide you with the tax deduction certificate from a new bank account he had opened during the year. HMRC find out about the account when processing the return.
2. Roger submits his return and it is processed by HMRC. He had deliberately omitted to provide you with the tax deduction certificate from a new bank account he had opened during the year. He advises you of the new account when you ask him about next year's return information and you advise HMRC at Roger's request.
3. Roger submits his return and it is processed by HMRC. He had deliberately omitted to provide you with the tax deduction certificate from a new bank account he had opened during the year. He does not tell you of the new account when you ask him about next year's return information. HMRC find out about the account when processing the return.
4. Roger submits his return and it is processed by HMRC. He had innocently forgotten to provide you with the tax deduction certificate from a new bank account he had opened during the year. He asks you to advise HMRC as soon as possible and to provide them with any information that they require in connection with the error.

Solutions to exam style questions

1.1 **Edward and Pat**

2010/11 Income tax liability

	Edward	*Pat*
	£	£
Trading income	96,600	10,000
Property income	5,000	
Total income	101,600	10,000
Less Deductible payments:		
Qualifying interest (paid basis)	(600)	
Net income	101,000	10,000
Less personal allowance (W)	(5,975)	(6,475)
Taxable income	95,025	3,525
Income tax		
£37,400 @ 20%	7,480	
£57,625 @ 40%	23,050	
£3,525 @ 20%		705
Income tax liability	30,530	705

(W) £6,475 – £((101,000 – 100,000) x ½) = £5,975

2.1 **Albert**

Add back to trading profit:

	£
Unsuccessful application for planning permission	1,720
Overhaul of printing press	5,200
Ladies toilets	12,500
	19,420

Explanations:

1. Planning permission relates to expenditure of a capital nature and therefore is not allowed, irrespective of the outcome of the application.
2. The repair was required to the printing press before it could be used. The expense is therefore disallowed as capital expenditure.
3. The expenditure brings into place a new asset and is capital in nature.

2.2 **Harry**

Allowable expenses = £3,750 (ie 2,700 + 300 + 250 + 500)

Explanations:

1. Entertaining customers is never allowable.
2. Gifts to customers are allowable if the cost is less than £50 per person, they carry an advert and do not consist of food, drink, tobacco or vouchers.
3. Trade subscriptions are allowable.
4. Charitable donations to small local charities are allowable provided they benefit the business eg good publicity.

2.3 **Paula**

(a) Goods own use

$560 \times \frac{140}{100}$ = £784 – add back to profit.

Explanation: Goods taken for own use treated as a sale.

(b) Impairments

	£
50% general provision	350
Loan to former employee - not wholly and exclusively for the purposes of the trade	125
Add back to profit	475

Explanation: Specific provisions are allowed.

2.4 **Mary**

Tax adjusted trading profit for the year ending 30 June 2010

		£	£
Net profit			54,050
Less:	Bank interest received		(2,500)
Plus:	Class 4 NIC	4,800	
	Free services to sister	–	
	Gift to employee	–	
	Loan to former employee written off	500	
			5,300
			56,850

Note. No adjustments are required for gifts of services or gifts to employees. The latter are assessed on the employee as a benefit.

2.5 **Richard**

(a) The advertising costs will be treated as incurred on 1 May 2010 and deducting from the profit per the accounts for the period ended 31 July 2011.

The expenditure is allowable as it was incurred in the 7 years before trade started and it would have been allowable if it had been incurred after the commencement of trade.

(b) Allowable lease costs

$300 \times 15 \times 85\%$ = £3,825

Explanation: The allowable lease costs are restricted as the car has CO_2 emissions exceed 160g/km.The % business use is irrelevant for the trader, where an employee uses the car.

2.6 **Olive**

Tax adjusted trading profit for the year ended 30 June 2010

	£
Profit per accounts	45,000
Legal fees (trade related)	–
Gifts (food disallowable)	300
IT course (disallowed as to acquire **new** skills)	500
Parking fine (allowed as employee)	–
Motor expenses (£8,000 x 5,000/10,000) (Note)	4,000
Tax adjusted trading profit	49,800

Note. Travel costs from home to place of business are not an allowable deduction.

3.1 **Wainwright**

Eligible for plant and machinery capital allowances:

	£
Car ramp	3,800
Partitions	8,400
Cabinets	2,000
	14,200

Explanation: The canopy and the light fittings are not eligible because they form 'part of the setting' in which the trade is carried on. The car ramp and cabinet perform a function in the business and therefore qualify. Also moveable office partitions were held to be plant in Jarrold v John Good & Sons Ltd. The light fittings, as part of an electrical system and so integral features, may be included in the special rate pool.

3.2 **Fielding**

Capital allowances – year to 30 April 2011

	Main pool	*Van (PU 20%)*	*Allowances*
	£	£	£
TWDV B/F	8,300		
Additions qualifying for AIA:			
Additions	750	8,000	
AIA	(750)	(8,000) × 80%	7,150
Disposal (restrict to cost)	(2,000)		
	6,300		
WDA at 20%	(1,260)		1,260
			8,410
TWDV c/f	5,040		

3.3 **John**

			£		*Allowances* £
Capital allowances – Y/e 31.3.11					
Volvo	Special rate car	Addition 1.5.10	16,000		
		WDA @ 10%	(1,600)		1,600
		TWDV c/f	14,400		
Cortina	PU car	TWDV b/f	4,200		
		Proceeds 10.5.10	(3,700)		
		Balancing allowance	500	× 90%	450
Fiesta	PU car	Addition 4.5.10	6,500		
	Main rate car	WDA @ 20%	(1,300)	× 90%	1,170
		TWDV c/f	5,200		3,220

Explanation: The Volvo car would enter the special rate pool – there was a nil balance on the pool as at 1 April 2010. Separate calculations for the other cars because they are used privately. No AIA for cars. There is no restriction for private use by an employee.

3.4 Maggie

Capital allowances computation for the year to 31 March 2011

	FYA	*Main pool*	*(PU 30%)*	*(PU 30%)*	*Allowances*
	£	£	£	£	£
TWDV at 1.4.10		40,000	18,000		
Additions qualifying for 100% FYAs:					
New Vauxhall car	11,000				
100% FYA	(11,000)				11,000
Additions qualifying for AIA/40% FYA:					
Van (Note)	13,000				
AIA	(13,000)				13,000
Other additions:					
Volvo car (main rate)				22,000	
Disposal			(13,000)		
			5,000		
Balancing allowance			(5,000) × 70%		3,500
		40,000		22,000	
WDA @ 20%		(8,000)		(4,400)× 70%	11,080
TWDV cfwd		32,000	–	17,600	
Total allowances					38,580

Note. The delivery van qualifies for a 40% FYA as it was acquired before 6 April 2010. It is more beneficial however to claim the 100% AIA.

3.5 Robert

Taxable trading profit for the 9 month period to 28 February 2011

	£
Adjusted trading profit	105,000
Less: HP finance charges (£20 x 8)	(160)
Capital allowances (W1)	(77,869)
Taxable trading profit	26,971

(W1) Capital allowances for the 9 months to 28 February 2011

	Main pool	*Special rate pool*	*Special rate car (PU 25%)*	*Allowances*
	£	£	£	£
3.6.10 Equipment	44,240			
1.7.10 Electrical system		40,000		
1.7.10 Photocopier (W)	5,760			
AIA (Max £100,000 x 9/12) (Note)	(35,000)	(40,000)		75,000
	15,000			
Other additions:				
1.6.10 PU Car (special rate)			11,000	
			11,000	
WDA at 20% x 9/12	(2,250)			2,250
WDA at 10% x 9/12			(825) x 75%	619
TWDV c/f	12,750		10,175	
Total allowances				77,869

(W) Cost of photocopier = 36 × £(180 – 20) = £5,760

Note: The AIA is allocated to the additions in the special rate pool (WDA 10%) in priority to the additions in the main pool (WDA 20%).

3.6 **Tintin**

Capital allowances – 8 months to 31 July 2010

	Main pool	*PU Car*		*Allowances*
	£	£		£
TWDV b/f	9,498			
Additions	1,500	6,000		
Disposals	(3,000)	(5,000)		
Balancing allowance	7,998	1,000	× 80%	8,798

Explanation: No AIA or WDAs are given in the final period of trading. The balancing allowance on the car is restricted by the private use.

3.7 **Cameron**

The tax adjusted trading profit for the year ended 31 December 2010 is:

	£
Profit per accounts	125,000
Add:	
Golf club membership	2,500
Legal fees (initial fees for short lease are disallowed)	750
Lease payment (£4,520 x 15%) (CO_2 emissions exceed 160g/km)	678
Parking fine (allowable as incurred by staff)	-
Tax adjusted trading profit	128,928

Note. The Annual Investment Allowance (Max £87,500 ((£50,000 x 3/12) + (£100,000 x 9/12))) is available in respect of the £24,000 spent on the equipment on 1 August 2010 (assuming no other plant and machinery acquired in the year). This allows a 100% deduction to be taken for the £24,000 incurred on the equipment. As the full cost of the equipment has already been deducted from the trading profit no adjustment is therefore required in calculating the taxable trading profit.

3.8 **Anne**

	FYA	*Main pool*	*Special rate pool*	*Special rate car (60%)*	*Allowances*
	£	£	£	£	£
TWDV b/f		136,733			
Additions eligible for AIA:					
14.4.10			95,000		
22.9.10		6,500			
AIA (W)		(834)	(95,000)		95,834
Additions (Cars):					
1.11.10				24,000	
Disposal (restricted to cost)		(12,000)			
		130,399		24,000	
WDA @ 20%		(26,080)			26,080
WDA @ 10%				(2,400)× 60%	1,440
c/f		104,319	-	21,600	
Total allowances					123,354

Working.

The maximum AIA is calculated as follows:

	£
1.3.10 – 5.4.10 = 1/12 × £50,000	4,167
6.4.10 – 28.2.11 = 11/12 × £100,000	91,667
Total AIA	95,834

4.1 **Stephen**

	Basis periods	*Basis of assessment*
2007/08	1 July 2007 – 5 April 2008	Actual basis
2008/09	1 July 2007 – 30 June 2008	First 12 months of trade
2009/10	year ended 30 April 2009	CYB
2010/11	year ended 30 April 2010	CYB
Overlap profits	1 July 2007 – 5 April 2008	
	1 May 2008 – 30 June 2008	

4.2 **Avril**

2010/11 Trading income assessment

Basis of assessment: 17 month period to 30 November 2010

	£	£
Year ended 30 June 2010 – taxable profit		38,000
5 months to 30 November 2010 – Adjusted trading profit	16,000	
Plus: Balancing charge (W1)	500	
		16,500
Less: Overlap profits		(2,500)
Trading income assessment		52,000

(W1) Capital allowances for the 5 months to 30 November 2010

	Main pool	*Allowances*
	£	£
TWDV bfwd	3,000	
Disposals:		
Van (MV)	(1,500)	
Plant and machinery	(2,000)	
	(500)	
Balancing charge	500	(500)

4.3 **Wayne**

	£	£	
2006/07 Actual 1.5.06 – 5.4.07			
11/12 × £15,000		13,750	(overlap profits)
2007/08 Y.e. 30.4.07		15,000	
2008/09 Y.e. 30.4.08		21,000	
2009/10 Y.e 30.4.09		23,000	
2010/11 Y.e. 30.4.10	24,000		
P/E 31.12.10	14,000		
Overlap profits	(13,750)	24,250	

4.4 Martina

The year of change is 2010/11.

The relevant period is 1 February 2010 to 30 June 2010, a period of 5 months. As this is less than 12 months, the basis period for 2010/11 is the 12 months ending 30 June 2010.

	£	£
2010/11 12 months to 30.6.10		
$^{7}/_{12} \times 21{,}000 + {}^{5}/_{17} \times 34{,}000$	22,250	
Overlap profits created = $^{7}/_{12} \times 21{,}000$ =		12,250
2011/12 CYB (Y/e 30.6.11)		
$^{12}/_{17} \times 34{,}000$	24,000	

4.5 Cecil

	Basis period	*Basis of assessment*	
			£
2009/10	1.9.09 – 5.4.10	Actual	
	£47,500 × 7/10		33,250
2010/11	1.9.09 – 31.8.10	First 12 months of trade	
	£47,500 + (£71,500 × 2/12)		59,417
2011/12	y/e 30.6.11	CYB	71,500

Taxable trading profits:

	£
10 months to 30.6.10: 52,500 – 5,000	47,500
Y.e. 30.6.11: 71,500	71,500

Capital allowances:	*TWDV*	*Allowances*
	£	£
10 months to 30.6.10	5,000	
AIA	(5,000)	
	-	5,000
Y.e. 30.6.11		
WDA 20%	-	-
	-	

4.6 Doug

(a) Trading income assessments

		£
2009/10	1.1.10 – 5.4.10 3/12 × £18,000	4,500
2010/11	CYB Y/E 31.12.10	18,000
2011/12	CYB Y/E 31.12.11	20,000

(b) Overlap profits

1.1.10 – 5.4.10
(3/12 × 18,000) = £4,500

Overlap profits are set off against the profits of the final tax year. In certain circumstances they can also be offset on a change of accounting date.

4.7 Olivia

(1) Tax adjusted trading profits for the eighteen months to 30 June 2011 are:

	£
Net profit per accounts	34,775
Add: Olivia's salary (appropriation of profit)	30,000
Rent and rates (private use £12,000 × 40%)	4,800
Depreciation	250
Less: capital allowances (pool < £1,000)	(950)
Tax adjusted trading profit	68,875

(2) 2010/11 Trading income assessment

The basis period for the 2010/11 trading income assessment is 6 April 2010 to 5 April 2011 (the actual basis as no accounting period ends in 2010/11).

12/18 × £68,875 = £45,917

(3) Overlap profits

Olivia's first year is 2009/10, when she will be taxed on 3 months' worth of the eighteen month period's profit.

Then in both 2010/11 and 2011/12 she will be taxed on 12 months of that same period's profit, ie 27 months in total. As the profit only relates to an 18 month period, 9 months' worth of profits will be taxed twice (ie overlap profits).

9/18 × £68,875 = £34,438

4.8 **Carrie**

The year of change is 2010/11.

The assessment for the years before the year of change are on the current year basis, ie 2008/09 = £24,500 and 2009/10 = £47,000.

The period of change is 15 months (1.10.09 – 31.12.10). Since we can never tax more than 12 months in any period we will need to relieve 3 months' worth of overlap profits. With an original accounts date of 30 September the business would have had 6 months' of overlap profits.

	£
15 m/e 31.12.10	84,000
Less: 3/6 × £17,490	(8,745)
Assessment	75,255

The overlap profits carried forward are £8,745 (£17,490 – £8,745)

4.9 **Chandler**

First, we need to deduct the capital allowances from the trade; we can then apply the opening year rules to determine the taxable trade profits.

	£	£
1.1.09 – 30.6.09	12,000	
Less: CAs	(16,000)	
		(4,000)
1.7.09 – 30.6.10	45,000	
Less: CAs	(22,000)	
		23,000

Opening year rules

2008/09

	£
1.1.09 – 5.4.09	
3/6 × £(4,000)	(2,000)
Trading assessment	Nil

2009/10

Period that ends in 2009/10 (ie 6 m/e 30.6.09) is < 12 months, so tax first 12 months of trade. Note that losses cannot be counted twice.

	£	£
1.1.09 – 30.6.09	(4,000)	
Less: already allocated	2,000	
	(2,000)	
1.7.09 – 31.12.09		
6/12 × £23,000	11,500	
		9,500

2010/11

	£
CYB – y/e 30.6.10	23,000

Overlap profits

The periods that are counted twice on commencement are:

	£
1.1.09 – 5.4.09 (3 months)	Nil
1.7.09 – 31.12.09 (6 months)	11,500
Total (9 months)	11,500

5.1 **Sophie**

2010/11	£
Trade profits (y/e 30.6.10)	12,000
s.83 relief – trading loss b/fwd	(3,000)
Other income:	9,000
Property income	1,000
Bank interest	500
	10,500
s.64 relief	(10,500)
	NIL

Loss c/f 14,000 – 10,500 = £3,500

5.2 **Brenda**

Trading income assessments

			Assessment
		£	£
2009/10	Basis period: Actual 1.1.10 – 5.4.10		
	3/6 x £(5,000) = £2,500 Loss		Nil
2010/11	Basis period: First 12 months		
	Six months to 30.6.10	(5,000)	
	Less allocated to 2009/10	2,500	
	Six months to 31.12.10		
	£12,000 x 6/12	6,000	
			3,500

5.3 **Darren**

The loss arises in 2010/11 and may be utilised as follows:

(1) Against total income for the year of the loss (2010/11) and/or preceding year (2009/10)

(2) After an offset against total income for 2010/11 to relieve the rental income, the loss can be set against the capital gain arising in that year

(3) Carry forward against the first available profits of the same trade.

5.4 **Parker**

Terminal loss:

	£
2010/11	
6.4.10 – 30.9.10 (6 April to date of cessation)	
$\frac{6}{9} \times 4{,}500$	3,000
Add: overlap profit	600
2009/10	
1.10.09 – 5.4.10 (12 months before cessation to 6 April)	
(7,200 × 3/12) – (3/9 × 4,500) = profit thus take nil	–
	3,600

5.5 **Keith**

s.72 against total income

	£
2007/08	6,000
2008/09	2,000
2009/10	1,000
	9,000

Explanation: s.72 loss relieved against earlier years before later years, total income in all years must be reduced to nil to the extent that there is available loss.

5.6 **Pipchin**

	2007/08	*2008/09*	*2009/10*	*2010/11*
	£	£	£	£
Trade profits	12,000	Nil	8,000	14,000
s.83			(3) (8,000)	(4) (3,600)
			–	10,400
Property income	10,400	11,000	11,000	11,000
General income	22,400	11,000	11,000	21,400
s.64	(1) (22,400)	(2) (11,000)		
Net income	–	–	11,000	21,400

Loss Memo

		£
Loss in 2008/09		45,000
s.64: 2007/08	(1)	(22,400)
s.64: 2008/09	(2)	(11,000)
c/f under s.83		11,600
s.83: 2009/10	(3)	(8,000)
		3,600
s.83: 2010/11	(4)	(3,600)
		–

5.7 **Alex**

The year of cessation is 2010/11.

On the cessation of a trade the usual current and prior year loss reliefs against general income are available.

In addition, it is possible to calculate a 'terminal' loss, which can be set against the trading profits of the preceding 3 years on a LIFO basis.

The final year of trade (1.1.10 – 31.12.10) is 'split' around the tax year:

	£	£
Penultimate tax year (1.1.10 – 5.4.10):		
3/ 12 × £12,000 (ignore as profit)		Nil
Final tax year (6.4.10 – 31.12.10)		
(i) 6.4.10 – 30.6.10: 3/12 × 12,000	3,000	
(ii) 1.7.10 – 31.12.10	(27,000)	
Less: overlap profits	(24,000)	
		(48,000)
Terminal loss		48,000

This can be set against the trading profits of 2009/10, 2008/09 and 2007/08 in that order.

6.1 **George**

2010/11	Based on 1 January to 5 April 2011		
	3/12 × 330,000 × 10%		£8,250
2011/12	Based on first 12 months		
	1 January 2011 to 31 December 2011		
	(6/12 × £330,000 + 6/12 × £420,000) × 10%		£37,500
2012/13	Based on accounts year ended in 2012/13		
	ie 30 June 2012		
	£420,000 × 10%		£42,000
Overlap period			
	1 January to 5 April 2011	8,250	
	1 July 2011 to 31 December 2011		
	(6/12 × £420,000 × 10%)	21,000	
			£29,250

6.2 **Peter and Paul**

Allocation of profits to partners – year to 31 December 2010

	Peter	*Paul*	*Total*
	£	£	£
6 months to 30.6.10			
Trading profit £220,000 x 6/12			
– allocated equally	55,000	55,000	110,000
6 months to 31.12.10			
Salary (x 6/12)	15,000	17,500	32,500
Trading profit ((£220,000 x 6/12) – 32,500)			
– allocated 3:4	33,214	44,286	77,500
	103,214	116,786	220,000
Trading income assessment 2010/11			
Basis of assessment			
– year ended 31 December 2010	103,214	116,786	

6.3 **Kenneth & Gail**

(a) Trading income assessments

		£
08/09	1.1.09 – 5.4.09	
	15,000 × 3/12 × ½	1,875
09/10	ye 31.12.09	
	15,000 × ½	7,500
10/11	ye 31.12.10	
	(28,000) × ½ = (14,000)	–
11/12	ye 31.12.11	
	20,000 × ¾	15,000

(b) Loss relief

Kenneth's share of the loss = ½ × 28,000 = 14,000

This can be c/back 3 years (FIFO) ie against total income of 2007/08, 2008/09 and 2009/10.

Explanation: Profits and losses split using PSR of *accounting period.*

6.4 **A, B and C**

2010/11 Trading income assessments

	A	*B*	*C*	*Total*
	£	£	£	£
5 months to 31.5.10				
Trading profit £72,000 x 5/12				
– allocated equally	15,000	15,000	–	30,000
7 months to 31.12.10				
Trading profit (£72,000 x 7/12)				
– allocated equally	14,000	14,000	14,000	42,000
	29,000	29,000	14,000	72,000
Trading income assessment 2010/11				
Basis of assessment:				
CYB – year ended 31 December 2010	29,000	29,000		
Actual – 1.6.10 – 5.4.11				
£14,000 + (£84,000 x 1/3 x 3/12)			21,000	

6.5 **Victor, Ann and Joan**

2010/11 Trading income assessments

	Victor	*Ann*	*Joan*	*Total*
	£	£	£	£
Year ended 31.12.10				
Salaries	35,000	25,000	–	60,000
Balance (20:30:50)	(3,000)	(4,500)	(7,500)	(15,000)
Profit	32,000	20,500	(7,500)	45,000
Reallocation of notional loss				
in ratio 32,000: 20,500	(4,571)	(2,929)	(7,500)	
Assessed in 2010/11	27,429	17,571	–	45,000

6.6 **Neil**

Loss relief available under s.64 ITA 2007

2008/09 £10,000 (unrelieved capital contribution £5,000) (Note 1)
2009/10 £5,000 (unrelieved loss £15,000) (Note 2)
2010/11 £18,000 (unrelieved loss £8,000) (Note 3)

Notes:

1. No restriction on loss relief as capital contributed (£15,000 exceeds loss)
2. Loss relief restricted to unrelieved capital contribution brought forward. Unrelieved loss of £15,000 is carried forward
3. Loss relief restricted to amount of capital contributed on 1 January 2011. Unrelieved loss carried forward are £8,000 (£15,000 + £11,000 – £18,000)

6.7 **Bill and Steve**

The accounting period must be time apportioned around the date that Molly joins the partnership.

First we need to calculate the partnership's taxable trade profits, after capital allowances.

	£
Trade profits	275,000
Less: CAs (W)	(68,300)
Taxable trade profits	206,700

Then we split this between the partners in their PSR:

1.4.10 – 30.4.10	*Total*	*Bill*	*Steve*	*Molly*
	£	£	£	£
Salary × 1/12	6,000	3,000	3,000	
Balance 50:50	11,225	5,613	5,612	
Total: 1/12 × £206,700	17,225	8,613	8,612	
1.5.10 – 31.3.11				
40:40:20				
Total: 11/12 × £206,700	189,475	75,790	75,790	37,895
Total	206,700	84,403	84,402	37,895

2010/11

Bill and Steve - £84,403 and £84,402 respectively (CYB)

Molly – opening year rules

1.5.10 – 31.3.11 (equivalent of 5.4.11 for exam purposes) = £37,895

Working

	Main pool	*Allowances*
	£	£
TWDV b/f	116,500	
Additions qualifying for AIA:	45,000	
AIA (max £100,000)	(45,000)	45,000
WDA @ 20%	(23,300)	23,300
c/f	93,200	
Total allowances		68,300

7.1 **Steven**

	£
Class 4 profits:	
Trade profits	49,000
less loss brought forward	(3,000)
less loss used against non-trading income in earlier years	(2,000)
	44,000
Class 4 liability	
(43,875 – 5,715) @ 8%	3,053
(44,000 – 43,875) @ 1%	1
	3,054

7.2 **Charlie**

2010/11 National insurance liability

(1) Class 2 NICs

Actual profits per the accounts for 2010/11:

	£
Year to 30 June 2010	
5.4.10 – 30.6.10 £4,000 x 3/12	1,000
Year to 30 June 2011	
1.7.10 – 5.4.11 £6,500 x 9/12	4,875
	5,875

Profit exceeds lower threshold of £5,075.

Class 2 payable: 52 x £2.40 = £125.

(2) Class 4 NICs

Basis period for 2010/11: Tax adjusted profit for y.e. 30.6.10

	£
Profit per accounts	4,000
Add: Depreciation	20,000
Tax adjusted trading profit	24,000

Class 4 payable: (£24,000 - £5,715) x 8% = £1,463.

Total NIC liability £1,588 (£125 + £1,463)

7.3 **Simon**

Taxable trading profit for the 9 month period to 31 May 2011

	£
Adjusted trading profit	70,000
Less: Capital allowances (W1)	(12,840)
Taxable trading profit	57,160

2010/11 Trading income assessment

	£
Basis period: 1 September 2010 to 5 April 2011	
7/9 x £57,160	44,458

2010/11 Class 4 National Insurance liability

	£
(£43,875 - £5,715) x 8%	3,053
(£44,458 - £43,875) x 1%	6
	3,059

(W1) Capital allowances for the 9 months to 31 May 2011

	Main pool £	*Special rate car (PU 30%)* £		*Allowances* £
Addition qualifying for AIA				
Equipment	12,000			
AIA	(12,000)			12,000
Addition not qualifying for AIA:				
Car (special rate)		16,000		
WDA x 10% x 9/12		(1,200)	× 70%	840
TWDV cfwd		14,800		
Total allowances				12,840

7.4 **John and Fred**

2010/11 Class 4 National Insurance liability

	John £	*Fred* £
(£43,875 - £5,715) x 8%	3,053	
(£49,000 - £43,875) x 1%	51	
(£41,000 - £5,715) x 8%		2,823
	3,104	2,823

Allocation of profits – Year ended 31 December 2010

	John	Fred	Total
	£	£	£
Salary	35,000	20,000	55,000
Trading profit (£90,000 – £55,000)			
– allocated 2:3	14,000	21,000	35,000
	49,000	41,000	90,000
Trading income assessment 2010/11			
Basis of assessment			
– year ended 31 December 2010	49,000	41,000	

7.5 **Lynne**

2010/11 Trading income assessment

	£
Basis period: 2nd tax year of assessment: No accounts ending in tax year:	
Actual basis 12/15 x £57,000	45,600

2010/11 Class 4 National Insurance liability

	£
(£43,875 – £5,715) x 8%	3,053
(£45,600 – £43,875) x 1%	17
	3,070

Payable under self-assessment rules:

- 31 January 2011: 50% of 2009/10 liability
- 31 July 2011: 50% of 2009/10 liability
- 31 January 2012: Balance of 2010/11 liability

7.6 **Malcolm, Pat and Rose**

Allocation of profits

	Rose
	£
Year to 30 April 2010	
£240,000 x 1/3	80,000
Year to 30 April 2011	
7 months to 30.11.10	
£250,000 x 7/12 x 1/3	48,611
5 months to 30.4.11	–
	48,611
Trading income assessment 2010/11	
Basis of assessment – final year	
Y.e. 30.4.10	80,000
Period to 30.11.10	48,611
Overlap profits	(12,000)
	116,611

2010/11 Class 4 National Insurance liability

	£
(£43,875 – £5,715) × 8%	3,053
(£116,611 – £43,875) × 1%	727
	3,780

7.7 **Miranda**

Although Miranda's accounting profit is below the small earnings exemption of £5,075 it must be adjusted for her salary (drawings) and for the goods taken for own use for this purpose. It need not be adjusted for depreciation, provided capital allowances are not also deducted. The profit clearly exceeds the exception limit.

C lass 2 payable: 52 x £2.40 = £125.

Her Class 4 contributions are based on the **taxable** profit:

	£
Profit per accounts	4,685
Add:	
Depreciation	280
Salary	5,435
MV of goods taken for own use £(350 – 150)	200
Customer entertaining	150
Less: CAs (small pool write off)	(900)
Tax adjusted trading profit	9,850

Class 4: £(9,850 – 5,715) @ 8% = £331

8.1 A racehorse is a wasting chattel and therefore is exempt from capital gains tax.

The limousine is exempt as all cars are exempt.

8.2 **Carl**

(1) Carl is ordinarily resident in the UK and is therefore subject to UK capital gains tax on the disposal of assets situated anywhere in the world. The sale of the house will be subject to capital gains tax as it is a chargeable disposal (sale) of a chargeable asset (not an exempt asset).

(2) Tracey is neither resident nor ordinarily resident in the UK. She is not therefore subject to UK capital gains tax.

(3) A greyhound is a wasting chattel (tangible moving property with a life of 50 years or less) and is therefore an exempt asset.

9.1 **Jeremy**

Capital gains tax liability 2010/11

		Pre 23.6.10	*Post 22.6.10*
Warehouse (May 2010)	£	£	£
Proceeds	220,000		
Less: cost	(120,000)		
Gain	100,000	100,000	
Property (August 2010)			
Proceeds	500,000		
Less: 31.3.82 MV	(60,000)		
Extension (May 1990)	(20,000)		
Gain	420,000		420,000
Annual exempt amount			(10,100)
Taxable gain		100,000	409,900
CGT @ 18%/28%		18,000	114,772
Total CGT		132,772	

Note. The annual exempt amount is set off against the gain arising on the investment property as this is taxed at 28% (as Jeremy is a higher rate taxpayer) whereas the gain on the warehouse is only taxed at 18%.

9.2 **Julie**

	£
Proceeds	30,000
Less: cost	
$\frac{30,000}{30,000 + 10,000} \times £8,000$	(6,000)
Gain	24,000
Less: Losses bfwd (restricted)	(13,900)
	10,100
Annual exempt amount	(10,100)
Taxable gain	NIL
Capital gains tax payable	£NIL
Losses cfwd (£15,000 – £13,900)	£1,100

9.3 **Felicity**

Felicity is connected with:

(1) Husband, sister (her relatives)
(2) Mother-in-law, step-father, brother-in-law (spouses of relatives or spouse's relatives)
(3) Business partner
(4) Civil partner of her business partner (Business partner's spouse/civil partner)

9.4 **Amber**

Share pool:

	No. of shares	*Cost*
		£
Purchase 19.2.83	2,000	10,000
Purchase 20.9.90	1,000	8,000
	3,000	18,000
Sale 15.11.10	(1,500)	(9,000)
c/f	1,500	9,000

Calculate gain:

	£
Proceeds	22,000
Cost	(9,000)
Chargeable gain	13,000

10.1 **Luther**

He can only claim the rollover relief against the purchase of the hovercraft as this is the only qualifying purchase.

Freehold factory: > 12 months before disposal

Forklift truck: not **fixed** P&M

Office: > 3 years after disposal.

10.2 **Henry**

Capital gain on sale of factory

	£
Proceeds	100,000
Cost	(40,000)
Gain	60,000
Less: Gain rolled over	(40,000)
Chargeable gain (proceeds not reinvested)	20,000
Base cost of new factory (£80,000 – 40,000)	40,000

10.3 **Steven**

(a) Steven has transferred **all** of the assets of the business, **as a going concern** in exchange for **consideration wholly in shares.**

Rollover relief for the transfer of a business to a company will therefore **automatically** apply unless Steven elects to disapply the relief.

(b) Base cost of shares in Carts Ltd

	£	£
Market value of shares		288,000
Less rollover relief on transfer of business:		
Gains arising on sale of business:		
Goodwill	40,000	
Freehold building	90,000	
		(130,000)
Base cost of shares		158,000

10.4 **Mr Terry**

(a) Gain on transfer of business

	£
Gain	46,000
Less: held-over	
$\frac{60,000}{16,000+60,000} \times £46,000$	(36,316)
Chargeable gain on transfer	9,684
Base cost of shares £(60,000 – 36,316) =	23,684

Explanation: s162 Incorporation relief available.

(b) Mr Terry must submit an election by 31 January 2014 (within two years of 31 January following the end of the tax year in which the business was transferred) if he wishes to disapply incorporation relief.

10.5 **Jeremy Brett**

(a) *Gain chargeable on Jeremy*

	£
Excess proceeds over 31.3.82 MV(50,000 – 42,000)	8,000
Base cost for John	
MV in August 2010	152,000
Less deferred gain (£110,000 – £8,000)	(102,000)
	50,000

(b) The claim must be made jointly by Jeremy and John on or before 5 April 2015 (ie 4 years from the end of the tax year of gift).

10.6 **Robert**

(a) *Chargeable gain*

	£
Proceeds (MV)	300,000
Less: cost	(160,000)
Gain	140,000
Gift relief (CBA/CA)	
$\frac{300}{300+50} \times £140,000$	(120,000)
Gain left in charge after gift relief	20,000

(b) Capital gains tax liability for 2010/11 is payable in full on 31 January 2012.

10.7 **Arthur – Capital gains computation 2010/11**

			Qualifying for ER	*Not qualifying for ER*
		£	£	£
1.	Gain on disposal of building			
	Proceeds	3,850,000		
	Less cost	(80,000)		
	Gain	3,770,000	3,770,000	
2.	Sale of business			
	Gains:			
	Goodwill	600,000		
	Business premises	800,000		
		1,400,000		
	Entrepreneurs' relief (Max £5m – £3.77m)		1,230,000	170,000
	Gains not qualifying for ER relief	180,000		180,000
	Chargeable gains		5,000,000	350,000
Annual exempt amount				(10,100)
Taxable gains			5,000,000	339,900
CGT @ 10%/28%			500,000	95,172
Total CGT			595,172	

Note. The annual exempt amount is set off against the gain arising on the gains not qualifying for entrepreneurs' relief as they are taxed at 28% (as Arthur is a higher rate taxpayer) whereas the gains qualifying for entrepreneurs' relief are only taxed at 10%, regardless of the taxpayer's level of income.

10.8 **Jen**

The disposal of the business as a going concern is a material disposal for entrepreneurs' relief purposes.

The disposal of the Matted Ltd shares is eligible for gift relief (sale at an undervalue of a 5% holding in an unquoted trading company). Any gain remaining chargeable after gift relief is also a material disposal for entrepreneurs' relief purposes (she is an officer of the company in her capacity as non-executive director and has held 5% of the shares for at least a year).

Entrepreneurs' relief reduces the chargeable gain for disposals prior to 23 June 2010. For disposals after 22 June 2010 gains qualifying for entrepreneurs' relief are taxed at a lower rate of 10%, regardless of the taxpayer's level of income.

Business

	£
Gain (per question)	950,000

Shares

	£
Proceeds (MV)	800,000
Less cost	(10,000)
Gain	790,000
Less: gift relief (balancing figure)	(610,000)
Gain remaining chargeable (W)	180,000

Capital gains tax computation 2010/11

	Pre 23.6.10	*Post 22.6.10*
	£	£
Business	950,000	
Shares		180,000
Less: entrepreneurs' relief 4/9 × £950,000	(422,222)	
Less: Annual exempt amount	(10,100)	
Taxable gain	517,678	180,000
CGT @ 18%/10%	93,182	18,000
Total CGT	111,182	

Note. The annual exempt amount is set off against the gain arising before 23 June 2010 as it is taxed at 18% whereas the gain arising after 22 June 2010 is only taxed at 10%.

Working

Gift relief - sale at an undervalue

	£
Actual proceeds	190,000
Less cost	(10,000)
Gain remaining chargeable	180,000

10.9 **Daryl**

Incorporation relief applies automatically when an individual incorporates their business (unless they elect to disapply the relief) to defer the gains arising into the base cost of any share consideration received.

Premises	£	£
Proceeds (MV)	790,000	
Less cost	(250,000)	
Gain		540,000
Goodwill		
Proceeds (MV)	500,000	
Less cost	(100,000)	
Gain		400,000
Total gains		940,000
Less: incorporation relief		
$£940,000 \times \frac{1{,}800{,}000}{1{,}800{,}000 + 200{,}000}$		(846,000)
Gain (qualifies for entrepreneurs' relief)		94,000
Less: annual exempt amount		(10,100)
Taxable gain		83,900
CGT payable @ 10%		8,390

Base cost of shares

	£
MV	1,800,000
Less incorporation relief	(846,000)
Cost c/f	954,000

11.1 **Paul, Jason and Susan**

Jason has effectively disposed of a 20% interest to Susan (reduced from 50% to 30%). There have been no adjustments in the accounts and the effective disposal takes place at no gain/no loss.

Susan acquires a base cost of £100,000 (£500,000 x 20%)

Jason is treated as disposing of part of the building for £100,000 on a no gain/no loss basis. His base cost for a future disposal is £150,000 (£250,000 - £100,000).

Sale of building:

	Paul	Jason	Susan
	£	£	£
Proceeds (5:3:2)	400,000	240,000	160,000
Less cost	(250,000)	(150,000)	(100,000)
Gain	150,000	90,000	60,000

11.2 **Millie, Whisper and Brooke**

Gain arising on transfer of building:

	Total	Each partner (1/3)
	£	£
Proceeds (Market value)	300,000	100,000
Less cost	(90,000)	(30,000)
Gain	210,000	70,000

The gain arising on Millie is not chargeable in 2010/11 but is deducted from the base cost of the building. The base cost of the building for future disposals is £ 230,000 (£300,000 – £70,000).

Entrepreneurs' relief is available to Whisper and Brooke on the disposal of their interest in the partnership and their share of the building transferred to Millie.

11.3 **Gary and Kevin**

When Veronica joins the partnership the existing partners make a disposal of 10% of their fractional ownership of the goodwill. Veronica is treated as acquiring each of their 10% fractions, giving a total of 20%. (W)

The disposal takes place at the balance sheet value. Entrepreneurs' relief is available as this is a material disposal (disposal of part of a business).

Chargeable gain	Gary	Kevin
Proceeds (10% × £585,000)	58,500	58,500
Less: cost: 10% × £240,000	(24,000)	(24,000)
Chargeable gain	34,500	34,500

The chargeable gains will be taxed at the lower rate of 10% as they qualify in full for entrepreneurs' relief.

Base costs c/f

	Gary	Kevin	Veronica
	£	£	£
Original (50% × £240,000)	120,000	120,000	
Less: used when Veronica joins	(24,000)	(24,000)	
c/f	96,000	96,000	
Veronica: £(58,500 × 2)			117,000

Working

Fractional entitlements

	Gary	Kevin	Veronica
Original	50%	50%	
After Veronica joins	(40%)	(40%)	20%
Disposal	10%`	10%	

12.1 **Jones**

(a) By 5 October 2013 (within 6 months of the end of the tax year in which his trade commenced).

(b) The standardised penalties for late notification of chargeability will apply. The penalty is based on a percentage of the potential lost revenue. The relevant percentage depends on the behaviour of the taxpayer. If the taxpayer has deliberately failed to notify HMRC the maximum penalty is 100% of the tax if the failure is concealed or 70% if it was not concealed. If the failure was not deliberate the maximum penalty is 30% of the tax.

(c) Notification is not required where:

(1) income tax has been suffered at source and there is no liability to higher rate tax and/or CGT; or

(2) where a tax return has been issued.

12.2 **Percy**

31.1.11	First payment on account for 2010/11 (W1)	£3,500
31.7.11	Second payment on account for 2010/11 (W1)	£3,500
31.1.12	Balancing payment for 2010/11 (W2)	£4,500

(W1)	Payments on account	10,500	IT
		(3,500)	deducted at source
		7,000	÷ 2 = £3,500
(W2)	Balancing payment	2,000	CGT
		12,500	IT
		(3,000)	deducted at source
		(7,000)	POA
		4,500	

12.3 **Jamie**

(a) The filing dates for the 2010/11 return depend on the filing method used by Jamie as follows:

- Paper return: later of 31 October 2011 and 3 months after the issue of a return
- Electronic return: later of 31 January 2012 and 3 months after the issue of a return.

(b) The return was submitted and payment of the tax made 7 months late.

There is an immediate £100 penalty. Daily penalties of £10 a day may be imposed as the return is more than 3 months late. The tax return was filed more than 6 months but less than 12 months late. A tax based penalty for late delivery of 5% of the tax due will be charged, or £300 if greater.

As the tax was paid more than 30 days late a penalty of 5% of the tax unpaid will be charged. A further 5% penalty will be charged as the payment was more than 6 months late.

12.4 **Donald**

Payment due on 31 January 2011

	£	£
2009/10		
Balance of income tax and Class 4 NIC liability :		
Income tax liability	22,000	
Class 4 NIC liability	5,000	
Less Tax deducted at source	(500)	
Income tax payable	26,500	
Less Payments on account	(11,000)	
		15,500
Capital gains tax liability		3,000
2010/11		
Income tax:		
First payment on account		
(50% of prior years income tax and Class 4 NIC payable)		
(£26,500 x 50%)		13,250
Payment due on 31 January 2011		31,750

12.5 **Dan**

2010/11 Income tax and Class 4 NIC liability

	£
Interest charges	
First payment on account due 31 January 2011. Paid 1 March 2011.	
Interest due: £11,500 x 1/12 x 3%	29
Second payment on account due 31 July 2011. Paid 1 October 2011	
Interest due: £11,500 x 2/12 x 3%	57
Balancing payment due 31 January 2012.	
Paid 31 January 2012. No interest charged.	–
	86

Penalties

Penalties do not apply to the late payment of payments on account.
The balancing payment was paid on time and therefore no penalties arise.

12.6 **Errors in returns**

The rates of penalties depend on the behaviour of the taxpayer in connection with the errors both when the error is made and when it is discovered.

In the first scenario Roger has not taken reasonable care and has made a careless error. As a result the penalty will be in the range 0% - 30%.

In the second scenario Roger has deliberately made the error but he has not concealed it when HMRC discovers it. As a result the penalty will be in the range 20% - 70%.

In the third scenario again Roger has deliberately made the error but he has concealed it. As a result the penalty will be in the range 30% - 100%.

In the 4th scenario there is a careless error which Roger tells HMRC about without being asked, and provides assistance in remedying the error. In this case HMRC have the power to "suspend" the penalty.

Awareness Paper
Corporation tax

Study Period Planner
Corporation Tax

Use this schedule and your exam timetable to plan the dates on which you will complete each Study Period. The letters 'H' and 'M' tell you whether the topic is high or medium priority.

Study Period	Topic		Due Date
1	Corporation tax basics (1)	H	
2	Corporation tax basics (2)	H	
3	Further CT/Land and buildings	M	
4	**Progress Test 1**	**H**	

Study Period	Topic		Due Date
5	Corporation tax losses	H	
6	Groups	H	
7	Special types of company/ Administration	M	
8	**Progress Test 2**	**H**	

COURSE EXAM 1

A practice exam covering Study Periods 1 – 3

COURSE EXAM 2

A practice exam covering all Study Periods

REVISION PHASE

Your revision phase will begin when **Course Exam 2** is complete. This should ideally be four months before the final exam

TQT Note: The Course Exams contain questions for all FIVE of the awareness paper modules. In your exam you must answer questions from THREE modules. We suggest that you identify the THREE modules you will study and then work through the Study Period Planners for each of those modules until the point where you are told to take Course Exam 1. When you have completed all THREE modules to that point, sit Course Exam 1. Similarly, you should complete all THREE modules before you sit course exam 2. Course Exam 2 covers all of the Study Periods, although it is weighted towards the second half of your studies.

Study Period 1

Corporation tax basics (1)

High Priority

Step 1 Exam Guidance

Any question on the calculation of corporation tax in the exam will rely on the background knowledge of the basic corporation tax computation in this study period.

A number of the topics covered in this period have been tested in:

- Sample Paper (Q2 and Q6)
- May 2009 exam (Q3 and Q10)
- Nov 2009 (Q3, Q6, Q12)
- May 2010 (Q4, Q7)

Step 2 Introduction to the session

The basics of the corporation tax computation are split across two study periods. Subsequent periods look at further aspects of this basic corporation tax computation.

In this study period we concentrate on calculating a company's taxable trade profit. In the next period we learn how to calculate the corporation tax liability.

Both are fundamental to your corporation tax studies so it is essential that you spend the time learning the basics.

Step 3 Guidance through the Study Text

Read through the relevant sections of Chapter 1 of the Study text after reading the following guidance:

Read Sections 1 and 2 carefully. You will study further detail on the overseas aspects of corporation tax (CT) (briefly covered in Section 2.2) in a later study period. Note the terminology: a '**period of account**' is the period for which the company draws up its financial statements; an '**accounting period** (AP)' is the period for which the company pays CT (which can never be longer than 12 months). Try Example 1.

Section 3 is very important as it takes you through the different items that make up the basis of the corporation tax computation. Make sure you can quickly reproduce a proforma corporation tax computation.

Section 3.3 refers to adjusting a company's accounting profit to turn it into the taxable profit, including the deduction available for capital allowances. At this point you must look at Chapters 2 and 3 of the '**Taxation of Unincorporated Businesses'** part of the Text which covers the rules for both in detail. Note also the specific rules which relate to companies set out in Sections 3.3.2 and 3.3.3 of this corporation tax text.

There are further rules in Section 3.3.4 for short life assets that you must know for the Corporation Tax Awareness Module. Try Example 2 to check your understanding.

You should now be able to attempt most questions requiring the calculation of a company's taxable trading profit.

Step 4 Quick Quiz

Attempt question 3 of the quick quiz at the end of Study Text Chapter 1 to reinforce your understanding.

You may also attempt the quick quizzes in Chapters 2 and 3 of the Taxation of Unincorporated Businesses Text.

You may find it best to do this after a break, so that you can see what you remember and what you don't.

Step 5 Workbook Questions

Now attempt exam style questions (ESQs) 1.4 to 1.7, which will help to reinforce your knowledge of the topics covered in this study period and give you examples of the types of question you may see in the exam.

You may also try the ESQs in Chapters 2 and 3 of the Taxation of Unincorporated Businesses Text.

Study Period 2

Corporation tax basics (2)

High Priority

Step 1 Exam Guidance

Remember that all questions in the exam will rely on your knowledge of the basic corporation tax computation.

A number of the topics covered in this period have been tested in:

- Sample Paper (Q4 , Q9 and Q11)
- May 2009 exam (Q1, Q4 and Q12)
- Nov 2009 (Q2, Q11)
- May 2010 (Q2, Q3, Q5, Q8, Q10, Q11)

Step 2 Introduction to the session

In the previous study period we learned how to calculate the taxable trade profit that enters the company's corporation tax proforma.

This study period continues our study of the basics of the computation of corporation tax. It deals with how to calculate the corporation tax liability.

Step 3 Guidance through the Study Text

Read through the rest of Chapter 1 the Study text after reading the following guidance:

Read Section 4 which explains how CT is calculated. Pay particular attention to the 'marginal relief' formula in Section 4.6 and how to deal with an accounting period of less than 12 months (Section 4.8). Work through Examples 3 to 7.

Section 5 deals with a company's CT accounting period 'straddling' two financial years. Read through this quickly as it is not a high priority for the exam.

Then read Section 6 which explains how companies are taxed if a period of account is more than 12 months long. Remember: an AP can **never** be longer than 12 months.

We now turn to Corporate Gains. Section 7 refers you to Chapters 9 and 10 of the '**Taxation of Individuals'** part of the Text for essential CGT background knowledge. You only need to read through Section 2 of Chapter 9. In Chapter 10 read sections 1, 6, 7, 9 and 10. Work through the examples in those sections. Note that indexation allowance is available to companies (see Section 7.3 of the **Corporation Tax** Text). If you have already studied the Taxation of Individuals module you should note that the rules for assets held at 31 March 1982 and shares are different from those for companies.

Step 4 Quick Quiz

Please attempt questions 1 and 2 of the quick quiz at the end of Study Text Chapter 1 to reinforce your understanding.

You should also attempt questions 4 and 6 of the quick quiz at the end of Chapter 10 of the Taxation of Individuals Text.

You may find it best to do this after a break, so that you can see what you remember and what you don't.

Step 5 Workbook Questions

Now attempt ESQs 1.1 to 1.3 and 1.8 to 1.11 of this chapter, which will help to reinforce your knowledge of the topics covered in this study period and give you examples of the types of question you may see in the exam.

Study Period 3

Further CT/Land and buildings

Medium Priority

Examined: Sample paper

Step 1 Exam Guidance

To succeed in the exam you must have a good knowledge of the principles covered in the first two study periods.

There may, however, be an additional mark or two, or sometimes a whole question on an area covered in this study period. These are additional aspects of the computation which you should only try to learn once you have completed the previous study periods.

The topics in this Study Period have been tested in:

- Sample Paper (Q1, Q3, Q8 and Q12)
- May 2009 (Q3, Q8 and Q11)
- Nov 2009 (Q1, Q8)

Step 2 Introduction to the session

In this session we consider a number of topics that could feature in the CT computation:

- Loan relationships
- Intangible fixed assets
- Research and Development expenditure
- Overseas aspects of CT
- Income from land and buildings.

Step 3 Guidance through the Study Text

Read Chapters 2 and 3 of the Study Text after reading the following guidance:

Read through Section 2 on the treatment of 'loan relationships'. The terminology here can make the topic seem tricky. Try and think of the loan relationship rules as the rules on how to treat interest paid and received by companies.

Section 3 then deals with the treatment of 'intangible fixed assets' (ie intellectual property such as patents, copyrights etc...). Attempt Example 1. Example 2 is comprehensive but is too long to be an Awareness module question. However, do attempt this question as it is a good test of your understanding so far.

Read through Section 4 on the treatment of research and development expenditure and attempt Example 3. This is the one time that more than 100% of an expense can be deducted in the corporation tax computation.

Section 5 covers the overseas aspects of CT. Work through Examples 4 to 6.

Finally read Chapter 3. This is a very short chapter and there isn't a lot to learn! Do pay particular attention to the rules for the taxation of lease premiums. Work through Examples 1 and 2 thoroughly.

Step 4 Quick Quiz

Please attempt the quick quizzes at the end of Study Text Chapters 2 and 3 to reinforce your understanding.

You may find it best to do this after a break, so that you can see what you remember and what you don't.

Step 5 Workbook Questions

Now attempt ESQs 2.1 to 2.9 and 3.1 to 3.4, which will help to reinforce your knowledge of the topics covered in this study period and give you examples of the types of question you may see in the exam.

Your TQT's i-Pass CD Rom also contains questions on the further aspects of the corporation tax computation.

Progress Test 1

In order to reinforce what you have learnt so far, answer the following questions. Try to answer them without referring to your Study Text or notes. The test should take you no longer than one hour and covers Study Periods 1–3. Solutions start on page 267.

1 Zac Ltd runs a manufacturing business. On 10 July 2010 the company sold an old office building for £250,000. The building had cost Zac Ltd £50,000 on 1 August 1981. It was extended in October 1981 at a cost of £10,000. Its value at 31 March 1982 was £80,000. After the sale the company rented office premises.

Calculate the chargeable gain arising on the disposal of the office block.

2 Meacham Ltd was incorporated on 1 March 2010 and commenced to trade on 1 April 2010. It drew up its first set of accounts for the period to 31 July 2011.

In its first period of trading it made an adjusted trading profit before capital allowances of £574,000 and made a gift aid payment of £46,000 on 1 July 2011. During the period it made the following capital additions:

1 April 2010	Equipment	£110,000
1 April 2010	New car for sales manager	£20,000

The sales manager's car had CO_2 emissions of 100g/km and was used 20% of the time for private purposes.

You are required to calculate the corporation tax liability of Meacham Ltd for the period to 31 July 2011. Assume that rates and allowances for FY2010 continue into the future.

3 Rowan Ltd prepares accounts to 31 December each year.

For the year ended 31 December 2010 the company had the following results:

	£
Taxable total profits	155,000
Gross exempt UK dividends received	35,000
Augmented profits	190,000

Rowan Ltd has two associates.

Calculate Rowan Ltd's corporation tax liability for the year ended 31 December 2010.

4 Molly Ltd had always made up accounts to 31 December. However the company decided to change its accounting reference date to 31 March. The company made up accounts for the following periods:

Year ended 31 December 2009
Fifteen months to 31 March 2011

State the corporation tax accounting periods for which Molly Ltd will prepare a corporation tax computation based upon the above accounting reference dates.

5 Unruly Ltd, a trading company, has owned 25% of the shares in Polite Ltd for many years. On 1 January 2008, Unruly Ltd disposed of a 20% holding in Polite Ltd and on 1 February 2011 the company disposed of the remaining 5% holding.

Describe the tax implications of each of these transactions, making reference to the availability of any reliefs.

6 **State the categories of revenue expenditure on research and development that qualify as allowable expenditure for the additional research and development trading deduction for corporation tax purposes.**

7 In the year to 31 July 2011 Bramble Ltd received rental income from an overseas property and exempt dividends in respect of a 20% holding of ordinary shares in an overseas trading company.

The rental income received, net of 30% withholding tax, was £75,000.

The dividends received, net of 15% withholding tax, were £85,000.

Explain how the above overseas income will be treated for UK corporation tax purposes.

8 Wite-up Ltd received bank interest of £13,500 and debenture interest from Black-out Ltd of £45,400 during its year ended 31 December 2010

It also paid debenture interest of £40,000 to Grey Ltd on a loan of £1,000,000. It issued the debentures to Grey Ltd in May 2009 to raise £750,000 for the purchase of a factory to use in the trade and £250,000 to purchase an investment property.

You are required to show how these amounts will be treated for tax purposes assuming all figures are gross and are the amounts shown in the accounts.

9 Carlsway Ltd, which prepares accounts to 31 December each year, owns an investment property that it has let out on a five year lease to Doorling Ltd from 1 June 2010. The property was empty before Doorling Ltd took occupation.

Doorling Ltd was required to pay a premium of £35,000 and an annual rent of £14,400, payable monthly, in arrears, on the last day of the month.

Carlsway Ltd had the following expenses in connection with letting out the property:

Repairs and maintenance	£775
Loan interest	£2,800

You are required to calculate Carlsway Ltd's taxable property income for the year ended 31 December 2010 and the deduction that Doorling Ltd can take against its trading income for its year ended 31 March 2011.

10 Splendour Ltd amortises its patents, which are valued at £235,000 and are not related to the company's trade, at a rate of 5% in its accounts. It receives patent royalties from other companies during the year in respect of these patents of £10,500.

You are required to calculate Splendour Ltd's loss and explain how it can be relieved.

11 The following expense items were incurred by a company by XYZ Ltd:

(a) Entertaining overseas suppliers;
(b) Dividends paid;
(c) Interest paid in the UK on an overdraft with a UK bank;
(d) Entertaining staff;
(e) Expense in acquiring a trade related patent;
(f) Professional charges in raising medium term loan finance to acquire plant and machinery;
(g) Charitable covenant;
(h) Amortisation of goodwill acquired 1 June 2003;
(i) Revenue expenditure incurred 20 months before the start of trading;
(j) Interest paid in respect of a bank loan taken out to acquire a property which will be rented out.

You are required to state, with reasons, which of the above expenses will not be deductible from the company's trading profits.

12 G Ltd owns all the ordinary shares in P Ltd (a UK resident trading company), Q Ltd (a UK resident investment company acquired two months before the end of the accounting period), R Ltd (a UK resident dormant company) and S Ltd (a non-UK resident trading company).

G Ltd prepared accounts for 11 months to 31 March 2011. Its results were:

	£
Trading income	130,000
Chargeable gains	15,000

You are required to compute the corporation tax liability of G Ltd for the 11 months to 31 March 2011.

You will find the answers to this test at starting on page 267. If you answer more than 6 questions correctly, your performance is satisfactory; if you answer more than 8 correctly, you are doing well. Once you have reviewed how you have performed, go back over topics where you feel your understanding is poor.

Study Period 5

High Priority

Corporation tax losses

Examined: Sample paper

Step 1 Exam Guidance

The examiner can consider a loss making company's corporation tax computation as well as a profitable one.

Corporation tax losses questions can test your knowledge of:

- The different ways in which losses can be used against the company's other income or gains, and
- The company's decision on how to use the loss to achieve the best tax position.

This topic has been tested in:

- Sample paper (Q10)
- May 2009 (Q6)
- May 2010 (Q9)

Step 2 Introduction to the session

In this Study Period, we consider the position of the loss making company.

If a company incurs a loss we must understand if and how any tax adjusted loss can be used for tax purposes.

We must also understand the company's decision making process for deciding which of a range of available loss reliefs it will use and in what order.

This is a brief chapter, but important, so take your time.

Step 3 Guidance through the Study Text

Read through Chapter 4 of the Study Text after reading the following guidance:

Read Section 1.1 for an overview of the treatment of a trading loss in the CT computation (ie the trading income assessment figure is 'nil').

Read through Sections 1.2 and 1.3 noting the main ways that a trading loss can be used including the temporary extension for losses in periods ending between 24 November 2008 and 23 November 2010. Focus on the accounting period(s) in which the loss can be used and where in the proforma the loss is deducted (ie after trading profits or after total profits?). Attempt Examples 1 to 3 to check your understanding. Section 1.4 deals with the use of the loss when a company ceases to trade.

Read Section 1.5 carefully. Do you understand the company's decision making process for using its loss(es)? Try and keep in mind that the company's main aim is to pay as little tax as possible and to obtain a refund if it has already unnecessarily paid tax in an earlier period. Try Example 4 to check your understanding.

Read Section 2 which covers the two main restrictions on the use of trading losses. Highlight the key ideas and terminology (eg 'major change in the nature or conduct of trade'). Finally read Sections 3 and 4 on first year tax credits and the relief for other losses.

Step 4 Quick Quiz

Please attempt the quick quiz at the end of Study Text Chapter 4 to reinforce your understanding.

You may find it best to do this after a break, so that you can see what you remember and what you don't.

Step 5 Workbook Questions

Now attempt ESQs 4.1 to 4.8, which will help to reinforce your knowledge of the topics covered in this study period and give you examples of the types of question you may see in the exam.

Study Period 6

Groups

High Priority

Step 1 Exam Guidance

It can be very beneficial from a tax perspective for a company to be in a 'group' of companies. The examiner will expect you to understand the level of shareholding required for each group relationship and the implications where a group exists.

Groups have been tested in:

- Sample Paper (Q5 and Q11)
- May 2009 exam (Q5 and Q7)
- Nov 2009 (Q4, Q7, Q10)
- May 2010 (Q6, Q12)

Step 2 Introduction to the session

This is a very important Study Period. We look at the group aspects of corporation tax.

You should concentrate on the rules for group relief for trading losses and those for chargeable gains groups.

Once you have understood these fully you should move onto the anti-avoidance rules for transfer pricing transactions and controlled foreign companies.

This session may take longer than the usual 3 hours.

Step 3 Guidance through the Study Text

Read through the relevant sections of Chapter 5 of the Study text after reading the following guidance:

Read Section 1 for background, then Section 2 on associated companies. Note the two tax consequences of a company having associates and try Example 1.

Read Sections 3.1 and 3.2 which deal with 75% group relief group companies. Try Examples 2 and 3 to check your understanding. This is an essential topic for the exam.

The read Section 3.3 on tax planning for group relief. You must understand the decision making behind group relief claims. Attempt Example 4. Then read Section 3.4 which deals with companies joining and leaving a group and try Examples 5 and 6.

Read Section 4 which deals with 75% chargeable gains groups. Note how the definition is different from a group relief group. Try Examples 7 and 8. Note carefully the rules for group elections and companies leaving a group and try Example 9. Read the rest of the section quickly.

Read through Sections 5 and 6 on transfer pricing and controlled foreign companies, highlighting the key ideas and terminology. Attempt Examples 10 to 12. These are lower priority than the previous sections.

Step 4 Quick Quiz

Please attempt the quick quiz at the end of Study Text Chapter 5 to reinforce your understanding.

You may find it best to do this after a break, so that you can see what you remember and what you don't.

Step 5 Workbook Questions

Now attempt ESQs 5.1 to 5.9, which will help to reinforce your knowledge of the topics covered in this study period and give you examples of the types of question you may see in the exam.

Study Period 7

Special types of company/Administration

Medium Priority

Step 1 Exam Guidance

The topics covered in the previous study periods are highly examinable and you must be comfortable with those rules before you move onto this period where we learn to identify particular types of companies, for example an investment company, and the special rules that apply to them.

We also cover the corporation tax administration rules which can form part of or an entire question.

Q9 in May 2009 exam tested personal service companies.

Q7 (Sample Paper). Q2 (May 2009), Q9 (Nov 2009), Q1 (May 2010) tested corporation tax administration.

Step 2 Introduction to the session

You have now covered the corporation tax rules that apply to mainstream companies. There are, however, a number of 'special' companies to which special rules apply. The rules you have already learnt do still apply to these 'special' companies but with some modification.

In this study period you learn to spot these companies in the exam and to apply the correct set of modified rules. You are also introduced to the administrative provisions that apply to companies.

Step 3 Guidance through the Study Text

Read through Chapters 6 and 7 of the Study text after reading the following guidance:

Start with Chapter 6. Read Section 1 on 'investment' companies and any companies with investments. Try Example 1 to test your understanding of the deductibility of management expenses.

Read Sections 2.1 to 2.3 for background on the Personal Service Company and Managed Service Company rules. Then read Section 2.4. Locate the relevant part of the legislation so that you can work through the proforma and Example 2.

Now turn to Chapter 7 on corporation tax administration. Read Section 1 on corporation tax returns and record keeping.

Now work through Section 2 on corporation tax payments for both large companies (ie those paying tax at the main rate of corporation tax) and non-large companies. It is essential that you know the different payment dates for each type of company. Carefully work Examples 1 to 4.

Finally read through Section 3 noting in your legislation the relevant penalties covered in this section.

You have now completed the technical material for the **Corporation Tax Awareness** module.

Step 4 Quick Quiz

Please attempt the quick quizzes at the end of Study Text Chapter 6 and 7 to reinforce your understanding.

You may find it best to do this after a break, so that you can see what you remember and what you don't.

Step 5 Workbook Questions

Now attempt ESQs 6.1 to 6.7 and 7.1 to 7.5, which will help to reinforce your knowledge of the topics covered in this study period and give you examples of the types of question you may see in the exam.

Progress Test 2

In order to reinforce what you have learnt so far, answer the following questions. Try to answer them without referring to your Study Text or notes. The test should take you no longer than one hour and covers Study Periods 5–7. Solutions start on page 273.

1 Badger Ltd submitted its corporation tax return in respect of the year ended 31 December 2008 on 1 February 2011. Tax due on this return amounted to £35,000 and was also paid on 1 February 2011. Badger Ltd had received a notice requesting submission of a corporation tax return for the year ended 31 December 2008 on 1 February 2009.

State the penalties chargeable on Badger Limited for the failure to submit a corporation tax return on time.

2 Matcham Ltd had the following profits for the year ended 31 March 2011:

Taxable total profits	295,000
Exempt dividends received on a 15% holding in a UK company	9,000

Matcham Ltd has no associated companies.

Calculate Matcham Ltd's corporation tax liability for the year ended 31 March 2011 and state the due date for payment of the tax due.

3 Palace Ltd has been making up accounts to 31 December for many years. On 1 January 2010 the company decided to change its accounting year end date to 31 March. The company can either make up:

- A set of accounts for the 3 months to 31 March 2010 and thereafter for twelve months periods to 31 March, or
- For the 15 months to 31 March 2011 and thereafter for twelve month periods to 31 March.

State the corporation tax accounting periods that will be taxed under each of the above options for the period 1 January 2009 to 31 March 2011 and state for each of the accounting periods when the corporation tax will be payable assuming payment is not due by instalments.

4 Opera Ltd has been a large company, paying tax at the main rate for many years. The company makes up accounts to 31 December each year. For the year ended 31 December 2010, it estimates that its corporation tax liability will be £10 million.

State the due date for the quarterly payments of corporation tax in respect of the accounting period ending on 31 December 2010 and state the amount due on each instalment date and explain how interest will be charged or paid if the corporation liability is greater or less than £10 million.

5 D'Oyley Carte Ltd has been suffering poor trading conditions and has made a tax adjusted trading loss for the year ended 31 March 2010. Taxable profits and losses for recent accounting periods have been as follows:

	Trading Profit/(Loss)
	£
Year ended 31 March 2009	25,000
Year ended 31 March 2010	(50,000)
Year ended 31 March 2011 (estimated)	35,000

D'Oyley Carte Ltd has no other taxable income in any of the years concerned.

State the ways in which D'Oyley Carte Ltd could use the trading loss of the year ended 31 March 2010. Briefly advise on the most tax efficient use of the loss.

6 Ralph Ltd makes up accounts to 31 December each year and owns the following shareholdings in other companies:

100% of Buttercup Ltd
75% of Porter Ltd, a dormant company, and
51% of Corcoran Ltd a company purchased on 1 May 2010

State, with reasons, the number of associated companies in the Ralph Ltd group for the year ended 31 December 2010 and calculate the small profits rate limits to be used by the group to calculate corporation tax for that year.

7 Ruth Ltd owns 75% of Badger Ltd, which in turn owns 75% of Bramble Ltd.

State which of these companies are:

- **In a 75% group relief for losses group**
- **In a 75% capital gains group.**

8 Metro Ltd owns 100% of the shares in Tropolis Ltd.

Metro prepares accounts to 31 December each year and in its accounting period ending 31 December 2010 it has a trading loss of £145,000.

Tropolis Ltd has total taxable profits of £250,000 in its year ended 31 March 2010 and £60,000 in its year ended 31 March 2011.

You are required to calculate the amount of group relief that Tropolis Ltd can claim from Metro Ltd.

9 Sarah owns her own company through which she contracts her services to a number of clients.

During the year ended 31 March 2011 the company received £55,000 from relevant engagements performed by Sarah and a further £25,000 from other engagements.

Sarah received a salary of £10,000 and the company paid employer's NIC in respect of this salary of £548.

The company also paid £2,000 into Sarah's personal pension and reimbursed her business travelling expenses of £350.

You are required to calculate the deemed employment payment Sarah will be treated as receiving on 5 April 2011.

10 Leopard Ltd has the following results for the 8 month period ending 31 March 2011:

Taxable total profits	£296,000
Exempt dividend received from UK company	£12,600

It has no associated companies.

You are required to calculate the corporation tax payable for the period ended 31 March 2011.

11 A Ltd has a wholly owned trading subsidiary B Ltd. In June 1986 A Ltd acquired a property for £50,000 which it transferred to B Ltd in July 2004, when its market value was £80,000. In May 2010 A Ltd sold all its shares in B Ltd to C Ltd an unconnected company. The property was then valued at £130,000.

You are required to explain how the above transactions will be treated for chargeable gain purposes. Your answer should include a calculation of any chargeable gains arising, stating in which company the gain arises, and when (ignore indexation allowance).

12 Widgets (UK) Ltd is a 100% subsidiary of Holdings Ltd. It has made trading losses over the past two years and expects to make a trading loss in the current accounting period.

Ventures Ltd intends to purchase Widgets (UK) Ltd. It is intended that the management of the company should be restructured, in which case the company will break even the following year and should then become profitable.

Widgets (UK) Ltd operates in the manufacturing side of the industry. Another of Ventures Ltd's subsidiaries runs a similar business and Ventures Ltd is considering diversifying Widgets (UK) Ltd's trade into the retail area.

You are required to comment briefly on the effects of these proposals on the use of the losses generated by Widgets (UK) Ltd.

You will find the answers to this test starting on page 273. If you answer more than 6 questions correctly, your performance is satisfactory; if you answer more than 8 correctly, you are doing well. Once you have reviewed how you have performed, go back over topics where you feel your understanding is poor.

Solutions

Progress Test 1

1 Gain on sale of old office building:

	Original cost	31.3.82 MV
	£	£
Disposal proceeds	250,000	250,000
Less: cost 1981	(50,000)	
enhancement cost 1981	(10,000)	
31.3.82 MV		(80,000)
Unindexed gain	190,000	170,000
Less: indexation allowance to July 2010 on 31.3.82 MV:		
$\frac{226.4 - 79.44}{79.44}$ (= 1.85)		
1.85 × £80,000	(148,000)	(148,000)
Gain	42,000	22,000
Chargeable gain (lower gain)		22,000

2 Meacham Ltd

First AP: 1 April 2010 (commencement of trade) to 31 March 2011 (end of 12 month period)
Second AP: 4 months to 31 July 2011 (end of period of account)

	12 mths to 31.3.11	4 mths to 31.7.11
	£	£
Adjusted trading profit: 12:4	430,500	143,500
Capital allowances (W1)	(122,000)	(533)
Trading profit	308,500	142,967
Qualifying charitable donation: Gift Aid		(46,000)
Taxable total profits	308,500	96,967
Corporation tax liability (W2)		
£308,500 x 28%	86,380	
7/400 × (1,500,000 – 308,500)	(20,851)	
£96,967 × 21% (assumes FY 10 rates apply)		20,363
	66,529	20,363

W1 Capital allowances

	FYA	Main pool	Allowances
	£	£	£
12 mths to 31.3.11			
Additions qualifying for 100% FYA:			
Low emission car	20,000		
FYA at 100%	(20,000)		20,000
Additions qualifying for AIA/:			
Equipment		110,000	
AIA (Max £100,000)		(100,000)	100,000
		10,000	
WDA at 20%		(2,000)	2,000
TWDV c/f		8,000	
Total allowances			122,000
4 mths to 31.7.11			
WDA at 20% x 4/12		(533)	533
TWDV c/f		7,467	
Total allowances			533

W2 Corporation tax liability

4 month accounting period ended 31.7.11:

Augmented profits limits: £1,500,000 × 4/12 = £500,000
£300,000 × 4/12 = £100,000

Company therefore pays tax at the small profits rate.

3 Rowan Ltd

Corporation tax payable for the year ended 31 December 2010

	£
£155,000 × 28%	43,400
Less: Marginal relief	
(500,000 – 190,000) × 155,000/190,000 × 7/400	(4,426)
	38,974

Working

Limits for small profits rate purposes

Upper limit £1,500,000/3 = £500,000
Lower limit £300,000/3 = £100,000

As augmented profits are £190,000 (therefore > lower limit and < upper limit) Rowan Ltd pays tax at the main rate with marginal relief.

4 Molly Ltd will calculate corporation tax for the following periods:

(a) 12 months to 31 December 2009
(b) 12 months to 31 December 2010
(c) 3 months to 31 March 2011

5 Unruly Ltd

The first disposal of shares in Polite ltd, on 1 January 2008 would have qualified for the substantial shareholdings exemption, as Unruly Ltd owned at least 10% of the shares in Polite Ltd for at least 12 months in the previous two years.

However, the substantial shareholding exemption would not apply to the sale of 5% of the shares in Polite Ltd on 1 February 2011, as Unruly Ltd had not owned at least 10% of the shares in Polite Ltd for a period of 12 consecutive months in the two previous years.

This sale would therefore result in a chargeable gain, or an allowable capital loss.

6 The categories of revenue expenditure qualifying for the additional trading deduction for companies are:

(a) Staff costs
(b) Consumables
(c) Computer software
(d) Fuel, power and water.

7 The rental income will be included gross (£75,000 x 100/70 = £107,143) as property income in the corporation tax computation. Double tax relief (DTR) will be available as the income has suffered UK and overseas tax. The DTR will be restricted to the lower of the UK tax and the overseas tax suffered (30%). As the highest marginal rate of UK corporation tax is 29.75% the DTR will be restricted to the amount of UK tax payable on the overseas rental income.

The dividends received will be exempt from UK tax. They will however be included as franked investment income (FII) in the calculation of augmented profits, used to determine the rate of tax paid by Bramble Ltd. The amount included as FII is the amount received x 100/90. Any overseas tax suffered is irrelevant.

8 Wite-up Ltd

Companies that receive interest (other than companies such as banks) are treated as receiving income in respect of non-trading loan relationships.

Interest payable for trade purposes is allowable as a deduction against trading income.

Other interest payable for non-trade purposes is allowable as a deduction against the income in respect of non-trading loan relationships.

The debenture interest payable to Grey Ltd was used partly for trade purposes and partly for non-trade purposes and must be split:

Non-trade purposes: £40,000 × £250,000/£1,000,000 = £10,000

Trade purposes: £40,000 × £750,000/£1,000,000 = £30,000

Trading deduction:		£(30,000)
Non-trading loan relationships		£
Income (credits) receivable:		
Bank interest		13,500
Debenture interest		45,400
		58,900
Less: interest payable		(10,000)
Profit on non-trading loan relationships		48,900

9 *Carlsway Ltd*

	£	£
Lease premium (W)		32,200
Rental income (accruals basis)		
1.6.010– 31.12.10 7/12 × £14,400	8,400	
Less: expenses (Note)	(775)	
		7,625
Property income		39,825

Note. The loan interest is dealt with under the loan relationship rules and will be a non-trading loan relationship debit.

Working

Lease premium

As the lease to Doorling Ltd is a short lease, part of the premium is taxable as property income in the year it is received.

$$£35,000 \times \frac{50-4}{50} = £32,200 \text{ assessable as property income}$$

Doorling Ltd

Doorling Ltd can take a deduction for its monthly rent expense and the proportion of the lease premium that relates to the period (accruals basis).

Rent: 1.6.10 – 31.3.11 = 10/12 × £14,400	12,000
Lease premium: £32,200/ 5 × 10/12	5,367
Total deduction	17,367

10 Splendour Ltd

As the patents are not related to the company's trade, all debits and credits are dealt with as miscellaneous income in respect of intangible fixed assets(IFAs).

	£
Miscellaneous income: patent income	10,500
Less: allowable debit: £235,000 × 5%	(11,750)
Deficit in respect of miscellaneous income (ie debit)	(1,250)

This loss can be relieved as follows:

(a) Set against current year total profits.
(b) Group relieve excess debit.
(c) Carry forward to next accounting period where it will be treated as if it were a non-trading debit arising in that period to be set against future profits on non-trading IFAs.

11 Not allowable are (a),(b),(g) and (j).

(a) – Entertainment is only allowable if it is entertaining staff.
(b) – Dividends are not allowable as they are an appropriation of profit.
(g) – Deductible from total profits as a qualifying charitable donation not as a trading expense.
(j) – Interest in respect of a non-trade related loan is deducted from income from non-trading loan relationships.

12 G Ltd – Corporation tax for 11 months to 31 March 2011

Three companies are associated, being P Ltd, Q Ltd and S Ltd. R Ltd is ignored as it is dormant.

Limits for small profits rate

	£
Upper limit $\times \dfrac{1{,}500{,}000}{4} \times \dfrac{11}{12}$	343,750
Lower limit $\times \dfrac{300{,}000}{4} \times \dfrac{11}{12}$	68,750

	£
Trading income	130,000
Chargeable gains	15,000
Taxable total profits	145,000
£145,000 × 28%	40,600
Less: Marginal relief	
7/400 × £(343,750 – 145,000)	(3,478)
Corporation tax due	37,122

1 Badger Ltd.

Corporation tax return for the year ended 31 December 2008 was due to be submitted by 31 December 2009.

As the return was not submitted until 1 February 2011, the penalties would be;

Late filing: £100 immediate penalty. A daily penalty of £10 may be imposed for up to 90 days as the return is more than 3 months late. As the return is more than 12 months late tax geared penalties will apply depending on the behaviour of the company ranging from 10% of the tax due where the withholding of the return is not deliberate up to 100% of the tax due where the withholding of the return is deliberate and concealed.

Late payment: As the tax is paid more than 12 months late a penalty of 15% of the unpaid tax may be charged.

2 Matcham Ltd

	£
Taxable total profits	295,000
Add: Exempt dividends from non-associated companies (£9,000 × 100/90)	10,000
Augmented profits	305,000

Compared to the limits for small profits rate purposes for the Financial Year 2010, the augmented profits fall in the marginal relief band.

Corporation tax payable:

	£
£295,000 x 28%	82,600
Less marginal relief	
(1,500,000 – 305,000) × 7/400 × 295,000/305,000	(20,227)
Corporation tax payable	62,373

This is payable nine months and one day after the end of the accounting period, that is by 1 January 2012.

3 Palace Ltd

Option 1 – 3 months accounts to 31 March 2010.

Corporation tax will be calculated for:
The 12 months to 31 December 2009, payable 1 October 2010.
The 3 months to 31 March 2010, payable 1 January 2011.
The 12 months to 31 March 2011, payable 1 January 2012.

Option 2 – 15 months accounts to 31 March 2011

Corporation tax will be calculated for:
The 12 months to 31 December 2009, payable 1 October 2010.
The 12 months to 31 December 2010, payable 1 October 2011.
The 3 months to 31 March 2011, payable 1 January 2012.

4 Opera Ltd

Payment dates:

14 July 2010
14 October 2010
14 January 2011
14 April 2011

The amount payable on each date will be £10,000,000/4 = £2,500,000.

If the liability is greater than £10 million, then interest will be charged on each underpaid instalment as if the due amount had been one quarter of the final liability. If the liability is less than £10 million, then interest will be paid by HMRC on each overpaid instalment on the same basis.

5 D'Oyley Carte Ltd

D'Oyley Carte Ltd could use its trading loss for the year ended 31 March 2010, as follows:

- Under S.45 (4) CTA 2010 the loss will be carried forward, if not used in any other way, against the next available trading profits of the same trade. In the year ended 31 March 2011 there are trading profits of £35,000 from which the loss can be deducted.
- Under S.37(3) CTA 2010 the loss can be deducted total profits, before deduction of qualifying charitable donations (QCDs) of the current accounting period (i.e. the year ended 31 March 2010). There are no profits of the current accounting period.
- Under S.37 (3) CTA 2010 the loss can be carried back and deducted from total profits of the twelve month period preceding the accounting period of loss provided a current year claim is made first. (i.e. the year ended 31 March 2009). There are profits of £25,000 in the year ended 31 March 2009, against which the loss could be used.
- As the loss arose in an accounting period ending between 24 November 2008 and 23 November 2010 it can be carried back against total profits (before deducting any QCDs) of the previous three years, provided a current year claim under S.37 (3) CTA 2010 is made first. The loss could therefore be carried back to year ended 31 Match 2009, then year ended 31 March 2008 and finally year ended 31 March 2007. There is no information provided in the question regarding the company's profits prior to the year ended 31 March 2009.
- The company is paying tax at the small profits rate (21%) throughout the three accounting periods for which information is available. However, carrying the loss back, rather than forward would use the loss as early as possible. This will result in a repayment of tax, rather than just the reduction of a future liability that has yet to be paid. The most efficient use of the loss is therefore to make a current year claim (no profits) followed by a carryback claim to offset the loss against the total profits of the year ended 31 March 2009.

6 Ralph Ltd

There are three associates:

Ralph Ltd

Buttercup Ltd – own more than 50%

Porter Ltd – not counted as an associate, as, although own >50% the company is dormant.

Corcoran Ltd – is an associate. Own more than 50% and it is an associate throughout the year, even though it is acquired part way through the accounting period.

The small profits limits for the group for the year ended 31 December 2010 are therefore:

£300,000/3 = £100,000

£1,500,000/3 = £500,000

TQT
Tax Qualification Training

7 Ruth Ltd

75% Group relief for losses group:

Ruth Ltd and Badger Ltd form one group and Badger Ltd and Bramble Ltd a separate group. All three companies cannot form one group relief for losses group, as for this purpose the effective interest held by the holding company needs to be at least 75%. In this case the effective interest is only 56.25% (75% x 75%).

75% capital gains group:

Ruth Ltd, Badger Ltd and Bramble Ltd all form one group for group capital gains purposes, as at each stage in the group structure there needs to be a 75% interest and the effective interest needs to be at least 51%.

8 Metro Ltd

Group relief can only be claimed for the current period. As Metro Ltd's and Tropolis Ltd's accounting periods are different we need to time apportion the loss to find the maximum relief available (ie the lower of Tropolis Ltd's profit and Metro Ltd's loss).

	£	£
Tropolis Ltd's y/e 31.3.10		
Profits: £250,000 × 3/12	62,500	
Metro Ltd's losses for that period:		
£(145,000) × 3/12	(36,250)	
Available loss		36,250
Tropolis Ltd's y/e 31.3.11		
Profits: £60,000 × 9/12	45,000	
Metro Ltd's losses for that period:		
£(145,000) × 9/12	(108,750)	
Available loss		45,000
Total loss available for group relief		81,250

9 Sarah

	£
Income from relevant engagements only	55,000
Less: 5% flat rate deduction	(2,750)
	52,250
Less: other deductions	
Salary	(10,000)
NIC on actual salary	(548)
Pension contribution	(2,000)
Reimbursed expenses	(350)
Gross deemed payment	39,352
Less: Employer's NIC on deemed payment	
£39,352 × 12.8/112.8	(4,465)
Deemed employment payment	34,887

10 Leopard Ltd

8 m/e 31 March 2011	£
Taxable total profits	296,000
Add: FII (gross dividend): £12,600 × 100/90	14,000
Augmented profits	310,000

Augmented profits are above £200,000 (W) but below £1,000,000, so marginal relief applies

	£
TTP @ 28%	82,880
Less: marginal relief	
7/400 × (1,000,000 – 310,000) × 296,000/310,000	(11,530)
CT due	71,350

Working

CT Limits	
£1,500,000 × 8/12	£1,000,000
£300,000 × 8/12	£200,000

11 A Ltd and B Ltd form a group for chargeable gains purposes. The transfer to B Ltd in July 2004 will take place at no gain/no loss.

When A Ltd sells its shares to C Ltd, B Ltd leaves the A Ltd gains group. As this happens within 6 years of the no gain/no loss transfer B Ltd will be assessed on a chargeable gain of £80,000 less £50,000 = £30,000. The gain is treated as arising at the start of the accounting period in which B Ltd leaves the group.

The disposal of B Ltd is likely to be exempt as the disposal of a substantial shareholding.

12 Widgets (UK) Ltd can only group relieve to the Ventures Ltd group any losses arising after the company joins the group.

Trading losses brought forward in Widgets (UK) Ltd (subject to any claim that the Holdings Ltd group makes for losses in the current accounting period but before Widgets (UK) Ltd leaves the group) can be carried forward in Widgets (UK) Ltd.

If however there is a major change in the nature or conduct of Widgets (UK) Ltd's trade within three years of being acquired by Ventures Ltd, the losses arising before the date of change of ownership will not be able to be carried forward and will therefore expire. Ventures Ltd should consider whether its proposals will be treated as a major change, in which case they could delay implementing them or restructure their plans.

Exam style questions

1.1 Buttercup Ltd, which makes up accounts to 31 March, purchased a 55% shareholding in an overseas company, Roote BV, and a 80% shareholding in a UK company, Petal Ltd, in 1988. In May 2010 it sold Petal Ltd and purchased 60% of another UK company, Stamen Ltd.

Buttercup Ltd produced the following results for the year ended 31 March 2011:

	£
Trading income	70,000
Dividend received	8,000

The dividend received was in respect of a 5% shareholding of ordinary shares in a UK company.

You are required to calculate the corporation tax payable for the year ended 31 March 2011.

1.2 Cal Limited had the following results for the year ended 30 September 2010:

	£
Trading income	600,000
Dividend received from Dal Limited	45,000
Dividend received from Thal Limited	90,000

Cal Limited owns 75% of the ordinary shares of Dal Limited and 35% of the ordinary shares of Thal Limited.

You are required to calculate Cal Limited's corporation tax liability for the year ended 30 September 2010.

1.3 Max Ltd has the following results for its 9 months ended 31 December 2010:

	£
Tax adjusted trading profits	62,000
Rental income	10,000
Bank interest actually received	23,000
Chargeable gain	9,000
Gift Aid paid (gross)	2,000
Dividend received from wholly owned subsidiary	28,000

As at 31 December 2010 accrued interest receivable was £5,000. No interest was accrued at 1 April 2010.

You are required to calculate Max Ltd's corporation tax liability for the period ended 31 December 2010.

1.4 Histon plc drew up accounts for the 15 month period to 30 June 2011. The trading profit figure for the 15 month period adjusted for tax but before capital allowances was £153,000. The company also had a chargeable gain of £20,000 in respect of a disposal on 1 February 2011 and made a payment under the Gift Aid scheme of £8,000 on 1 May 2011.

The balance on the capital allowances main pool as at 1 April 2010 was £20,000. On 1 June 2010 the company purchased a car (CO_2 emissions 164g/km) for £16,000 and a machine for £110,000.

You are required to calculate the taxable total profits chargeable to corporation tax for the period. Assume that rates and allowances for FY 2010 continue into the future.

1.5 Ramble Ltd was incorporated in the UK on 1 March 2009 and commenced to trade on 1 April 2009. It drew up its first set of accounts to 30 April 2010. The shares are wholly owned by Robert Ramble. Robert works full time for the company.

In the year to 30 April 2011 the company acquired the following assets:

- car acquired on 1 June 2010 for £20,000. The car had CO_2 emissions of 158g/km and is used 20% of the time for personal purposes by Robert.
- a computer on 1 July 2010 for £105,000 including £800 for software.

Robert expects to sell both of the above assets for less than their original cost in 2 years time.

You are required to:

(a) **State, with reasons, the corporation tax accounting periods arising in respect of the period from incorporation to 30 April 2011.**

(b) **Explain the capital allowances that will be available to Ramble Ltd in respect of the above assets and advise whether it would be appropriate to claim short life asset treatment in respect of the assets.**

Assume that rates and allowances for FY 2010 continue into the future.

1.6 Overt Ltd prepares accounts to 31 March. An extract from the company's profit and loss account for the year to 31 March 2011 shows the following:

	£	£
Gross operating profit		5,600,000
Depreciation	65,000	
Rent, rates and utilities (Note 1)	105,000	
Repairs (Note 2)	40,000	
Professional fees (Note 3)	55,000	
Gain on sale of office building	(85,000)	
Sundry expenses (All allowable)	45,000	
		(225,000)
		5,375,000
Bank interest received		48,000
Profit before tax		5,423,000

Notes:

(1) Rent includes a premium of £50,000 which Overt Ltd paid on 1 April 2011 for the grant of a 30 year lease on office premises.

(2) Repairs includes £2,500 on replacing a rotten window in the factory.

(3) Professional fees includes £2,000 in connection with the 30 year lease acquired on the office premises and £5,000 in connection with setting up an Approved Share Incentive Plan to allow employees to acquire shares in the company.

(4) Capital allowances claimed for the year were £95,000.

You are required to calculate Overt Ltd's taxable trading income for the year to 31 March 2011.

1.7 Mariner Ltd prepares accounts to 31 December. During the year to 31 December 2010 the following transactions took place:

		Cost/Proceeds
		£
1 January 2010	Car sold (original cost £10,000)	4,000
15 March 2010	Van acquired	16,000
1 May 2010	Volvo car acquired	25,000
1 June 2010	Computer sold (original cost £25,000)	10,000

The car acquired on 1 May 2010 had CO_2 emissions of 171g/km and was for the use of the managing director. 30% of his annual mileage was for private purposes.

The balances on the capital allowance pools as at 1 January 2010 were:

Main pool	£85,000
Short-life asset (acquired 1 May 2006)	£24,000

You are required to calculate the capital allowances available to Mariner Ltd for the year ended 31 December 2010.

1.8 Albatross Ltd operates a manufacturing business and draws up its accounts to 30 September each year.

In the year to 30 September 2010 it made the following disposals:

(1) On 1 March 2010 it sold a 5% shareholding in Magpie Ltd, a trading company, for £80,000. It had acquired a 20% shareholding in Magpie Ltd for £60,000 on 1 June 2007.

(2) On 1 June 2010 it sold an office building for £1,200,000. The building had been acquired on 1 May 1994 for £200,000.

(3) On 1 July 2010 it sold 5 acres of a 15 acre piece of land for £50,000. The company had acquired the land for £10,000 on 1 April 2003. On 1 July 2010 the remaining 10 acres of the car park were valued at £120,000.

You are required to calculate the chargeable gains to be included in the company's corporation tax computation for the year ending 30 September 2010 in respect of the above transactions.

1.9 Angel Ltd, an unquoted trading company, prepares accounts to 31 December each year.

On 1 September 2007 Angel Ltd had purchased 20% of the shares in Scooby Ltd, an unquoted trading company for £17,000. On 1 November 2009 it had sold a 14% holding and it sold the remainder of the shares for £42,800 on 1 August 2010.

On 1 August 2010 Angel Ltd sold a factory for £1,850,000. It had purchased the factory in May 2000 for £575,000. On 1 June 2010 Angel Ltd had purchased a replacement factory in a less expensive area for £1,225,000.

You are required to calculate the company's total chargeable gains for its year ended 31 December 2010 and to state the base cost of the factory purchased on 1 June 2010 assuming all possible reliefs are claimed.

1.10 Specialty Suds Ltd prepares accounts to 30 September each year.

During the year ended 30 September 2010 it had the following capital transactions:

11 November 2009	Machinery purchased	£57,500
6 December 2009	Machinery sold (original cost £22,000)	£12,000
2 April 2010	Car purchased for employee (CO_2 emissions 152g/km)	£9,500
16 April 2010	Equipment purchased	£20,000

The tax written down value of the main pool at 1 October 2009 was £68,000 and of the long life asset pool was £119,000.

You are required to calculate the capital allowances available to Specialty Suds Ltd for the year ended 30 September 2010.

1.11 Seedy Ltd changed its accounting date and had the following results for the 8 month period ending 30 November 2010:

	£
Trading profit	910,000
Profit on non-trading loan relationships	40,000
Chargeable gains	32,000
Exempt dividends received from non-associated companies	22,500

Seedy Ltd paid tax at the main rate for its year ended 31 March 2010.

You are required to state the due date(s) for payment of the company's corporation tax liability for the 8 months ended 31 December 2010 and the amount(s) due.

2.1 Iron Ltd, a large company as defined for R&D purposes, spent £200,000 on qualifying research and development in the year to 31 March 2011. Tax adjusted trading profits before deducting any amount for research and development expenditure are £1,300,000 for the year.

Lead Ltd, a small company as defined for R&D purposes, spent £6,000 on qualifying research and development during the year to March 2011. Tax adjusted trading profits for the year before deducting any amount for research and development expenditure are £80,000.

You are required to:

(a) **Calculated the taxable trading profits, after relief for research and development expenditure for both Iron Ltd and Lead Ltd for the year to 31 March 2011.**

(b) **Give three examples of the type of revenue expenditure which qualifies for research and development relief.**

2.2 Plate Ltd buys goodwill for £50,000 on 1 May 2010. £5,000 is written off immediately to the profit and loss account. The goodwill is sold on 1 December 2010 for £65,000.

You are required to calculate the profit arising on the sale of the goodwill and to state how much of the gain will be eligible for rollover relief.

2.3 Muxton Ltd has charged the following items in arriving at its net profit per the accounts for the year ended 31 March 2011:

	£
Goodwill acquired 1 August 2008 written off	5,000
Interest on late payment of corporation tax (AP ended 31.3.09).	1,000
Interest payable on loan taken out to acquire machinery	10,000
Interest payable on loan taken out to acquire a rental property	8,000

You are required to explain how the above items will be treated in the company's corporation tax computation for the year ended 31 March 2011.

2.4 A Inc is incorporated overseas. In the year to 31 March 2011 it had tax adjusted trading income of £1,200,750 arising from its operations in the UK and tax adjusted trading income of £250,000 arising from its overseas manufacturing plants. Its only other income was a dividend of £50,000 it received from an overseas company in which it owns a 5% holding and rental income of £9,000 in respect of an overseas property .

15% withholding tax was suffered on both the dividend and rental income.

You are required to:

(a) **State the rules for determining whether A Inc will be regarded as UK resident.**

(b) **Assuming that A Inc is UK resident calculate its UK corporation tax liability for the year to 31 March 2011.**

Assume that the foreign dividend is an exempt dividend for UK corporation tax purposes.

2.5 B Inc, is incorporated overseas. It is wholly owned by a company resident overseas. On 1 January 2010 B Inc transferred its central management and control from the UK to Switzerland.

The company owned two chargeable assets as at the date of migration. The first was a factory situated in the UK, which was acquired for £200,000 in April 2003. The company continued to operate from this factory until 1 March 2011 when it was sold for £800,000. The market value of the factory on 1 January 2010 was £700,000.

The second asset was a factory in Switzerland, which was acquired on 1 June 2009 for £600,000. Its market value on 1 January 2010 was £900,000 and it was sold on 1 June 2011 for £1,100,000.

You are required to explain the UK corporation tax implications of the above events.

2.6 Bronco Ltd, a small company as defined for R&D purposes, had a trading loss of £200,000 and property income of £18,000 for the year ended 31 March 2011.

During December 2010 it spent £120,000 on qualifying research and development and its PAYE bill for the year was £26,000.

You are required to calculate Bronco Ltd's surrenderable loss and the R&D tax credit that the company may claim for the year to 31 March 2011. State the effect of the claim on the amount of any trading losses available to carry forward as at 31 March 2011.

2.7 Gerald Maine set up a company, Maine Ltd, on 1 December 2009 and commenced to trade on that date. He is the sole shareholder.

The company drew up its first accounts to 31 December 2010 and had the following results:

	£
Adjusted trading profits (before capital allowances)	156,000
Bank interest receivable	19,500
Loan interest payable (non trading)	13,000
Chargeable gain (disposal date 13 November 2010)	32,000

On 1 December 2009 the company acquired equipment for £55,000. On 1 December 2010 the company purchased a company car (CO_2 emissions 165g/km) for Gerald for £14,500 which he will use 40% of the time for private purposes.

Maine Ltd made a donation to charity under the Gift Aid scheme on 1 January 2010 of £10,000.

You are required to calculate the taxable total profits chargeable to corporation tax in respect of the period to 31 December 2010

2.8 Monulife Ltd makes up its accounts to 31 December each year.

In the year to 31 December 2010, Monulife Ltd received and paid the following:

	£
Bank interest	25
Repayment interest from HMRC on overpaid tax	157
Interest paid on bank loan taken out to acquire an investment property	3,250
Debenture interest paid	50,000

At 31 December 2010 there was interest accrued but not yet received on the bank account of £1,250.

Monulife Ltd had issued the debentures on 1 August 2007 to raise money to purchase equipment for the business. The amounts of interest paid are the amounts shown in the accounts.

You are required to calculate the taxable trading profit and the profit/deficit on non-trading loan relationships figures for Monulife Ltd for the year ended 31 December 2010

2.9 Amiable Ltd has the following income during its year ended 31 March 2011:

	£
Taxable trading profits	530,000
Chargeable gain	124,750
Profit on non-trading loan relationships	26,225
Rental income from overseas property (net of 25% tax)	250,000

It made a donation of £25,000 under the gift aid scheme on 21 January 2010.

You are required to calculate Amiable Ltd's corporation tax liability for the year ended 31 March 2011, stating the amount of double taxation relief available.

3.1 Alter Ltd owns a house which is let furnished at a rent of £1,500 per quarter payable in advance.

During the year ended 31 March 2011 Alter Ltd received the following rents:

	£
10 April 2010 – arrears of rent due on 31 March 2010	800
30 June 2010 – quarter commencing 1 July 2010	1,500
30 Sept 2010 – quarter commencing 1 October 2010	1,500

The tenants left on 31 January 2011 without paying the rent due on 31 December. Alter Ltd was unable to recover this from them and therefore wrote off the debt in the accounts

During the year the following expenses were incurred:

	£
Agent's commission	360
Mortgage repayments (including interest of £500)	800
Council tax	1,100
	2,260

You are required to calculate Alter Ltd's taxable property income for the year to 31 March 2011. Explain your treatment of the mortgage repayments.

3.2 Staple Ltd owns two rental properties. In the year to 31 December 2010 the company received the following rents and incurred the following expenses in connection with the properties:

Property 1 Furnished flat

Rent: Rented from 1 April 2010 for an annual rent of £10,000 payable quarterly in advance. Previous tenants moved out on 31 December 2009

Expenses: Professional fees in preparing rental agreement £1,000
Decorating prior to new tenants moving in £2,000

Property 2 Unfurnished office

Rent: Acquired 1 October 2010 and rented from 1 December 2010 for £15,000 per annum payable monthly in advance.

Expenses: Agent's fees £5,500
Insurance premium for the year to 30 September 2011 £1,500.

During the year to 31 December 2010 the company also had tax adjusted trading profits of £250,000 and chargeable gains of £8,000.

You are required to calculate Staple Ltd's taxable total profits for the year to 31 December 2010.

3.3 During the year to 31 December 2010 Aspen Ltd received the following income:

(1) Received a premium of £60,000 from Fairmount Ltd for the grant of a 25 year lease on an office property.

(2) Received a dividend from a Real Estate Investment Trust of £20,000 on 1 June 2010.

You are required to explain how the above income will be treated for corporation tax purposes in the tax computations of Aspen Ltd for the year to 31 December 2010.

3.4 Ghost Ltd received the following income during its year ended 31 December 2010:

	£
Rental income from 245 Main Street	30,000
Rental income from 134 George Street	18,720
Lease premium in respect of new 15 year lease of George St property	60,000

The company incurred expenses of £1,765 in connection with the Main Street property, which is let furnished, including £1,650 for council tax. It also incurred expenses of £3,000 in connection with the George Street property, which is let unfurnished.

Ghost Ltd's total annual interest payments in respect of both properties were as follows:

	£
245 Main Street	5,265
134 George Street	3,125

Ghost Ltd also received dividends of £33,750 from a REIT. The dividends were paid out of the REIT's tax exempt income.

You are required to calculate the company's taxable property income for the year ended 31 December 2010.

4.1 Tunbridge Ltd has the following results:

Year ended	*31 December 2007*	*31 December 2008*	*31 December 2009*	*31 December 2010*
	£	£	£	£
Trading profit/(loss)	5,000	1,500	(10,000)	500
Interest received	1,500	500	2,000	1,000

The amount of interest received is the same as the amount accrued for each period.

The company claims relief for the loss sustained in 31 December 2009 as early as possible.

You are required to calculate the taxable total profits, after loss relief, for each of the above periods, and state the amount, if any, of unused losses carried forward at 31 December 2010. State by when the appropriate loss relief elections must be made.

4.2 Green Ltd has the following results for the year ended 31 March 2011:

	£
Trading income	175,000
Profit on non-trading loan relationships	30,000
Capital gains	20,000
Gift Aid donation paid (gross)	10,000
Exempt dividend received	15,000

The amount of interest received is the same as the amount accrued for the period. Green Ltd has no associated companies.

The company has trading losses brought forward of £210,000 and capital losses brought forward of £30,000.

You are required to calculate Green Ltd's corporation tax liability for the year ended 31 March 2011 and state the amount, if any, of unrelieved losses carried forward.

4.3 Montrelle Ltd has the following results for the three accounting periods to 31 December 2010:

Year ended:	*31.12.08*	*31.12.09*	*31.12.10*
	£	£	£
Trading profit/(loss)	490,000	(550,000)	150,000
Property income	28,000	15,000	18,000
Chargeable gain	-	9,000	-
Qualifying charitable donation – Gift Aid	5,000	10,000	10,000

You are required to show the taxable total profits for all years assuming that losses are set off under S. 37(3) Corporation Tax Act 2010. Ignore the temporary extended loss carry back provisions of Finance Act 2009.

4.4 Tanui Ltd had always prepared accounts to 31 December until 2010 when it changed its accounting date to 30 June and prepared a six month set of accounts to 30 June 2010. On 30 June 2011 the company ceased to trade. The company has had the following results in recent accounting periods:

	Year to 31.12.07	*Year to 31.12.08*	*Year to 31.12.09*	*6 mths to 30.6.10*	*Year to 30.6.11*
	£	£	£	£	£
Trading profit/(loss)	350,000	300,000	290,000	100,000	(950,000)
Bank interest income	12,000	10,000	18,000	5,000	2,000
Capital gain/(loss)	(10,000)	-	5,000	-	20,000
Qualifying charitable donation – Gift Aid	8,000	8,000	8,000	4,000	-

You are required to show the taxable total profits for all years assuming that losses are set off as soon as possible. Ignore the temporary extended loss carry back provisions of Finance Act 2009.

4.5 Mott Ltd commenced to trade on 1 April 2009 and has had the following results in recent accounting periods:

	Year to 31.3.10	*Year to 31.3.11*
	£	£
Trading profits/(loss)	400,000	(80,000)
Bank interest income	20,000	8,000

The company is forecasting to make a profit of £100,000 in the year to 31 March 2012.

You are required to explain the loss relief options available to Mott Ltd and advise the company which option would be the most beneficial. Assume that tax rates for Financial year 2010 continue into the future.

4.6 Morvel Ltd, a highstreet retailer, has had the following results in recent accounting periods:

	Year to 31.10.09	*Year to 31.10.10*
	£	£
Trading profit/(loss)	50,000	(180,000)
Bank interest income	5,000	2,000

On 1 March 2011 100% of the company's share capital was acquired by Amble Ltd, a UK trading company. Amble Ltd has considerable expertise in internet selling. Consequently after the acquisition 85% of Morvel Ltd's customers were obtained via the company's new website. Prior to the acquisition all sales had been made via highstreet retail stores. As a consequence of the change in selling method Morvel Ltd is forecasting to make a trading profit of £120,000 in the year to 31 October 2011.

You are required to explain the loss relief options available to Morvel Ltd.

4.7 Droma Ltd had the following results for the accounting periods to 31 March 2011.

	Y/e 31.10.06	*Y/e 31.10.07*	*Y/e 31.10.08*	*Y/e 31.10.09*	*Y/e 31.10.10*
	£	£	£	£	£
Trading profits	45,000	60,000	41,000	55,000	(177,000)
Gains	10,000	–	2,000	–	15,000
Property income	5,000	7,000	4,000	16,000	32,000

You are required to explain how the trading losses could be utilised assuming Droma Ltd wishes to claim any loss relief as early as possible and compute the taxable total profits for all the above periods.

4.8 Cassel Ltd commenced to trade on 1 January 2010 and made up its first accounts to 31 December 2010. In 2011 it changed its year end to 31 March.

It has had the following trading results:

	£
y/e 31.12.10	88,000
p/e 31.3.11	24,500
y/e 31.3.12	(195,000)
y/e 31.3.13 (est)	116,000

Its only other income each year was £20,000 of interest income. It makes an annual gift aid donation of £10,000 on 1 June each year.

You are required to:

(1) State how much loss is used in each relevant year assuming relief is taken as early as possible.

(2) Calculate the loss carried forward at 31 March 2012.

(3) State whether the loss, if any, can be set against taxable total profits or trading profits only in the year ended 31 March 2013.

5.1 Holding Ltd owns 100% of the ordinary share capital of Sub Ltd and there are no other companies in the group. Both companies have traded for several years. In the two years ended 31 March 2010 and 2011, the companies' tax adjusted trading profits and losses were

	2010	*2011*
	£	£
Holding Ltd	109,000	(119,000)
Sub Ltd	95,000	268,000

You are required to explain how the loss of Holding Ltd should be utilised to maximise the group tax saving and to state the order in which the claims should be made.

5.2 Mr Phillips owns shares in the following UK resident companies:

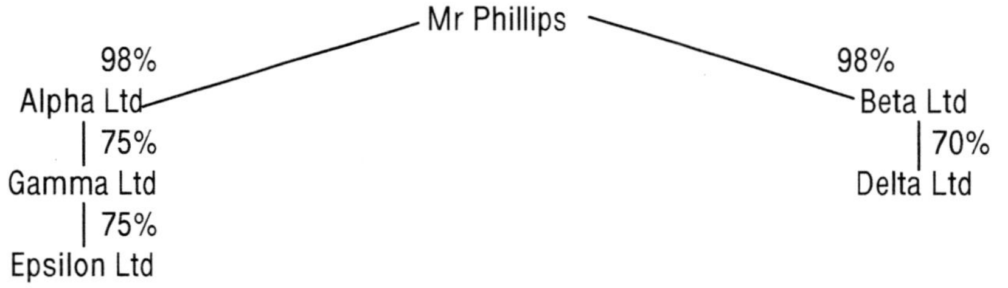

You are required to state which companies are associated with Alpha Ltd and which are within the same group for group relief and chargeable gains purposes.

5.3 James Ltd is a UK resident company and a member of a group. For the year to 30 September 2010, it has made profits of £700,000, and the group agrees that James Ltd should claim as much group relief as possible from other group companies. The following information is available about the other group companies:

(1) Edward Ltd is the parent company, and is an investment company. For the year ended 30 September 2010, its tax computations show:

	£
Chargeable gains	5,000
Management expenses	(20,000)

(2) Gordon Ltd joined on 1 January 2010, and has an accounting date of 31 March. In its year to 31 March 2010, its tax adjusted trading losses were £80,000. It was profit making in the year to 31 March 2011.

You are required to calculate the maximum amount of group relief which can be claimed by James Ltd.

5.4 Wind Ltd and Sail Ltd, its 85% owned subsidiary, prepare accounts to 31 March. In February 1994 Wind Ltd bought an asset for £80,000 and sold it to Sail Ltd in June 2010 for its market value of £200,000. On 1 April 2011 Sail Ltd sold the asset to an unconnected company for £300,000.

You are required to explain how the sale in June 2010 will be treated for corporation tax purposes and to calculate the chargeable gain arising on the sale on 1 April 2011.

5.5 Force Ltd owns 80% of the shares of Power Ltd. Force Ltd had acquired the 80% holding for £450,000 in April 2008. Both companies are UK resident trading companies with 31 March year ends.

On 1 June 2009 Force Ltd sold a factory to Power Ltd for £200,000 when its market value was £500,000. Force Ltd had acquired the factory on 1 June 2003 for £80,000.

On 1 March 2011 Force Ltd sold a 15% holding in Power Ltd to an unconnected company for £200,000.

You are required to explain, with calculations, the corporation tax implications of the above transactions. Ignore the gain, if any, arising on the sale of shares in Power Ltd.

5.6 Overseas Ltd is a company resident in Overseasland. It is owned 65% by Expansion Ltd, a company incorporated in the UK and 35% by Mr Offshore, who is non-UK resident.

The rate of corporation tax in Overseasland is 8%.

Overseas Ltd has not paid any dividends in the year to 31 March 2011.

You are required to explain with reasons how, if at all, the profits of Overseas Ltd will be taxed in the UK.

5.7 Tweet Ltd has the following shareholdings:

Pounce Ltd	100%
Feeder Ltd	90%

Feeder Ltd owns 80% of the shares in Booker Ltd.

The companies' results for the year ended 31 March 2011 are as follows:

	Tweet	*Pounce*	*Feeder*	*Booker*
	£	£	£	£
Trading (profit/ loss)	875,000	(145,000)	189,000	21,000
Bank interest	12,000		8,000	400
Rental income		12,000		
Chargeable gains/ (loss)			65,000	(25,000)
Gift Aid payments	(25,000)	(2,500)	(12,000)	(1,000)

You are required to calculate the corporation tax payable by each company following any beneficial loss relief claims.

5.8 Chill Ltd has owned all of the share capital of Freeze Ltd since 15 May 2003 when it purchased the shares for £275,000. Both companies are unquoted trading companies and make up accounts to 31 December.

On 17 August 2010 Chill Ltd sold its entire holding in Freeze Ltd to an unconnected third party for £899,999.

On 21 April 2005 Chill Ltd had transferred a property to Freeze Ltd when its market value was £425,000. The property had originally cost Chill Ltd £219,000 in June 2000 and it was valued at £687,000 in August 2010.

You are required to calculate, in connection with the sale of the Freeze Ltd shares:

(1) The gain arising for Chill Ltd.

(2) The gain arising for Freeze Ltd.

You should assume that Freeze Ltd does not take any steps to mitigate its tax position in August 2010.

5.9 Sand Ltd has owned the whole of the share capital of Pebble Ltd for a number of years. On 1 March 2011 Sand Ltd transferred a capital asset to Pebble Ltd when its value was £80,000. Sand Ltd had acquired the asset for £50,000. The asset is treated as trading stock by Pebble Ltd and will be sold to an unconnected third party for £90,000.

You are required to explain how these transactions will be treated for corporation tax purposes, assuming all beneficial elections are made.

6.1 **You are required to explain how the following are treated for companies whose business consists wholly of making investments.**

(1) Incidental cost of raising loan finance
(2) Contributions to a training and enterprise council
(3) Accountants fees for preparation of annual accounts
(4) Capital allowances in respect of let properties
(5) Payment to registered occupational pension scheme.

6.2 Moriarty Ltd has one wholly owned subsidary Watson Ltd.

Watson Ltd results for the year ended 31 March 2011 were as follows:

	Moriarty Ltd	*Watson Ltd*
	£	£
Trading profit	–	90,000
Expenses of management	(300,000)	–
Capital gain	–	10,000
Qualifying charitable donations	–	(30,000)

Moriarty Ltd's expenses of management include £220,000 brought forward.

You are required to calculate how much group relief Watson Ltd can claim.

6.3 Carp Ltd, a company whose business consists wholly of making investments, had the following results for the year ended 31 December 2010:

	£
Rental income	300,000
Interest income	50,000
Management expenses:	
– Re property management	65,000
– General expenses	15,000
Interest payable re rental properties	22,000
Chargeable gains	264,000

The interest payable is in respect of loans taken out to fund the acquisition of rental properties.

Carp Ltd had unrelieved expenses of management of £25,000 as at 31 December 2009.

You are required to compute the taxable total profits for the year to 31 December 2010.

6.4 Albert owns all of the share capital of Sledge Consulting Ltd and works full-time for the company.

He was employed by Apollo plc as an IT manager until 1 March 2010 when he left the company and set up Sledge Consulting Ltd.

In 2010/11 Albert received a salary of £6,000 from Sledge Consulting Ltd on which employer's NIC of £36 was paid. He was also reimbursed business related travel expenses of £477. In addition Sledge Consulting Ltd paid £2,000 into a registered pension scheme for Albert.

In the year to 5 April 2011 Sledge Consulting Ltd received income of £85,000 from Apollo plc for IT consultancy services and £5,000 from sundry other clients.

You are required to calculate the deemed employment payment made to Albert on 5 April 2011.

6.5 The following is a summary of the main points arising from a telephone conversation you have recently had with one of your clients, Robert Archer.

1. Until recently he was employed as a proof reader by Robin Publications plc.
2. Robert has decided to resign from his employment on 6 April 2011 and set up a company, Archer Ltd, wholly owned by him, which will provide proofing reading services.
3. Robert is expecting that 80% of the company's income will be from services provided to Robin Publications plc.
4. Robert is planning to take a small annual salary of approximately £7,000 out of the company. Any other income that he receives from the company will be in the form of dividends.

You are required to briefly outline how the personal service companies legislation will affect Robert's plans.

6.6 Cheryl worked for five years at Argonaut Plc, an information technology (IT) firm.

She left Argonaut Ltd on 31 December 2009 and set up her own IT consultancy firm, Cherub Consulting Ltd, on 1 April 2010. She is the sole shareholder and the managing director.

In the year ended 31 March 2011, Cherub Consulting Ltd received £65,000 for a number of contracts completed for Argonaut Plc, on their premises, using Argonaut Plc's equipment.

Cherub Consulting Ltd also received £20,000 from other single-contract clients.

Cheryl receives a monthly salary of £1,000 from Cherub Consulting Ltd, on which £804 of employer's NIC was paid. The company also paid £5,000 into Cheryl's personal pension and reimbursed £1,250 of travel expenses.

Cherub Consulting Ltd incurred a further £3,600 of allowable business expenses in the year. It received no other income during the year.

HMRC has confirmed that the company is caught by the IR35 provisions.

You are required to calculate Cheryl's deemed employment payment for 5 April 2011 and the company's taxable total profits for the year ended 31 March 2011.

6.7 Investalot Ltd, a non-trading company, is owned equally by Mr and Mrs Drake.

During its year ended 31 December 2010 it had the following results:

	£
Rental income	150,000
Chargeable gains	14,000
Interest	3,500
Dividends	119,000
Management expenses:	
Property management	41,040
General	68,000
Capital allowances:	
In connection with the property	1,500
General	2,225
Gift aid donation	15,000

Investalot Ltd had no unrelieved expenses of management brought forward at 1 January 2010.

In addition to the disposal that gave rise to the chargeable gain above, Investalot Ltd also sold its entire holding of 200,000 £1 shares in Enterprise Ltd for £120,000 on 14 May 2010. It had purchased the shares on 1 June 2006 at par. There are 1.5 million shares issued.

You are required to calculate Investalot Ltd's corporation tax liability for the year ended 31 December 2010 assuming any beneficial claims are made.

7.1 Jasmine Ltd prepares accounts to 31 December each year.

Its corporation tax liability for the year to 31 December 2009 was £2,600,000.

Its budgeted corporation tax liability for the year to 31 December 2010 was £3,400,000. Its actual corporation tax liability for the year ended 31 December 2010 was £3,550,000.

The company made the following payments on account of its corporation tax liability for the year to 31 December 2010:

	£
14 July 2010	650,000
14 October 2010	1,050,000
14 January 2011	850,000
14 April 2011	850,000
1 October 2011	150,000
	3,550,000

You are required to state how any interest charges will be calculated in respect of the tax liability for the year ended 31 December 2010.

7.2 New Venture Ltd commenced to trade on 1 April 2010 and prepared its first set of accounts for the 9 months to 31 December 2010.

In the 9 months to 31 December 2010 the company had a tax adjusted trading profit of £210,000 and a profit on non-trading loan relationships of £10,000. It received dividends of £10,000 from a 10% holding of ordinary shares in a UK company..

You are required to:

(a) **Calculate New Venture Ltd's corporation tax liability for the 9 month period to 31 December 2010 and state when it is payable.**

(b) **State by when the company's tax return for the period to 31 December 2010 must be submitted.**

7.3 Taranaki Ltd prepared accounts to 31 December each year until 2010 when it changed its accounting date and prepared a 7 month set of accounts to 31 July 2010.

The company's taxable total profits were £2,000,000 in the year to 31 December 2009 and £950,000 in the 7 months to 31 July 2010. The company did not receive any dividend income in either of the accounting periods.

You are required to state when Taranaki Ltd should pay its corporation tax liability for the 7 month period to 31 July 2010 in order to avoid any interest charges accruing.

7.4 Brooke Ltd commenced to trade on 1 January 2010 and prepared its first set of accounts for the 14 month period to 28 February 2011.

The company's only income in the period was trading income of £150,000.

You are required to:

(a) **State the due dates for filing the tax return and paying the corporation tax liability in respect of the 14 month period to 28 February 2011.**

(b) **State the penalty which would be payable if Brooke Ltd submitted a tax return 8 months late.**

7.5 Dynamo Ltd commenced trading on 1 October 2009 and prepared its first set of accounts for the 15 month period to 31 December 2010.

Its results for the period to 31 December 2010 were as follows:

	£
Trading profit	3,000,000
Chargeable gain	500,000

The chargeable gain arose on the sale of a piece of land on 1 December 2010.

You are required to:

(a) **Calculate Dynamo Ltd's corporation tax liability for the 15 month period to 31 December 2010.**

(b) **State when the corporation tax liability for the period should be paid by Dynamo Ltd to avoid interest charges accruing.**

Solutions to exam style questions

1.1 **Buttercup Ltd**

Buttercup Ltd has 3 associated companies.

Include companies bought and sold during the period.

Include non-resident companies.

FY10: Upper limit $\frac{1,500,000}{4} = 375,000$

Lower limit $\frac{300,000}{4} = 75,000$

	£
Taxable total profits	70,000
FII (8,000 × 100/90)	8,889
	78,889
CT: 70,000 × 28%	19,600
7/400 (375,000 – 78,889) × $\frac{70,000}{78,889}$	(4,598)
	15,002

1.2 **Cal Limited**

Cal Limited is associated with Dal Limited

Upper limit 1,500,000/2 = 750,000 Lower limit 300,000/2 = 150,000

	£
TTP	600,000
FII (90,000 × 100/90) (Exclude dividend from associate)	100,000
Augmented profits	700,000
FY09 (6m) and FY10 (6m): Rates and small profits limits are the same	
£600,000 × 28%	168,000
7/400 × (750,000 – 700,000) × $\frac{600,000}{700,000}$	(750)
Liability	167,250

Note. 2 associated companies in the group.

1.3 **Max Ltd**

Corporation tax computation – 9 months to 31 December 2010

	£
Trading income	62,000
Property income	10,000
Profit on non-trading loan relationships (23,000 + 5,000)	28,000
Chargeable gain	9,000
Less QCDs: Gift Aid	(2,000)
Taxable total profits	107,000
£107,000 × 21%	22,470

FY10 rates and limits apply:

Upper limit $\frac{1,500,000}{2} \times 9/12 = 562,500$

Lower limit $\frac{300,000}{2} \times 9/12 = 112,500$

1.4 **Histon plc**

Corporation tax – 15 months to 30 June 2011

	12m to 31.3.11	*3m to 30.6.11*
	£	£
Trading income (W1)	14,800	29,040
Gain	20,000	–
Qualifying charitable donation: Gift aid	–	(8,000)
Taxable total profits	34,800	21,040

(W1) Trading profit

	12m to 31.3.11	*3m to 30.6.11*
	£	£
Tax adjusted profits before capital allowance (12.3)	122,400	30,600
Capital allowances (W2)	(107,600)	(1,560)
Tax adjusted trading profit	14,800	29,040

(W2) Capital allowances computation

	FYA	*Main pool*	*Special rate pool*	*Allowances*
	£	£	£	£
Year ended 31.3.11				
TWDV at 1.4.10		20,000		
Additions qualifying for AIA:				
Machine		110,000		
AIA max £100,000		(100,000)		100,000
		30,000		
Other additions:				
Special rate car			16,000	
WDA @ 20%		(6,000)		6,000
WDA @ 10%			(1,600)	1,600
TWDV cfwd		24,000	14,400	
Total allowances				107,600
3 months ended 30.6.11				
WDA @ 20%/10% x 3/12		(1,200)	(360)	1,560
TWDV cfwd		22,800	14,040	
Total allowances				1,560

1.5 **Ramble Ltd**

(a) **Accounting periods:**

- 1 April 2009 to 31 March 2010 – starts on commencement of trade and ends 12 months thereafter.
- 1 April 2010 to 30 April 2010 – starts after the end of the previous period and ends at the end of the company's period of account.
- 1 May 2010 to 30 April 2011 – starts after the end of the previous period and ends at the end of the company's period of account.

(b) **Capital allowances**

– *Car*

CO_2 emissions are less than 160g/km. It is therefore a main rate car and will enter the main capital allowances pool qualifying for WDAs at 20% per annum. As the car is owned by a company there is no restriction for private use by Robert. Robert will be assessed to employment income on the private use of the car.

Short life asset treatment is not available for cars.

– *Computer*

Cost of computer and software is eligible for the 100% Annual Investment Allowance in the year to 30 April 2011 up to a maximum of £100,000. The balance of £5,000 enters the main pool and is eligible for 20% WDA in the year to 30 April 2011. The remaining balance remains in the main pool and continues to receive WDAs at 20% in future years.

Short life asset treatment is available. However whether this treatment is beneficial depends on whether the company is expecting to dispose of the asset for less than its tax written down value, not its original cost. As the short life asset election does not need to be made until 30 April 2013 the company is likely to know whether it will be beneficial to make the election before the deadline for submitting the election.

1.6 **Overt Ltd**

Taxable trading income for the year ended 31 March 2011

	£	£
Profit before tax		5,423,000
Add back:		
Depreciation	65,000	
Lease premium	50,000	
Repairs (repair to part of building allowable)	-	
Professional fees re new lease (capital)	2,000	
Less:		
Lease premium allowable deduction (W1)	(700)	
Gain on sale of office building	(85,000)	
Bank interest (not trading income)	(48,000)	
Capital allowances	(95,000)	
		(111,700)
Taxable trading profit		5,311,300

(W1) Lease premium – allowable deduction

Amount assessable on landlord as property income:

$$£50,000 \times \frac{50 - 29}{50} = £21,000$$

	£
Allowable deduction:	
£21,000/30	700

1.7 **Mariner Ltd**

Capital allowances computation for the year to 31 December 2010

	FYA	*Main pool*	*Special rate pool*	*Short life asset (SLA)*	*Allowances*
	£	£	£	£	£
TWDV at 1.1.10		85,000		24,000	
Additions qualifying for AIA/40% FYA:					
Van	16,000				
AIA	(16,000)				16,000
Other additions:					
Special rate car			25,000		
Disposals:					
Computer		(10,000)			
Car		(4,000)			
		71,000	25,000	24,000	
WDA at 20%		(14,200)		(4,800)	19,000
WDA at 10%			(2,500)		2,500
TWDV c/f		56,800	22,500	19,200	
Total allowances					37,500

Note: Prior to 1 April 2009 cars costing ≤ £12,000 were allocated to the main pool. Disposals of these cars after 1 April 2009 are also dealt with through the main pool. It is more beneficial to claim the AIA on the van than the 40% FYA.

1.8 **Albatross Ltd**

Chargeable gains – year ending 30 September 2010

(1) **Sale of shares**

Albatross Ltd, trading company, has disposed of shares out of a substantial shareholding (10% or more) in a trading company, which it has held for 12 months in the previous two years. The gain is therefore exempt.

(2) **Office building**

	£
Proceeds	1,200,000
Less: Cost (1 May 1994)	(200,000)
Unindexed gain	1,000,000
Less indexation allowance	
(225.0 – 144.7)/144.7 = 0.555 × £200,000	(111,000)
Indexed gain	889,000

(3) **Land**

	£
Proceeds	50,000
Less: Cost (April 2003)	
$£10,000 \times \dfrac{£50,000}{£50,000 + £120,000}$	(2,941)
Unindexed gain	47,059
Less indexation allowance	
(226.4 – 181.2)/181.2 = 0.249 × £2,941	(732)
Indexed gain	46,327
Total chargeable gains	935,327

1.9 **Angel Ltd**

The disposal of the shares in Scooby Ltd comes within the substantial shareholding exemption as Angel had held at least 10% for 12 months out of the last 2 years.

Factory

	£
Proceeds	1,850,000
Less: cost	(575,000)
Less: IA	
227.8-170.7/170.7 = 0.335 × £575,000	(192,625)
Gain	1,082,375
Less: rollover relief	(457,375)
Chargeable now (W)	625,000

Base cost of new factory

Cost	1,225,000
Less: rollover relief claimed	(457,375)
c/f	767,625

Working

Chargeable now = proceeds not reinvested

	£
Proceeds received	1,850,000
Less: proceeds spent	(1,225,000)
Chargeable now	625,000

1.10 **Speciality Suds Ltd**

1.10.09 – 30.9.10	*FYA*	*Main pool*	*LLA pool*	*Allowances*
	£	£	£	£
TWDV b/f		68,000	119,000	
Additions qualifying for AIA/40% FYA:				
11.11.09	57,500			
16.4.10 (no FYA)		20,000		
AIA Max (Note)	(50,000)	(20,000)		70,000
	7,500			
FYA at 40%	(3,000)			3,000
Addition (Cars):				
2.4.10 Main rate car		9,500		
Disposal 6.12.09		(12,000)		
		65,500	119,000	
WDA @ 20%		(13,100)		13,100
WDA @ 10%			(11,900)	11,900
Transfer to main pool	(4,500)	4,500		
c/f		56,900	107,100	
Total allowances				98,000

Note. The maximum AIA for the year ended 30 September 2010 is £75,000 ((£50,000 × 6/12) + (£100,000 × 6/12)). However a maximum of only £50,000 can be claimed in respect of expenditure incurred before 1 April 2010. The maximum AIA that Suds Ltd can claim is therefore £70,000 (£50,000 plus £20,000 (expenditure incurred after 1 April 2010)).

1.11 **Seedy Ltd**

	£
Trading profit	910,000
Profit on non-trading loan relationships	40,000
Chargeable gains	32,000
Taxable total profits (TTP)	982,000
Add FII £22,500 × 100/90	25,000
Augmented profits	1,007,000
Tax @ main rate (W)	
£982,000 × 28%	274,960

The tax must be paid by quarterly instalments. The due dates with the due amounts are as follows:

	Explanation	£
14.10.10	Month 7 of AP (3/8 × TTP)	103,110
14.01.11	3 months after 1st payment (3/8 × TTP)	103,110
14.03.11	4 months after end of AP (Balance)	68,740
Total		274,960

Working

The corporation tax limits for the 8 month period are:

£1,500,000 × 8/12 = £1,000,000

£300,000 × = £200,000

2.1 **Iron Ltd**

(a) *Iron Ltd –year ended 31.3.11*

	£
Adjusted trading profits before R & D relief	1,300,000
Less R&D relief £200,000 × 130%	(260,000)
Tax adjusted trading profits	1,040,000

Lead Ltd – year ended 31.3.11

	£
Adjusted trading profits before R & D relief	80,000
Less R&D Expenditure	(6,000)
Tax adjusted trading profits	74,000

Lead Ltd is not be able to claim the additional 75% relief as it did not spend at least £10,000 in the year.

(b) Allowable revenue expenditure. Any three of:

(i) Staff costs
(ii) Consumables
(iii) Computer software
(iv) Fuel, power and water

2.2 **Plate Ltd**

Plate Ltd will have an accounting profit on sale of goodwill of:

	£	£
Proceeds		65,000
Cost	50,000	
Written off	(5,000)	(45,000)
		20,000

The profit taken to the P&L account will be £20,000.

The profit available for rollover is found by comparing proceeds to cost and not taking account of any write offs.

Eligible for rollover	£
Proceeds	65,000
Cost	(50,000)
	15,000

2.3 **Muxton Ltd**

(i) The goodwill is an intangible asset which has been acquired for the purpose of the trade. Under the IFA rules the amount written off is an allowable deduction from trading profits.

(ii) The interest on late payment of corporation tax is a non-trade related payment of interest. Under the loan relationship rules it is a non-trading loan relationship debit and is not deductible from trading profits.

(iii) The interest on the loan to acquire machinery is a trade related payment of interest. It is an allowable trading deduction on an accrual basis.

(iv) The interest on the loan to acquire a rental property is a non-trade related payment on interest. It is an allowable non-trading loan relationship debit. It is not an allowable deduction from property income.

2.4 **A Inc**

(a) A Inc is incorporated overseas. It will be deemed UK resident if it is controlled and managed from the UK.

(b) *Corporation tax computation – Year ended 31 March 2011*

	£	£
Trading income:		
– UK trade	1,200,750	
– Overseas trade	250,000	
		1,450,750
Property income (£9,000 x 100/85)		10,588
Taxable total profits		1,461,338
FII (£50,000 x 100/90)		55,556
Augmented profits		1,516,894
Corporation tax payable @ 28%		409,175
Less DTR: Lower of:		
– UK tax (10,588 x 28%) = 2,965		
– Overseas tax = (10,588 x 15%) = 1,588		(1,588)
Corporation tax payable		407,587

Note: Exempt dividends from non-associated companies are included in FII. The amount received is grossed up by 100/90 (any overseas tax suffered is ignored).

2.5 **B Inc**

The company becomes non-UK resident when it transfers its central management and control overseas. On this date it is deemed to have disposed of and reacquired all of its chargeable assets at market value, thus giving rise to potential chargeable gains.

On 1 January 2010 a chargeable gain will arise on the factory situated in Switzerland calculated by reference to its market value at that date. When the factory is sold in June 2011 the company is not UK resident and no further chargeable gain will arise in the UK.

The factory situated in the UK continued to be used in a trade carried on in the UK for a period after migration. On 1 January 2010 there is no deemed disposal of the UK factory. The charge to tax is deferred until the factory is sold in March 2011. The gain on disposal is calculated in the usual way using sale proceeds and the original cost of the factory.

2.6 **Bronco Ltd**

Surrenderable loss

Lower of:

– Trading loss less amount set against other income £182,000 (200,000 – 18,000)

– 175% of R&D expenditure £210,000 (120,000 x 175%)
i.e. £182,000

R&D tax credit

Lower of:

– 14% of the surrenderable loss £25,480 (182,000 x 14%)
– PAYE bill of £26,000

The company can therefore claim £25,480.

Trading losses

The trading losses available to carry forward are reduced by £182,000, the amount of the surrenderable loss.

2.7 **Gerald Maine**

	1.12.09 – 30.11.10	1.12.10 – 31.12.10
	£	£
Adjusted profits before CAs (12:1)	144,000	12,000
Less: CAs (W1)	(52,000)	(170)
Adjusted trading profit	92,000	11,830
Profit on non-trade loan relationship (W2) (12:1)	6,000	500
Chargeable gain	32,000	–
Less: QCD (Gift Aid)	(10,000)	
Taxable total profits	120,000	12,330

Workings

(1) CAs

	FYA	Main pool	Special rate car	Allowances
1.12.09 – 30.11.10	£	£	£	£
Acquisition qualifying for AIA/40% FYA:				
Equipment	55,000			
AIA (Note)	(50,000)			50,000
	5,000			
FYA @ 40%	(2,000)			2,000
Transfer to main pool	(3,000)	3,000		
		3,000		
Allowances				52,000
1.12.10 – 31.12.10				
Acquisition			14,500	
WDA @ 20% × 1/12		(50)		50
WDA @ 10% × 1/12			(120)	120
c/f		2,950	14,380	
Total allowances				170

Note. The maximum AIA for the year ended 30 November 2010 is £83,334 ((£50,000 × 4/12) + (£100,000 × 8/12)). However a maximum of only £50,000 can be claimed in respect of expenditure incurred before 1 April 2010. The maximum AIA that Suds Ltd can claim is therefore £50,000.

(2) Profit on non-trade loan relationship

	£
Interest receivable	19,500
Less: interest payable	(13,000)
	6,500

2.8 **Monulife Ltd**

Interest paid and receivable in connection with the trade is dealt with as trading items while that payable or receivable in connection with non-trade activities is dealt with under the 'loan relationship' rules.

Bank interest received and HMRC repayment interest are always income from non-trading loan relationships. The amount receivable, including any accruals, is the taxable amount.

The interest paid on the loan taken out to acquire the investment property also relates to a non-trading loan relationship, so is netted off against any income on non-trading loan relationships, while the debenture interest is paid in respect of a trading loan relationship, so is taken as a trading deduction.

	£
Bank interest £(25 + 1,250)	1,275
Repayment interest from HMRC on overpaid tax	157
Less: interest on loan to acquire property	(3,250)
Deficit on non-trading loan relationships	(1,818)
Trading deduction: debenture interest	(50,000)

Note: The figures shown in the accounts include any relevant accruals and are the figures also used for tax purposes.

2.9 **Amiable Ltd**

Rental income from an overseas property is taxed as property income. It is included in the computation gross and double taxation relief is available being the lower of the UK and the overseas tax suffered.

	Total	*UK*	*Overseas*
	£	£	£
Taxable trading profits	530,000	530,000	
Chargeable gain	124,750	124,750	
Profit on non-trading loan relationships	26,225	26,225	
Property income from overseas property net of 25% tax)			
£250,000 × 100/75	333,333		333,333
Less: QCD (Gift Aid)	(25,000)	(25,000)	
Taxable total profits (TTP)	989,308	655,975	333,333
TTP @ 28%	277,006	183,673	93,333
Less: marginal relief (< £1.5m, > £300,000)			
7/400 × £(1,500,000 – 989,308)	(8,937)	(5,926)	(3,011)
CT liability	268,069	177,747	90,322
Less: DTR			
Lower of			
(i) UK tax : £90,322			
(ii) Overseas tax: 25% × £333,333 = £83,333	(83,333)		
CT due	184,736		

3.1 **Alter Ltd**

		£	£
Rent accrued: 1.4.10 – 31.1.11			
£6,000 × 10/12			5,000
Less bad debt relief			
£1,500 × 1/3			(500)
			4,500
Less expenses:	Commission	360	
	Council tax	1,100	
	Wear and tear (10% × (4,500 – 1,100)	340	(1,800)
Property income assessment			2,700

Interest on loans taken out to purchase let property is relieved as a non-trading loan relationship debit.

3.2 **Staple Ltd**

Corporation tax computation – Year ended 31 December 2010

	£
Trading profit	250,000
Chargeable gains	8,000
Total profits	258,000
Property business losses (W1)	(875)
Taxable total profits	257,125

(W1) Property business loss

	Property 1	*Property 2*	*Total*
	£	£	£
Rent:			
9/12 x £10,000	7,500		7,500
1/12 x £15,000		1,250	1,250
	7,500	1,250	8,750

Less expenses:			
Wear and tear allowance (£7,500 x 10%)	(750)		(750)
Professional/agent's fees	(1,000)	(5,500)	(6,500)
Decorating	(2,000)	–	(2,000)
Insurance £1,500 x 3/12	–	(375)	(375)
Profit/(loss)	3,750	(4,625)	(875)

3.3 **Aspen Ltd**

(1) Lease premium

As the premium is received in respect of the grant of a short lease part of the premium will be assessed as property income in the year ended 31 December 2010.

Amount assessable as property income:

$$£60{,}000 \times \frac{50 - 24}{50} = £31{,}200$$

(2) Dividend from Real Estate Investment Trust (REIT)

Dividends paid out of a REIT's property income and gains are taxed as property income and not as dividends. Income of (£20,000) will be assessed as property income in the year ended 31 December 2010 (income tax is not deducted from distributions paid to other UK companies).

If the dividend is paid out of the REIT's other income (not property income or gains) the income will be treated as normal dividend income and will be treated as an exempt dividend for corporation tax purposes.

3.4 **Ghost Ltd**

	£
245 Main Street	25,400
134 George Street	58,920
REIT dividends	33,750
Property income	118,070

Notes:

(1) The loan interest paid is dealt with under the loan relationship rules.

(2) REIT dividends are paid gross to companies and come with a basic rate tax credit when paid from the REIT's tax-exempt income.

Workings

(1) 245 Main St

	£
Income	30,000
Less: expenses	(1,765)
Less: Wear & tear allowance (30,000 – 1,650) @ 10%	(2,835)
Property income	25,400

(2) *134 George St*

	£	£
Income	18,720	
Less: expenses	(3,000)	
Rental income		15,720
Add: premium assessable as property income		
$£60,000 \times \frac{50-14}{50} =$		43,200
Total property income		58,920

4.1 **Tunbridge Ltd**

	y/e 31.12.07	*y/e 21.12.08*	*y/e 31.12.09*	*y/e 31.12.10*
	£	£	£	£
Trading income	5,000	1,500	Nil	500
Profit on non-trading loan relationship	1,500	500	2,000	1,000
	6,500	2,000	2,000	1,500
S.37 (3) – CY			(2,000)	
S.37 (3) – PY		(2,000)		–
FA09 extended carry back	(6,000)			
Taxable total profits	500	Nil	Nil	1,500
Loss memo:				
Trading loss – y.e 31.12.09				10,000
Current year offset				(2,000)
				8,000
Carry back				(2,000)
Extended loss carry back				(6,000)
Carried forward at 31 December 2010				-

The loss relief elections must be submitted by 31/12/11. There are no losses to carry forward as at 31 December 2009.

4.2 **Green Ltd**

	£	£
Trading income		175,000
Loss carried forward (s 45(4))		(175,000)
		–
Profit on non-trading loan relationship		30,000
Gains	20,000	
Capital losses b/f	(20,000)	–
Gift Aid		(10,000)
Taxable total profits		20,000
FII (15,000 × 10/9)		16,667
Augmented profits		36,667
Corporation tax payable		
£20,000 × 21%		4,200
Trading losses carried forward (210,000 – 175,000)		35,000
Capital losses carried forward (30,000 – 20,000)		10,000

4.3 Montrelle Ltd

Taxable total profits

Year ended	*31.12.08*	*31.12.09*	*31.12.10*
	£	£	£
Trading income	490,000	–	150,000
Losses bfwd against trading profits			(8,000)
Property income	28,000	15,000	18,000
Chargeable gain	–	9,000	–
Total profits	518,000	24,000	160,000
Loss offset against total profits:			
– CY		(24,000)	
– PY	(518,000)		
QCDs – Gift Aid	unrelieved	unrelieved	(10,000)
Taxable total profits	–	–	150,000

Loss memorandum

	£
Loss – y.e. 31.12.09	550,000
Offset against total profits:	
– CY – 31.12.09	(24,000)
– PY – 31.12.08	(518,000)
	8,000
Carried forward against trading profits:	
– y.e.31.12.10	(8,000)
	–

4.4 Tanui Ltd

Taxable total profits

	Year to 31.12.07	*Year to 31.12.08*	*Year to 31.12.09*	*6 mths to 30.6.10*	*Year to 30.6.11*
	£	£	£	£	£
Trading income	350,000	300,000	290,000	100,000	–
Profit on non-trading loan relationship	12,000	10,000	18,000	5,000	2,000
Chargeable gain (20,000 – 5,000)	–	–	–	–	15,000
Total profits	362,000	310,000	308,000	105,000	17,000
Loss offset against total profits:					
– CY					(17,000)
– PY – 3 years	(181,000)	(310,000)	(308,000)	(105,000)	
QCDs – Gift Aid	(8,000)	wasted	wasted	wasted	–
Taxable total profits	173,000	–	–	–	–

Loss memorandum

		£
Loss – y.e. 30.6.11		950,000
Offset against total profits:		
– CY	– 30.6.11	(17,000)
– PY	– 30.6.10	(105,000)
	– 31.12.09	(308,000)
	– 31.12.08	(310,000)
	– 31.12.07 (6 mths)	(181,000)
Losses unrelieved		29,000

4.5 **Mott Ltd**

Loss relief options

(1) Relief against total profits of year ended 31 March 2011 followed by a carryback claim to 31 March 2010.

This would save tax at the small profits rate (21%) in the current year and at the small profits marginal rate (29.75%) in the prior year. It would also result in a tax repayment in respect of the year ended 31 March 2010.

(2) Relief against total profits of the current year and carry the balance forward against trading profits in the year ended 31 March 2012.

This would save tax at the small profits rate (21%) in both years and there would be a delay in obtaining relief for most of the loss until year ended 31 March 2012.

(3) Carry forward losses against trading profits in the year ended 31 March 2012.

This would save tax at the small profits rate (21%).

Recommendation

Option (1) is most beneficial as it saves the most tax and obtains relief as soon as possible.

4.6 **Morvel Ltd**

Loss relief options

(1) Offset against total profit of year ended 31 October 2010 and carry back to offset against total profits of prior year. Remaining losses are carried forward against future trading profits (see comments below).

(2) Offset against total profit of year ended 31 October 2010 and carry back to offset against total profits of previous three years under the temporary loss carry back relief in Finance Act 2009, if there are profits available to offset (not known from question). The offset in two earlier years is restricted to a maximum of £50,000. Remaining losses are carried forward against future trading profits (see comments below).

(3) Offset against total profit of year ended 31 October 2010 and carry forward against future trading profits.

It is likely however that there has been a major change in the conduct of the company's trade, due to the change in the method of selling the company's products. As this has occurred within 3 years of a change in ownership of the company the losses arising before the change in ownership cannot be carried forward to offset trading profits arising after the date of change in ownership. The losses can therefore only be offset against trading profits arising in the 4 months to 28 February 2011 i.e. £120,000 x 4/12.

(4) Carry forward against first available trading profits. This option is also subject to the change in ownership point set out in point (3).

4.7 **Droma Ltd**

As the loss arises in an accounting period ending between 24 November 2008 and 23 November 2010 it can be carried back against total profits (before deducting any qualifying charitable donations) of the previous three years, subject to a maximum offset in the earlier two years of £50,000.

	Y/e 31.10.06	Y/e 31.10.07	Y/e 31.10.08	Y/e 31.10.09	Y/e 31.10.10
	£	£	£	£	£
Trading profits	45,000	60,000	41,000	55,000	–
Gains	10,000	–	2,000	–	15,000
Property income	5,000	7,000	4,000	16,000	32,000
	60,000	67,000	47,000	71,000	47,000
CY					(47,000)
PY				(71,000)	
Extended c/b		(3,000)	(47,000)		
Taxable total profits	60,000	64,000	–	–	–

Loss memorandum:	
Loss y/e 31.10.10	177,000
Less: current year	(47,000)
Less: prior year	(71,000)
Extended carry back claim:	
C/b to 31.10.08	(47,000)
C/b to 31.10.07 (Max £50,000 - £47,000)	(3,000)
Loss to c/f	9,000

4.8 **Cassel Ltd**

To carry a trading loss back, the company must first claim to set the loss against its current year income, even if this wastes a gift aid donation (as it does here).

The maximum loss that can be carried back to the year ended 31 December 2010 is the lower of the available loss and nine month's worth of the profits of that period, as the loss can only be carried back against a total of 12 months worth of profits.

	y/e 31.12.10	*p/e 31.3.11*	*y/e 31.3.12*
	£	£	£
Trading profits	88,000	24,500	
Profit on non-trading loan relationships	20,000	20,000	20,000
Total profits	108,000	44,500	20,000
Less: CY loss relief			(i) (20,000)
Less: CB loss relief	(iii) (81,000)	(ii) (44,500)	
Revised total profits	27,000	Nil	Nil
Less: QCD (Gift Aid)	(10,000)	*	*
Taxable total profits	17,000	Nil	Nil

* Gift Aid is wasted

Loss memo

		£
Loss of y/e 31.3.12		195,000
(i) CY		(20,000)
(ii) p/e 31.3.11		(44,500)
(iii) y/e 31.12.10	9/12 × £108,000 = 81,000 (max)	(81,000)
c/f		49,500

The loss must be carried forward against future trading profits of the same trade.

The extended loss relief under FA09 is not available as the loss making accounting period ended after 23 November 2010.

5.1 Group relieve £118,000 to Sub Ltd to bring it down to lower profits limit of £150,000 (ie £300,000 ÷ 2). This saves tax at 29.75%.

Then choice between a carry back of the remaining loss of £1,000 to y/e 31 March 2010 to save tax at 21% or group relief in y/e 31 March 2011 to also save tax at 21%. Do the former to generate a cashflow advantage from obtaining a repayment in the prior year.

Only a group relief claim is required. Note that if a carry back claim were made technically the group relief claim should be made first, as the carry back claim is an 'all or nothing' claim.

5.2 **Mr Phillips**

Associates – all companies – as Mr Phillips has common control.

Group relief – Alpha & Gamma only as must have 75% relationship via other companies and the holding company must have an effective 75% holding in all sub-subsidiaries.

Chargeable gains – Alpha Ltd, Gamma Ltd and Epsilon Ltd. Group can include Epsilon Ltd as the principal company (Alpha Ltd) has a 56.25% holding in the company (i.e. at least 51%).

5.3 **James Ltd**

Group relief:

	£	£
From Edward = excess management expenses (20 – 5)		15,000
From Gordon – part of the group from 1.1.10 – 31.3.10		
Lower of:		
Loss 3/12 × £80,000	20,000	
Profits 3/12 × £700,000	175,000	20,000
		35,000

5.4 **Wind Ltd**

Transfer from Wind Ltd to Sail Ltd

Wind Ltd and Sail Ltd form a chargeable gains group as Wind Ltd owns 85% (at least 75%) of the ordinary share capital of Sail Ltd. The sale to Sail Ltd therefore automatically takes place at no gain/no loss. The deemed proceeds on the transfer will be the original cost plus indexation to the date of transfer (W1).

Chargeable gain – Sale of asset 1 April 2011

	£
Proceeds	300,000
Less: Cost (W1)	(126,640)
Unindexed gain	173,360
Less Indexation allowance	
(237.7 – 225.0)/225.0 = 0.056 x £126,640	(7,092)
Chargeable gain	166,268
(W1) Cost	
Original cost (Feb 1994)	80,000
Indexation to June 2010	
(225.0 – 142.1)/142.1 = 0.583 x £80,000	46,640
Deemed proceeds/deemed cost to Sail Ltd	126,640

5.5 **Force Ltd**

Sale to Power Ltd

Force Ltd and Power Ltd form a chargeable gains group at the date of the sale of the factory as Force Ltd owns 80% (at least 75%) of the ordinary share capital of Power Ltd. The sale to Power Ltd therefore automatically takes place at no gain/no loss. The deemed proceeds on the transfer will be the original cost plus indexation to the date of transfer (W1).

Degrouping charge on leaving group

Power Ltd ceases to be a member of Force Ltd's chargeable gains group when Force Ltd reduced its shareholding to 65% on 1 March 2011.

As the factory was transferred to Power Ltd within 6 years of it leaving the group and it still owns the building at that date a degrouping charge will arise.

The degrouping charge will arise in Power Ltd in the year to 31 March 2011. It will be calculated by reference to the market value at the date of transfer and the original cost of the building as follows:

	£
Market value on 1.6.09	500,000
Less: Cost (W1)	(94,160)
Chargeable gain	405,840

(W1) Cost

Original cost (June 2003)	80,000
Indexation to June 2009	
(213.4 – 181.3)/181.3 = 0.177 x £80,000	14,160
	94,160

5.6 **Overseas Ltd**

Overseas Ltd is likely to be a controlled foreign company (CFC) because it is:

(1) resident outside of the UK

(2) controlled by persons resident in the UK (Expansion Ltd, incorporated in the UK)

(3) subject to a lower level of taxation in Overseasland. A tax rate of 8% is likely to be lower than 75% of the tax which would be payable in the UK as the minimum UK tax rate is 21%.

If Overseas Ltd is a CFC the income profits (not gains) of the company will be apportioned to (65%) and taxed on Expansion Ltd. There are specified situations when the profits are not apportioned eg when the profits of the CFC for the accounting period do not exceed £50,000.

5.7 **Tweet Ltd**

Only Tweet Ltd, Pounce Ltd and Feeder Ltd are in a loss relief group, as Tweet Ltd's effective interest in Booker Ltd is only 72% (90% × 80%). Feeder and Booker Ltd are in a separate loss relief group, but Feeder Ltd cannot surrender any losses received from Pounce Ltd to Booker Ltd. Pounce Ltd does not have to use any of the losses itself.

All companies are in a gains group. It is preferable for Feeder Ltd's gain to be included in the results of the company with capital losses and/ or the lowest rate of tax. An election can be made to transfer the gain to Booker Ltd.

There are 4 associates, so the CT limits are:

£1,500,000 / 4 = £375,000

£300,000/ 4 = £75,000

	Tweet	*Pounce*	*Feeder*	*Booker*
	£	£	£	£
Trading (profit/ loss)	875,000		189,000	21,000
Bank interest	12,000		8,000	400
Rental income		12,000		
Chargeable gains/ (loss)				40,000
Total profits	887,000	12,000	197,000	61,400
CT rate	28%	21%	29.75% then 21%	21%
Total profits	887,000	12,000	197,000	61,400
Less: CY loss				
Less: Group relief	(35,000)		(110,000)	
	852,000	12,000	87,000	61,400
Less: Gift Aid payments	(25,000)	(2,500)	(12,000)	(1,000)
Taxable total profits	827,000	9,500	75,000	60,400
CT due	231,560	1,995	15,750	12,684

Loss memo – Pounce Ltd

	£
y/e 31.3.11	145,000
To Feeder Ltd (note)	(110,000)
To Tweet Ltd	(35,000)
c/f	Nil

Note: Use sufficient loss to bring the taxable total profits down to the level where the company only pays 21%. Remember to factor in the gift aid donation.

5.8 **Chilli Ltd**

Chill Ltd and Freeze Ltd are in a group for chargeable gains purposes (=75%). At the date of the original transfer of the property, the disposal took place at no gain/ no loss, ie Freeze Ltd took over Chill Ltd's original cost and indexation.

However, Freeze Ltd is sold within 6 years of that intra-group transfer so the gain that would have arisen at the date of the transfer becomes chargeable now on Freeze Ltd when it leaves the group (a 'de-grouping charge'). Freeze Ltd could elect to transfer the charge to Chill Ltd, but we are told that Freeze Ltd does not do anything to improve its tax position, so we can assume it does not make an election.

	£
Proceeds (MV)	425,000
Less: cost	(219,000)
Less: IA (191.6 – 171.1)/171.1 = 0.120 x £219,000	(26,280)
Gain	179,720

As both Chill Ltd and Freeze Ltd are trading companies, the gain for Chill Ltd on the disposal of the Freeze Ltd shares is exempt (substantial shareholding exemption). This is because Chill Ltd has owned at least 10% of the shares for at least 12 months in the prior 2 years.

5.9 **Sand Ltd**

There is a no gain/no loss disposal by Sand Ltd. The deemed proceeds equal original cost (£50,000) plus indexation allowance to the date of the transfer.

Pebble Ltd acquires the capital asset and appropriates it into trading stock realising a chargeable gain based on the assets market value at the date it is transferred into stock . Ignoring indexation allowance the gain would be £30,000 (£80,000 – £50,000).

When the asset is disposed of Pebble Ltd realises a trading profit of £10,000. It can however elect under s.161(3) TCGA 1992 to treat the whole gain as trading income. Thus there would be no chargeable gain on the appropriation into stock and a trading profit of £40,000. This may be beneficial if the company has trading losses to reduce the trading profit.

6.1 **Investment companies**

(1) The cost of raising loan finance will be a non-trading loan relationship debit. It is normally written off over the period of the loan.

(2) The cost of contributions to a training and enterprise council, the accountant's fees and the pension payments are allowed as specifically allowed as expenses of management.

(3) Capital allowances on let properties are relieved as expenses deductible from property income.

6.2 **Moriarty Ltd**

		£
Management expenses		300,000
Less bfwd		(220,000)
Current year available for group relief		80,000
Profits available in claimant	Trading income	90,000
	Gain	10,000
	Qualifying charitable donations	(30,000)
		70,000

Only £70,000 can be surrendered.

6.3 **Carp Ltd**

Corporation tax computation – Year ended 31 December 2010

	£	£
Property income:		
Rent	300,000	
Less property management expenses	(65,000)	
		235,000
Profit on non-trading loan relationship (50,000 – 22,000)		28,000
Chargeable gains		264,000
		527,000
Less Expenses of management:		
General expenses	15,000	
Expenses of management brought forward	25,000	
		(40,000)
Taxable total profits		487,000

6.4 **Albert**

Deemed employment payment – 2010/11

	£
Income from relevant engagements	85,000
Less: Deduction at 5% (5% x 85,000)	(4,250)
Deductible travel expenses	(477)
Pension scheme contributions	(2,000)
Employer's NIC	(36)
Salary paid	(6,000)
Gross deemed employment income (gross of NIC)	72,237
Less: Employer's NIC	
72,237 x 12.8/112.8	(8,197)
Deemed employment payment	64,040

6.5 **Archer Ltd**

Implications of personal service companies legislation:

1. The services provided to Robin Publications plc are likely to be regarded as a relevant engagement. If Robert had contracted directly with Robin Publications plc the relationship would probably have been deemed to be in the nature of an employment.

2. On the assumption that it is a relevant engagement a deemed employment payment will arise in Archer Ltd on 5 April each year based on the income received from the relevant engagement.

3. The deemed employment payment is broadly based on the income received from the relevant engagement less the salary actually paid to Robert less a flat rate deduction of 5% of income plus other specified items.

4. PAYE and NIC is payable by Archer Ltd on the deemed employment payment.

5. Dividends paid to Robert in relation to income included in the deemed employment payment will not be taxable on Robert.

6.6 **Cheryl**

Cheryl is treated as receiving a deemed employment payment on 5 April 2011.

		£	£
Income from relevant engagements			65,000
Less :	5% flat rate deduction	3,250	
	Salary	12,000	
	Employers' NIC on actual salary	804	
	Pension contribution	5,000	
	Reimbursed expenses	1,250	
			(22,304)
Gross deemed employment payment			42,696
Less: Employer's NIC			
£42,696 × 12.8%/112.8%			(4,845)
Net deemed employment payment			37,851

Cherub Consulting Ltd's PCTCT:

		£	£
Trading profits: £65,000 + 20,000			85,000
Less :	Salary	12,000	
	Employers' NIC on actual salary	804	
	Pension contribution	5,000	
	Reimbursed expenses	1,250	
	Other expenses	3,600	
			(22,654)
Taxable total profits			62,346

Note: The deemed employment payment and associated NIC cannot be deducted until the period in which the payment is deemed to be made, ie in the year ended 31 March 2012.

6.7 **Investalot Ltd**

Investalot Ltd is a close investment company. It is taxable at the main rate of corporation tax regardless of its level of profits.

Although the shares in Enterprise Ltd are a substantial shareholding the loss is allowed because Investalot Ltd is not a trading company and therefore the substantial shareholding exemption does not apply. Had the shares been subscribed for the loss could have been offset against total profits, assuming Enterprise Ltd satisfied the criteria of the Enterprise Investment Scheme.

Any remaining loss will be carried forward against future gains.

CORPORATION TAX

	£	£
Property income	150,000	
Less: expenses	(41,040)	
Less: CAs	(1,500)	
		107,460
Profit on non-trading loan relationships		3,500
Gains (W)		–
Total		110,960
Less: Expenses of management		
General		(68,000)
Capital allowances		(2,225)
		40,735
Less: Gift aid donation		(15,000)
Taxable total profits		25,735
Tax:		
£25,735 × 28%		7,206

Loss on unquoted shares

	£
Proceeds	120,000
Less: cost	(200,000)
Loss	(80,000)

Net gains

	£
Gains	14,000
Current year loss	(14,000)
Net gains	nil

Capital loss carried forward

	£
Loss	(80,000)
Current year offset	14,000
	(66,000)

7.1 **Jasmine Ltd**

The level of Jasmine Ltd's corporation tax liability indicates that it pays tax at the main rate. Its tax liability is therefore payable in instalments, based on its actual tax liability for the year, as follows:

	Due	*Paid*	*Shortfall/ (Over payment)*	*Cumulative*
	£	£	£	£
14 July 2010 £3,550,000 x ¼	887,500	650,000	237,500	237,500
14 October 2010	887,500	1,050,000	(162,500)	75,000
14 January 2011	887,500	850,000	37,500	112,500
14 April 2011	887,500	850,000	37,500	150,000
1 October 2011		150,000	(150,000)	
	3,550,000	3,550,000		

Interest will be charged as follows:

Interest period	*Charged on*
	£
14 July 2010 to 13 October 2010	237,500
14 October 2010 to 30 September 2011	75,000
14 January 2011 to 30 September 2011	37,500
14 April 2011 to 30 September 2011	37,500

7.2 **New Venture Ltd**

(a) *Corporation tax computation – 9 months ended 31 December 2010*

	£
Trading income	210,000
Profit on non-trading loan relationships	10,000
Taxable total profits	220,000
FII £10,000 x 10/9	11,111
Augmented profits	231,111
Corporation tax payable:	
£220,000 x 28%	61,600
Less: Marginal relief	
7/400 x (1,125,000 – 231,111) x 220,000/231,111	(14,891)
	46,709

Small profits limits:
Upper limit: £1,500,000 x 9/12 = £1,125,000
Lower limit: £300,000 x 9/12 = £225,000

Tax payable: 1 October 2011 (9 months and 1 day after the end of the accounting period.

(b) The company's tax return for the 9 months to 31 December 2010 must be submitted by 31 December 2011 (within 12 months of the end of the accounting period).

7.3 **Taranaki Ltd**

Payment due dates

Taranaki Ltd paid tax at the main rate in the year ended 31 December 2009 and the 7 months to 31 July 2010. The reduced upper small profits rate limit for a 7 month accounting period is £875,000 (1,500,000 x 7/12). The company's tax liability for the 7 month period to 31 July 2010 is therefore payable by instalments as follows:

	£
14 July 2010 £950,000 x 28% x 3/7	114,000
14 October 2010 £950,000 x 28% x 3/7	114,000
14 November 2010 (balance of liability)	38,000
Total liability (950,000 x 28%)	266,000

7.4 **Brooke Ltd**

(a) Filing and payment dates

There are two accounting periods in the 14 month period of account to 28 February 2011:

- Year to 31 December 2010
- Two months to 28 February 2011

	Filing date	Payment date
	(12 months after end of period of account)	*(9 months and one day after end of accounting period)*
Year to 31 December 2010	28 February 2012	1 October 2011
Two months to 28 February 2011	28 February 2012	1 December 2011

(b) The penalty for late filing would be an immediate £100 penalty. In addition daily penalties of £10 per day may be charged as the return is more than 3 months late (max 90 days). A tax geared penalty of 5% of the tax due (minimum £300) will also be charged as the return is more than 6 months but less than 12 months late.

7.5 **Dynamo Ltd**

(a) *Corporation tax computation – 15 month period to 31 December 2010*

	Year to 30.9.10	*3 mths to 31.12.10*
	£	£
Trading income (12:3)	2,400,000	600,000
Chargeable gain (December 2010)		500,000
Taxable total profits	2,400,000	1,100,000
Corporation tax payable		
£2,400,000 × 28%	672,000	
£1,100,000 × 28% (Note 1)		308,000

(b) Due payment dates:

9 months after end of AP (Note 2)	1 July 2011	
Instalment basis (Note 3)		14 April 2011

Notes:

(1) Adjusted small profits upper limit £375,000 (1,500,000 × 3/12)

(2) In the first accounting period the company is large but its taxable total profits do not exceed £10 million. Payment is therefore not due by instalments.

(3) Payment due on earlier of 14th day of month 7 from the start of the AP (14 April 2011) and 14th day of month 4 from the end of the AP (14 April 2011).

Awareness Paper
VAT and Stamp Taxes

Study Period Planner
VAT and Stamp Taxes

Use this schedule and your exam timetable to plan the dates on which you will complete each Study Period. The letters 'H' and 'M' tell you whether the topic is high or medium priority.

Study Period	Topic		Due Date
1	VAT basics	H	
2	Treatment of supplies	H	
3	Input tax	H	
4	Land and buildings	M	
5	**Progress Test 1**	**H**	

Study Period	Topic		Due Date
6	Overseas matters	M	
7	Miscellaneous VAT issues	H	
8	Administration	H	
9	Stamp Taxes	M	
10	**Progress Test 2**	H	

COURSE EXAM 1

A practice exam covering Study Periods 1 – 4

COURSE EXAM 2

A practice exam covering all Study Periods

REVISION PHASE

Your revision phase will begin when **Course Exam 2** is complete. This should ideally be four months before the final exam.

TQT Note: The Course Exams contain questions for all FIVE of the awareness paper modules. In your exam you must answer questions from THREE modules. We suggest that you identify the THREE modules you will study and then work through the Study Period Planners for each of those modules until the point where you are told to take Course Exam 1. When you have completed all THREE modules to that point, sit Course Exam 1. Similarly, you should complete all THREE modules before you sit course exam 2. Course Exam 2 covers all of the Study Periods, although it is weighted towards the second half of your studies.

Study Period 1

VAT basics

High Priority

Step 1 Exam Guidance

This study period considers the basics of VAT, ie the background information fundamental to your study of VAT.

These topics have examined in:

The contained the following questions covering these areas of the syllabus:

- Sample Paper (Q5 and Q7)
- May 2009 exam (Q1 and Q5)
- Nov 2009 (Q5)
- May 2010 (Q2, Q9)

Step 2 Introduction to the session

In this study period we begin our study of VAT by looking at the basics of VAT. These topics provide background information essential to your understanding of this syllabus.

Step 3 Guidance through the Study Text

Read through Chapter 1 of the VAT Awareness Study Text after reading the following guidance:

Sections 1 to 3 should be read through quickly, as background information. Follow through Illustrations 1 to 4. You need to know these details to understand the mechanics of VAT, but these areas might not be examined in their own right.

Read Section 4 on registration and deregistration carefully. You must be able to determine when a trader should or could register for VAT and identify the penalties for late registration. You must also be aware of the rules for deregistration from VAT. This is an important area of the syllabus. Work through the remaining illustrations and attempt Examples 1 to 3 to help reinforce your understanding of the section.

Step 4 Quick Quiz

Please attempt the quick quiz at the end of Study Text Chapter 1 to reinforce your understanding.

You may find it best to do this after a break, so that you can see what you remember and what you don't.

Step 5 Workbook Questions

Now attempt the VAT exam style questions (ESQs) 1.1 to 1.7 which will help to reinforce your knowledge of the topics covered in this study period and give you examples of the types of question you may see in the exam.

Study Period 2

Treatment of supplies

High Priority

Step 1 Exam Guidance

This Study Period covers background information to the calculation of VAT liabilities. It is the source of many potential exam questions.

This topic was examined in:

- Q5 of the sample paper
- Q6 & Q7 May 2010

Step 2 Introduction to the session

In this study period we learn how to identify which rate of VAT applies to a particular supply. We must be able to determine when a supply has been made and whether it is:

- Exempt from VAT, or
- Zero rated, or
- Standard rated, or
- A lower rated supply.

Step 3 Guidance through the Study Text

Read through Chapter 2 of the Study Text, after reading the following guidance:

Read through Section 1 of the Chapter to understand the difference between zero rated and exempt supplies, working through Illustrations 1 and 2. This Section gives you the references within the legislation for the lists of zero rated, exempt and reduced rate supplies. Take this opportunity to locate these lists in your copy of the legislation so that you can easily find and use them in the exam. There is no need to memorise the lists in the chapter. Try Example 1.

Read quickly through Section 2 to understand the circumstances in which supplies can be treated as having taken place.

Finally, read quickly through Section 3 to understand the VAT implications of transactions made by charities.

Step 4 Quick Quiz

Please attempt the quick quiz at the end of Study Text Chapter 2 to reinforce your understanding.

You may find it best to do this after a break, so that you can see what you remember and what you don't.

Step 5 Workbook Questions

Now attempt ESQs 2.1 to 2.7 which will help to reinforce your knowledge of the topics covered in this study period and give you examples of the types of question you may see in the exam.

Study Period 3

Input tax

High Priority

Step 1 Exam Guidance

This study period covers the recoverability of input VAT. It is the source of many potential exam questions.

These topics were tested in:

- Sample Paper (Q1 and Q8)
- May 2009 (Q6)
- November 2009 (Q2, Q9)
- May 2010: Q4, Q10

Step 2 Introduction to the session

In this study period we look at input VAT in detail.

You must be able to identify recoverable input VAT, which can be deducted when calculating the VAT liability, and irrecoverable input tax, which is 'blocked' from recovery (ie it cannot be deducted).

You must also be comfortable with the input VAT recovery position of traders who make both taxable and exempt supplies.

Step 3 Guidance through the Study Text

Read through Chapter 3 of the Study Text after reading the following guidance:

Quickly read Sections 1 and 2, which introduce the concept of input tax and then go on to set out the rules for the deductibility of input tax.

Read Section 3 carefully. This section deals with the situations when input tax is **not** recoverable and you must be able to identify these in the exam. Attempt Examples 1 and 2 as you work through this section.

Quickly read through Sections 4 and 5, but do pay particular attention to Section 4.2 on pre-registration input tax.

Carefully work through Section 6. This deals with 'partial exemption', which is one of the more complex (and examinable) VAT topics. You must be able to deal confidently with the VAT position of a partially exempt trader in the exam. Work through Examples 3 to 5 to reinforce your understanding.

Finally, read through Section 7 on the capital goods scheme, which deals with input VAT recovery for certain capital items (ie computers and land and buildings). Work through Illustrations 3 to 6 as you go along to test your understanding.

Step 4 Quick Quiz

Please attempt the quick quiz at the end of Study Text Chapter 3 to reinforce your understanding.

You may find it best to do this after a break, so that you can see what you remember and what you don't.

Step 5 Workbook Questions

Now attempt ESQs 3.1 to 3.12 which will help to reinforce your knowledge of the topics covered in this study period and give you examples of the types of question you may see in the exam.

Study Period 4

Land and buildings

Medium Priority

Step 1 Exam Guidance

The VAT implications of transactions involving land and buildings can easily be examined as a whole question.

VAT on land and buildings was examined in Q2 (Sample paper), Q3 (Nov 2009) and Q5 (May 2010).

Step 2 Introduction to the session

In this Study period we continue our study of VAT by looking at the rules for calculating VAT on transactions involving the supply of land and buildings.

Step 3 Guidance through the Study Text

Read through Chapter 4 of the Study text after reading the following guidance:

Section 1 sets out the general rules for zero rated transactions involving land and buildings. Work through Illustration 1 to test your understanding.

Section 2 covers the transactions involving land and buildings that are exempt, and the exceptions from the exemption. Work through Example 1 to check you have understood the section.

Quickly read Sections 3 and 4. Make sure you understand the general rule that leases are exempt supplies for VAT purposes and try Example 2.

Section 5 deals with the VAT position for transactions involving exempt commercial land and buildings if the trader 'opts to tax' them. Read through carefully to ensure that you are comfortable with the concept of the 'option to tax' and work through Illustration 2 to test your understanding.

Finally, read quickly through Section 6.

Step 4 Quick Quiz

Please attempt the quick quiz at the end of Study Text Chapter 4 to reinforce your understanding.

You may find it best to do this after a break, so that you can see what you remember and what you don't.

Step 5 Workbook Questions

Now attempt ESQs 4.1 to 4.7 which will help to reinforce and give you examples of the types of question you may see in the exam.

Progress Test 1

In order to reinforce what you have learnt so far, answer the following questions. Try to answer them without referring to your Study Text or notes. The test should take you no longer than one hour and covers Study Periods 1-4. Solutions start on page 333.

1 Mr Gillott is in business selling garden statues. He checks his turnover level regularly to ensure that he is still below the VAT registration threshold. At the end of October, his average monthly turnover of taxable supplies was £3,000. On 14 November 2010, he received a letter from a national magazine agreeing to use his products in reader offers, and ordering goods worth £71,000, to be supplied and invoiced within the next 28 days. The magazine intends to use his products in offers regularly from now on.

State the dates by which Mr Gillott should notify HMRC of the need to register for VAT and which date the VAT registration will be effective from. Explain the maximum penalty that he could be charged for late notification of registration.

2 **State the advantages and disadvantages of voluntarily registering for VAT.**

3 Betty opens a catering business on 1 September 2010. Her cumulative turnover for the five months to 31 January 2011 is £55,000. She is asked to cater for a large party in February 2011. The turnover from this alone will be £20,000.

Explain when Betty will need to notify her liability to register for VAT and the date she will be registered from.

4 Kenwood Ltd incurred the following VAT-inclusive expenditure in the quarter to 31 December 2010:

(a) £1,578 entertaining clients.

(b) £294 entertaining employees.

(c) £1,833 on repairs to a property occupied by one of its directors.

(d) £899 on lease payments for a car provided to an employee. The employee uses the car 20% of the time for private purposes.

You are required to calculate how much VAT input tax is not recoverable by the company.

5 Billy started trading on 1 October 2010 as a greeting cards designer and applied to register for VAT with effect from 1 December 2010. Prior to registration, he had incurred the following VAT inclusive expenditure:

	£
Computer for business use purchased new on 1 July 2010	700
Fees for market research on invoice dated 1 June 2010	400
Printing inks purchased on 1 August 2010	300

Of the £300 of printing inks purchased on 1 August 2010, £200 (VAT inclusive) worth were still in stock on 1 December 2010.

You are required to explain what input VAT Billy can reclaim in respect of these items.

6 Cradle Financial Services Ltd is partially exempt for VAT purposes and uses the standard method of apportioning input tax. Input tax for the quarter ended 31 December 2010 is:

Attributable to taxable supplies	*Attributable to exempt supplies*	*Unattributable*
£	£	£
800	1,800	600

The total amounts invoiced for the period were £22,800 (including VAT) of which £4,000 relates to exempt supplies.

The company did not satisfy the annual test for the previous VAT year and does not use the recovery percentage for the previous year.

What is the deductible input tax for the period?

7 **Briefly state the consequences for a trader who fails to register for VAT when required to do so.**

8 Zebra Ltd has been registered for VAT for many years and is partly exempt. Its partial exemption year ends on 31 March.

During the year ended 31 March 2011 Zebra Ltd incurs the following input tax:

	£
Attributable to taxable supplies	47,000
Attributable to exempt supplies	23,000
Residual input tax	14,000

The total value of supplies during the year was £700,000 of which £500,000 were taxable.

How much input tax is recoverable for the year ended 31 March 2011?

9 Treemendous Ltd purchased a computer for £57,500 (inclusive of VAT) on 1 May 2010. It used the computer 65% for taxable use in the quarter of purchase and 70% for taxable purposes in the year to 31 December 2010.

In the year to 31 December 2011 taxable use decreased to 60%.

Treemendous Ltd sold the computer for £10,000 plus VAT on 6 May 2012. Its taxable use in the period from 1 January 2012 to the date of sale was 60%.

You are required to calculate the initial input recovery for the year to 31 December 2010 and adjustments required for all other years.

10 Supplies of goods and services can be categorised as standard rated, exempt, zero rated or reduced rate for VAT purposes.

You are required to state how the following are categorised for VAT purposes.

- **(a) Investment advice**
- **(b) Accountancy services**
- **(c) Insurance**
- **(d) Children's clothing**
- **(e) Newspapers**
- **(f) Fuel for domestic use**
- **(g) Hot take-away meal**
- **(h) Burial services**

(i) **Professional accountancy course**

(j) **Exports outside the EU**

11 The following transactions occurred in December 2010:

1. Perky Ltd grants a 90 year lease from its freehold interest in a factory that was completed in early 2010.
2. Jenny sells a factory for £340,000, excluding VAT, that she bought 12 years ago. She had been letting out part of the factory and so had previously opted to tax this building.
3. Perred Ltd sells a 99 year lease in a new residential building that it had constructed.

You are required to explain how these transactions are treated for VAT purposes.

12 A supply is acquired partly for business purposes and partly for the private use of an employee.

You are required to describe how this should be dealt with for VAT.

You will find the answers to this test starting on page 333. If you answer more than 6 questions correctly, your performance is satisfactory; if you answer more than 8 correctly, you are doing well. Once you have reviewed how you have performed, go back over topics where you feel your understanding is poor.

Study Period 6

Medium Priority

Overseas matters

Examined: Sample Paper

Step 1 Exam Guidance

The VAT implications of overseas transactions is a topic which can be examined as a whole question.

VAT on overseas transactions is examined in Question 6 on the sample paper.

Step 2 Introduction to the session

In this study period we consider the VAT implications of buying goods and selling goods overseas, both within and outside the EU.

Step 3 Guidance through the Study Text

Read through Chapter 5 of the Study text after reading the following guidance:

Section 1 is a long and detailed Section which describes the VAT position of imports and exports of goods both inside and outside the EU. Make sure you are aware of the VAT implications of each of the different circumstances. Work through Illustration 1 and attempt Examples 1 and 2.

Section 2 considers international services. Note the general rule for supplies of services which depends on whether the customer is in business or not. Note the situations when the supply is treated as being made somewhere else. Follow through Illustrations 2 to 5. Use your legislation to help you as you read through this section, so that you know where to find the details in the exam.

Step 4 Quick Quiz

Please attempt the quick quiz at the end of Study Text Chapter 5 to reinforce your understanding.

You may find it best to do this after a break, so that you can see what you remember and what you don't.

Step 5 Workbook Questions

Now attempt ESQs 5.1 to 5.7 which will help to reinforce and give you examples of the types of question you may see in the exam.

Study Period 7

Miscellaneous VAT issues

High Priority

Step 1 Exam Guidance

A number of the topics covered in this study period have been examined on the sample paper as whole questions and are essential for your exam.

These topics have been tested as follows:

- Transfer of a going concern: Sample Paper Q3, May 2009 Q9, May 2010 Q1
- VAT groups: Sample Paper Q9, May 2009 Q4

Step 2 Introduction to the session

In this study period we consider a number of outstanding technical VAT issues. These are:

- The VAT position of traders who use certain VAT schemes
- The VAT treatment when a business is transferred as a going concern
- Group VAT registration for companies.

Step 3 Guidance through the Study Text

Read through Chapter 6 of the Study Text after reading the following guidance:

Sections 1 to 4 deal with various VAT schemes for certain traders. Carefully read Section 1, which covers the flat rate scheme, and work through Illustration 1. Quickly read through Section 2, which is a brief section that deals with the second-hand goods scheme, and Section 3, which deals with the farmers' flat rate scheme, working through Illustration 2. Then read through Section 4 on schemes for retailers. Try not to get bogged down with the detail, but work through slowly, using Illustrations 3 to 6 to help reinforce your understanding of the topic. Concentrate on understanding how the schemes work.

Section 5 deals with the VAT treatment when there is a disposal of a business as a going concern. Can you identify when a business is transferred as a going concern? Work through Illustrations 7 to 9 to help you learn the consequences of such a transfer.

Finally, read carefully through Section 6 ensuring you understand the VAT consequences of a group of companies registering as a single group entity for VAT purposes.

Step 4 Quick Quiz

Please attempt the quick quiz at the end of Study Text Chapter 6 to reinforce your understanding.

You may find it best to do this after a break, so that you can see what you remember and what you don't.

Step 5 Workbook Questions

Now attempt ESQs 6.1 to 6.11 which will help to reinforce and give you examples of the types of question you may see in the exam.

Study Period 8

Administration

High Priority

Step 1 Exam Guidance

There are a number of administrative rules to learn in the VAT Awareness syllabus.

The examiner could tack an administrative point at the end of another question for, say, one mark, or make the topic the focus of a question.

These topics have been tested as follows:

- Sample Paper: Q4, Q10 and Q11
- May 2009 exam: Q4, Q7 and Q10
- November 2009: Q1, Q4, Q7, Q8, Q10
- May 2010: Q3, Q8

Step 2 Introduction to the session

In this Study Period we complete our study of VAT by looking at how a VAT return is completed, the records and returns that need to be maintained, the penalties imposed if traders do not comply with their obligations, bad debt relief and VAT accounting schemes to assist small businesses.

We also consider the system by which VAT assessments can be raised and the mechanism by which a VAT registered trader can appeal against a VAT assessment.

Step 3 Guidance through the Study Text

Read through Chapter 7 of the Study text, which covers a number of administrative topics, after reading the guidance below:

Read carefully through Section 1, which covers some basic administrative provisions, such as the period for which VAT returns are required, the contents of a VAT return and the determination of the tax point of a transaction. Follow through Illustrations 1 and 2 and attempt Example 1 to check your understanding of the section.

Read Section 2 covering the rules for keeping VAT records and the contents of a valid VAT invoice. Take this opportunity to locate the relevant part of the legislation referred to at the start of the section so that you can easily find and use it in the exam.

You can read quickly through Sections 3 to 7 on assessments and HMRC powers, interest, penalties and disclosure schemes. Section 4 refers you to Section 7 of Chapter 15 of the CTA Awareness Taxation of Individuals Study Text. You should study section 7 of that chapter before continuing with your study of this VAT and stamp taxes text. Again instead of learning the detail for these topics, learn where it is in your legislation.

Finally, work carefully through Sections 8 and 9, which deal with the relief available for bad debts and the two main schemes available to small businesses to help with VAT accounting: the cash accounting scheme and the annual accounting scheme. Use the examples and illustrations to check your understanding of these topics.

Step 4 Quick Quiz

Please attempt the quick quiz at the end of Study Text Chapter 7 to reinforce your understanding.

You may find it best to do this after a break, so that you can see what you remember and what you don't.

Step 5 Workbook Questions

Now attempt ESQs 7.1 to 7.11 which will help to reinforce and give you examples of the types of question you may see in the exam.

Study Period 9

Stamp Taxes

Medium Priority

Examined: Sample Paper

Step 1 Exam Guidance

This Study Period covers the three stamp taxes: Stamp duty (SD), stamp duty reserve tax (SDRT) and stamp duty land tax (SDLT).

Stamp duty land tax was examined in Q12 (Sample paper), Q11 & Q12 (May 2009),Q11 & Q12 (Nov 2009) and Q11 & Q12 (May 2010).

Step 2 Introduction to the session

In this study period we consider the stamp tax implications of transactions:

- involving shares (SD and SDRT) and
- land (SDLT)

Step 3 Guidance through the Study Text

Read through Chapter 8 of the Study text after reading the following guidance:

Section 1 is a useful brief summary of the scope of each of the stamp taxes. Read this for background information.

Read through Section 2 which covers stamp duty on share transactions where shares are transferred using a stampable instrument eg a stock transfer form. Section 2.5 covers an important relief from stamp duty for transactions involving groups of companies. This is an important section to study.

Read through Section 3 on stamp duty reserve tax. Make sure you understand the interaction of SD and SDRT. SDRT applies to all share transactions however the transfer of ownership is implemented, eg electronically as for quoted shares dealt with on the Stock Exchange or by a stock transfer instrument for private company shares. In the latter case SD is also payable on the stock transfer instrument and the SDRT liability is cancelled upon presentation of a stamped stock transfer form.

Stamp duty land tax is covered in Section 4. Read this and ensure you understand to what transactions it applies, who pays the tax and how the tax is calculated. Note in particular the treatment of leases and the relief available for groups of companies.

Finally quickly read through the administration of the taxes in Section 5.

Step 4 Quick Quiz

Please attempt the quick quiz at the end of Study Text Chapter 8 to reinforce your understanding.

You may find it best to do this after a break, so that you can see what you remember and what you don't.

Step 5 Study Text Questions

Now attempt ESQs 8.1 to 8.4 which will help to reinforce and give you examples of the types of question you may see in the exam.

Progress Test 2

In order to reinforce what you have learnt so far, answer the following questions. Try to answer them without referring to your Study Text or notes. The test should take you no longer than one hour and covers Study Periods 6-9. Solutions start on page 337.

1 Hamish, a VAT registered trader, owns a property in Edinburgh which is let to a builders merchant. He has made an option to tax in respect of the property. The following transactions take place in the quarter ended 31 December 2010:

(a) Hamish charges quarterly rent of £3,000.
(b) The tenant pays Hamish £10,000 for the surrender of his lease.

All figures are exclusive of VAT.

How much VAT will Hamish need to charge in respect of the above transactions for the quarter ended 31 December 2010?

2 **State how the time of supply of goods is determined for VAT purposes.**

3 Exceedingly Big Builders Ltd constructed a new bottling plant for Kipling Ltd. Work began on 1 August 2010. The construction work was completed on 17 April 2011. Payment was received on 12 April 2011 and a VAT invoice was issued on 3 May 2011, reflecting the full consideration already paid.

State and explain the VAT tax point for the supply of the bottling plant.

4 Shadowplay Ltd has opted for cash accounting for VAT purposes. In the VAT quarter ended 31 December 2010 the following transactions take place:

(a) Receipt of £5,000 as payment on account of invoice of £10,000 plus VAT issued on 30 September 2010.

(b) Write off of a debt of £6,000 plus VAT which was due on 30 April 2010.

(c) Payment of £400 against invoice of £2,000 plus VAT dated 28 November 2010 received from a supplier.

What is the VAT payable/repayable for Shadowplay Ltd in respect of the quarter ended 31 December 2010? Calculate to the nearest penny.

5 White Horse Ltd is preparing its VAT return for the quarter ended 31 October 2010. This quarter, White Horse Ltd has written off the following bad debts:

Debtor	*Date of supply*	*Amount (Inclusive of VAT)*	*Payment received*
		£	£
A Ltd	1 June 2010	1,150	Nil
B Ltd	1 November 2009	2,350	300
C Ltd	10 January 2010	2,300	Nil

Invoices are due for payment within 28 days of the invoice date.

White Horse Ltd has already accounted to HM Revenue & Customs for all of the VAT charged on the supplies.

How much VAT bad debt relief is due to White Horse Ltd for the quarter ended 31 October 2010?

6 Cardart Ltd, a VAT registered trader, supplies a batch of greetings cards, on approval, to a new customer on 31 January 2011. The arrangement is that the customer will either pay for the goods on 31 March 2011 or return them intact. The cards are a great success and the customer pays Cardart Ltd for the cards on 28 February 2011. Cardart Ltd issues a VAT invoice dated 31 March 2011.

State and explain the tax point for the above sale by Cardart Ltd.

7 Silk Ltd manufactures textiles. The company is VAT registered and operates the cash accounting scheme. In the quarter to 31 December 2010 the company undertakes the following transactions:

(a) Invoices sales of £4,000 plus VAT
(b) Purchases raw materials for cash of £2,000 plus VAT
(c) Receives cash from trade debtors of £3,525 in respect of invoices dated 1 February 2010.

How much VAT is due for payment by Silk Ltd in respect of the quarter to 31 December 2010?

8 Mr Dashwood submits his quarterly VAT return on time. He sent in his previous three returns late and had to pay a default surcharge. Unfortunately, although he has correctly calculated the VAT due as £1,520, he accidentally writes the cheque for £1,250 instead, when submitting his return. He does not realise his mistake in time to pay the balance before the deadline of 30 days after the return date.

How much default surcharge will HM Revenue and Customs be entitled to collect?

9 Frank is a sole trader who manufactures garden chairs. He is registered for VAT. He received an order for six chairs on 30 July 2010. The chairs were delivered to the customer on 20 August 2010 and an invoice was issued on 30 August 2010. Payment was received on 13 September 2010.

Explain what is the tax point for the sale of the garden chairs.

10 **You are required to state the three conditions that must be satisfied for a supply of goods to another EU member state to be zero rated for VAT purposes.**

11 XYZ Ltd is registered for VAT in the UK and has recently entered into the following transactions:

- Sale of goods located in India which were delivered to America
- Sale of goods located in Wales and delivered to Australia

Discuss the place of supply for VAT purposes and their subsequent treatment for VAT.

12 **You are required to explain the stamp taxes implications of the following transactions:**

1. Ray sold 2,000 shares in Apple Ltd for £81,300 to Pear plc using a stock transfer form.

2. Pluto Ltd sold some residential land to Saturn plc, an unconnected company, for £260,000.

3. Sun Ltd paid £80,000 for the grant of a 30 year lease of a warehouse. The net present value of the rental was £510,000 and the annual rent was £10,000. The factory was not in a disadvantaged area.

You will find the answers start on page 337. If you answer more than 6 questions correctly, your performance is satisfactory; if you answer more than 8 correctly, you are doing well. Once you have reviewed how you have performed, go back over topics where you feel your understanding is poor.

Progress Test 1

1 Turnover is expected to exceed £70,000 in 30 days following 14 November 2010 ∴ must notify HMRC by 13 December 2010 (end of 30 day period).

He will be registered from 14 November 2010 (beginning of 30 day period).

If Mr Gillot is late in notifying HMRC of his liability to register he could be charged a maximum penalty of 30% of the net tax due from the date when the trader should have been registered to the date of actual notification. This assume that as Mr Gillott has been monitoring his turnover that any failure to register is careless and not deliberate .

2 Voluntary registration for VAT:

Advantages:

- Can claim back input VAT incurred.
- Improves the image of the business (can make the business look older and more established than it is).

Disadvantages:

- Increases prices to non VAT registered customers.
- Burden of administration.

3 Betty's cumulative turnover in the preceding 12 months will exceed the £70,000 turnover limit on 28 February 2011. She needs to notify HMRC by 30 March 2011.

She will be registered from the start of the following month (ie by 1 April 2011).

4 Kenwood Ltd

	£
The irrecoverable input VAT is as follows:	
Client entertaining: £1,578 × 7/47	235
Staff entertaining (all recoverable)	Nil
Director's accommodation services: £1,833 × 7/47	273
Leased car payment 50% × £899 × 7/47 (Note)	67
Total irrecoverable VAT	575

Note. 50% of the lease payment is irrecoverable because there is private use of the vehicle. The level of private use is irrelevant.

5 Billy can reclaim the input VAT suffered as follows:

– Computer £104 – as a fixed asset and assumed still held at the date of registration.
– Market research £60 – as a service provided within the 6 months prior to registration
– Inks £30 – VAT recoverable on the stock still held at the date of registration (£200)

6 Input tax

Firstly you should determine whether either Test 1 or Test 2 are satisfied for the quarter.

Test 1 is not satisfied because total input tax exceeds £625 per month (£3,200/3) = £1,067).

Test 2 is not satisfied because total input tax less that directly attributable to taxable supplies exceeds £625 per month ((£2,400)/3 = £800).

A partial exemption calculation must be performed to determine how much input tax is recoverable for the quarter as follows.

	Taxable supplies £		Exempt Supplies £
Directly attributable	800	600	1,800
Unallocated			
$\frac{16,000}{16,000 + 4,000}$	480		120
⇒ 80%	1,280		1,920

- >£625pm
- > 50% of total input tax

∴ not de minimis

∴ £1,280 deductible

W: Net taxable supplies = (22,800 – 4,000) × 40/47 = £16,000

Tutorial note.

40/47 was used rather than the 7/47 in order to create a 1 step solution rather than a 2 step solution.

7
- The trader will be personally liable for output VAT due on taxable supplies from the due date of registration.
- Sales prices during the above period will be considered to have been VAT inclusive.
- A late registration penalty for the period of the default is payable unless there is a reasonable excuse for the delay. The penalty is a percentage of the potential lost tax depending on the behaviour of the taxpayer eg 70% where the failure is deliberate but not concealed. The penalty is reduced for the quality of disclosure by the taxpayer.

8 Firstly you should determine whether either Test 1 or Test 2 are satisfied for the year.

Test 1 is not satisfied because total input tax exceeds £625 per month (£84,000/12) = £7,000).

Test 2 is not satisfied because total input tax less that directly attributable to taxable supplies exceeds £625 per month ((£37,000)/12 = £3,083).

A partial exemption calculation must be performed to determine how much input tax is recoverable for the quarter as follows.

Partial exemption 500/700= 72% (round up) of residual input tax is recoverable.

47,000 + (72% x 14,000)

= £57,080

Note: The VAT relating to exempt supplies clearly exceeds the de minimis.

9 For the first VAT year to 31 December 2010, the recovery is:

£57,500 × 7/47 = £8,564 × 70% = £5,995.

For the second VAT year to 31 December 2011 the adjustment is:

£8,564 × 10% (ie 70% - 60%) × 1/5 = £171 payable to HMRC.

For the third VAT year to 31 December 2012 there are two adjustments:

(a) £8,564 × 10% × 1/5 = £171, payable to HMRC

(b) £8,564 × 30% (ie 100% - 70%) × 2/5 = £1,028, restricted to the VAT charged on the sale of the computer, ie £10,000 × 20% = £2,000. So, can recover the full £1,028 from HMRC.

The net adjustment for this third year is:

£(171) + £1,028 = £857 recoverable from HMRC.

10

(a)	Investment advice	Standard rated
(b)	Accountancy services	Standard rated
(c)	Insurance	Exempt
(d)	Children's clothing	Zero rated
(e)	Newspapers	Zero rated
(f)	Fuel for domestic use	Reduced rate
(g)	Hot take-away meal	Standard rated
(h)	Burial services	Exempt
(i)	Professional accountancy course	Standard rated
(j)	Exports outside the EU	Zero rated

Tutorial note. You may not be able to remember all of the detail necessary to answer a question in the exam. There may also be questions where the detail required exceeds that provided in the study text. In these circumstances you will need to use the legislation to find the detail you require and you should practice doing this during your studies. For example in this question the answer is contained in Schedules 7A, 8 and 9 of VATA 1994.

11 The grant of the lease is an exempt supply. Perky Ltd could opt to tax the grant, making it a standard rated supply.

The sale of the factory will be standard rated supply as Jenny has opted to tax the building. Output VAT will be £340,000 x 17.5% = £59,500

The grant of a major interest (freehold or lease exceeding 21 years) of newly constructed residential property is zero rated.

12 Generally the input tax should be apportioned between business and private use, and only the business proportion treated as deductible input tax.

The strict position under EU law, however, is that all of the input tax should be treated as recoverable but that there is a deemed supply of the private use, and output tax should be charged on the deemed supply.

Where the supply is of road fuel a scale rate is used to calculate the deemed supply.

Progress Test 2

1 Hamish

	£
Rent	3,000
Surrender	10,000
	13,000

£13,000 @ 17.5% = £2,275.

Tutorial note.

Rent and payment for surrender are VATable.

2 Supply takes place on the date the goods are removed or made available to the customer. This is also known as the basic tax point.

If an invoice is issued, or payment is received, **prior** to this date, then this earlier date becomes the tax point for the amount invoiced or payment received. The normal rule will apply to any balance.

If an invoice is issued within 14 days *after* the basic tax point, then this becomes the tax point, unless the trader elects for this treatment not to apply. (This rule only applies if an 'earlier' date has not already fixed the tax point.) This period may be extended by HMRC to allow for, say, monthly invoicing.

3 The tax point is the earliest of

(a) completion date = 17 April 2011

(b) payment date = 12 April 2011

(c) invoice date - if before the date of completion and payment. As it is later, then the tax point is 12 April 2011.

4 VAT only accounted for when cash is received or paid

(a) Total invoice 10,000 + (17.5% × 10,000) £11,750.00

Receipt of $\frac{5,000}{11,750} \times$ £1,750 £744.68

(b) No cash involved

(c) Total invoice £2,000 + (17.5% × 2,000) = £2,350

Payment of $\frac{400}{2,350} \times 350$ (£59.57)

∴ VAT payable to HMRC £744.68– £59.57 = £685.11

5 B Ltd (2,350 – 300) x 3/23 = £267

C Ltd 2,300 x 7/47 = £343

Total bad debt relief = £610

Tutorial note.

Invoices over 6 months old are eligible for bad debt relief, ie B Ltd and C Ltd.

6 Tax point is the date of receipt of the cash ie 28 February 2011.

The 14 day rule only overrides the basic tax point if the invoice is dated within 14 days.

7

		VAT	
	£	£	
Received from debtors	3,525	525	(7/47 × 3,525)
Paid to suppliers	2,000	350	(17½% × 2,000)
VAT payable amounts to		175	

8 Greater of:

£(1,520 – 1,250) = 270 @ 10% = £27

(3rd default in notice period)

Or minimum £30

∴ £30

9 Basic tax point = date goods removed 20 August 2010.

But invoice issued within 14 days of basic tax point therefore tax point is 30 August 2010.

10 Conditions for despatch to be zero rated:

- Supply must be made to a registered trader,
- The supplier must quote the customer's VAT number on the invoice (to prove he is registered), and
- The supplier must hold evidence that the goods were actually delivered to the other member state.

11 India to America: Goods located outside the UK and therefore outside the scope of UK VAT.

Wales to Australia: Goods located within the UK and so UK supply liable to UK VAT, but zero rated as an export.

12 The stamp taxes implications are:

1. Stamp duty of 0.5% x £81,300 rounded to the nearest £5 is payable by Pear plc i.e. £410. No stamp duty reserve tax will be payable if the stamp transfer document is presented within 6 years of the contract date.

2. Stamp duty land tax (SDLT) of £7,800 (£260,000 x 3%) is payable by Saturn plc.

3. SDLT payable by Sun Ltd:

   Premium: £80,000 × 1% = £800 – The zero rate is not available as the annual rent exceeds £1,000 and the property is non-residential.

   NPV of rents: (£510,000 – £150,000) x 1% = £3,600.

Exam style questions

1.1 In his first year of trading to 31 December 2009 Monty's turnover from his restaurant was £3,500 a month.

For the first seven months of 2010 his turnover was as follows:

	£
January 2010	4,000
February 2010	5,600
March 2010	7,000
April 2010	9,000
May 2010	10,000
June 2010	13,700
July 2010	14,000

You are required to state, with reasons, the date by which Monty is required to notify HMRC that he is liable to register for VAT.

Due to a careless oversight Monty actually registers for VAT on 30 November 2010 and the net tax due on his first VAT return is £900.

You are required to outline the maximum penalty for late registration that Monty is liable for.

1.2 Big Ltd has acquired the rights to sell miniature televisions in the UK. The company was formed on 2 July 2010 and obtained the marketing rights on 3 July 2010. Its budgeted turnover for the first 12 months is:

Quarter ended	*Turnover*
	£
30 September 2010	2,000
31 December 2010	18,500
31 March 2011	210,000
30 June 2011	150,000

Turnover is expected to arise evenly within each quarter.

You are required to state:

By what date must the company inform HMRC of the need to register for VAT and from what date will registration be effective?

If the business terminates at a later date, within how many days must Big Ltd notify HMRC that it must deregister?

1.3 Banbury plc issues an invoice on 1 February 2011 as follows:

	£	£
Goods		1,000
Less: trade discount	100	
cash discount	60	(160)
		840

The cash discount is only available if the invoice is settled within thirty days. The client pays within 10 days.

Banbury plc also sells an item on which standard-rated VAT is due on 1 March 2011. The item costs £600 excluding VAT before any discounts. The client is entitled to a 5% trade discount and a further 2.5% (on cost after trade discount) discount if he pays within 30 days. The client pays 60 days later.

You are required to state what VAT is due on both sales.

1.4 Richard commenced trading on 11 January 2010, and his first two years' monthly turnover (excluding VAT) is set out below. He does not wish to register unless he has to do so.

	2010	*2011*
	£	£
January	2,200	10,420
February	2,690	10,700
March	3,590	10,630
April	4,690	12,290
May	5,370	14,980
June	4,960	12,990
July	5,240	11,920
August	6,920	12,540
September	6,380	9,300
October	8,060	12,230
November	9,410	11,920
December	10,930	13,440

You should assume that the registration thresholds are the same for 2011 as they are for 2010.

You are required to state the action Richard should take, and when, assuming all of his turnover is zero-rated.

1.5 Xilo Ltd made the following taxable supplies after its incorporation on 1 May 2010:

	2010	*2011*
	£	£
January	nil	90,000
February	nil	102,000
March	nil	152,000
April	nil	170,000
May	8,000	
June	10,000	
July	17,000	
August	21,000	
September	24,000	
October	50,000	
November	60,000	
December	100,000	

You are required to outline (with explanations) the date on which the business should notify HMRC of its need to register for VAT and the date from which the business will be VAT registered.

1.6 Mr Cassell begins to run his own stationery shop on 1 November 2009. He makes the following supplies during his first year of trade:

	£
November 2009	1,200
December 2009	2,400
January 2010	3,800
February 2010	6,600
March 2010	8,250
April 2010	16,200
May 2010	18,900
June 2010	18,750
July 2010	19,100
August 2010	18,900
September 2010	19,600
October 2010	19,450

He incurred expenses of £3,000 (inclusive of standard rate VAT) each month.

You are required to:

(1) State the date by which Mr Cassell must notify HMRC of his liability to register for VAT.
(2) State the date from which he will be registered to charge VAT.
(3) The maximum amount of any penalty if, due to lack of reasonable care, he does not notify HMRC until 1 November 2010.

1.7 **You are required to state five situations which will result in compulsory deregistration.**

2.1 **You are required to discuss briefly the difference between a mixed supply and a compound supply. In your discussion give one example of each type of supply.**

2.2 **You are required to:**

(a) explain the difference between zero-rated and exempt supplies.

(b) outline what type of supply are the following for VAT purposes?

(i) Food sold for consumption away from the premises but where a microwave oven is made available to heat up the food either before or after the till point

(ii) Pet food which is canned, packaged or prepared

(iii) Santa flight to Lapland

(iv) A coach excursion to a theme park

2.3 Ade Sleightholme is the managing director of one of your clients, Stimpson Group plc, which trades in the health sector owning and running two nursing homes for the elderly and infirm.

Stimpson Group plc has paid full rate VAT on all its fuel supplies since it commenced trading on 1 January 2000 and estimates that its costs, excluding VAT, are £30,000 per annum. A business contact has suggested to Ade that it should be possible for the Group to only pay the reduced rate of VAT on all its fuel supplies in the future and to recover the amount overpaid in full from the suppliers.

You are required to consider the proposition, commenting on the technical position with detailed reference to the legislation.

2.4 Iain is an employee of ABC Ltd. He has the use of a car with CO_2 emissions of 176g/km for one month and a car with CO_2 emissions of 208g/km for two months during the quarter ended 31 December 2010.

ABC Ltd pay all the petrol costs in respect of both cars without requiring Iain to make any reimbursement in respect of private fuel. Total petrol costs for the quarter amount to £300 (including VAT).

You are required to state what the VAT effect of the above on ABC Ltd is.

VAT Scale rates (VAT inclusive) for 3 month periods

	£
CO_2 emissions	
175	340
205	425

2.5 **How would the following supplies be treated for VAT purposes?**

(a) Plain, wholesome biscuits sold in a novelty 1940s biscuit tin.
(b) A subscription to a satellite TV provider which includes a weekly magazine.
(c) A ticket to fly to Rome which includes in-flight catering.

2.6 (a) Sale of a stamp by the post office.
(b) Sale of a child's car seat.
(c) A dentist's bill for a filling.
(d) Sale of a mars bar.
(e) A newspaper.

You are required to outline how the above supplies will be treated for VAT with legislative references to support your answer.

2.7 **A gift of goods is a deemed supply for VAT purposes. You are required to state and explain the two exceptions to this rule.**

3.1 Ben commenced trading on 1 August 2010 repairing electrical equipment and applied to register for VAT with effect from 1 October 2010.

Prior to registration, he had incurred VAT as follows:

	£
Van purchased new on 3 May 2010	500
Accountancy fees on invoice dated 5 September 2010	30
Stock of spare parts as on 30 September 2010	240

Ben also incurred the following capital expenditure during his first VAT quarter:

	Net	*VAT*
	£	£
Two cars for employees (available for private use)	14,234	2,491
Motor van	10,500	1,837
Second hand transit van	26,254	4,594

You are required to state how much VAT can be reclaimed by Ben in respect of the above items.

3.2 Kate's business was registered for VAT from 1 January 2011. The following transactions took place in the quarter ended 31 March 2011.

	£
Sales at standard rate (including VAT)	240,000
Sales at zero rate	50,000
Exempt sales	75,000
Sales are stated inclusive of VAT	
Her input tax has been attributed as follows:	
Attributed to taxable supplies	60,000
Attributed to exempt supplies	17,000
Unattributed	73,000
	150,000

You are required to state what the recoverable input tax is. Assume that all supplies took place after 4 January 2011.

3.3 Giles Ltd is a partially exempt trader for VAT purposes. The company makes up its accounts and VAT returns for the year to 31 March. The company's partial exemption recovery percentage for the year to 31 March 2010 was 79%.

During the quarter to 30 June 2010 the following amounts of VAT were charged on the company's purchases and other expenses.

	£
Wholly attributable to making taxable supplies	12,500
Wholly attributable to making exempt supplies	1,500
Non-attributable VAT	4,000

During the quarter the company made the following supplies.

	£
Standard rated supplies (excluding VAT)	140,000
Zero-rated supplies	20,000
Exempt supplies	40,000

You are required to compute the amount of input tax that can be reclaimed for the quarter assuming:

(1) The company chooses to use the recovery percentage for the previous year and

(2) The company does not use the previous years' recovery percentage.

3.4 Mr J Cake is a VAT registered trader. In the quarter to 31 August 2010 he makes net standard rated supplies of £40,000, zero-rated of £20,000 and exempt supplies of £23,000. His total input VAT is £45,000 of which £27,000 can be matched with taxable supplies and £9,000 with exempt supplies.

Mr Cake did not satisfy the annual test for the previous VAT year and does not use the recovery percentage for the previous year.

You are required to state how much input VAT Mr Cake can recover in the quarter.

3.5 Nordon Ltd makes wholly taxable supplies and is registered for VAT. In the period ended 31 December 2010 it incurs the following input tax:

	£
Re supplies for contracts to be fulfilled in the first quarter of 2011	15,200
Re overheads in factory	3,300
Re purchases of new company car for sales manager	5,100
Re entertainment	
Clients	1,100
Employees	850

You are required to calculate the amount of deductible input tax for the quarter ended 31 December 2010.

3.6 Keith runs a large grocery store in a small village in Hertfordshire. The store sells all types of groceries and also has a post office counter, which is managed by his wife Julie.

Total input tax suffered by Keith's business was £35,000 for the year ended 31 December 2010.

This can be analysed as follows:

	£
Attributable to taxable supplies	20,000
Attributable to exempt supplies	10,000
Relating to general overheads and thus not directly attributable	5,000
	35,000

Turnover (VAT exclusive) can be analysed as follows:

	£
Groceries: standard rated	21,500
zero rated	80,200
Postal services	20,300
	122,000

You are required to calculate the amount of input tax recoverable for the year ended 31 December 2010.

3.7 Trusty Car Sales Ltd (TCS) is a car dealership, which also provides finance and insurance to customers on request.

On 19 May 2009 TCS purchased a computer to be used in the business for both operational and accounting purposes. The purchase invoice showed the total amount of VAT (at 15%) to be £26,250, of which £11,250 related to software.

TCS is partly exempt as a result of its services of arranging finance and insurance and it operates the partial exemption standard method. Its tax year ends on 31 March and the recovery rates in the tax years 2009 to 2011 were as follows:

2009	*2010*	*2011*
80%	70%	85%

You are required to:

(a) Explain whether or not the purchase of the computer and the related software falls within the Capital Goods Scheme.

(b) Calculate, with explanations, the input tax which should have been recovered/paid in respect of the computer purchase in the tax years ending 31 March 2010 and 31 March 2011 and state on which return any adjustment required should have been made.

3.8 Z Ltd purchased a computer for £100,000 + VAT on 1 January 2010. It used it 58% for taxable use in the quarter of purchase and 60% for taxable purposes in the year to 31 March 2010.

The taxable use in the year to 31 March 2011 was 50%. The computer was sold for £6,000 + VAT on 10 August 2011. The taxable use in the period 1 April 2011 to 10 August 2011 was 50%.

You are required to calculate the initial input recovery and adjustments required for all other years.

3.9 In her first VAT quarter to 31 March 2011 Alice made the following supplies:

Exempt supplies	£86,000
Taxable supplies	£325,000

Her input VAT for the period was as follows:

		£
Wholly attributable to:	Taxable supplies	1,895
	Exempt supplies	420
Overheads		1,545

You are required to calculate how much input VAT Alice can claim on her return for the quarter ended 31 March 2011.

3.10 Spice Ltd purchased a computer server for £75,000 (exclusive of VAT) on 1 May 2010. It used the server 61% for taxable use in the quarter of purchase and 68% for taxable purposes in the year to 31 March 2011.

The taxable use in the year ended 31 March 2012 was 49%.

Spice Ltd sold the server on 21 September 2012 for £19,000 (plus VAT). The taxable use for the period to the date of sale was 45%.

You are required to calculate the recovery in the year ended 31 March 2011 and the adjustments required for all other years.

3.11 Patchwork Ltd makes widgets and made standard rated supplies of £247,000 (plus VAT) in the VAT year ended 31 December 2010.

The company also incurred the following VAT-inclusive expenditure during the year:

Client entertaining	£2,124
Staff entertaining	£2,258
Renovation work on property occupied by director	£15,575
Car with 80% business use	
Cost of the car	£16,800
Servicing costs	£3,021
Other wholly business expenses	£35,600

You are required to calculate the net VAT payable to HMRC by Patchwork Ltd.

3.12 **You are required to give five examples of supplies of goods and services on which input tax is not recoverable.**

4.1 **You are required to outline how the following supplies will be treated for VAT purposes:**

(a) Peter the plasterer sends an invoice to the builder BIG Homes Ltd for his work on 10 houses in a new housing estate the company is building.

(b) The services of a lawyer used by BIG Homes Ltd to draw up contracts for employees working on the development mentioned in (a).

(c) Juniper Ltd sells the freehold of a five year old restaurant to a property developer.

Give legislative references in your answer.

4.2 **You are required to state what type of supply the following are for VAT purposes. (Note that no options to tax have been made unless otherwise stated.)**

(a) **Electrician's supply of services in relation to the conversion of a warehouse to luxury apartments.**

(b) **Supply of services of installing energy saving materials in residential accommodation or in a building intended for use solely for a relevant residential purpose.**

(c) **The grant of a 99-year lease in a new commercial building.**

(d) **The first grant of a major interest, by the person constructing, in a building designed as a dwelling.**

(e) **The sale of a freehold interest in a commercial building built in 1993 on which the landlord has 'opted to tax'.**

4.3 Tim Clarke, a developer, is proposing to construct an office building for letting on land that he has recently purchased. Construction would commence on 1 July 2011. He is unsure whether to opt to tax the development or not. On completion of the development on 31 December 2012, Tim intends granting leases over one or more floors of the building to tenants.

The estimated costs of the development are as follows.

	Cost (excluding VAT)	*VAT*
	£	£
Land	800,000	–
Construction costs	7,200,000	1,440,000
Professional costs	600,000	120,000
Interest costs	1,200,000	–

You are required to calculate the impact, both in terms of input tax recovery and its timing, of Tim deciding to opt to tax the development.

4.4 Mr Heart owns an eight storey office block in Manchester, which is currently let out to various tenants.

The building is in need of renovation and Mr Heart has been quoted a VAT (at 17.5%) inclusive cost of £750,000 to do this.

You are required to discuss Mr Heart's position in relation to the building outlining any planning point(s) which may benefit him.

4.5 **You are required to outline whether the option to tax can be made in relation to each of the following supplies:**

(a) **Sale of 20 acres of farmland**
(b) **Sale of a 30 year old house in Salford**
(c) **Lease of a one year old factory**
(d) **Freehold sale of a 1 year old office block**
(e) **99 year lease of a newly refurbished show room**

4.6 Girth Ltd purchases a new warehouse on 1 August 2010 and immediately decides to opt to tax the building.

Girth Ltd plans to purchase a number of other buildings in the future.

You are required to state:

(1) **The date by which the option to tax must be notified to HMRC.**

(2) **The date on which the cooling off period for revoking the option to tax ends.**

(3) **The earliest date on which the option to tax can be revoked if it is not revoked during the cooling off period.**

(4) **The name of the election that Girth Ltd can use to include any future properties within the option to tax.**

4.7 **You are required to state five examples where the grant of an interest in or right over land or a licence to occupy land is treated as a standard rated supply.**

5.1 Jane Moss, a UK based designer registered for VAT in the UK, made the following supplies of hand made jewellery in the quarter ended 31 August 2010:

	£
To Canadian based purchasers	2,500
To Italian based purchasers	
- Registered for VAT in Italy	5,200
- Not registered for VAT in Italy	1,800

Jane also acquired £15,000 of ceramics and gem stones from a supplier based in Portugal.

You are required to state what the VAT implications are for Jane in respect of the above supplies and purchases.

5.2 ABC Ltd is registered for VAT in the UK and has recently sold the following.

(1) A set of furniture which was in India and was delivered from India to a customer in Australia;

(2) A table which was in Edinburgh and was delivered to a customer in America; and

(3) An armchair which was supplied to a customer in Hong Kong out of a batch of 100 received from China and re-exported.

You are required to:

(a) Outline the general rules in respect of the place of supply of goods;
(b) Discuss the place of supply of the goods supplied by ABC Ltd;

5.3 **You are required to state whether the following supplies are a dispatch, acquisition, export or import for VAT purposes.**

1 Sale of lamb to France
2 Purchase of lamb from New Zealand
3 Purchase of books from Brazil
4 Sale of children's clothes to Germany
5 Sale of chocolate to Italy
6 Purchase of wine from Australia
7 Purchase of wine from Germany
8 Sale of bird houses to USA
9 Purchase of green beans from Kenya
10 Sale of bacon to Portugal

5.4 On 1 March 2011 Alladyce Services Ltd instructs a firm of management consultants based in Jersey to perform a review of its business. The management consultants charge £100,000 to the company in respect of this service.

You are required to outline the VAT impact of the above scenario.

5.5 **You are required to briefly outline the difference between an export and a dispatch from a VAT point of view.**

5.6 Purse Ltd, a UK VAT registered business selling leather goods, recently had the following transactions:

(1) Sale of goods located in a warehouse in Canada which were delivered to the USA.
(2) Sale of goods located in a warehouse in Milton Keynes which were delivered to Mexico.

You are required to state whether the place of supply is inside or outside the UK in each instance and whether the transaction is:

(A) Zero rated, or
(B) Outside the scope of VAT.

5.7 The place of supply of a service to a business customer is generally treated as the place where the customer belongs and for supplies to non-business customers it is generally where the supplier belongs. However various services are treated as exceptions to these general rules.

You are required to give five examples of services which do not follow the general rule and for each example state the prescribed place of supply.

6.1 Where the assets of a business are transferred in connection with all or part of the business as a going concern, the transfer is not treated as a taxable supply and no VAT is payable.

You are required to state four conditions that must be met in order for this treatment to apply.

6.2 Steve, an estate agent, undertakes work for individuals and for business clients. In the VAT year to 31 December 2010, the business client work amounted to £55,000 plus VAT. Turnover from work for individuals totalled £28,000 plus VAT.

The flat rate percentage for an estate agency or property management business is 10.5%.

You are required to:

(1) Briefly describe the optional flat rate scheme.

(2) Calculate the VAT payable by Steve under the optional flat rate scheme for the year to 31 December 2010.

6.3 On 30 April 2010 Sparks Ltd ordered a new printing machine and on 16 May 2010 paid a deposit of £10,000. The machine was dispatched to Sparks Ltd on 31 May 2010. On 18 June 2010 an invoice was issued to Sparks Ltd for the balance due of £45,000. This was paid on 20 June 2010.

You are required to outline (and explain why you have reached this answer):

(a) the tax point for the £10,000 deposit

(b) the tax point for the balance of £45,000

6.4 Farmer Bard has an annual turnover of £70,000 from sales of potatoes grown on his land. He sells £65,000 to supermarkets and £5,000 from a roadside stall. In the year to 31 December 2010 he purchased seed potatoes costing £1,000 and manure for £5,000 from a neighbour, who is retired but runs a refuge for elderly horses. He also bought a new tractor for £40,000 (excl VAT) to replace his old tractor which had collapsed after 20 years of use and was towed away free of charge by the local scrap merchant.

Farmer Bard dreads completing his VAT return and finds VAT administration a 'real headache'.

You are required to explain how the flat-rate scheme would affect Farmer Bard.

6.5 Julip Cleaners operates a dry-cleaning outlet in Charlton undertaking work for individuals but also business clients such as a local hotel.

In the VAT year to 31 December 2010 the business client work amounts to £52,000 net of VAT and the individuals work has brought in cash takings of £72,000.

Julip Cleaners operates the flat rate scheme with an 9.5% flat rate applying.

You are required to outline how the flat rate scheme will apply to the business using the above figures.

6.6 The structure of Red Group is as follows:

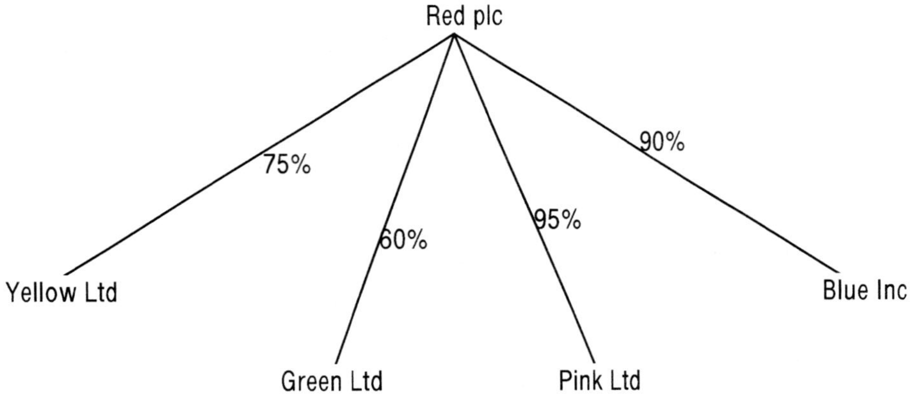

All the companies make electrical products except Yellow Ltd which is a finance company making only exempt supplies.

Blue Inc is an American company.

You are required to:

(a) **Discuss which companies are eligible to form a VAT group.**

(b) **Outline two effects of making a VAT group registration.**

6.7 Slick Tony sells prestige cars. He bought a Porsche from a member of the public for £8,000 in June 2010. He spent £550 plus VAT on restoration by a local garage he often uses. He sold the car to a member of the public for £12,500 in August 2010.

Slick Tony is preparing his quarterly VAT return to 31 August 2010.

You are required to:

(a) **outline briefly how the second hand goods scheme operates.**

(b) **state the output tax/input tax to be entered onto Tony's return in respect of the above car.**

6.8 Stan is an accountant. He provides his services to individuals and businesses.

During his VAT year to 31 December 2010 Stan provides services as follows:

Business clients	£78,000
Individual clients	£32,500

These figures are shown exclusive of VAT.

Stan also incurs expenses during the year of £11,745, inclusive of VAT at the standard rate.

The flat rate percentage for accountancy businesses is 13%.

You are required to calculate:

(1) **Stan's VAT due using the normal VAT rules.**

(2) **Stan's VAT due using the flat rate scheme rules.**

6.9 Jason had the following sales and purchases in his quarter ended 31 December 2010:

	£	
Standard rated sales	690,000	(inclusive of VAT)
Standard rated purchases	112,890	(plus VAT)
Zero rated purchases	95,750	

You are required to calculate the output VAT due for the quarter ended 31 December 2010, assuming Jason operates retail Apportionment Scheme 1.

6.10 Alone Ltd, which makes standard rated supplies, has the following shareholdings:

100% in Bone Ltd
80% in Clone Ltd
50% in Drone Ltd

It makes the following supplies of goods during its quarter ended 30 September 2010:

Amount	*To*
£54,000	Bone Ltd
£112,000	Clone Ltd
£99,000	Drone Ltd
£78,000	Individuals

All figures are exclusive of VAT. A VAT group registration is in effect which includes all those companies which are eligible to be included.

You are required to:

(1) **State which companies are eligible to be in a group for VAT purposes.**

(2) **Calculate the output VAT to be shown on Alone Ltd's return for the quarter ended 30 September 2010.**

6.11 **You are required to state five circumstances where a flat rate trader ceases to be eligible to account for VAT using the flat rate scheme**

7.1 Conway Ltd sends taxable goods to Payne Ltd on a sale or return basis. The goods are dispatched on 1 July 2010 and Payne Ltd accepts them on 30 September 2010. A tax invoice is issued on 23 October 2010 which is settled by Payne Ltd on 15 November 2010.

You are required to outline the tax point for this transaction giving your reasons.

7.2 Kindlyco Ltd sells goods to Meanieco Ltd on 12 June 2010 (VAT accounting period ended 31 July 2010) and raises an invoice for the supply on that day. The amount of the invoice is £2,600 including VAT and must be paid within 30 days. By December 2010, despite chasing, the invoice has not been paid.

You are required to state:

(a) two of the conditions for a VAT registered trader to claim bad debt relief

(b) on what VAT return Kindlyco Ltd can claim VAT bad debt relief, how much it can claim and where this should be included on the VAT return.

7.3 Derek submitted his recent VAT returns and payments as follows:

Period ended	*Date submitted*	*Payment due*
31 March 2010	15 May 2010	£17,500
30 June 2010	21 July 2010	£18,000
30 September 2010	20 December 2010	£22,000

A surcharge liability notice was issued on 10 June 2010.

Derek submitted his VAT return for the period ended 31 December 2010, 3 months late with tax outstanding of £25,000.

You are required to:

(a) State what the consequences are for the return for the period ended 30 September 2010 being submitted late.

(b) State the consequences of the December 2010 return being submitted late.

7.4 Peter Popper has an annual turnover of around £300,000. His VAT return for the quarter to 31 December 2009 is late. He then submits returns for the quarters to 30 September 2010 and 31 March 2011 late as well as making late payment of the tax due of £12,000 and £500 respectively.

Peter's VAT return to 31 March 2012 is also late and the VAT due of £1,100 is also paid late. All other VAT returns and VAT payments are made on time.

You are required to outline Peter Popper's exposure to default surcharge.

7.5 Jack is a VAT registered plumber. He submits his VAT return to 30 June 2011 on time showing VAT due of £14,000. However Jack deliberately increased the input tax deduction on this return by £3,000 of false invoices for purchases of plumbing supplies. HMRC initiate a review into Jack's return which prompts Jack to make a disclosure of his wrong doing.

State the maximum and minimum penalties that could be charged by HMRC on Jack.

7.6 The managing director of Charlie Ltd, Stanley Laurel, has written to you about various VAT matters. He has received notification of a control visit from the local VAT office and a review of the company's affairs prior to the visit has brought to light certain transactions which Mr Laurel suspects have not been correctly treated for VAT purposes. The transactions which he has queried are:

(1) Catering provided in the staff restaurant, where employees can purchase a two-course lunch for £2. The company subsidises the restaurant at a cost of approximately £1 per meal. No VAT has been accounted for on the restaurant sales.

(2) Bottles of whisky given to customers at Christmas. The cost to the company was £12 per bottle, although the full retail price would be £16. Again no VAT has been accounted for on these gifts.

(3) The company offers cash discounts for prompt payment, varying from 1.5% to 3.5%. Mr Laurel has discovered that the person who prepares the invoices has been calculating output tax on the full value of each invoice and then issuing a credit note if a discount is taken up.

(4) The company has sold two cars, formerly used by directors. The first is a BMW, which cost £22,000 and was sold to a private buyer for £15,000. The second is a Lotus which cost £30,000 and was sold, again to a private buyer, for £37,000. Mr Laurel has assumed that there is no VAT to account for on these sales, since no input tax credit was available when they were purchased.

You are required to briefly discuss the matters Stanley Laurel has raised. You are not required to deal with the interest or penalty implications of any errors made by the company. Assume a standard VAT rate of 17.5% applied where applicable.

7.7 Anthony Brown, who is registered for VAT, made the following supplies in 2010 to Jessica Heath. Ms Heath then moved away from the town but before she left she sent a note saying that she was unable to pay Anthony's bill in full but could only afford £5,200 and enclosed a cheque for that sum. She did not allocate the payment to any supply. The supplies made to her were as follows:

Tax point (date order)	*Type of supply*	*Net value*	*VAT*	*Gross consideration*
		£	£	£
2 April 2010	zero-rated	2,000	zero	2,000
4 May 2010	standard-rated	1,000	175	1,175
30 May 2010	standard-rated	5,000	875	5,875
12 June 2010	zero-rated	2,000	zero	2,000

Anthony has heard on the grapevine that he may receive a future payment in respect of the outstanding amount from her accountant in the future. His normal terms of business allow 30 days from the invoice date for payment and he submits returns to 31 May and quarterly thereafter.

You are required to calculate the VAT refund due to Anthony Brown and outline how Anthony would treat any future payment received in respect of the bad debt written off.

7.8 Dilatory Ltd has an annual turnover of approximately £1.2 million. The following is a summary of the last three VAT returns submitted by Dilatory Ltd.

	£	£	£
Output tax due	89,383	67,621	120,567
Input tax	20,396	32,564	79,972
Net tax due	68,987	35,057	40,595
Date due	30 June 2010	30 September 2010	31 December 2010
Date submitted and tax paid	19 July 2010	25 October 2010	14 February 2011

You are required to set out your calculations of the maximum default surcharge to which Dilatory Ltd is liable.

7.9 Rob Moore has an annual turnover of £450,000. His VAT return for the quarter to 30 September 2009 is late. He is late in submitting his return for the quarter ended 30 June 2010 and is late paying the VAT of £20,500. He is also late paying the VAT for the quarter to 31 December 2010 of £400 although he submits his return on time.

Rob's VAT return for the quarter ended 31 December 2011 is also late and the VAT due of £1,900 is also paid late. All other VAT returns and VAT payments are made on time.

You are required to:

(1) State the date to which the original surcharge liability notice will run and the amount of any penalty due on that date.

(2) Calculate the penalties due on each relevant date thereafter and state the date to which the penalty period will extend.

7.10 Deborah Hall runs a pet food distribution business. During her VAT quarter ended 31 March 2011 she ran a 10% discount promotion and one of her regular customers placed an order for £15,000 of goods on 21 March 2011.

Deborah always offers a 5% early payment discount regardless of any promotions being run. To obtain the discount, payment must be received within 30 days.

The goods arrived in Deborah's warehouse on 29 March 2011 and they were delivered to the customer on 30 March 2011. Deborah raised an invoice for the whole amount on 10 April 2011, which the customer paid in full on 1 June 2010.

You are required to:

(1) State the tax point for this transaction.
(2) State the return in which any output VAT must be reported.
(3) Calculate the amount of VAT due in respect of the transaction.

7.11 **You are required to list eight particulars which a registered person should shown on a VAT invoice supplied to another registered person and to state the deadline by when such a tax invoice should be issued.**

8.1 **You are required to explain the stamp taxes implications of the following transactions:**

1. Pat sold 200 shares in Bridge Ltd to Tom for £800 on 1 June 2010. The transfer was effected using a stock transfer form.

2. Plum Ltd sold 10,000 shares in Jam Ltd to Damson plc, an unconnected company, for £450,252 on 1 July 2010.

3. Peach Ltd acquired a warehouse from Albert for £280,000 on 1 June 2010. The warehouse was not in a disadvantaged area.

8.2 Samson Ltd paid £170,000 for the grant of a 20 year lease of a factory on 1 July 2010. The net present value of the rental was £620,000 and the annual rent was £30,000. The factory was not in a disadvantaged area.

You are required to explain the stamp taxes implications of the above transaction and state the due date for filing the stamp taxes return.

8.3 Beach Ltd owns 80% of Sand Ltd and 75% of Pebble Ltd. Pebble Ltd owns 60% of Shingle Ltd.

On 1 June 2010 Beach Ltd sold a factory to Shingle Ltd for £100,000 and a warehouse to Sand Ltd for £300,000.

On 1 October 2011 Beach Ltd sold the shares in Sand Ltd to an unconnected company for £1,200,000. Sand Ltd still owned the warehouse at this date.

You are required to explain the stamp taxes implications of the transfer of the properties.

8.4 Lionel granted a 25 year lease on a commercial property to Bill on 17 April 2010.

Bill paid a premium of £86,000 on 17 April 2010. The net present value of the rent is £154,000. Bill will also pay rent of £1,250 per month.

You are required to:

(a) Calculate the Stamp Duty Land Tax payable on the grant of the lease.
(b) State the payment date.
(c) State who it is payable by.

Exam style answers

1.1 When the value of taxable supplies in any previous twelve months exceeds £70,000 he is required to notify HMRC within 30 days ie 30 July 2010 (30 days after the 12 months to 30 June 2010).

As Monty did not deliberately fail to register the maximum penalty is 30% of the potential lost tax ie £900 x 30%

1.2 Notification by 30 January 2011, ie 30 days after the start of a 30 day period (ie January 2011) in which turnover is anticipated to exceed £70,000. But registration will be effective from 1 January 2011.

If Big Ltd decides to terminate the business it must notify HMRC within 30 days of ceasing to trade.

1.3 On first sale:

£168 (£840 × 20% = £168)

VAT based on fully discounted price (even if settlement discount not actually taken by the customer).

On the second sale VAT is due as follows:

£600 × 95% = £570 cost after trade discount
£570 × 97.5% = £556 after settlement discount
£556 × 20% = £111

All possible discounts are taken into account when calculating the VAT payable irrespective of when the customer actually pays.

1.4 All turnover zero-rated

Zero-rated supplies are taxable supplies and therefore taken into account in determining liability to registered. The first point at which past annual turnover exceeds the registration limit (then £70,000) is at the end of December 2010 (£70,440).

He must therefore notify HMRC of his liability by 30 January 2011 and is registered with effect from 1 February 2011.

However, as Richard's turnover will be wholly zero-rated he may apply to HMRC to be exempted from the requirement to register (VATA 1994 Sch 1 para 14). His application should accompany the notice of liability to register (form VAT 1). If HMRC think fit, they will exempt him from registration.

However it is likely that being VAT registered will allow a significant reclaim of input VAT which will outweigh the administrative burden of registration.

1.5 Under the historic test cumulative taxable turnover at the end of August 2010 is £56,000 and at the end of September 2010 is £80,000.

Thus the registration limit is first exceeded at the end of September 2010.

HMRC must be notified of this within 30 days, so by 30 October 2010.

The business will be registered for VAT from 1 November 2010.

Although under the future test supplies of £100,000 in December alone would force the business to VAT register, an earlier registration date applies under the historic test – thus HMRC will use the earlier date.

1.6 Mr Cassell exceeds the VAT threshold of £70,000 in June. He must notify HMRC by 30 July 2010 and will be registered from 1 August 2010.

If he does not notify HMRC until 1 November 2010 he will be liable to a penalty of 30% × the net VAT due since the date he should have been registered, ie 30% × £7,291 (W) = £2,187

Working – net VAT due

	£
August 2010	18,900
September 2010	19,600
October 2010	19,450
Total	57,950
VAT @ 7/47	8,631
less: input VAT: £3,000 × 3 × 7/47	(1,340)
Net VAT due	7,291

1.7 The following situations will result in compulsory deregistration:

1. Where a person ceases to make taxable supplies
2. If HMRC were misled into granting registration ie registration is void from the start
3. Where a registered person, who could voluntarily deregister, has failed to make a return or account for VAT
4. Where a person who has registered voluntarily is no longer entitled to be registered
5. Certain changes in business circumstances eg sole trader becoming a partnership, incorporation of a business

2.1 A mixed supply is where there are individual elements within the supply that are treated separately for VAT. An example of this would be where a student enrols on a BPP revision course and has to purchase some books as part of the course. A course is standard rated and books are zero-rated. They are effectively treated as separate supplies, even though the student might purchase them together. The individual elements are treated separately for VAT. With a mixed supply, there is the need to perform some sort of apportionment to apportion the individual elements of the supply in order to calculate the VAT due.

A compound supply is just a single supply although it might be made up of several different things. A compound supply is a single supply with a single VAT liability. An example of this is a plane ticket. The traveller will also probably be provided with a meal on the flight. Air transport is zero-rated and catering is standard rated. However the traveller is buying a complete package and it is difficult to separate the two elements plus the meal is just a small insignificant piece of the overall larger flight. In such a case, this compound supply would just be treated as a single zero-rated supply of a flight ticket. With a compound supply only a single rate of VAT applies to the whole supply.

2.2 (a) Zero-rated supplies are taxable at 0%. A trader who sells taxable supplies, whether at the zero or standard rate, may reclaim VAT paid on related purchases.

Exempt supplies are not chargeable to VAT. A person making exempt supplies is unable to recover VAT on related purchases.

(b) VAT supply

(i) Standard-rated (supply is of hot food and must be standard-rated regardless of whether a charge is made for the use of the oven)

(ii) Standard-rated (excepted Item Group 1, Schedule 8, VAT Act 1994)

(iii) Zero-rated (Item 4, Group 8, Schedule 8, VAT Act 1994)

(iv) Zero-rated (Notice 744A)

Tutorial note. You may not be able to remember all of the detail necessary to answer a question in the exam. There may also be questions where the detail required exceeds that provided in the study text. In these circumstances you will need to use the legislation to find the detail you require and you should practice doing this during your studies.

2.3 The reduced rate of VAT, of 5%, is charged under VATA 1994 s.29A on any supplies falling within Sch 7A of that Act. Sch 7A Group 1 covers a wide range of fuel supplies, including, inter alia, electricity, gas, oil and coal. To obtain the reduced rate, Stimpson Group plc must be able to demonstrate that the fuel is supplied for 'qualifying use' (Group 1 Item 1) – as it is a commercial undertaking, this has to be for 'domestic use' (Note 3). In turn, as the premises in question are commercial, they must be 'used for a relevant residential purpose' (note 6).

'Relevant residential purpose' is defined in note 7 to include seven categories of premises; in addition there is an exclusion where the use is as a hospital, a prison or similar institution or an hotel or inn or similar establishment. Unfortunately the term 'residential accommodation' (note 7(1)) is not defined. The key issue to determine is whether or not the trading premises it runs come within any of the categories, and, if so, the impact of the exclusion.

Considering the nursing homes run by Stimpson Group plc these appear to fall clearly within note 7(1)(b), 'being a home... providing residential accommodation with personal care for persons in need of personal care by reason of old age, disablement ...'. Consequently the reduced rate of VAT should apply to all supplies of fuel made to the homes.

2.4 Value for the quarter:

	£
Car 1	
£340 × 1/3	113
Car 2	
£425 × 2/3	283
	396

Output tax: 7/47 × £396 = £59

Input tax: 7/47 × £300 = £45

2.5 (a) Biscuits sold in a fancy tin are a compound supply. This would be a single zero rated supply.

(b) The subscription to satellite TV with a monthly magazine was held in the *British Sky Broadcasting Ltd* case to be a compound supply with the supply of the zero rated magazine being only incidental to the main standard rated supply.

(c) An airline ticket is a compound supply – it is a zero rated supply of transport with an incidental (hence ignored) standard rated supply of catering.

2.6 (a) Postal services provided by the Post Office are exempt under Group 3 Schedule 9 VATA 1994.

(b) Children's car seats are charged to VAT at the reduced rate of 5% under Group 5 Schedule 7A VATA 1994.

(c) Services provided by registered medical practitioners such as Dentists are exempt under Group 7 Schedule 9 VATA 1994.

(d) Although food is normally zero rated under Group 1 Schedule 8 VATA 1994 sweets are specifically excluded from zero rating, so this supply will be a standard rated supply.

(e) Newspapers are zero rated for VAT under Group 3 Schedule 8 VATA 1994.

2.7 A gift of goods is not a supply where the transfer or disposal is a:

(1) Business gift the cost of which, together with the cost of any other business gifts made to the same person in the same year was not more than £50 or a

(2) Sample of any goods

The cost of business goods is the cost to the donor of acquiring or producing them.

Where a person is given a number of samples, which are identical, then only the first gift is not treated as a supply.

3.1 Regarding the pre-registration input tax Ben may recover £770 (all of it)

Stock – if unsold on registration date
Fixed assets – if within four years and still held and used in business

Services – if within six months prior to registration

When looking at the purchase of motor vehicles Ben may recover (1,837 + 4,594) = £6,431

VAT on cars with private use is not reclaimable. VAT on vans and lorries can be reclaimed

3.2 Firstly you should determine whether either Test 1 or Test 2 are satisfied for the quarter.

Test 1 is not satisfied because total input tax exceeds £625 per month (£150,000/3) = £50,000).

Test 2 is not satisfied because total input tax less that directly attributable to taxable supplies exceeds £625 per month ((£90,000)/3 = £30,000).

A partial exemption calculation must be performed to determine how much input tax is recoverable for the quarter as follows.

Taxable supplies = $240{,}000 \times \frac{100}{120} + 50{,}000 = £250{,}000$

Total supplies = £250,000 + £75,000 = £325,000

	£
Share of unattributed input tax	
$\frac{250{,}000}{325{,}000} \times 100 = 77\%$ (rounded) × £73,000	56,210
Attributed to taxable supplies	60,000
	116,210

The input tax attributable to exempt supplies is not *de minimis*.

3.3 (1) Previous years' recovery percentage used

	£
Non attributable input VAT attributed to making taxable supplies	
79% × 4,000	3,160
Input VAT specifically attributable to making taxable supplies	12,500
Total input VAT reclaimed for the quarter	15,660

The VAT attributable to making exempt supplies (1,500 + 840), exceeds the de-minimis of £625 a month or £1,875 a quarter.

(2) Previous years' recovery percentage not used

	£
Non attributable input VAT attributed to making taxable supplies	
$\frac{160{,}000}{200{,}000}$ (80% × 4,000)	3,200
Input VAT specifically attributable to making taxable supplies	12,500
Total input VAT reclaimed for the quarter	15,700

The VAT attributable to making exempt supplies (1,500 + 800), exceeds the de-minimis of £625 a month or £1,875 a quarter.

3.4 Firstly you should determine whether either Test 1 or Test 2 are satisfied for the quarter.

Test 1 is not satisfied because total input tax exceeds £625 per month (£45,000/3) = £15,000).

Test 2 is not satisfied because total input tax less that directly attributable to taxable supplies exceeds £625 per month ((£18,000)/3 = £6,000).

A partial exemption calculation must be performed to determine how much input tax is recoverable for the quarter as follows.

Total taxable supplies: £40,000 + £20,000 = £60,000

Partial recovery fraction: $\frac{60,000}{60,000+23,000}$ = 72.289 rounded up to 73%

Input tax – taxable supplies

	£
Direct	27,000
Apportioned (45,000 – 27,000 – 9,000) × 73%	6,570
Total	33,570

Exempt VAT

	£
Direct	9,000
Apportioned (9,000 – 6,570)	2,430
Total	11,430

Exempt input VAT greater than £625 per month therefore irrecoverable.

3.5 Amount of deductible input tax:

	£
Re supplies for contract to be fulfilled in first quarter of 2010	15,200
Re overheads in factory	3,300
Re employee entertainment	850
	19,350

3.6 Firstly you should determine whether either Test 1 or Test 2 are satisfied for the year.

Test 1 is not satisfied because total input tax exceeds £625 per month (£35,000/12) = £2,917).

Test 2 is not satisfied because total input tax less that directly attributable to taxable supplies exceeds £625 per month ((£15,000)/12 = £1,250).

A partial exemption calculation must be performed to determine how much input tax is recoverable for the quarter as follows.

Recoverable input tax

	£
Input tax attributed to taxable supplies	20,000
Unallocated input tax attributed to taxable supplies (£5,000 × 84 %) (W)	4,200
	24,200

Potentially not recoverable

	£
Input tax attributed to exempt supplies	10,000
Balance of unallocated £(5,000 – 4,200)`	800
	10,800

This amount of exempt input tax will be recoverable if it is small, ie, < £625 per month on average or £625 × 12 = £7,500 per annum. As the amount (£10,800) exceeds the de minimis limits it will not be recoverable. Thus, only £24,200 of input tax is recoverable.

Working

% of taxable to total supplies $\frac{21,500+80,200}{122,000} = 83.36\%$

Round up to next whole % = 84%

3.7 (a) The input tax incurred on the purchase of the computer was £15,000 (£26,250 – £11,250), giving the computer itself a VAT exclusive value of £100,000. The computer is therefore a capital item for the purposes of the Capital Goods Scheme as its value is £50,000 or more.

The Capital Goods Scheme (CGS) does not apply to the purchase of software.

(b) The computer was purchased on 19 May 2009 (which falls within the tax year ending 31 March 2010) which means the first interval for CGS purposes run from 19 May 2009 to 31 March 2010.

Input tax is recoverable in the first interval using the 2010 recovery rate of 70%. The calculation is therefore:

£15,000 × 70% = £10,500

Input tax incurred on the purchase of a computer within the capital goods scheme may be adjusted over five successive intervals. As there is a change in the level of partial exemption recovery, an adjustment is required in the second interval adjustment (ie year ended 31 March 2011) as follows:

$$\frac{£15,000}{5} \times (70\% - 85\%) = £450$$

The adjustment, ie additional input tax claim, should have been included on the VAT return for the second period after the end of the tax year ie in this case the period ended 30 September 2011.

3.8 For the first VAT year to 31 March 2010 the recovery (after the annual partial exemption adjustment) is £100,000 × 17.5% = £17,500 × 60% = £10,500.

For the second VAT year to 31 March 2011 the adjustment is £17,500 × 10% (ie 60%-50%) × 1/5 = £350, payable to HMRC.

For the third VAT year to 31 March 2012 there are two adjustments:

(a) £17,500 × 10% × 1/5 = £350, payable to HMRC.

(b) £17,500 × 40% (ie 100%-60%) × 2/5 = £2,800, restricted to the VAT charged on the sale of the computer ie £6,000 × 20% = £1,200, recoverable from HMRC.

The net adjustment for the third VAT year to 31 March 2012 is (£(350) + £1,200) = £850 recoverable from HMRC.

3.9 The partial exemption rules apply.

Firstly you should determine whether either Test 1 or Test 2 are satisfied for the quarter.

Test 1 is not satisfied because total input tax exceeds £625 per month (£3,860/3) = £1,287).

Test 2 is not satisfied because total input tax less that directly attributable to taxable supplies exceeds £625 per month ((£1,965)/3 = £655).

A partial exemption calculation must be performed to determine how much input tax is recoverable for the quarter as follows.

	£
Wholly attributable to taxable supplies	1,895
Partly attributable to taxable supplies	
$\frac{325,000}{325,000 + 86,000}$ = 79.08% rounded up to 80% × £1,545	1,236
Total	3,131
Add: exempt input VAT: £(420 + (1,545 – 1,236))	729
Total recoverable input VAT	3,860

ie all input VAT is recoverable (W)

Working – exempt input VAT

De minimis test:

Monthly average: $\frac{729}{3}$ = £243 ie not more than £625

Proportion of total $\frac{729}{3,860}$ = 18.9% ie not more than 50%

Therefore all the exempt input VAT can be recovered.

3.10 Computers costing at least £50,000 are inside the capital goods scheme and are dealt with over a 5 year period.

For the first VAT year to 31 March 2011, the recovery (after the annual partial exemption adjustment) is:

£75,000 × 17.5% = £13,125 × 68% = £8,925

For the second VAT year to 31 March 2012, the adjustment is:

£13,125 × (49% - 68%) × 1/5 = £499 payable to HMRC.

For the third VAT year to 31 March 2013 there are two adjustments:

(i) £13,125 × (45% - 68%) × 1/5 = £604, payable to HMRC
(ii) £13,125 × (100% - 68%) × 2/5 = £1,680 recoverable from HMRC.

Note: The second adjustment (£1,680) is restricted to the VAT actually charged on the sale of the server, ie £19,000 × 20% = £3,800. Therefore in this case there is no restriction and the £1,680 is recoverable in full.

The net adjustment for the third VAT year to 31 March 2013 is:

£((604) + 1,680) = £1,076 recoverable from HMRC

3.11 Input VAT incurred on client (but not staff) entertaining is always disallowed as is expenditure on accommodation for directors. Input VAT on cars is also blocked, but the input VAT on the servicing costs can be reclaimed in full.

	£	£
Output VAT: £247,000 × 17.5%		43,225
Less: reclaimable input VAT		
Other expenses: £35,600 × 7/47	5,302	
Client entertaining	-	
Staff entertaining £2,258 × 7/47	336	
Renovation work on property occupied by director	-	
Car with 80% business use		
Cost of the car	-	
Servicing costs £3,021 × 7/47	450	
		(6,088)
Net VAT due		37,137

3.12 Examples (only five required by the question) of supplies of goods and services on which input tax is not recoverable are:

(1) Goods/services to be used for the purposes of business entertainment (Art 5 SI1992/3222)

(2) Goods installed in houses by a builder other than articles ordinarily installed as builder's fixtures (Art 6 SI1992/3222)

(3) Motor cars (subject to a number of exceptions) (Art 7 SI1992/3222)

(4) Goods purchased under a margin scheme where no VAT invoice is provided by the supplier (Art 4 SI 1992/3222)

(5) Goods and services purchased to provide domestic accommodation for a director (s.24(3) VATA 1994)

(6) Goods imported for private purposes (s.24(5) VATA 1994)

Tutorial note: Note the legislative references in the answer above. You may need to refer to your legislation in the exam to be able to provide the level of detail required by a question. Get used to using it now.

4.1 (a) Peter will be allowed to zero rate his services provided to BIG Homes Ltd as they are constructing new residential properties and Peter is a sub-contractor working on those properties. [Schedule 8 Group 5 VATA 1994]

(b) Services of lawyers are standard rated despite the overall project being zero rated. The lawyers' services do not fall with Schedule 8 Group 5 VATA 1994.

(c) The building is 'old' so the supply is exempt from VAT although Juniper Ltd may make an option to tax over the building and standard rate this supply. [Schedule 9 Group 1 and Schedule 10 VATA 1994]

4.2 VAT supply

(a) Reduced rate applies (item 1, Group 6, Schedule 7A, VAT Act 1994. Supply in the course of conversion not eligible for zero-rating under item 2, Group 5, Schedule 8, VAT Act 1994)

(b) Reduced rate applies (item 1, Group 2, Schedule 7A, VAT Act 1994)

(c) Exempt (item 1, Group 1, Schedule 9, VAT Act 1994)

(d) Zero-rated (item 1(a), Group 5, Schedule 8, VAT Act 1994)

(e) Standard-rated.

In general the supply would be exempt (Group 1 Schedule 9 VATA 1994) but the option to tax has been made (Schedule 10 VATA 1994) so that the supply becomes taxable at the standard rate.

4.3 If Tim opts to tax (under Sch 10 VATA 1994) the development at the outset, the VAT incurred by him will be recoverable in full as the project progresses. The net cost to him would therefore be £9.8 million. However, on letting the property he must charge VAT on any premium and rent received. Tim should be aware that this course of action might be unattractive to a potential tenant who is partially or completely exempt. He should also be aware that he will have to charge VAT on any future disposal of the building.

If Tim decides not to opt to tax the development and instead grants exempt leases, the VAT of £1.56 million charged on the supply will not be recoverable by Tim as it is directly attributable to the exempt supply of the lease on the building. Therefore the total cost of the development to Tim becomes £11.36 million.

Tim may be able to obtain a higher premium or rent for an exempt lease. However, whether this would be sufficient to give him the same yield from the increased capital cost of development, as he would achieve from a taxed building, is questionable. Therefore opting to tax may be the preferred route.

4.4 Since Mr Heart is leasing out a commercial property he is making an exempt supply of the office block.

The building needs renovation, costing £750,000. Renovating and building services are standard rated supplies so VAT will be charged on this supply to Mr Heart.

Because Mr Heart leases out the building and hence makes an exempt supply the £111,702 of input tax incurred on the renovation will relate to making an exempt supply of that office block and hence will be irrecoverable.

Mr Heart should consider making an option to tax over the property. If Mr Heart opts to tax the building he will make a taxable supply of that office building from the date of the option onwards. Thus, when the renovation occurs the £111,702 of input tax paid will relate to making a taxable supply of the building and hence will be recoverable in full.

Once the option to tax is made all future invoices for rent sent to the tenants must include VAT at 17.5%.

4.5 (a) The sale of land is an exempt supply and the option to tax can be made on this supply.

(b) The sale of a 30 year old house is an exempt supply. A house is a building in domestic rather than commercial use and so the option to tax cannot be made.

(c) The lease of a one year old factory is an exempt supply because although it is a new commercial property, the supply is of a lease rather than the freehold. Because the building is commercial the option to tax can be made.

(d) The freehold sale of a one year old office block being freehold, commercial and new is a standard rated supply. Since the supply is not exempt the option to tax does not apply here.

(e) A 99 year lease on a newly refurbished showroom is an exempt supply. The option to tax can be made over such a supply.

4.6 (1) Girth Ltd must notify HMRC that it has 'made' an option to tax by 30 August 2010.
(2) The cooling off period ends on 31 January 2011.
(3) The option to tax can only be revoked from 1 August 2030.
(4) Girth Ltd can make a 'Real Estate Election' (REE) to include all of its properties within the option to tax.

The option to tax must be notified within 30 days of being 'made'.

The company has a 6 month cooling off period.

After the cooling off period ends, the option to tax can only be revoked after 20 years.

4.7 The following supplies are treated as standard rated:

(1) The sale of the freehold (fee simple) in a new or partly completed commercial property.

(2) The provision of accommodation in a hotel

(3) The right to occupy holiday accommodation

(4) The provision of seasonal pitches for caravans

(5) The grant of facilities for playing any sport or participating in any physical recreation

Tutorial note. They are other examples which you could have listed. Refer to Group 1 Sch 9 VATA 1994 for a full list of standard rated supplies.

5.1 Zero-rated export to Canadian customers – export evidence to be obtained and retained.

Zero-rated dispatch to VAT registered customer in Italy, provided customer's Italian VAT registration number is obtained and shown on the invoice and export evidence is obtained.

Standard-rated sale to non-registered customer.

Provided Jane gives the supplier her UK VAT registration number she will not be charged Portuguese VAT by the supplier. Instead, she will be required to account for output tax in her next VAT return and reclaim the same amount as input tax on the same return.

5.2 (a) *Place of supply of goods*

If the supply of any goods does not involve their removal from or to the UK they are treated as being supplied in the UK if they are in the UK at the time of the supply. If they are not in the UK at the time of the supply they are treated as being supplied outside the UK and the supply is therefore outside the scope of VAT.

Where the supply of any goods involves their removal from the UK, as, for instance, where they are exported, they are treated as being supplied in the UK.

If the supply involves the removal of goods to the UK, as where goods are imported, the place of supply is deemed to be outside the UK. However, the goods are subject to VAT on importation.

(b) *Place of supply for ABC Ltd*

The place of the supplies made by ABC Ltd is as follows:

(i) the furniture was supplied outside the UK because it was outside the UK when allocated to the supply;

(ii) the table was supplied in the UK because it was in the UK when allocated to the supply; and

(iii) the armchair was supplied in the UK because it was only allocated to the supply in the UK, ie once the stock had arrived from China.

5.3
1 Sale of lamb to France – dispatch
2 Purchase of lamb from New Zealand – import
3 Purchase of books from Brazil – import
4 Sale of children's clothes to Germany – dispatch
5 Sale of chocolate to Italy – dispatch
6 Purchase of wine from Australia – import
7 Purchase of wine from Germany – acquisition
8 Sale of bird houses to USA – export
9 Purchase of green beans from Kenya – import
10 Sale of bacon to Portugal – dispatch

5.4 Alladyce Services Ltd is a UK based company receiving services from management consultants based in Jersey, which is not in the UK and hence the UK company is receiving an international service. As the supply is between two businesses the place of supply is deemed to be where the customer (Alladyce Services Ltd) belongs i.e. the UK.

This means that Alladyce Services Ltd will have to apply the reverse charge procedure. The company will therefore account for output tax of £20,000, which is calculated as the £100,000 for the service at the standard rate of VAT. It will also account for input tax of £20,000. The normal input tax recovery rules apply to this input tax. So on the VAT return this will be output VAT of £20,000 and input VAT of £20,000, assuming that the input tax can be recovered in full by Alladyce Services Limited.

5.5 Exports are where a trader sells goods to a customer based in a country outside the UK but not in the European Union. An export is a zero-rated supply irrespective of what type of goods are being sold overseas. Exports of goods are always a zero-rated supply.

To apply zero rating to an export a trader must obtain the necessary evidence that the goods sold have been exported within three months of the time of the supply.

A dispatch is where a trader sells goods to a customer in the European Union. How the trader treats the dispatch depends on the status of his European customer. If the European customer is VAT registered in this EU member state and he gives the UK trader his VAT registration number, then the UK trader will zero-rate the supply of goods to his business customer.

If, however, the customer is not VAT registered in his EU member state, then the UK trader treats him in the same way as a UK customer and charges him UK VAT at the rate that would be appropriate to the goods being sold. Thus for example, if a trader is selling DVD players he would charge standard rate VAT. If he was selling wheat he would charge 0% VAT because food is zero-rated.

5.6 *Sale of goods from Canada to the USA*

The goods are located outside the UK so the place of supply is Canada, ie outside the UK. The supply is therefore outside the scope of UK VAT.

Sale of goods from Milton Keynes to Mexico

The goods are located inside the UK so the place of supply is the UK. The supply is therefore liable to UK VAT but it is an export so is zero rated.

5.7 Examples of supplies of services where the place of supply does not follow the general rules are:

(1) Certain services in relation to land eg the grant of an interest in land - the country where the land is situated

(2) The transportation of passengers – country in which the transportation takes place

(3) Short term hiring of transport – in the country where the transport is made available

(4) The supply of cultural, educational and entertainment facilities eg fairs and exhibitions – country where the services are physically carried out

(5) Telecommunication and broadcasting services – country where they are used and enjoyed if they would otherwise be treated as supplied in the UK and they are used and enjoyed outside the EU or they would otherwise be treated as supplied in a country outside the EU and they are used and enjoyed in the UK

Tutorial note. They are other examples which you could have listed. Refer to Sch 4A VATA 1994 for a full list of the exceptions

6.1 The transfer of business assets is not treated as a taxable supply and no VAT is charged if the following conditions are met:

- The assets must be used by the transferee in carrying on the same kind of business as carried on by the transferor.
- The business transferred must be a going concern at the time of the transfer;
- There must not be a series of consecutive transfers (A to B then to C);
- There must be no significant break in trading after the transfer;
- If property is involved then if the transferor has opted, the purchaser must also opt and notify that option prior to the transfer date.
- If the purchaser has to opt to tax, they must give a declaration that their option will not be disapplied
- Where the transferor is a taxable person, the transferee must be a taxable person or become one when the transaction takes place.

- If part of a business is transferred that part must be capable of separate operation.

(Only four of the above are required).

6.2 (1) The optional flat rate scheme is a simplification measure which enables businesses to calculate the net VAT due simply by applying a flat rate percentage to their tax-inclusive turnover ie the total turnover generated, including all reduced, zero-rated and exempt income.

The flat rate percentage will depend upon the trade sector into which a business falls for the purposes of the scheme. In the tax year to 31 December 2010 the percentages ranged from 3.5% for retailing food, confectionery, tobacco, newspapers or children's clothing to 13% for labour-only building construction services. The flat rate percentage for accountancy and book-keeping was 13% and for financial services was 12%.

Businesses using the scheme still need to issue VAT invoices to their VAT registered customers but do not have to record all the details of the invoices issued or purchase invoices received to calculate the VAT due. Invoices issued will show VAT at the normal rate rather than the flat rate.

(2) Gross sales:

	£
Business customers	
£55,000 × $\frac{117.5}{100}$	64,625
Individuals	
£28,000 × $\frac{117.5}{100}$	32,900
	97,525

VAT payable:

Flat rate 10.5% applies

10.5% × £97,525 = £10,240

6.3 (a) 16 May 2010

Date deposit is paid (as this is earlier than the dispatch date)

(b) 31 May 2010

Dispatch date (for the invoice date to apply it must have been issued within 14 days of the date of dispatch)

6.4 Farmer Bard (FB) made zero-rated sales of potatoes of £70,000. FB also made some purchases. The seed potatoes and manure will not have had the addition of VAT to their price but the tractor will have cost £40,000 plus £7,000 of VAT. His position over the whole year will thus have been a VAT recovery of £7,000.

If he joins the flat-rate scheme (FRS), he will not be able to recover the £7,000 of VAT on the tractor but will now charge 4% on the £65,000 of sales to his VAT registered customers (the supermarkets) totalling £2,600. No flat-rate is charged to the presumably non-VAT registered stall customers.

Comparing the two, the FRS has no VAT administration but only £2,600 is recovered, whereas when VAT registered £7,000 was recovered. However if FB is not planning any large asset purchases (and hence large input tax bills) in the next few years then the FRS will give him a better result in the future.

6.5 As business client work amounts to £52,000 Julip Cleaners will issue VAT invoices totalling £61,100 (£52,000 plus 17.5% VAT).

Individual work totals £72,000 (inclusive of VAT).

The total gross sales are £133,100.

VAT due to HMRC under the scheme will therefore amount to £12,644 (£133,100 × 9.5%).

VAT invoices are issued to customers in the normal way showing 17.5% VAT.

No input tax is recovered from purchases under the scheme unless a purchase costs over £2,000 (VAT inclusive).

6.6 (a) The companies eligible to form a VAT group are:

Red plc
Yellow Ltd
Green Ltd
Pink Ltd

Since Red plc controls all the companies the 'common control' definition is satisfied. However, a group can only consist of UK established companies so Blue Inc cannot be part of the VAT group.

Yellow Ltd may be included in the VAT group even if it makes exempt supplies. It may however impact the group as including it would make the group partially exempt.

(b) (i) The group is treated as a single taxable person for VAT with one company (the representative member) responsible for all VAT accounting.

(ii) All the members of the group are jointly and severally liable for the VAT liability of the whole group.

6.7 (a) The second hand goods scheme involves calculating a profit (known as the margin) made on each item that is bought or sold. The margin is effectively the difference between the price paid and the sale proceeds. Under the Scheme, the profit margin is VAT inclusive so, when multiplied by 7 over 47, gives the output VAT due on the individual sale. If the sale is made at a loss, in other words there is no profit margin, then there is no VAT due.

If the trader has incurred any costs, for example, repairing or improving the item before it is sold, these costs are not taken into account when calculating the profit margin. However, once all the output tax is calculated, any VAT incurred, for example on these costs, is treated as input tax and can be deducted from the output tax in the normal way.

A normal VAT invoice is not issued for sales under the Scheme. Thus any purchasers cannot reclaim any of the VAT charged. If a purchaser wants a VAT invoice and wants to recover any VAT charged, then the item must be accounted for outside of the scheme in the normal way.

(b) Margin

£(12,500 – 8,000) = £4,500

£4,500 × 7/47 = £670

Return to August 2010

Output tax = £670

Input tax

£550 × 17.5% = £96

The above entries would be made in respect of the Porsche on the VAT return to 31 August 2010.

6.8 Stan's VAT liability, using the normal VAT rules, is:

	£
Output VAT: £(78,000 + 32,500) × 17.5%	19,337
Less: input VAT: £11,745 × 7/47	(1,749)
Net VAT due	17,588

If he were to use the flat rate scheme, he would apply the flat rate percentage to his gross turnover (ie inclusive of VAT) and ignoring input VAT:

	£
£78,000 + 32,500 + 19,337	129,837
@ 13%	16,879

6.9 Apportionment scheme 1 is available to traders with VAT-exclusive annual sales of up to £1 million.

The estimated gross takings are split between the different types of turnover based on the types of expenditure incurred.

The fraction used is based on the VAT-inclusive standard rated purchases over the total purchases:

$$\frac{112{,}890 + 19{,}756 \text{ (VAT)}}{112{,}890 + 19{,}756 + 95{,}750} = \frac{132{,}646}{228{,}396} = 0.5807719$$

Standard rated supplies: £690,000 × 0.5807719 = £400,733

Output VAT is therefore: £400,733 × 7/47 = £59,684 due to HMRC

6.10 Companies can join a VAT group where there is common control, ie over 50%, so Alone Ltd, Bone Ltd and Clone Ltd are all eligible to be in the VAT group.

The output VAT due is:

	£
Output VAT	
(£99,000 + £78,000) @ 17.5%	30,975

6.11 A flat rate trader ceases to be eligible to account for VAT using the flat rate scheme in the following circumstances:

(1) If in the previous 12 months the total value of his income exceeded £225,000

(2) There are reasonable grounds to believe that the total value of his income in the next 30 days will exceed £225,000

(3) He becomes a tour operator

(4) He intends to acquire or construct a capital asset which falls within the capital goods scheme

(5) He becomes eligible to be registered as part of a VAT group

Tutorial note. There are other circumstances which could have been given. Refer to SI 1995/2518 Reg 55M for a full list of circumstances.

7.1 30 September 2010.

The earlier of:

(a) Acceptance date

(b) Invoice date

(c) Cash received

(d) 12 months after dispatch

7.2 (a) Two of the following:

(i) He must have supplied goods or services and accounted for and paid VAT on the supply.

(ii) All or part of the consideration must have been written off in the accounts.

(iii) Six months must have elapsed from the later of the date of supply and the time when the consideration became due and payable.

(b) VAT bad debt relief can be claimed on the VAT return for the period ended 31 January 2011 (payment outstanding for six months)

The amount of the claim will be 7/47 of £2,600 which equals £387

This sum should be added to the input tax figure claimed for the period (included in box 4 on the VAT return)

7.3 (a) The surcharge liability notice (SLN) will be extended to the period ended 30 September 2011. Derek will be liable to a surcharge of £440 (£22,000 × 2%)

(b) The SLN will be extended to the period 31 December 2011 and a penalty of £1,250 (5% × £25,000) will be levied.

7.4 A surcharge liability notice will be issued after the late filing on the 31 December 2009 return outlining a surcharge period extending to 31 December 2010.

The late 30 September 2010 return is in the surcharge period so the period is extended to 30 September 2011. The late VAT payment triggers a 2% penalty. 2% × £12,000 = £240. Since £240 is less than the £400 de minimis limit it is not collected by HMRC.

The late 31 March 2011 return is in the surcharge period so the period is now extended to 31 March 2012. The late payment triggers a 5% penalty. 5% × £500 = £25. Since £25 is less than the £400 de minimis limit it is not collected by HMRC.

The late 31 March 2012 return is in the surcharge period. The period is extended to 31 March 2013. The late payment triggers a 10% penalty. 10% × £1,100 = £110. This is collected by HMRC since the £400 de minimis does not apply to penalties calculated at the 10% (and 15%) rate.

Peter will have to submit all four quarterly VAT returns to 31 March 2013 on time and pay the VAT on time to 'escape' the default surcharge regime.

7.5 The potential lost revenue as a result of Jack's error is; £3,000

Jack's error was deliberate and concealed so the maximum penalty is £3,000 × 100% = £3,000

However, Jack made a prompted disclosure so the minimum penalty is £3,000 × 50% = £1,500

7.6 (1) Catering

The company should have accounted for output tax on the provision of catering to staff. The amount paid by the employee is treated as the VAT-inclusive value of the supply. Hence where the cost to the employee is £2, the amount of output tax due is 30p (£2 × 7/47).

(2) Gifts

Gifts of goods are generally deemed to be supplies on which output tax must be paid. There is however an exception, which applies to the present case, for small gifts which are made in the course or furtherance of business. A gift is small if the total cost of gifts given to the same person in a twelve month period is less than £50.

It seems likely that there will be no requirement for the company to account for tax on these gifts.

(3) Cash discounts

The current treatment is incorrect. Output tax should be accounted for on the amount due from the customer net of the maximum possible cash discount (provided that this is shown on the invoice), regardless of whether that discount is taken up.

(4) Sale of cars

Your assumption about the car sales is correct. For many years, sales of cars at above cost were thought to give rise to a VAT charge. However, a European Court ruling confirmed that no VAT should be charged on sales if no VAT was recovered on purchase. The sales are exempt from VAT. Thus no VAT is due on either the loss making sale or the profit making sale. Any input tax incurred in making the sales will be irrecoverable, subject to the de minimis rules.

7.7 Refund of VAT due to Anthony Brown

Tax point (date order)	*Type of supply*	*Net value*	*VAT*	*Gross consideration*
		£	£	£
2 April 2010	zero-rated	2,000	zero	2,000
4 May 2010	standard-rated	1,000	175	1,175
30 May 2010	standard-rated	5,000	875	5,875
12 June 2010	zero-rated	2,000	zero	2,000
		10,000	1,050	11,050

payment on account = £5,200

To calculate bad debt relief, the payment is allocated to the supplies on a 'first-in, first-out' basis. Thus, later debts are treated as bad rather than earlier ones. The bad debt of £5,850 (being £11,050 less £5,200) and the refund is identified as follows:

Tax point	*Bad debt (gross consideration)*	*VAT bad debt refund*
	£	£
12 June 2010	2,000	zero
30 May 2010	3,850	573
	5,850	

The refund of VAT due under the bad debt relief legislation for Mr Brown is £573. This claim may be made once six months after the due date for payment of the debt has lapsed, ie in the return for the period to 28 February 2011.

Any bad debt refund must be repaid to HMRC to the extent of the VAT element of any full or part payment subsequently received (Value Added Tax Regulations 1995 (SI 1995/2518), reg. 171(1)). The claimant must include the VAT element on the VAT return for the period in which he received the payment. It is included in the box opposite the legend 'VAT due in this period on sales and other outputs'. A part payment would be treated as a part of £3,850 on which the VAT is £573, unless the debtor allocated the payment specifically to the zero-rated invoice which has not yet been included in any claim.

7.8 Computation of default surcharge

Quarterly Return to 31 May 2010:

No surcharge, but surcharge liability notice issued

Quarterly Return to 31 August 2010:

Default surcharge liability 2% × £35,057 = £701

Quarterly Return to 30 November 2010:

Default surcharge liability 5% × £40,595 = £2,030

7.9 If a business is late in submitting its return and/ or paying its VAT the surcharge liability notice (SLN) rules apply.

When Rob is late submitting his return for the quarter to 30 September 2009, the surcharge liability notice period will initially run to 30 September 2010. As the VAT is not paid late, no penalty is due.

As Rob is then late submitting his return and paying the tax for the quarter to 30 June 2010, which is within the SLN period, the period extends to 30 June 2011 and he will pay a penalty of £20,500 × 2% = £410.

The return for the quarter to 31 December 2010 is on time but the payment is late, so the SLN period is extended to 31 December 2011 and the penalty is now 5% × £400 = £20, which is below the de minimis limit of £400 so it is not collected by HMRC.

Rob's return for the quarter ended 31 December 2011 is late and the tax is paid late too. The SLN period is extended to 31 December 2012 and the penalty of 10% × £1,900 = £190 is due (the £400 limit does not apply to the 10% (or 15%) penalties).

Rob must submit four returns on time and pay the VAT on time before the SLN period can end.

7.10 The basic tax point for VAT purposes is the delivery date of the goods (ie when they are made available to the customer), ie 30 March 2011. However, as the invoice was raised within 14 days of this basic tax point, the invoice date, ie 10 April 2011, becomes the tax point. This amount will be reported on the June 2011 VAT return.

The VAT due is based on the discounted figure, even where the discount is not given:

	£
Value	15,000
Less: 10%	(1,500)
	13,500
Less: 5%	(675)
	12,825
Output VAT @ 20%	2,565

7.11 A VAT invoice should show:

(1) A unique and sequential identifying number
(2) The time of supply
(3) The date of issue of the invoice
(4) Details of the supplier (ie name, address and registration number)
(5) Details of the customer (ie name and address)
(6) A description sufficient to identify the goods or services supplied
(7) The total amount payable (excluding VAT)
(8) The total amount of VAT chargeable

A VAT invoice must be issued within 30 days of the tax point (SI 1995/2518 Reg 13 (5))

Tutorial note. For a complete list of particulars which must be shown on a VAT invoice see SI 1995/2518 Reg 14

8.1 The stamp taxes implications are:

1. No stamp duty is payable as the transaction was after 13 March 2008 and the consideration was less than £1,000. There will be no stamp duty reserve tax charge if the stock transfer form is presented as being exempt from stamp duty.

2. Stamp duty reserve tax (SDRT) of 0.5% x £450,252 (£2,251) is payable by Damson plc. If the transfer of shares was effected using a stock transfer stamp duty of 0.5% x £450,252 rounded to the nearest £5 (£2,255) is payable. The SDRT liability will be cancelled when Damson plc provides a stamped stock transfer form provided this is within six years of the transfer.

3. Stamp duty land tax (SDLT) of £8,400 (£280,000 x 3%) is payable by Peach Ltd.

8.2 Stamp duty land tax (SDLT) is payable by Samson Ltd as follows:

Premium: £170,000 x 1% = £1,700 – The zero rate is not available as the annual rent exceeds £1,000 and the property is non-residential.

NPV of rents: (£620,000 - £150,000) x 1% = £4,700.

The SDLT return must be filed by 31 July 2010 i.e. within 30 days of the transaction.

8.3 Beach Ltd, Sand Ltd and Pebble Ltd form a group for stamp duty land tax purposes, as Sand Ltd and Pebble Ltd are 75% subsidiaries of Beach Ltd.

The sale of the warehouse to Sand Ltd therefore falls within the SDLT group relief exemption. However group relief will be withdrawn when Sand Ltd leaves the Beach Ltd group on 1 October 2011 still owning the land as Sand Ltd has left the group within three years of the transfer.

SDLT of £300,000 x 3% = £9,000 will therefore be payable.

Shingle Ltd is not part of the Beach Ltd SDLT group. SDLT is therefore payable on the sale of the factory. However no SDLT arises as the consideration of £100,000 falls within the zero rate band.

8.4 As the rent exceeds £1,000 and the land is non-residential property, the zero rate charge cannot apply.

The SDLT on the lease is:

	£
On premium: £86,000 × 1% (see above)	860
On rent: £(154,000 – 150,000) × 1%	40
Total	900

The due date is 30 days from completion, ie no later than 17 May 2010.

Bill must pay the SDLT.

You must tick in the boxes below which THREE Modules you have answered.

A	B	C	D	E
☐	☐	☐	☐	☐

The Chartered Tax Adviser Examination

Sample Paper

AWARENESS

TIME ALLOWED – 3 HOURS

- You should answer **THREE** out of the five following modules:

    Module A – VAT including Stamp Taxes
    Module B – Inheritance Tax, Trusts & Estates
    Module C – Corporation Tax
    Module D – Taxation of Individuals
    Module E – Taxation of Unincorporated Businesses

- Each module consists of 12 questions and each question carries 5 marks.
- You must answer all the questions from the modules you choose.
- You should answer questions in brief bullet points and/or summary computations where appropriate.
- You must answer questions in the spaces provided.
- You may not need all the space provided.
- You should make all calculations to the nearest month and pound unless stated otherwise.

NB In the actual examination candidates will be required to answer in the space under each question. There are no spaces shown in this sample paper.

You must tick the box below if you have answered this Module.

☐

The Chartered Tax Adviser Examination

Sample Paper

AWARENESS

MODULE A – VAT INCLUDING STAMP TAXES

- Each question carries 5 marks.
- You must answer all the questions from the modules you choose.
- You should answer questions in brief bullet points and/or summary computations where appropriate.
- You must answer questions in the spaces provided.
- You may not need all the space provided.
- You should make all calculations to the nearest month and pound unless stated otherwise.

1 Alpha Developments owns a number of properties which it leases to tenants. The company purchased a mainframe computer for £140,000 plus VAT on 29 June 2008, and used this for general business purposes.

Under Alpha Developments' partial exemption method, the level of taxable use has been determined as follows.

Year to 31 March	*Rate*
2008	80%
2009	70%
2010	85%
2011	75%

The computer was sold on 7 August 2010 for £47,000 inclusive of £7,000 VAT.

You are required to:

(1) **Compute the amount of input tax recoverable in respect of the purchase of the computer as well as any subsequent adjustments which must be made.** **(2)**

(2) **Compute the additional input tax, if any, reclaimable from HMRC following the sale of the computer.** **(3)**

Total (5)

2 (1) The sale of the freehold in a warehouse built 18 months ago and used to store manufactured products since then.

(2) Sale of 20 acres of land at the edge of his farm by Farmer Giles. The land has been in his family since 1800s.

(3) Sale of the freehold of a semi-detached post WWII house by the current owner a VAT registered plumber.

(4) 24 month lease of newly built apartment by the builder Kimple Builders to Mr Smith.

(5) 99 year lease of a newly built office block by the builder Stats Construction.

You are required to categorise the above supplies of land and buildings for VAT and state whether an option to tax could be made. **(5)**

3 Horricks Ltd is selling its business as a going concern to a major competitor JL Industries Ltd on 1 January 2011.

The assets of the business comprise:

	£'000
Freehold interest in a two-year old warehouse	250
Goodwill	50
Plant and machinery	50
	350

You are required to:

(1) **State how the transfer will be treated for VAT assuming both businesses are VAT registered.** **(3)**

(2) **Calculate the VAT due (if any) and state any planning points available to reduce the VAT chargeable.** **(2)**

Total (5)

4 Lancashire Candles Ltd sells candles to both the wholesale and retail trade. The bad debts account at 30 June 2011 reflects the following:

Date of invoice	*Debtor*	*Details*	*Amount*
			£
30 June 2010	Scents Ltd	Retail sales	2,000
30 November 2010	Hope Ltd	Sale of now obsolete plant	10,000
20 December 2010	Dot Ltd (in liquidation)	Wholesale	5,000
15 April 2011	Jingle Ltd	Retail sales	3,000
30 April 2011	N/A	Increase in general provision	7,000
			27,000

Notes

(1) No adjustment has been made for any VAT relief.
(2) Lancashire Candles Ltd has terms requiring payment within 10 days of the invoice date.
(3) On 15 May 2011, a dividend of £1,500 was received from the liquidators of Dot Ltd.

In accordance with normal accounting practice, debtors are shown inclusive of VAT in the accounts.

You are required to calculate the amount of bad debt relief for VAT that can be claimed on the quarterly return to 30 June 2011. **(5)**

5 Charlie and Bella Royle have been in business as partners acting as Personal Trainers for over 10 years. However, due to their age, they decide to retire on 30 April 2011. On that date the assets held by the business (valued at replacement cost for identical items) are:

	£
Van	12,000
Motor car (owned outright and used for both business and private purposes)	14,000
Sports training equipment	1,000

The van and equipment items will be sold over the next few months. Charlie will keep the car for his own personal use.

You are required to outline for VAT purposes how Charlie and Bella must proceed following their decision to retire. **(5)**

6 In December 2011 Simply Bags Ltd made the following transactions of which the new chief accountant requires advice as to their VAT treatment.

(1) Sale of 600 ladies handbags to Cordes SARL – a company based in France.
(2) Purchase of fine leather from a supplier in Brazil.
(3) Purchase of 1,000 metal hinges for bags from a supplier in Italy.

You are required to discuss the VAT implications of the above three transactions. **(5)**

7 Hermione opened a clothes shop on 1 July 2009. Since then her sales have been consistent at £5,200 per month, apart from each December when, due to Christmas demand, turnover is £24,000. Hermione does not sell children's clothes.

Due to the pressure of work Hermione forgot to monitor whether she was required to register for VAT. She didn't register for VAT until 29 March 2011. Her monthly input tax is £500.

You are required to calculate the maximum penalty HMRC will charge for the late registration. **(5)**

8 Olivia runs a village post office and general store. In her first VAT quarter of the year ie the quarter to 31 December 2010, she had the following:

	£
Standard rated supplies (excluding VAT)	53,000
Zero-rated supplies	7,000
Exempt supplies	12,500
Input tax:	
Attributable to taxable supplies	6,800
Attributable to exempt supplies	1,500
Residual	1,000

Taxable supplies include £4,000 (excluding VAT) for the sale of a computer, printer and scanner, which Olivia had previously used in her business.

Olivia did not satisfy the annual test for the previous VAT year and does not use the recovery percentage for the previous year.

You are required to calculate the VAT payable by/repayable to Olivia in her return for the quarter to 31 December 2010. **(5)**

9 The structure for the Marlowe Group is as below.

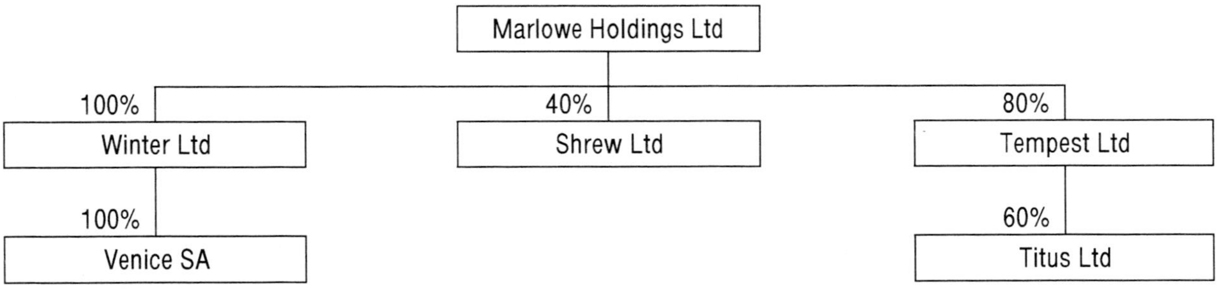

All companies except Venice SA have a place of business in the UK.

Titus Ltd runs children's day nurseries and makes wholly exempt supplies. All other companies make taxable supplies.

Which companies can be included in a VAT group registration and what are the effects of a group VAT registration? **(5)**

10 Tempest Ltd ordered a consignment of widgets from Caliban Ltd on 12 November 2010 paying a £2,000 deposit.

The widgets are dispatched from Caliban Ltd's factory on 15 December 2010.

An invoice is issued on 20 December 2010. Tempest Ltd paid the balance of £18,000 on 29 December 2010.

Briefly explain the VAT tax points for the deposit and for the balance? **(5)**

11 Gower Ltd submits its VAT returns and pays its VAT as follows:

Quarter ended	*VAT due* £	*Date return submitted*	*Date VAT paid*
30 June 2010	22,000	25 August 2010	25 August 2010
30 September 2010	28,000	25 October 2010	25 October 2010
31 December 2010	30,000	14 February 2011	14 February 2011
31 March 2011	(5,000)	31 May 2011	-
30 June 2011	7,000	29 July 2011	5 August 2011

You are required to outline how the default surcharge rules will apply to Gower Ltd. **(5)**

12 Harry granted a 45-year lease on a commercial property to Richard on 12 June 2011. The premium was £95,000 and the net present value of the rent is £180,000. Annual rents under the lease are £1,100 per month.

What is the Stamp Duty Land Tax payable on the grant of the lease and what is the due date for payment? **(5)**

You must tick the box below if you have answered this Module.

☐

The Chartered Tax Adviser Examination

Sample Paper

AWARENESS

MODULE B – INHERITANCE TAX, TRUSTS & ESTATES

- Each question carries 5 marks.
- You must answer all the questions from the modules you choose.
- You should answer questions in brief bullet points and/or summary computations where appropriate.
- You must answer questions in the spaces provided.
- You may not need all the space provided.
- You should make all calculations to the nearest month and pound unless stated otherwise.

1 Paul gifts £275,000 to an interest in possession trust on 3 April 2011. The beneficiaries of the trust are his three teenage children.

His only other lifetime gifts have been a gross chargeable transfer of £115,500 on 14 June 2007 and gifts of £100 to each of his four nieces and nephew at Christmas every year since 2002.

Paul always pays any Inheritance Tax due in connection with his lifetime gifts.

You are required to calculate how much Inheritance Tax Paul must pay. You should also state Paul's gross chargeable transfer in respect of the April 2011 gift. **(5)**

2 Anne is a very wealthy 62 year old looking for Inheritance Tax advice.

She is UK domiciled and intends to leave all her assets to her husband, Gus, aged 47.

Gus was born in New Zealand. He moved to England when he married Anne, eleven years ago, and has told Anne that he intends to return to New Zealand if Anne dies before him.

Anne has no other relations and has made no other substantial gifts.

You are required to advise Anne on her Inheritance Tax position and any potential planning opportunities available to her. **(5)**

3 In May 2005 Lisa sold her family home for £650,000. She gave £400,000 to her son, David, who bought a property for Lisa to live in.

The property is currently worth £475,000 and has an annual rental value of £18,525. Lisa does not pay rent to David.

Lisa is a higher rate taxpayer.

You are required to calculate Lisa's tax liability for 2010/11 in respect of the property and to advise her how she can avoid paying this tax charge. **(5)**

4 Kari dies on 8 October 2010.

In her estate were the following assets:

(1) *15,000 Smoky plc shares*

At the date of her death the shares were quoted at 230.25 – 235, with bargains at 231, 233.25 and 234.

The shares had gone ex-dividend on 28 September 2009 and the dividend of 19p per share was paid on 12 October 2009.

(2) *Holiday home in France*

Kari had purchased the property for €127,500 when the buying exchange rate was €1.39 and the selling rate was €1.20. At the date of her death the villa is worth €622,000. The buying exchange rate is €1.51 and the selling rate is €1.32.

(3) *1,000 shares in Fire Ltd*

Fire Ltd is an unquoted trading company valued at £725,000. Kari had owned the shares for ten years. The company does not hold any investments.

The costs of dealing with the overseas property came to €5,852.

Funeral expenses were £1,200.

Kari had made no gross chargeable lifetime transfers and left her entire estate to her son, Nick.

You are required to calculate the Inheritance Tax liability on Kari's estate. **(5)**

5 The trustees of the Conn Family Discretionary Trust pass a property worth £725,000 out of the trust to one of the beneficiaries on 1 June 2010. The trust had been set up by Janet Conn on 12 April 2004 with cash of £450,000.

Janet's only other lifetime gift had been a gift of £50,000 to her daughter on her wedding day on 25 April 2003.

You are required to calculate the exit charge when the property leaves the trust, assuming the beneficiary pays any Inheritance Tax due. **(5)**

6 The trustees of the Slocombe Discretionary Trust have a tax pool brought forward at the beginning of the tax year of £625.

They receive dividend income of £19,800 and have no trust management expenses.

They make an income payment of £9,000 to a beneficiary.

You are required to calculate the trustees' Income Tax liability and state the balance on the tax pool at the end of the year. (5)

7 Alan sets up a discretionary trust on 15 May 2010 for his two children, Samantha (age 12) and Jake (age 9).

The trust property consists of 50,000 shares in Loaded plc, a quoted trading company, and an investment property that is currently rented out. The annual trust income is expected to be in the region of £25,000 and expenses are expected to be approximately £1,500.

The plan is for the trustees to pay the children's school fees from trust income.

You are required to explain to Alan how the trust income will be taxed. You should ignore both Capital Gains Tax and Inheritance Tax. (5)

8 Henry acquired some shares in York Ltd (an unlisted trading company) in June 2009. In March 2011 he settled them on to a trust for his children and grandchildren.

Briefly explain the circumstances in which Business Property Relief will be available to reduce the transfer of value made by Henry to the trust. (5)

9 **Give five instances where a donor can give away an asset, be able to benefit from the use of the asset after the gift and not be caught by the rules regarding Gifts With Reservation of Benefit. (5)**

10 William is a company director earning £100,000 per annum. In June 2007, William created a discretionary trust for the benefit of his three nephews by settling an investment property (then worth £400,000). The chargeable gain of £120,000 on settlement was held over under S.260 TCGA 1992.

In March 2011 the trustees sold the property for £600,000. This was their only disposal in 2010/11.

You are required to explain (with appropriate calculations) the Capital Gains Tax position in respect of the above. (5)

11 Mrs Hathaway died on 5 April 2010 leaving her estate to her daughter Anne. The estate consisted of the family home, an investment property and a bank deposit.

The Executors completed the administration of the estate on 31 January 2011. The income and expenses during the administration period were as follows;

	£
Rental income	24,000
Bank deposit interest (net)	4,800
Letting expenses	(4,000)
Estate management expenses	(400)
Interest on short term loan to pay the IHT	(2,500)

You are required to show the entries required for form R185 (Estate Income) to be given to the residuary beneficiary. (5)

12 (1) Small-holding of arable pasture in northern France. Farmed by a tenant under a long-lease since 1997.

(2) Cattle farm in North Yorkshire farmed by the taxpayer and his wife in partnership.

(3) Farmhouse (situated on the farmland) in which they live.

(4) Cattle herd.

(5) Tenanted land used by a sheep farmer in North Wales. 30-year lease signed in 1993 (due for renegotiation in 2013).

Briefly explain whether the above assets will qualify for agricultural property relief and (if so) at what rate. You should assume all assets have been held for many years. (5)

You must tick the box below if you have answered this Module.

☐

The Chartered Tax Adviser Examination

Sample Paper

AWARENESS

MODULE C – CORPORATION TAX

- Each question carries 5 marks.
- You must answer all the questions from the modules you choose.
- You should answer questions in brief bullet points and/or summary computations where appropriate.
- You must answer questions in the spaces provided.
- You may not need all the space provided.
- You should make all calculations to the nearest month and pound unless stated otherwise.

1 Harrap Ltd recently acquired 100% of the shares in Overseas Inc, a company incorporated in a country which is not in the European Union. Following the acquisition, a number of directors of Harrap Ltd will join the board of directors of Overseas Inc.

Overseas Inc's main trading operations are outside of the UK but it operates a small manufacturing unit in the UK.

You are required to advise Harrap Ltd on how the UK residency position of Overseas Inc will be determined and the corporation tax implications of Overseas Inc being UK or non-UK resident. **(5)**

2 Gardener Ltd prepares accounts to 31 October. During the year to 31 October 2010 the following transactions took place:

		Cost/proceeds
		£
1 May 2010	Car acquired (CO_2 emissions 158g/km)	11,000
1 June 2010	Van acquired	13,000
1 June 2010	Mercedes car sold	15,000
1 July 2010	Machine sold (original cost £35,000)	40,000

The car acquired on 1 May 2010 was for the use of the sales manager and 25% of his annual mileage was for private purposes.

The balances on the capital allowance pools as at 1 November 2009 were:

	£
Main pool	45,000
Mercedes car (Old expensive car)	24,000
Short-life asset (acquired 1 May 2004)	4,000

You are required to calculate the capital allowances available to Gardener Ltd for the year ended 31 October 2010. **(5)**

3 Marine Ltd manufactures speedboats and prepares accounts to 31 March. In the year to 31 March 2011 the following transactions took place:

(1) On 1 April 2010 the company issued £200,000 10% debentures. The funds were used to purchase an investment property which was rented out from 1 June 2010 at an annual rent of £25,000, payable quarterly in advance. The company incurred professional fees of £1,800 in connection with the issues of the debentures.

(2) On 1 June 2010 the company took out a bank loan to fund the purchase of plant and machinery. Interest of £2,000 was paid during the year. Interest payable of £800 was accrued as at 31 March 2011.

You are required to explain how the above income and expenditure will be treated in the corporation tax computation of Marine Ltd for the year to 31 March 2011. **(5)**

4 Mammoth Ltd, an electrical engineering company, has always prepared accounts to 30 June. In 2010 it decided to change its accounting date and prepared accounts for the six months to 31 December 2010.

The company's trading profit for the six months to 31 December 2010 was £200,000. This figure is adjusted for tax purposes, with the exception of the following items:

(1) An amortisation charge of £20,000 in relation to the goodwill of a business acquired in May 2008 has not yet been charged in the profit and loss account.

(2) Capital allowances for the year have not yet been computed. The balance on the capital allowance main pool as at 1 July 2010 was £50,000.

On 1 August 2010 the company acquired plant and machinery for £15,000.

Mammoth Ltd has no other income in the period.

You are required to calculate Mammoth Ltd's corporation tax liability for the six months to 31 December 2010. **(5)**

5 Circle Ltd owns 100% of the share capital of Oblong Ltd and 80% of Square Ltd. Square Ltd owns 80% of the share capital of Triangle Ltd.

All companies are UK resident.

The results of Circle Ltd and Oblong Ltd for the year ended 31 December 2010 are as follows:

Year ended:	*Circle Ltd*	*Oblong Ltd*
	£	£
Trading profit/(loss)	50,000	(220,000)
Chargeable gain/(loss)	15,000	(20,000)
Bank interest	10,000	5,000
Qualifying charitable donation – Gift Aid	2,000	6,000

You are required to:

(1) **State, giving reasons, whether Square Ltd and Triangle Ltd are in a group for group loss relief purposes with Circle Ltd and Oblong Ltd.** **(2)**

(2) **Calculate the amount of losses of Oblong Ltd which are available for group relief and the maximum amount of loss that Circle Ltd could claim from Oblong Ltd.** **(3)**

Total (5)

6 Hotspur Ltd was incorporated on 1 January 2010. Its shares are wholly owned by Mr Percy.

Hotspur Ltd opened a bank account and began trading on 1 April 2010. The first accounts were drawn to 31 May 2011 and showed the following results;

	£
Adjusted trading profits before capital allowances	448,000
Bank interest receivable	7,000
Rental income (see below)	120,000

Plant and equipment was bought on 1 April 2010 for £103,000. Some equipment was sold in April 2011 for £1,600.

An investment property was acquired on 1 December 2010 and was immediately leased out at an annual rent of £120,000 payable in advance.

Compute the taxable total profits in respect of the period to 31 May 2011 and show the due date(s) for the submissions of forms CT 600. **(5)**

7 Verona Ltd (a large company) has traditionally drawn up accounts to 30 April. It joined the Swan plc group on 1 May 2010 and, to coincide with that of its new parent company, duly changed its accounting reference date to 31 December.

Verona Ltd estimated that its taxable total profits for the eight months to 31 December 2010 would be £5 million. At their board meeting on 6 April 2011, the directors signed off the accounts and provisional tax computations showing taxable total profits of £6 million.

You are required to calculate the corporation tax payment required to be made on 14 April 2011. **(5)**

8 **Give four ways in which a deficit on a non-trading loan relationship may be relieved.** **(5)**

9 Orsino Ltd incorporated a new wholly owned subsidiary (Viola Ltd) on 1 January 2010. Viola Ltd opened a bank account and started to trade on 1 February 2010. First accounts are drawn to 30 September 2010. Orsino Ltd has one other subsidiary.

The accounts of Viola Ltd for its first accounting period show the following:

	£
Tax adjusted profit	125,000
Bank interest receivable	8,000
Dividend received on quoted investment	1,000

Viola Ltd's only capital acquisition was a car, with CO_2 emissions of 163g/km, costing £9,000 on 1 May 2010.

You are required to calculate the corporation tax payable by Viola Ltd for the period ended 30 September 2010. **(5)**

10 **Briefly outline the circumstances in which the carry forward of trading losses could be denied on a change of ownership of a company.** **(5)**

11 Lysander Ltd is a property investment company, wholly owned by Theseus Ltd. Theseus Ltd had incorporated Lysander Ltd in 2003 when it subscribed for 100,000 £1 ordinary shares at par.

In 2011, Quince Ltd paid £10m for all of the share capital of Lysander Ltd.

The main asset of Lysander Ltd is an office block that it rents out to various third party tenants.

The office block was originally owned by Puck Ltd, another 100% subsidiary of Theseus Ltd. Puck Ltd had constructed the office block for £1 million in 2002. It was transferred to Lysander Ltd in 2008 for £3 million, when its market value was £6 million.

You are required to calculate the chargeable gains arising as a result of the above transactions, stating clearly which company will be chargeable. You should ignore indexation allowance. **(5)**

12 Cressida Ltd is a small company which manufactures paint. In its year ended 31 December 2010, it had the following income and expenditure:

	£	£
Income		
Paint sales		312,000
Patent royalty received from Mr Paris (UK trader)		8,000
		320,000
Expenses		
General manufacturing costs	120,000	
Research expenditure into new paint making methods	40,000	
Acquisition cost of business goodwill (Note)	100,000	
		(260,000)
Profit		60,000

Note: On 1 July 2010, Cressida Ltd paid £100,000 for the goodwill of a tin-making company. It will write the goodwill off over 5 years.

Calculate the corporation tax payable by Cressida Ltd for the year ended 31 December 2010. **(5)**

You must tick the box below if you have answered this Module.

☐

The Chartered Tax Adviser Examination

Sample Paper

AWARENESS

MODULE D – TAXATION OF INDIVIDUALS

- Each question carries 5 marks.
- You must answer all the questions from the modules you choose.
- You should answer questions in brief bullet points and/or summary computations where appropriate.
- You must answer questions in the spaces provided.
- You may not need all the space provided.
- You should make all calculations to the nearest month and pound unless stated otherwise.

1 A new client, Reginald, has advised you that he purchased an investment property and started receiving rental income of £10,000 per month from 1 January 2011. He notified HMRC of this new source of income on 15 September 2011 and was issued with a 2010/11 tax return on 10 November 2011. He filed this return online on 13 February 2012.

You are required to advise Reginald on the following matters, providing reasons for your conclusions:

(1) Whether he notified HMRC of his new source of income on time
(2) Whether he filed his 2010/11 tax return on time
(3) The deadline for Reginald to make amendments to his tax return
(4) The deadline for HMRC to open an enquiry into Reginald's 2010/11 tax return
(5) Any penalties which Reginald may have incurred in respect of the above matters.

(5)

2 Mr Falstaff is 76. In 2010/11 he received the following income:

	£
State pension	5,200
Employers pension (PAYE deducted £1,850)	14,000
Rental profits	4,800
Bank interest	750

On 15 November 2010 he married Celia (63). Celia has self-employed trading profits of £30,000.

On 1 January 2011 Mr Falstaff made a donation to charity of £500 under Gift Aid.

You are required to calculate the income tax payable by Mr Falstaff for 2010/11. **(5)**

3 Antony joined Cleo plc as a HR manager on 1 July 2010 on a salary of £60,000. His benefits package included the following:

(1) Company car, list price £20,000, CO_2 emissions 163 g/km, all petrol costs reimbursed by the company.

(2) Use of an unfurnished company-owned flat until such time as he found suitable family accommodation in the area. The flat cost £250,000 in 2008 and has an annual rental value £1,000. Antony paid a notional rent of £200 per month for the use of the flat. He bought a family house on 31 January 2011 and duly moved out of the flat.

You should assume HM Revenue & Customs' official interest rate is 4%.

You are required to calculate the taxable benefits arising in 2010/11. Assume Cleo plc has paid other relocation costs for Antony in excess of £8,000. **(5)**

4 Eleanora was born in Australia, but moved to the UK 19 years ago to work for a UK company and has lived here ever since. She plans to return to Australia on her retirement in around five years' time.

During 2010/11, Eleanora had the following income:

UK employment income	£70,000
Rent from letting out her house in Sydney	£12,000 (credited to her Australian bank account)
Dividend income from an overseas company	£20,000 (of which £11,000 was transferred to her UK account)

You are required to discuss Eleanora's current residence and domicile status for UK tax purposes and explain the UK tax treatment of her various sources of income in 2010/11. You may assume that no overseas tax is payable on any of Eleanora's income and that she makes any beneficial claims. **(5)**

5 On 15 March 2008, Jemima was granted share options to acquire 5,000 shares in her employer company, Puddle plc, at a price equal to the March 2008 market value of £6.80 per share. The options were granted under the company's Enterprise Management Incentive scheme.

Jemima exercised her options in November 2010, by which time the shares were valued at £14.50 each. She sold the shares one month later for £14.70 per share.

Jemima's shareholding represents less than 1% of the company's shares. Jemima is a higher rate taxpayer.

You are required to explain (with supporting calculations where appropriate) Jemima's income tax, National Insurance Contributions and capital gains tax position on grant and exercise of the options and on sale of the shares, assuming that she is a higher rate taxpayer and that she made no other chargeable gains during 2010/11. **(5)**

6 Roderigo sold some quoted shares in 2008 making a substantial capital gain. In 2009 he subscribed for shares in a qualifying EIS company and elected to defer the gain arising.

You are required to list five events which will result in the deferred gain becoming chargeable. **(5)**

7 Jamie lets out a furnished flat in the UK and received the following rent:

	£
18 December 2009: Annual rental to 31 December 2010	15,000
22 December 2010: Annual rental to 31 December 2011	15,600

He also incurred the following expenditure on the property:

(1) Insurance premiums paid in advance for the next 12 months: £3,600 on 1 August 2009 and £4,200 on 1 August 2010.

(2) Council tax of £1,100 for the year to 31 March 2011.

(3) Replacement of a chimney in November 2010 at a cost of £800, following damage in a storm.

(4) Interest at 3% per annum on the outstanding loan of £200,000 which Jamie took out a few years ago in order to finance the purchase of the property.

You are required to calculate Jamie's taxable property income for the 2010/11 tax year. **(5)**

8 Emily is a director of Arcite Ltd with a salary of £50,000 per annum. During 2010/11 she also received the following remuneration:

(1) Bonus of £36,000 for year ended 31 March 2010 paid on 20 July 2010.

(2) Private medical insurance costing the company £480.

(3) Free accommodation in a flat which has a market value of £180,000 and is rented by the company at a rate of £10,800 per annum.

(4) Reimbursement of personal telephone bills totalling £650.

You are required to calculate the 2010/11 National Insurance Contributions payable by Emily and the company in respect of her remuneration, assuming that Emily is not contracted out of S2P. **(5)**

Question 9 has been amended to accommodate changes to capital gains tax legislation.

9 Maria made a number of disposals in February 2011, realising the following gains.

Date of purchase	*Type of asset*	*Gain*
		£
6 May 1971	Painting	Note
14 August 2008	Shares in West Ltd (20% shareholding)	45,000
2 November 2005	Shares in Coach plc (1% shareholding)	24,000

Note

The painting was acquired for £3,000. It was sold for £6,860, net of 2% auctioneers' fees. It was valued for insurance purposes at £4,000 in March 1982.

Both West Ltd and Coach plc are trading companies. Maria has been employed by West Ltd since 2005. Maria had capital losses brought forward at 6 April 2010 of £5,000. Her taxable income in 2010/11 was £35,000.

You are required to calculate Maria's capital gains tax payable for 2010/11. (5)

10 Henry Percy sold his house in Scotland on 30 September 2010 realising a gain (after selling expenses) of £272,000.

He had bought the house in October 1978. On 1 April 1998 he bought a flat in Newcastle and elected for this property to be his main residence. He worked in Newcastle but continued to use the house in Scotland on occasional weekends. He sold the Newcastle flat in September 2009 and returned permanently to the house in Scotland.

In 2010/11, Henry had self-employed trading profits of £37,500 and made no other gains.

You are required to calculate Henry's capital gains tax payable for 2010/11. (5)

11 Oswald gave the following assets to his family members in 2010/11:

(1) In January 2011 he sold his shares in Shrew Ltd (an unlisted trading company) to his son Edmund for £40,000. He had bought the shares in February 2010 for £12,000 and they were worth £95,000 at the date of transfer. Oswald has never worked for Shrew Ltd.

(2) On 3 February 2011 he sold a painting to his daughter Cordelia for £10,000. He had inherited it in 2007 when it has a probate value of £25,000. It was worth £20,000 at the date of the transfer.

(3) In March 2011 he gave some shares in Southern Stone plc to his nephew Edgar. The shares had cost him £20,000 in May 2002 and were worth £8,000 at the date of the gift.

You are required to calculate the net gains arising. Assume all appropriate claims are made. (5)

12 Miranda bought 10,000 shares in Tempest plc in June 2008 for £80,000. On 1 July 2009, Tempest plc was taken over by Prospero plc. For each of their Tempest plc shares, the shareholders received the following:

Two new Prospero plc ordinary shares worth £4.75 each
£10 of non-convertible loan stock (valued at par)
£5.50 cash

In December 2010, Miranda redeemed her loan stock and received £85,000.

Miranda's shareholdings in Tempest plc and Prospero plc represented less than 1% of the companies' shares.

You are required to calculate the chargeable gain/allowable loss on redemption of the stock. (5)

You must tick the box below if you have answered this Module.

☐

The Chartered Tax Adviser Examination

Sample Paper

AWARENESS

MODULE E – TAXATION OF UNINCORPORATED BUSINESSES

- Each question carries 5 marks.
- You must answer all the questions from the modules you choose.
- You should answer questions in brief bullet points and/or summary computations where appropriate.
- You must answer questions in the spaces provided.
- You may not need all the space provided.
- You should make all calculations to the nearest month and pound unless stated otherwise.

1 Albert is in business running a café. His accounts for the year to 30 June 2010 show a trading profit of £35,000, this is after deducting the following:

(1) Legal fees of £500 in respect of renewing the ten year lease on the cafe.

(2) Repair costs of £200 in respect of a second-hand refrigeration unit which was acquired during the year. The repairs were required prior to using the unit in order to comply with health and safety regulations.

(3) Cost of acquiring a delivery van on 1 June 2010 for £6,000. The van is used 20% of the time by Albert for private purposes.

(4) Parking fine of £50 incurred by Albert whilst making a delivery of sandwiches to a local business.

You are required to calculate Albert's taxable trading profit for the year to 30 June 2010 giving an explanation for your treatment of the repair costs. **(5)**

2 Maggie commenced business as a self-employed beautician on 1 February 2010. Her results for her first set of accounts for the fifteen month period to 30 April 2011 are as follows:

	£	£
Gross operating profit		120,000
Less : Wages (Note 1)	80,000	
Rent and rates (Note 2)	10,000	
Depreciation	2,000	
Telephone and utilities	2,500	
Sundry expenses (all allowable)	800	
		(95,300)
Net profit		24,700

Notes

(1) Wages includes £45,000 in respect of Maggie and £10,000 in respect of Maggie's daughter who works full-time in the business.

(2) Rent and rates relate to the whole of the building. The beauty salon occupies three of its rooms; Maggie's son lives in the fourth room.

(3) During the period Maggie used goods which had cost £500 for her own personal use. The usual retail price of these goods was £850. No adjustments have been made in the accounts for the goods removed.

You are required to calculate Maggie's taxable trading profit for the fifteen month period to 30 April 2011 and to state the basis period for the trading income assessment in 2010/11. **(5)**

3 Karen operates a dress-making business as an unincorporated trader. The following capital transactions took place in the year to 31 August 2011:

		£
Acquisitions		*Cost*
1 October 2010	New Jaguar car (CO_2 emissions 175g/km, 40% private use)	25,000
1 December 2010	New Ford car (CO_2 emissions 105g/km, 20% private use)	10,000
1 March 2011	Second hand delivery van	15,000
Disposals		*Proceeds*
15 September 2010	Expensive car (Volvo) (CO_2 emissions 175g/km ,40% private use)	12,000

The Jaguar car acquired and the Volvo car disposed of during the year were used by Karen. The Ford car was used by the sales manager.

The original cost of the Volvo car was £22,000.

The value of the capital allowance pools as at 1 September 2010 were:

Main pool	£25,000
Expensive car (Volvo)	£16,000

You are required to calculate the capital allowances available to Karen for the year to 31 August 2011. Assume tax rates and allowances for 2010/11 continue into the future. (5)

4 Gerald has traded as a self-employed carpenter for a number of years. On 31 December 2010 he ceased to trade.

Gerald's taxable trading profits had been as follows:

Year to 30 June 2009	£38,000
Year to 30 June 2010	£34,000

His final accounts for the six months to 31 December 2010 show a tax adjusted trading profit before capital allowances of £15,000.

The only assets used in the business were a van, which he retained for his personal use, and items of plant and machinery which he sold for £6,500. Gerald had only ever used the van for business purposes.

The van had cost £15,000 in April 2005 and had a market value of £8,500 at 31 December 2010. None of the individual items of plant and machinery were sold for more than their original cost.

The tax written down value of the main capital allowances pool as at 1 July 2010 was £4,000.

Gerald had overlap profits in respect of his opening years' assessments of £8,000.

You are required to calculate Gerald's trading income assessment for 2010/11. (5)

5 Brooke has been trading as a self-employed hairdresser for a number of years.

Her recent tax adjusted trading results have been as follows:

Year to 31 May 2008	£45,000
Year to 31 May 2009	£26,000
Year to 31 May 2010	£(10,000) loss

Brooke expects to have a tax adjusted trading profit of £500 for the year to 31 May 2011.

In addition to her trading income Brooke has other taxable income of £5,000 each year.

You are required to set out the options available to Brooke to utilise the loss arising in the year to 31 May 2010 and to explain the implications of each of the options. You do NOT need to quantify the amount of tax saved under each option. (5)

6 Richard sold a freehold building for £850,000 on 1 August 2010. The building had always been used for business purposes. Richard had acquired the building on 1 July 2002 for £400,000.

On 1 September 2010 he acquired a new freehold building, for use in his business, for £750,000.

You are required to:

(1) **Calculate the chargeable gain arising on the sale of the building assuming that Richard will not claim to rollover the gain into the cost of the building acquired on 1 September 2010.** (2)

(2) **Calculate the revised base cost of the building acquired on 1 September 2010 assuming that Richard elects to rollover the gain arising on the old building into the cost of the new building.** (3)

Total (5)

7 Antonio and Bassanio are in partnership sharing profits equally. Their only asset is the business goodwill, which they purchased in April 1991 for £200,000.

On 1 January 2011, Portia was admitted to the partnership and profits were thereafter split 50:30:20 between Antonio, Bassanio and Portia. No adjustment was made to the partnership accounts, although Portia made a direct payment of £80,000 to Bassanio for his share of the goodwill.

You are required to explain (with calculations) the capital gains consequences of Portia joining the partnership and show the base cost of her 20% share. (5)

8 Horatio and Claudius have been in partnership for many years preparing accounts annually to 30 November. Profits are split 3:2 after a salary of £15,000 to Claudius.

Horatio retired on 31 December 2010, so Claudius took the opportunity to move the accounts date to 31 December and thereafter continue as a sole trader. Profits for the period 1 December 2009 to 31 December 2010 were £260,000.

There were four months of overlap profits arising on the commencement of trade. These amounted to £15,000 and £10,000 for Horatio and Claudius respectively.

You are required to calculate the taxable trading profit for 2010/11 for Horatio and Claudius. (5)

9 Toby started trading on 1 May 2009. His results have been as follows:

	Profit/(loss)
	£
1 May 2009 to 31 January 2010	60,000
1 February 2010 to 30 April 2010	(30,000)
1 May 2010 to 30 April 2011	90,000

You are required to calculate the National Insurance Contributions payable by Toby for 2010/11. (5)

10 Florence owned a gift shop. She retired on 31 March 2011 and sold the business to an unconnected buyer, Oliver. Oliver paid Florence £400,000 for the business and the two parties agreed that this be broken down as follows.

	£
Business premises	220,000
Goodwill	100,000
Stock	60,000
Plant & machinery	20,000
	400,000

The stock cost £10,000 and had an estimated market value of £25,000. Florence has trading losses brought forward to offset any trade profits arising.

You are required to show the adjustment, if any, which should be made to Florence's final trading profits in respect of her stock. (5)

11 Warwick started trading as a wedding singer on 1 January 2010. His tax adjusted profits have been as follows;

Year ended 31 December 2010	12,000
Period ended 30 April 2012	30,000

His only asset is his car bought in December 2009 for £6,000 (130g/km CO_2 emissions), which he uses solely for business purposes.

You are required to calculate the taxable trading profits for 2011/12 and show any overlap profits to be carried forward. (5)

12 Morgan started trading on 1 May 2008. He notified his chargeability to income tax in July 2009 and was duly sent a 2008/09 tax return, which he filed on 29 January 2010. The income tax and Class 4 National Insurance Contributions due for 2008/09 was £16,000.

Within the return, Morgan made a claim to reduce his payments on account for 2009/10 to £5,500 each.

Morgan submitted his 2009/10 return on 27 February 2011 showing tax and National Insurance Contributions due for the year of £13,000. No claim was made to reduce his payments on account for 2010/11.

The following tax payments have been made;

	£
29 January 2010	21,500
30 September 2010	5,500
31 March 2011	8,500

Assume HM Revenue & Customs' interest rate is 3%.

You are required to calculate the interest and penalties for which Morgan is liable. You may do interest calculations on a monthly basis. **(5)**

The Chartered Tax Adviser Examination

Sample Paper

Awareness

Suggested Answers

Module A – VAT including stamp taxes: answers

1 **Alpha Developments**

(1) Recovery on computer:

In year to 31 March 2009 (interval 1 – initial recovery): (70% £24,500) = £17,150
In year to 31 March 2010 (interval 2 – annual adjustment): 1/5 × £24,500 × (85% – 70%) = £735

In both cases, the input tax can be reclaimed.

(2) The sale of the computer is a taxable supply and the VAT on the remaining adjustment periods will be made on the basis that the computer was wholly used for taxable purposes (Regulations 115(3)).

In the year to 31 March 2011 the adjustment percentage is 75% (ie. taxable use of computer in period prior to sale).

Adjustment (credit) is (75 – 70)% × £24,500 × 1/5 = £245

For the years to 31 March 2012 and 2013 the adjustment is (100 – 70)% × 24,500 × 2/5 = £2,940

As the VAT charged on the sale of the computer is £7,000, the whole of the sale credit of £2,940 can be reclaimed (Regulation 115(3)).

Total adjustment (credit to business) = £3,185

2 **Categorise**

(1) Standard rated supply of the freehold of a 'new' (less than 3 years old) commercial building. As this supply is already standard rated an option to tax is not applicable.

(2) Exempt supply of land, however, Farmer Giles may make the option to tax prior to the sale to standard rate the supply.

(3) Exempt supply. Option to tax cannot apply to buildings which will be used as a dwelling.

(4) Exempt supply of lease. Zero rating does not apply since 'major interest' has not been supplied by constructor. Option to tax cannot apply to buildings which will be used as a dwelling.

(5) Exempt supply of a commercial lease. Option to tax can be made prior to sale by Stats Construction to standard rate the sale.

3 **Horricks Ltd**

(1) The sale of the business is a transfer of a going concern and is therefore not treated as a supply of goods or services, assuming certain conditions are met, eg JL Industries Ltd uses the assets acquired from Horricks Ltd for the same kind of business, there is no significant break in trade, etc. However, unless JL Industries complies with additional obligations, TOGC treatment will not apply to the warehouse since it is 'new' (less than three years old) and if sold in isolation would be a standard rated supply.

(2) VAT due

Warehouse £250,000 × 17.5% = £43,750

Goodwill and plant/machinery are not treated as a supply of goods on this transfer.

However, if JL Industries Ltd complies with certain additional obligations , the sale of the warehouse will fall within the TOGC and will therefore will not be subject to VAT. In order for this to be the case, JL Industries must:

- Opt to tax the warehouse
- Notify HMRC of this option to tax; and
- Notify Horricks that this option to tax will not be disapplied under special anti-avoidance rules

JL Industries must do all of this by the 'relevant date' (usually the date of completion).

If JL Industries Ltd does opt to tax, it will have to charge VAT on any supplies it makes in the future with respect to the warehouse (eg if it leases the building to another party).

4 **Lancashire Candles Ltd**

Scents Ltd

The debt is over six months old. VAT due is 7/47 × £2,000 = £298. This can be claimed as bad debt relief on next return to 30 June 2011 if debt is written off in company's accounts.

Hope Ltd

The VAT relating to the debt would have been £1,489 (£10,000 × 7/47). The date on which the debt can be written off for BDR purposes is 10 December 2010 so the debt is over six months old. As for Scents above bad debt relief is available if the debt is written off in the company's accounts.

Dot Ltd

£5,000 was due and £1,500 is repaid (by way of dividend) so £3,500 is outstanding. The debt is six months old (the date on which the debt can be written off for BDR purposes is 30 December 2010) so, as above, bad debt relief is due for £521 (£3,500 × 7/47) if the debt is written off in the company's books.

Jingle Ltd

The debt is not yet six months old (the date on which the debt can be written off for BDR purposes is 25 April 2011) so bad debt relief is not available on either the quarter ended June 2011 return or the quarter ended September 2011 return. The company must wait until the quarter ended 31 December 2011 return to claim £500 (£3,000 × 1/6).

General provision

Cannot satisfy the VAT bad debt conditions, so no bad debt relief is due.

5 **Charlie and Bella Royle**

The business must notify HMRC of a need to deregister by 30 May 2011 as the business ceased to trade on 30 April 2011.

The following assets had input tax reclaimed on them and were in the business on the last day of registration.

	£
Van	12,000
Sports equipment	1,000
	13,000

Note: VAT was not recovered on the purchase of the car so it is ignored in the above calculation.

As the VAT which would be charged (ie £13,000 x 1/6 = £2,167) is not below the de minimis of £1,000, the partnership must account for output VAT in respect of the van and equipment on the final VAT return of the business.

When the van and equipment are later sold VAT is not charged as the business is no longer VAT registered.

6 **Simply Bags Ltd**

The VAT implications of the transactions are as follows:

(1) This is a dispatch to an EU customer in France. If Simply Bags Ltd has the French VAT registration number of Cordes SARL it may zero rate the sale of bags. If not it must charge VAT at the standard rate. It must also obtain and retain commercial evidence to show that the goods were despatched to another member state.

(2) This is an import. The goods will be held at the port of entry until Simply Bags Ltd pays the standard rate VAT (and other taxes) due to release the goods. This VAT is input tax and can be recovered in the normal way on the VAT return covering the date of importation.

(3) This is an acquisition from an EU supplier. If Simply Bags Ltd gave the supplier its UK VAT registration number the goods will arrive at the premises of the company VAT free. Simply Bags Ltd must charge itself standard rate VAT on these goods. This will be in the form of acquisition tax which must be declared on the VAT return covering the date of acquisition. Subject to the usual rules, Simply Bags may deduct this as input tax on the same VAT return.

7 **Hermione**

2009	£
July	5,200
August	5,200
September	5,200
October	5,200
November	5,200
December	24,000
2010	
January	5,200
February	5,200
March	5,200
April	5,200
Total	70,800

Hermione should have notified her liability to register for VAT by 30 May 2010 and should have charged VAT on sales from 1 June 2010. She is therefore 10 months late.

	£
Output tax	
£(6 × £5,200) + £(1 × 24,000) = £55,200 × 7/47 + (3 x £5,200 x 1/6)	10,821
Input tax (£500 × 10)	(5,000)
VAT due	5,821
As Hermione did not deliberately fail to register the maximum penalty is 30% of the potential lost tax ie £5,821 x 30%	£1,746

8 **Olivia**

Firstly you should determine whether either Test 1 or Test 2 are satisfied for the quarter.

Test 1 is not satisfied because total input tax exceeds £625 per month (£9,300/3) = £3,100).

Test 2 is not satisfied because total input tax less that directly attributable to taxable supplies exceeds £625 per month ((£2,500)/3 = £833).

A partial exemption calculation must be performed to determine how much input tax is recoverable for the quarter as follows.

$$\frac{\text{Taxable supplies}}{\text{Total supplies}} = \frac{60{,}000 - 4{,}000}{60{,}000 - 4{,}000 + 12{,}500} = 81.75\% \text{ (round to 82\%)}$$

Note: exclude supplies of capital items in partial exemption fraction.

	£
Input tax recoverable:	
Taxable supplies	6,800
Non-attributable (£1,000 × 82%)	820
Recoverable input tax	7,620
Exempt input tax is:	
Exempt	1,500
Non attributable £(1,000 – 820)	180
De minimis (< £625 per month and less than 50% of the total input VAT for the period) thus recoverable in this period)	1,680

VAT due:

	£
Output tax	
£53,000 × 17.5%	9,275
Input tax recoverable £(7,620 + 1,680)	(9,300)
VAT repayable	(25)

9 **Marlowe Group**

The following companies CANNOT be within the VAT Group:

- Shrew Ltd (not under common control – ie < 50% owned)
- Venice SA (no UK place of business / fixed establishment in the UK)

The other companies can form a VAT Group (including the exempt company, Titus Ltd).

The main effects of group VAT registration are:

(a) The group is treated as one single taxable person.

(b) One company (the 'representative member') is responsible for all VAT accounting including the completion and submission of VAT returns.

(c) All the companies within the group registration are jointly and severally liable for any VAT due.

(d) Any supplies made between members of the VAT group are ignored (ie such supplies are outside the scope of VAT).

10 **Tempest Ltd**

Deposit

The basic tax point is the date the goods are dispatched – ie 15 December 2010.

However, a deposit is paid before this date, so the earlier date becomes the tax point but only to the extent of the deposit paid.

The tax point for the deposit is therefore 12 November 2010.

Balance

The basic tax point is the date the goods are dispatched – ie 15 December 2010.

An invoice is issued within 14 days of the basic tax point, so the invoice date becomes the tax point.

The tax point for the balance is therefore 20 December 2010.

The date of payment of the balance has no impact here.

11 **Gower Ltd**

30.6.10	Late return and VAT. SLN issued covering period from 1.7.10 to 30.6.11. No penalty charged.
30.9.10	Return & VAT on time.
31.12.10	Late return and VAT. 2% penalty applies. 2% × £30,000 = £600. Surcharge period extended to 31.12.11.
31.3.11	Return late. Repayment return so no penalty charged but surcharge period extended to 31.3.12.
30.6.11	Late payment of VAT. 5% penalty applies. 5% × £7,000 = £350. This is less than £400 so it will not be collected. Surcharge period extended to 30.6.12

12 **Harry**

The SDLT on the lease is:

	£
Duty on premium: £95,000 × 1% (note)	950
Duty on rent: £(180,000 – 150,000) × 1%	300
Total duty	1,250

Note

The zero rate charge does not apply because the annual rental exceeds £1,000 and the land is non-residential property.

The SDLT is payable by Richard no later than 12 July 2011 (30 days from completion).

Module B – Inheritance tax, trusts & estates: answers

1 **Paul**

Any gift to a trust during a person's lifetime (except to a bare trust or a trust for a disabled person) is a chargeable lifetime transfer as the trust is a relevant property trust. This trust cannot be a bereaved minor trust or age 18-25 trust as it is being set up during Paul's lifetime.

The tax due is:

	£	£
Transfer of value		275,000
Less: AE 2010/11 (Note)		(3,000)
AE 2009/10 b/f		(3,000)
CLT		269,000
Less: nil rate band	325,000	
GCT in previous 7 years	(115,500)	
		(209,500)
Chargeable		59,500
Tax @ 20/80 or 25%		14,875

Note. The full annual exemption for both 2010/11 and 2009/10 are available as the Christmas gifts to Paul's nieces and nephews come within the small gifts exemption as they are below £250.

The GCT is the total amount that leaves Paul's estate as a result of the gift (ie the chargeable gift PLUS the tax):

£269,000 + £14,875 = £283,875

2 **Anne**

Gifts between spouses are usually exempt from IHT. However, Gus has arguably retained his New Zealand domicile of origin because he intends to return to New Zealand if Anne dies before him, which is likely considering the age difference. He has no intention to make England his permanent home.

Since only the first £55,000 of transfers from a UK domiciled spouse to a non-UK domiciled spouse are exempt, only gifts up to this amount from Anne to Gus will be exempt.

Anne should consider making gifts up to this amount now. She will be able to use her annual exemption of £3,000 for the year of the gift and the exemption from the previous year as this has not already been used. The annual exemption is not available for transfers on death.

If she gifts more than the £55,000 limit, the excess will be a potentially exempt transfer (PET) for IHT purposes. A PET is exempt during the donor's lifetime and only becomes chargeable if they die within seven years of making the gift. So, if Anne survives more than seven years from making the gift, it will be completely exempt.

A final planning consideration could be for Anne to make regular gifts out of income. These are fully exempt from IHT so long as she can show a regular pattern of giving and that the gifts do not affect her standard of living.

3 **Lisa**

As Lisa provided the funds for the purchase of the property that she now lives in the property is caught by the Pre-Owned Asset Tax (POAT) rules.

There is an income tax charge based on the annual value of the land less any amount paid by the individual for their use of it.

The taxable amount in respect of Lisa's occupation of the property is:

£18,525 @ 40% = £7,410.

There are two possible ways in which Lisa can avoid an income tax charge:

(1) Lisa can pay David a market rent for her occupation of the property, or

(2) She can notify HMRC that the property should come within the gift with reservation rules. Notification should be made by the self assessment return filing deadline for the year the charge first applied, although HMRC may accept late notifications.

Lisa should be aware that this second option does not avoid tax entirely as making the election brings the asset into her estate for IHT purposes.

4 **Kari**

Death estate	£
Quoted shares (W1)	37,566
Holiday home (W2)	411,921
Unquoted shares (W3)	nil
Total	449,487
Less: administration costs	
$5,852 ÷ 1.51	(3,875)
	445,612
Less: reasonable funeral expenses	(1,200)
Death estate	444,412
Less: nil rate band	(325,000)
	119,412
Tax @ 40%	47,765

Workings

1 *Quoted shares*

Quoted shares are valued at the lower of the quarter-up and mid bargain values. As the shares had gone ex-div at the date of death, the value of the next dividend must be included in the value.

15,000 shares @ lower of:

(i) ¼-up:

(235 – 230.25) ÷ 4 + 230.25 = 231.4375

(ii) Mid bargain:

$$\frac{231+234}{2} = 232.50$$

	£
ie £2.314375 × 15,000 =	34,716
Add: dividend 15,000 × 19p	2,850
Probate value	37,566

2 Foreign property

Valued at the buying (ie the lower) exchange rate: €622,000 ÷ €1.51 = £411,921

3 Unquoted shares

BPR is available for the shares as they are unquoted trading company shares that Kari has owned for more than two years.

	£
Shares:	725,000
Less: BPR @ 100%	(725,000)
	nil

5 **Conn Family Discretionary Trust**

	£
Exit charge	
Transfer to trust	450,000
Less: nil rate band (Note)	(325,000)
	125,000
Tax @ 20%	25,000

Effective rate:
25,000/450,000 × 100 = 5.55555%

Actual rate:
5.55555% × 30% × 24/40 = 0.99999%

Exit charge:	
0.99999% × £725,000	£7,250

Note. The PET to her daughter on her wedding day does not use up any of the nil rate band as it is exempt during lifetime.

6 **Slocombe Discretionary Trust**

Income payments to discretionary trust beneficiaries come with a 50% tax credit. The trustees must have paid sufficient tax to cover this tax credit. They keep a tally of all the tax paid to HMRC in the 'tax pool'.

If there is insufficient tax paid to HMRC in the tax pool, the trustees have an additional liability that must be paid over with any other income tax liability. If there is sufficient tax, the balance is carried forward to cover payments in future years.

	£
Dividend income × 100/90	22,000
Taxable income	22,000
Basic rate band:	
£1,000 @ 10%	100
£21,000 @ 42.5%	8,925
Income tax liability	9,025
Less: 10% tax credit: £22,000 × 10%	(2,200)
Income tax due (and entering the tax pool)	6,825

The balance on the tax pool is:

	£
Tax pool b/f	625
Add tax paid in current year:	6,825
Available tax credits	7,450
Less: tax required to cover beneficiary's £9,000 payment:	(9,000)
Additional tax liability	(1,550)
Total tax liability: £1,550 + £6,825	8,375
Tax pool c/f	nil

7 **Alan**

The first £1,000 of non-savings income will be taxed at the basic rate.

In addition any income used to pay trust expenses is also taxed at the basic rate depending on the type of income used to pay them (usually dividend income first).

The balance of non-savings income will be taxed at 50% and the dividends at 42.5%.

When the beneficiaries either receive income from the trust or funds are used for their benefit (eg when the trustees pays their school fees) that income is usually taxable on them. Such payments come with a 50% tax credit.

However, as Alan's unmarried minor children can benefit from the trust it is a settlor interested trust. This means that any income paid to or used for the benefit of the children will be taxed on Alan unless it is below the annual de minimis limit of £100 (gross).

It is unlikely that the school fees will be below this limit so the income used to pay the fees will not be taxed on the children but instead on Alan.

8 **Henry**

Where relevant business property has not been owned for 2 years, BPR will still be given if:

(a) 'Old' business property has been sold in the prior 3 years and replaced with the York Ltd shares. BPR will be given on the York Ltd shares if the aggregated ownership periods total at least two of the five years immediately preceding the transfer; or

(b) If Henry had acquired the York Ltd shares on the death of his spouse and the joint ownership period was at least 2 years; or

(c) Henry has acquired the shares on the death of a person within the last 2 years and that death transfer had qualified for BPR.

[see s.107 – 109 IHTA 1984]

9 **Gifts with Reservation of Benefit**

- Where the donor pays full consideration for the use of the asset;
- Where the donor gives away half of a house then shares that house with the donee (provided that the donor pays a reasonable share of all outgoings);
- Where the donor gives away a house and stays with the donee for less than one month a year in total (or less than 2 weeks if the donee is not present);
- Where the donor gives a house to a donee then stays with the donor for a short-term purpose (eg while convalescing after medical treatment);
- Where the donor gives away land then uses that land to walk dogs etc, as long as this does not restrict the donee's use.

(+ marks for other examples in HMRC Tax Bulletin November 1993).

10 **William**

Capital gain arising

	£	£
Proceeds		600,000
Cost	400,000	
Less: held over gain	(120,000)	
		(280,000)
Trustees gain		320,000
Less: Annual exempt amount		(5,050)
Taxable gain		314,950
CGT @ 28%		£88,186

11 **Mrs Hathaway**

2010/11	*Non savings*	*Interest*
	£	£
Rental profit (£24,000 - £4,000)	20,000	
Interest (× 100/80)		6,000
Less: loan interest	(2,500)	
Taxable income	17,500	6,000
Less: tax suffered at 20%	(3,500)	(1,200)
Net income	14,000	4,800
Less: estate expenses		(400)
Net distributable income	14,000	4,400

R185 (Estate income)	*Net*	*Tax*
	£	£
Non-savings	14,000	3,500
Interest	4,400	1,100

12 **Agricultural property relief**

- Yes – APR available on land situated in UK, Channel Islands, Isle of Man or within the European Economic Area. Relief given at 100% × agricultural value, post 1.9.95 lease.
- Yes – relief given at 100% × agricultural value. BPR may be available on residual value.
- Yes – assuming that the farmhouse is 'of a character appropriate to the property', at 100% × agricultural value.
- No – livestock may qualify for BPR.
- Yes - relief given at 50% × agricultural value as lease signed pre 1.9.95 and has more than 2 years left to run.

1 **Overseas Inc**

Overseas Inc is incorporated outside of the UK. It will therefore only be resident in the UK if its central management and control is exercised in the UK. If the central management and control is exercised by the board of directors, the place where the board meetings are held will be an important factor in determining the residence of the company.

If Overseas Inc is deemed to be UK resident it will be subject to UK corporation tax on its worldwide profits. The profits arising from both the UK and overseas operations will therefore be taxed in the UK.

A non-UK resident company is only taxed in the UK on profits arising from a trade carried on through a permanent establishment in the UK, eg the manufacturing unit. If Overseas Inc is non-UK resident it will only be taxed in the UK on the profits arising from the UK manufacturing operations.

Double tax relief may be available for income which is taxed both in the UK and overseas.

2 **Gardener Ltd**

Capital allowances computation for the year to 31 October 2010

	Main Pool	*Old Expensive Car*	*Short life asset (SLA)*	*Allowances*
	£	£	£	£
TWDV at 1.11.09	45,000	24,000	4,000	
SLA transfer (held > 5 APs)	4,000		(4,000)	
Additions qualifying for AIA/ 1.6.10 Van	13,000			
AIA	(13,000)			13,000
Additions (Cars): 1.5.10 Main rate car	11,000			
Disposals: 1.7.10 Machine (limited to cost)	(35,000)			
1.6.10 Old expensive car		(15,000)		
	25,000	9,000		
Balancing allowance		(9,000)		9,000
WDA @ 20%	(5,000)			5,000
TWDV cfwd	20,000	–	–	
Total allowances				27,000

3 **Marine Ltd**

(1) The debentures were issued to raise funds for non-trade related purposes and are therefore a non-trading loan relationship. The interest payable, on an accrued basis, of £20,000 will be a debit in respect of a non-trading loan relationship. The associated professional fees will be treated in the same way.

The accrued rent for the 10 months to 31 March 2011 of £20,833 (£25,000 × 10/12) will be taxed as property income.

(2) The bank loan was used for trading purposes and is therefore a trade related loan relationship. Interest payable is an allowable trading deduction. The interest is deductible on accrued basis and £2,800 will therefore be an allowable deduction from trading profits.

4 **Mammoth Ltd**

Corporation tax liability for the six months ended 31 December 2010

	£
Taxable trading income:	
Trading profit per accounts	200,000
Amortisation charge	(20,000)
Capital allowances:	
Pool WDA £50,000 × 20% × 6/12	(5,000)
Plant AIA £15,000 × 100%	(15,000)
Taxable trading profits	160,000
Corporation tax liability (W):	
£160,000 × 28%	44,800
Less marginal relief:	
7/400 × (£750,000 – £160,000)	(10,325)
	34,475

Working

Rate of corporation tax

The accounting period is 6 months long. The limits used to determine the rate of corporation tax are therefore multiplied by 6/12:

Upper limit: £1,500,000 × 6/12	£750,000
Lower limit £300,000 × 6/12	£150,000

The company therefore pays tax at the main rate with marginal relief.

5 **Circle Ltd**

(1) Loss relief group

Circle Ltd owns at least 75% of Square Ltd. They therefore form a loss relief group.

Triangle Ltd is not in a loss relief group with Circle Ltd as Circle Ltd's indirect holding in Triangle Ltd is less than 75% ie 64% (80% × 80%).

Square Ltd and Triangle Ltd can form a separate loss relief group.

(2) Group relief – Year ended 31 December 2010

Oblong Ltd can surrender its current year trading loss of £220,000 and its excess qualifying charitable donations (QCDS) of £1,000 (£6,000 – £5,000). Capital losses cannot be group relieved.

Circle Ltd can claim losses of £73,000 from Oblong Ltd, ie the amount of its taxable total profits (ie total profits (including gains) less QCDs).

Tutorial note. This question is concerned with the group relief provisions and the answer correctly states that capital losses cannot be group relieved. It should be noted however that as the companies are also within a chargeable gains group the companies can elect to transfer chargeable gains/capital losses around the group under the provisions of s. 171A TCGA 1992. You were not however required to consider this in the question.

6 **Hotspur Ltd**

	12 m/e 31.3.11	2 m/e 31.5.11
	£	£
Adjusted profit before CAs (12:2)	384,000	64,000
CAs: AIA £100,000 (max)	(100,000)	
Balance £3,000 × 20% WDA	(600)	
£(3,000 – 600 – 1,600) × 20% × 2/12		(27)
Taxable trading income	283,400	63,973
Profit on non-trading loan relationship (12:2)	6,000	1,000
Property income (12 :2 Note)	51,429	8,571
Taxable total profits	340,829	73,544
Due dates for CT 600	31.5.12	31.5.12

Note: Property income is calculated on the accruals for the period of account ie the 14 months to 31 May 2011 ie £120,000 x 6/12 (Rented from 1 December 2010 to 31 May 2011). It is allocated to the different accounting periods for tax purposes on a time apportionment basis (in the same way as trading profits).

7 **Verona Ltd**

8 month CAP, therefore 3 payments on account required.

Initial payments based on profit estimate of £5m.

Instalment	*Due*	*Working*	£
1	14.11.10	£5m × 28% × 3/8	525,000
2	14.2.11	£5m × 28% × 3/8	525,000
			1,050,000
3	14.4.11	Balance required (Note)	630,000
Total tax payable			1,680,000

Note: Revised tax due = £6m × 28% = £1,680,000.

8 **Non-trading loan relationship**

(1) Against profits of the same accounting period before qualifying charitable donations and a current year trading loss.
(2) Surrendered as group relief.
(3) Carried back 12 months against profit on non-trading loan relationships.
(4) Against non-trading profits of the next accounting period.

9 **Orsino Ltd**

The chargeable accounting period is 1.2.10 to 30.9.10 (ie 8 months)

	£	£
Tax adjusted profit	125,000	
Less; capital allowances		
Special rate car: £9,000 × 10% x 8/12	(600)	
Trading profit		124,400
Profit on non-trading loan relationship		8,000
Taxable total profits		132,400
FII (£1,000 × 100/90)		1,111
Augmented profits		133,511

There are 3 associated companies:

	£
Upper limit (£1.5 m × 1/3 × 8/12)	333,333
Lower limit (£300,000 × 1/3 × 8/12)	66,667

Marginal relief applies.

	£
CT due:	
£132,400 × 28%	37,072
$7/400 \times £(333,333 - 133,511) \times \frac{132,400}{133,511}$	(3,468)
Corporation tax payable	33,604

10 **Trading losses**

The carry forward of trading losses is denied where within a three year period there is BOTH

(1) a change of ownership of a company; AND
(2) a 'major change in the nature or conduct of the trade' carried on by the company.

A change will be 'major' if there is a change in any of the following:

- the type of property dealt in
- the type of services provided
- the facilities provided
- customers
- outlets
- markets

The carry forward of trading losses is also denied where:

(1) the company's activities had become small or negligible; and
(2) there is a change of ownership of the company; and
(3) following the change of ownership there is a considerable revival in the scale of activities.

11 **Lysander Ltd**

The sale of the shares in Lysander Ltd will result in a gain chargeable on Theseus Ltd.

	£
Proceeds	10,000,000
Less: cost 2003	(100,000)
Gain chargeable	9,900,000

The substantial shareholding exemption does not apply as Lysander Ltd is not a trading company.

There will also be a de-grouping charge as the office block had been transferred to Lysander Ltd in a NGNL transfer within 6 years of Lysander leaving the group:

	£
Market value at transfer in 2008	6,000,000
Less: Cost to group in 2002	(1,000,000)
Gain chargeable	5,000,000

This gain will be chargeable on Lysander Ltd.

12 **Cressida Ltd**

	£	£
Trading income:		
Paint sales		312,000
Patent royalty (× 100/80)		10,000
		322,000
Expenses:		
General manufacturing costs	120,000	
R&D expenditure (£40,000 × 175%)	70,000	
Amortisation of goodwill:		
£100,000 × 1/5 × 6/12	10,000	
		(200,000)
Taxable total profits		122,000

Small profits rate applies.

	£
Tax:	
£122,000 × 21%	25,620
Less: income tax suffered on patent royalty income	(2,000)
	23,620

TQT Tax Qualification Training

Module D – Taxation of individuals: answers

1 **Reginald**

Reginald has notified chargeability on time. The deadline is 5 October 2011 for 2010/11.

As HMRC issued the tax return after 31 October, the deadline for filing online was 3 months after the tax return was issued ie by 10 February 2012. Therefore, Reginald filed his return late.

Reginald can amend his return within 12 months of the filing deadline – ie up until 10 February 2013.

If a return is filed late, HMRC has until the quarter day following the first anniversary of the actual filing date to open an enquiry ie 30 April 2013.

As Reginald filed his return less than three months late, he will incur a late filing penalty of £100.

2 **Mr Falstaff**

	Non savings	*Savings*
	£	£
State pension	5,200	
Employers pension	14,000	
Rental profits	4,800	
Bank interest (× 100/80)		937
Net income	24,000	937
Less: PAA (W1)	(8,934)	
Taxable income	15,066	937

Tax	
15,066 @ 20%	3,013
937 @ 20%	187
Tax liability	3,200
Less: PAYE	(1,850)
Tax on interest	(187)
Tax payable	1,163

Working

	£
Income	24,937
Less: gift aid (£500 × 100/80)	(625)
Income for PAA purposes	24,312
PAA (>75)	9,640
Less ½ × (24,312 – 22,900)	(706)
	8,934

Note: as marriage takes place after 5 December 2005, the married couples allowances goes to the one with the highest income (in this case this is Celia).

3 **Antony**

	£	£
Car:		
$\frac{(160-130)}{5}$ + 15 = 21% £20,000 x 21% × 9/12		3,150
Fuel:		
£18,000 × 21% × 9/12		2,835
Accommodation:		
Annual value	1,000	
Additional yearly rent		
£(250,000 – 75,000) × 4%	7,000	
	8,000	
× 7/12	4,667	
Less: rents paid (£200 × 7)	(1,400)	
		3,267
Total taxable benefits		9,252

4 **Eleanora**

Eleanora is currently resident and ordinarily resident, but non-domiciled in the UK. Even though she has lived here for many years, she retains her non-domicile status because she has a clear intention to return to live in Australia.

Her UK employment income will be taxable in full in the UK on an arising basis.

As a non-domiciled individual, she may claim for her overseas rental income to be taxable in the UK only to the extent that it is remitted to the UK. So the rental income of £12,000 is not taxable in the UK.

The overseas dividend income will also only be taxable to the extent that it has been remitted to the UK (ie £11,000 x 100/90 (grossed up by a 10% non-repayable UK tax credit)). This amount will be taxed as non-savings income at a rate of 40%.

However, as Eleanora has been resident in the UK for at least 7 out of the preceding 9 tax years she will be subject to the £30,000 remittance based charge if she claims to be taxed on the remittance basis. This is in addition to the tax charged on her remitted income. It would not therefore be beneficial for Eleanora to claim the remittance basis in respect of 2010/11 and she will be taxed on all her foreign income on an arising basis. (The overseas dividends will be grossed up by the 10% non-repayable tax credit, but will only be taxed at the rate of 32.5%.)

5 **Jemima**

Grant

There is no tax or NIC on the grant of options under the EMI scheme.

Exercise

There is no tax or NIC on the exercise of the EMI options, because the exercise price was not less than the market value of the shares at the date of grant.

Sale of shares

The gain on the sale of shares is subject to capital gains tax, as follows:

	£
Proceeds (£14.70 × 5,000)	73,500
Cost (£6.80 × 5,000)	(34,000)
	39,500
Annual exempt amount	(10,100)
	29,400
CGT @ 28%	8,232

6 **Roderigo**

The deferred gain will crystallise if;

(1) Roderigo disposes of the shares (other than by way of a gift to his spouse/civil partner);

(2) After transferring the shares to his spouse/civil partner, the spouse/civil partner then disposes of the shares;

(3) Roderigo becomes neither resident nor ordinarily resident within 3 years from the issue of the shares;

(4) After giving the shares to the spouse/civil partner, the spouse/civil partner becomes neither resident nor ordinarily resident within 3 years from the issue of the shares;

(5) The EIS shares cease to be eligible for relief.

7 **Jamie**

		£	£
Rent	(9/12 × £15,000)	11,250	
	(3/12 × £15,600)	3,900	
			15,150
Less allowable expenses:			
Insurance	(4/12 × £3,600)		(1,200)
	(8/12 ×£4,200)		(2,800)
Council tax			(1,100)
Chimney replacement (Note)			(800)
Interest	(3% × £200,000)		(6,000)
Wear and tear allowance	(10% × (15,150 – 1,100))		(1,405)
Property income (2010/11)			1,845

Note: Replacement of a subsidiary part of an asset (eg chimney) is treated as revenue expenditure and therefore allowable.

8 **Emily**

Class 1 primary – payable by Emily

		£
Earnings		
Salary		50,000
Bonus		36,000
Telephone bills		650
		86,650
Class 1 primary:	(43,875 – 5,715) × 11%	4,198
	(86,650 – 43,875) × 1%	428
		4,626

Class 1 secondary – payable by Arcite Ltd

(86,650 – 5,715) × 12.8% = £10,360

Class 1A – payable by Arcite Ltd

		£
Accommodation	10,800	
Medical insurance	480	
	11,280 × 12.8%	£1,444

9 **Maria**

Capital gains tax computation 2010/11

			Qualifying for ER	Not qualifying for ER
		£	£	£
1	Painting			
	Proceeds	6,860		
	31.3.82 MV	(4,000)		
	Gain	2,860		
	Restricted to:			
	5/3 × (7,000 – 6,000) (Note gross proceeds used)	1,667		1,667
2	West Ltd			
	Gain (qualifies for ER)	45,000	45,000	
3	Coach plc			24,000
Total gains				25,667
Less losses brought forward				(5,000)
Less Annual exempt amount				(10,100)
Taxable gain			45,000	10,567
CGT at 10%/28%			4,500	2,959
Total CGT			7,459	

Note. The capital losses and annual exempt amount are set off against the gains not qualifying for entrepreneurs' relief as they are taxed at 28% rather than 10%.

The remaining basic rate band of £2,400 is used firstly by the gain qualifying for entrepreneurs' relief (ER). The gains not qualifying for ER are therefore taxed in full at 28%.

10 **Henry Percy**

	£
Gain	272,000
Less: PPR relief 19/28.5 × £272,000 (W1)	(181,333)
Gain	90,667
Less: Annual exempt amount	(10,100)
Taxable gain	80,567
CGT: Basic rate band remaining = £6,375 (£37, 400 – (£37,500 - £6,475))	
£6,375 @ 18%	1,147
£74,192 @ 28%	20,774
	21,921

Working

	Occupied years	*Absent years*
1.4.82 – 31.3.98	16	
1.4.98 – 30.9.07		9.5
1.10.07 – 30.9.10 (last 3 years)	3	
Total	19	9.5

11 **Oswald**

	£	£
Shares to son:		
MV	95,000	
Less: cost	(12,000)	
Gain	83,000	
Less: s.165 gift relief	(55,000)	
Chargeable gain £(40,000 – 12,000)	28,000	
		28,000
Painting to daughter:		
MV	20,000	
Less: cost	(25,000)	
Loss	(5,000)	
'Connected persons' loss so no relief against other gains		NIL
Shares to nephew:		
MV	8,000	
Less: cost	(20,000)	
Loss	(12,000)	
Nephew not a 'connected person' so general loss relief allowed		(12,000)
Net gains 2010/11		16,000

12 **Miranda**

Apportionment of consideration on takeover

	Value £	%
20,000 ordinary shares in Prospero plc	95,000	38%
£100,000 of loan stock in Prospero plc	100,000	40%
Cash	55,000	22%
Total	250,000	100%

Gain on receipt of loan stock in 2009/10 will be frozen until loan stock is sold / redeemed:

	£
Value of loan stock at takeover	100,000
Less: base cost	
£80,000 × 40%	(32,000)
Frozen gain	68,000

This gain crystallises in 2010/11 when the loan stock is redeemed.

The loss on redemption (£85,000 - £100,000) is not allowable as the loan stock is exempt from CGT.

1 **Albert**

Tax adjusted trading profit for the year ended 30 June 2010

	£
Profit per accounts	35,000
Add:	
Legal fees	–
Repair costs (Note)	200
Delivery van -cost	6,000
Parking fine	50
	41,250
Capital allowances (AIA) on van £6,000 × 100% × 80%	(4,800)
Tax adjusted trading profit	36,450

Note: The repair costs were initial repairs to a recently acquired asset and were necessary in order for the asset to be used in the business. The costs are therefore disallowed as capital.

2 **Maggie**

Tax adjusted trading profit for the fifteen months to 30 April 2011

	£
Net profit per accounts	24,700
Plus: Maggie's wages (appropriation of profit)	45,000
Rent and rates (private use £10,000 × ¼)	2,500
Depreciation	2,000
Goods own use	850
Tax adjusted trading profit	75,050

2010/11 Trading income assessment

The basis period for the 2010/11 trading income assessment is 6 April 2010 to 5 April 2011 (the actual basis as no accounting period ends in 2010/11).

3 **Karen**

Capital allowances computation for the year to 31 August 2011

	FYA £	*Main pool* £	*Old expensive Car (PU 40%)* £	*Special rate Car (PU 40%)* £		*Allow-ances* £
TWDV at 1.9.10		25,000	16,000			
Addition qualifying for 100% FYA:						
New low emission car (Ford)	10,000					
100% FYA	(10,000)					10,000
Addition qualifying for AIA:						
Van		15,000				
AIA		(15,000)				15,000
Additions not qualifying for AIA:						
Jaguar car (special rate)				25,000		
Disposal			(12,000)			
		25,000	4,000	25,000		
Balancing allowance			(4,000)x 60%			2,400
WDA @ 20%		(5,000)				5,000
WDA @ 10%				(2,500)	x 60%	1,500
TWDV c/fwd	-	20,000	-	22,500		
Total allowances						33,900

4 **Gerald**

2010/11 Trading income assessment

Basis of assessment: 18 month period to 31 December 2010

	£	£
Year ended 30 June 2010 - taxable profit		34,000
6 months to 31 December 2010 - Adjusted trading profit	15,000	
Plus: Balancing charge (W)	11,000	
		26,000
Less: Overlap profits		(8,000)
Trading income assessment		52,000

Working

Capital allowances for the 6 months to 31 December 2010

	Main pool	*Allowances*
	£	£
TWDV bfwd	4,000	
Disposals:		
Van (MV)	(8,500)	
Plant and machinery	(6,500)	
	(11,000)	
Balancing charge	11,000	11,000

5 **Brooke**

The loss arises in the tax year 2010/11.

Options available

(1) Carry forward against the first available future trading profits of the same trade.

Under this option £500 of the loss would be offset in 2011/12 (year ended 31 May 2011). The balance of £9,500 would be carried forward to future years. The benefit of the loss will therefore be delayed into the future.

(2) Offset against general income

The loss can be offset against general income of the current tax year (2010/11) and/or the previous tax year (2009/10).

In 2010/11 Brooke's other income is £5,000 which would be covered by the personal allowance. Offsetting the loss in this year would waste most of the personal allowance and is not therefore advisable.

In 2009/10 Brooke has trading income of £26,000 (year ended 31 May 2009) and other income of £5,000. The loss would be fully utilised, save tax at the basic rate and result in a repayment of tax.

6 **Richard**

(a) *Disposal of building – August 2010*

	£
Proceeds	850,000
Less: Cost (July 2002)	(400,000)
Chargeable gain	450,000

(b) *Base cost of new building - assuming rollover relief claimed*

	£
Rollover relief - restricted as proceeds are not fully reinvested.	
Proceeds not reinvested (£850,000 – £750,000)	100,000
Gain eligible to be rolled over (£450,000 – £100,000)	350,000
Cost of new building	750,000
Less: Gain rolled over	(350,000)
Revised base cost	400,000

7 **Antonio, Bassanio and Portia**

Portia is acquiring a 20% interest in the partnership goodwill on 1 January 2011.

Bassanio is disposing of a 20% interest in the partnership goodwill on 1 January 2011.

No adjustment is made via the partnership accounts, so the transaction takes place at no gain, no loss under SP D12 para 4.

As Portia makes a payment to Bassanio outside the accounts, this payment is treated as additional consideration.

Bassanio's CGT computation is therefore as follows:

Gain on 1.1.11:	*Bassanio*
	£
'Deemed proceeds' (20% share)	40,000
Less: cost (£200,000 × 20%)	(40,000)
Gain	NIL
Actual consideration paid	80,000
Gain	80,000

Bassanio is therefore deemed to have sold his 20% interest to Portia for £(40,000 + 80,000) = £120,000. This is Portia's CGT base cost for her 20% share.

8 **Horatio and Claudius**

	Total	*Horatio*	*Claudius*
	£	£	£
P/e 31.12.10 (13 m)	260,000		
Salary (× 13/12)	16,250		16,250
Balance (3:2)	243,750	146,250	97,500
	260,000	146,250	113,750
2010/11:			
P/e 31.12.10		146,250	113,750
Less: overlap relief (W)		(15,000)	(2,500)
Taxable profits		131,250	111,250

(W) Overlap:	£
Horatio	
Overlap profits arising on commencement	15,000
Claudius	
Overlap profits arising on commencement (4 mths)	10,000
Used on change of accounts date:	
£10,000 × ¼	2,500

9 **Toby**

	£
2009/10:	
1.5.09 – 5.4.10	
£60,000 + £(30,000) × 2/3	40,000
2010/11:	
1.5.09 – 30.4.10	
£60,000 + £(30,000)	30,000
Add: losses allocated in 2009/10	20,000
	50,000
NIC 2010/11:	
Class 2 (£2.40 × 52)	125
Class 4 £(43,875 – 5,715) × 8%	3,053
£(50,000 – 43,875) × 1%	61
	3,239

10 **Florence**

As stock is transferred along with other assets, under s.176 ITTOIA 2005, the value placed on stock has to be 'just & reasonable' to prevent manipulation of consideration to obtain a tax advantage.

HMRC will therefore expect the value to be placed on the stock at cessation to be its market value of £25,000.

As £60,000 has been accounted for in respect of the stock, £35,000 will therefore need to be deducted from the final trading profit.

The cost of the stock for Oliver will now be £25,000 (not £60,000 as agreed).

11 **Warwick**

	£	£	£
Capital allowances:			TWDV
Year ended 31 December 2010	£6,000 × 20% (WDA) = £1,200	1,200	4,800
Period ended 30 April 2012	£4,800 × 20% × 16/12	1,280	3,520
Trading profits:			
Year ended 31 December 2010	£(12,000 – 1,200)	10,800	
Period ended 30 April 2012	£(30,000 – 1,280)	28,720	

Assessable profits & overlap

		£	£
2009/10	1.1.10 – 5.4.10		
2010/11	1.1.10 – 31.12.10		
Overlap	1.1.10 – 5.4.10		
	3/12 × £10,800	2,700	
2011/12	1.5.10 – 30.4.11		
	8/12 × £10,800		7,200
	+ 4/16 × £28,720		7,180
			14,380
Overlap	1.5.10 – 31.12.10		
	8/12 × £10,800	7,200	
2011/12	1.5.11 – 30.4.12		
Overlap c/f	From opening years		2,700
	Created on change of accounts date		7,200
			9,900

12 **Morgan**

Interest charges:

	£
2nd POA for 2009/10 (due 31.7.10)	
£5,500 × 2/12 × 3%	27
Balancing payment for 2009/10 (due 31.1.11)	
£2,000 × 2/12 × 3%	10
Over-reduction of POAs for 2009/10 (by £1,000 each)	
£1,000 × 12/12 × 3%	30
£1,000 × 6/12 × 3%	15
1st POA for 2010/11 (due 31.1.11)	
£6,500 × 2/12 × 3%	32
Total interest charges	114
Penalties:	
Late filing penalty: 2009/10 return filed 1 month late, immediate penalty	100
Late payment penalty: 2009/10 balancing payment over 30 days late:	
£2,000 × 5%	100
Grand total	314

CTA EXAMINATIONS

MAY AND NOVEMBER 2011

TAX TABLES

THE CHARTERED INSTITUTE OF TAXATION

INCOME TAX

	2010/11	2009/10
Rates	%	%
Starting rate for savings income only	10	10
Basic rate for all income	20	20
Higher rate for non-savings and savings income only	40	40
Higher rate for dividends	32.5	32.5
Additional rate for non-savings and savings income only	50	–
Additional rate for dividends	42.5	–
Trust rate	50	40
Dividend trust rate	42.5	32.5
Thresholds	£	£
Savings income starting rate band	1 – 2,440	1 – 2,440
Basic rate band	1 – 37,400	1 – 37,400
Higher rate band	37,401 – 150,000	N/A
Standard rate band for trusts	1,000	1,000
Reliefs	£	£
Personal allowance(1)	6,475	6,475
– age 65–74(1)	9,490	9,490
– age 75 or over(1)	9,640	9,640
Married couple's allowance(2)	6,965	6,965
– Maximum income before abatement of relief - £1 for £2	22,900	22,900
– Minimum allowance	2,670	2,670
Blind person's allowance	1,890	1,890
'Rent-a-room' limit	4,250	4,250
Enterprise investment scheme relief limit(3)	500,000	500,000
Venture capital trust relief limit(4)	200,000	200,000
Employer supported childcare	£55 per week	£55 per week

Notes (1) From 2010/11, the personal allowance of any individual with income above £100,000 is reduced by £1 for every £2 of income above the £100,000 limit.

(2) Only available where at least one partner was born before 6 April 1935. Relief restricted to 10%.

(3) Relief at 20%.

(4) Relief at 30%.

Pension contributions

	Annual allowance(1)	Lifetime allowance	Minimum pension age
	£	£	
2009/10	245,000	1,750,000	50
2010/11	255,000	1,800,000	55

Basic amount qualifying for tax relief £3,600

Notes (1) Individuals with incomes above £130,000 (excluding employer pension contributions) may be subject to a Special Annual Allowance which restricts tax relief on their pension contributions in excess of normal patterns to basic rate relief.

ITEPA Mileage Rates

Vehicles		**2010/11 and 2009/10**
Car or van(1)	First 10,000 business miles	40p
	Additional business miles	25p
Motorcycles		24p
Bicycles		20p
Passenger payments		5p

Note (1) For NIC purposes, a rate of 40p applies irrespective of mileage.

Company cars and fuel

Emissions 2010/11	Emissions 2009/10	Car benefit percentage[(1)(2)(3)]
0g/km	**N/A**	**0%**
1 – 75g/km	**N/A**	**5%**
76 – 120g/km	**1 – 120g/km**	**10%**
121 – 130g/km	**121 – 135g/km**	**15%**
131 – 230g/km	**136 – 235g/km**	**15% + 1% for every additional whole 5g/km above 130g/km (135 g/km in 2009/10)**
Over 230g/km	**Over 235g/km**	**35%**

	2010/11	2009/10
Fuel benefit base figure [(2)]	**£18,000**	**£16,900**

Notes (1) Apply the car benefit percentage to list price of the vehicle.

(2) Apply the same car benefit percentages to the fuel benefit base figure to calculate the fuel benefit.

(3) 3% supplement for diesel cars.

Taxable benefits for vans	2010/11	2009/10
	£	£
Van benefit – No CO_2 emissions	**0**	**3,000**
Van benefit – CO_2 emissions > 0g/km	**3,000**	**3,000**
Fuel benefit	**550**	**500**

Official rate of interest	2010/11	2009/10
	4.00%	**4.75%**

CAPITAL GAINS TAX	**2010/11**		**2009/10**
	From 23.6.10	**Until 22.6.10**	
Annual exempt amount	£10,100	£10,100	£10,100
CGT rates for individuals[(1),(2)]			
Gains qualifying for entrepreneurs' relief (see final section of table below)	10%	18%	18%
Gains falling within remaining basic rate band[(3)]	18%	18%	18%
Gains exceeding basic rate band	28%	18%	18%
CGT rates for trusts & individuals paying the remittance basis charge			
Gains qualifying for entrepreneurs' relief	10%	18%	18%
Other gains	28%	18%	18%
CGT rate for PRs			
All gains[(4)]	28%	18%	18%
Entrepreneurs' relief			
Relevant gains (lifetime maximum)	£5 million	£2 million	£1 million
Reducing fraction	NA	$\frac{4}{9}$	$\frac{4}{9}$

Notes (1) For individuals, gains are taxed as if they are the top slice of income.

(2) Capital losses and the annual exempt amount may be offset in the most beneficial manner, ie against gains not qualifying for entrepreneurs' relief first.

(3) The remaining basic rate band is calculated as £37,400 less taxable income less any gains on which entrepreneurs' relief has been claimed.

(4) Personal representatives of deceased persons cannot claim entrepreneurs' relief.

Lease percentage table

Years	Percentage	Years	Percentage	Years	Percentage
50 or more	100.000	33	90.280	16	64.116
49	99.657	32	89.354	15	61.617
48	99.289	31	88.371	14	58.971
47	98.902	30	87.330	13	56.167
46	98.490	29	86.226	12	53.191
45	98.059	28	85.053	11	50.038
44	97.595	27	83.816	10	46.695
43	97.107	26	82.496	9	43.154
42	96.593	25	81.100	8	39.399
41	96.041	24	79.622	7	35.414
40	95.457	23	78.055	6	31.195
39	94.842	22	76.399	5	26.722
38	94.189	21	74.635	4	21.983
37	93.497	20	72.770	3	16.959
36	92.761	19	70.791	2	11.629
35	91.981	18	68.697	1	5.983
34	91.156	17	66.470	0	0.000

Retail Prices Index

Where Retail Price Indices are required, it should be assumed that they are as follows.

	Jan	Feb	Mar	Apr	May	Jun	Jul	Aug	Sep	Oct	Nov	Dec
1982	–	–	79.44	81.04	81.62	81.85	81.88	81.90	81.85	82.26	82.66	82.51
1983	82.61	82.97	83.12	84.28	84.64	84.84	85.30	85.68	86.06	86.36	86.67	86.89
1984	86.84	87.20	87.48	88.64	88.97	89.20	89.10	89.94	90.11	90.67	90.95	90.87
1985	91.20	91.94	92.80	94.78	95.21	95.41	95.23	95.49	95.44	95.59	95.92	96.05
1986	96.25	96.60	96.73	97.67	97.85	97.79	97.52	97.82	98.30	98.45	99.29	99.62
1987	100.0	100.4	100.6	101.8	101.9	101.9	101.8	102.1	102.4	102.9	103.4	103.3
1988	103.3	103.7	104.1	105.8	106.2	106.6	106.7	107.9	108.4	109.5	110.0	110.3
1989	111.0	111.8	112.3	114.3	115.0	115.4	115.5	115.8	116.6	117.5	118.5	118.8
1990	119.5	120.2	121.4	125.1	126.2	126.7	126.8	128.1	129.3	130.3	130.0	129.9
1991	130.2	130.9	131.4	133.1	133.5	134.1	133.8	134.1	134.6	135.1	135.6	135.7
1992	135.6	136.3	136.7	138.8	139.3	139.3	138.8	138.9	139.4	139.9	139.7	139.2
1993	137.9	138.8	139.3	140.6	141.1	141.0	140.7	141.3	141.9	141.8	141.6	141.9
1994	141.3	142.1	142.5	144.2	144.7	144.7	144.0	144.7	145.0	145.2	145.3	146.0
1995	146.0	146.9	147.5	149.0	149.6	149.8	149.1	149.9	150.6	149.8	149.8	150.7
1996	150.2	150.9	151.5	152.6	152.9	153.0	152.4	153.1	153.8	153.8	153.9	154.4
1997	154.4	155.0	155.4	156.3	156.9	157.5	157.5	158.5	159.3	159.5	159.6	160.0
1998	159.5	160.3	160.8	162.6	163.5	163.4	163.0	163.7	164.4	164.5	164.4	164.4
1999	163.4	163.7	164.1	165.2	165.6	165.6	165.1	165.5	166.2	166.5	166.7	167.3
2000	166.6	167.5	168.4	170.1	170.7	171.1	170.5	170.5	171.7	171.6	172.1	172.2
2001	171.1	172.0	172.2	173.1	174.2	174.4	173.3	174.0	174.6	174.3	173.6	173.4
2002	173.3	173.8	174.5	175.7	176.2	176.2	175.9	176.4	177.6	177.9	178.2	178.5
2003	178.4	179.3	179.9	181.2	181.5	181.3	181.3	181.6	182.5	182.6	182.7	183.5
2004	183.1	183.8	184.6	185.7	186.5	186.8	186.8	187.4	188.1	188.6	189.0	189.9
2005	188.9	189.6	190.5	191.6	192.0	192.2	192.2	192.6	193.1	193.3	193.6	194.1
2006	193.4	194.2	195.0	196.5	197.7	198.5	198.5	199.2	200.1	200.4	201.1	202.7
2007	201.6	203.1	204.4	205.4	206.2	207.3	206.1	207.3	208.0	208.9	209.7	210.9
2008	209.8	211.4	212.1	214.0	215.1	216.8	216.5	217.2	218.4	217.7	216.0	212.9
2009	210.1	211.4	211.3	211.5	212.8	213.4	213.4	214.4	215.3	216.0	216.6	218.0
2010	217.9	219.2	220.7	222.8	223.6	225.0*	226.4*	227.8*	227.9*	229.3*	230.7*	232.1*
2011*	233.5	234.9	236.3	237.7	239.1	240.5	241.9	243.3	244.7	246.1	247.5	248.9

* = assumed

NATIONAL INSURANCE CONTRIBUTIONS

Class 1 Limits		2010/11			2009/10	
	Annual	Monthly	Weekly	Annual	Monthly	Weekly
Lower earnings limit (LEL)	£5,044	£421	£97	£4,940	£412	£95
Earnings threshold (ET)	£5,715	£476	£110	£5,715	£476	£110
Upper accruals point (UAP)	£40,040	£3,337	£770	£40,040	£3,337	£770
Upper earnings limit (UEL)	£43,875	£3,656	£844	£43,875	£3,656	£844

Class 1 primary contribution rates	2010/11	2009/10
Not contracted out		
Earnings between ET and UEL	11%	11%
Earnings above UEL	1%	1%
Contracted out		
Earnings between ET and UAP	9.4%	9.4%
Earnings between UAP and UEL	11%	11%
Earnings above UEL	1%	1%
Rebate on earnings between LEL and ET	1.6%	1.6%

Class 1 secondary contribution rates	2010/11	2009/10
Not contracted out		
Earnings above ET	12.8%	12.8%
Contracted out – salary related		
Earnings between ET and UAP	9.1%	9.1%
Earnings above UAP	12.8%	12.8%
Rebate on earnings between LEL and ET	3.7%	3.7%
Contracted out – money purchase		
Earnings between ET and UAP	11.4%	11.4%
Earnings above UAP	12.8%	12.8%
Rebate on earnings between LEL and ET	1.4%	1.4%

Other contribution limits and rates	2010/11	2009/10
Class 1A contributions	12.8%	12.8%
Class 1B contributions	12.8%	12.8%
Class 2 contributions		
Normal rate	£2.40 pw	£2.40 pw
Small earnings exception	£5,075 pa	£5,075 pa
Class 3 contributions	£12.05 pw	£12.05 pw
Class 4 contributions		
Annual lower profits limit (LPL)	£5,715	£5,715
Annual upper profits limit (UPL)	£43,875	£43,875
Percentage rate between LPL and UPL	8%	8%
Percentage rate above UPL	1%	1%

CORPORATION TAX

Financial year	2011	2010	2009
Main rate	27%	28%	28%
Small profits rate	20%	21%	21%
Augmented profit limit for small profits rate	£300,000	£300,000	£300,000
Augmented profit limit for marginal relief	£1,500,000	£1,500,000	£1,500,000
Standard fraction	$\frac{7}{400}$	$\frac{7}{400}$	$\frac{7}{400}$
Marginal rate	28.75%	29.75%	29.75%

EU definition of small and medium sized enterprises(1)(2)(3)

	Small From 1.1.05	Medium From 1.1.05
Employees	≤ 50	≤ 250
Turnover	≤ €10m	≤ €50m
Balance sheet assets	≤ €10m	≤ €43m

Notes (1) Small and medium sized enterprises (SMEs) must meet the employees criteria and *either* the turnover *or* the balance sheet assets criteria.

(2) These thresholds apply as given for transfer pricing and distributions received by small companies.

(3) For the purposes of research and development expenditure the definition of a SME is extended with effect from 1 August 2008 to: Employees 500; Turnover €100m; Balance sheet assets €86m.

CAPITAL ALLOWANCES

	6.4.10 – 5.4.11(1)	6.4.09 – 5.4.10(1)
Annual investment allowance (AIA)(2)	100%	100%
First year allowance (FYA)(3)	–	40%
WDA on plant and machinery in main pool(4)	20%	20%
WDA on plant and machinery in special rate pool(5)	10%	10%
Writing down allowance on patent rights and know-how	25%	25%

Notes (1) Dates for companies are 1 April – 31 March.

(2) 100% on the first £100,000 (£50,000 in 2009/10) of investment in plant and machinery (except cars).

(3) A FYA was available for expenditure on assets other than cars in the main pool in 2009/10. The FYA was given after and in addition to the AIA.

(4) A rate of 20% applies to cars with CO_2 emissions greater than 110g/km but not more than 160 g/km acquired on or after 6 April 2009 (1 April for companies).

(5) A rate of 10% applies to cars with CO_2 emissions greater than 160 g/km acquired on or after 6 April 2009 (1 April for companies).

(6) Cars acquired before 6 April 2009 (1 April for companies) continue to be written down based on cost rather than emissions.

100% First year allowances available to all businesses

1) New energy saving plant and machinery, and water efficient plant and machinery.
2) New cars registered between 16 April 2002 and 31 March 2013 if the car either emits not more than 110 g/km of CO_2 or it is electrically propelled.
3) Renovation or conversion of vacant business premises, in a designated Enterprise Area, for the purpose of bringing those premises back into business use.
4) Converting or renovating an empty or under-used space above a commercial property into qualifying residential accommodation.
5) Capital expenditure incurred by a person on research and development.

INHERITANCE TAX

Death rate	40%	**Lifetime rate**	20%

Nil rate bands

6 April 1999 – 5 April 2000	up to £231,000	6 April 2005 – 5 April 2006	up to £275,000
6 April 2000 – 5 April 2001	up to £234,000	6 April 2006 – 5 April 2007	up to £285,000
6 April 2001 – 5 April 2002	up to £242,000	6 April 2007 – 5 April 2008	up to £300,000
6 April 2002 – 5 April 2003	up to £250,000	6 April 2008 – 5 April 2009	up to £312,000
6 April 2003 – 5 April 2004	up to £255,000	6 April 2009 – 5 April 2015	up to £325,000
6 April 2004 – 5 April 2005	up to £263,000		

Taper relief

Death within 3 years of gift	Nil%
Between 3 and 4 years	20%
Between 4 and 5 years	40%
Between 5 and 6 years	60%
Between 6 and 7 years	80%

Quick Succession relief

Period between transfers less than one year	100%
Between 1 and 2 years	80%
Between 2 and 3 years	60%
Between 3 and 4 years	40%
Between 4 and 5 years	20%

Lifetime exemptions

Annual exemption	£3,000
Small gifts	£250
Wedding gifts – Child	£5,000
– Grandchild or remoter issue or other party to marriage	£2,500
– Other	£1,000

VALUE ADDED TAX

	From 4.1.11	**From 1.1.10 to 3.1.11**	**1.12.08 to 31.12.09**
Standard rate	20%	17½%	15%
VAT fraction	1/6	7/47	3/23

Limits	**From 1.4.10**	**1.4.09 to 31.3.10**
Annual registration limit	£70,000	£68,000
De-registration limit	£68,000	£66,000

Thresholds	**Cash accounting**	**Annual accounting**
Turnover threshold to join scheme	£1,350,000	£1,350,000
Turnover threshold to leave scheme	£1,600,000	£1,600,000

OTHER INDIRECT TAXES

	2010/11	2009/10
Insurance Premium Tax[(1)]		
Standard rate	5% (6% from 4.1.11)	5%
Higher rate	17.5% (20% from 4.1.11)	17.5%
Landfill Tax (pro rated for part tonnes)		
Standard rate	£48 per tonne	£40 per tonne
Lower rate	£2.50 per tonne	£2.50 per tonne
Landfill Communities Fund[(2)] (LCF)	5.5% × landfill tax liability	6.0% × landfill tax liability
Aggregates Levy (pro rated for part tonnes)	£2.00 (£2.10 from 1.4.11) per tonne	£2.00 per tonne
Climate Change Levy[(3)]		
Electricity	0.470p per kwh	0.470p per kwh
Gas	0.164p per kwh	0.164p per kwh
Liquid hydrocarbons	1.050p per kg	1.050p per kg
Any other taxable commodity	1.281p per kg	1.281p per kg

Notes (1) Premium is tax inclusive – IPT is 1/21 (3/53 from 4.1.11) or 7/47 (1/6 from 4.1.11) of the premium.

(2) Relief for 90% of qualifying contributions

(3) Where the reduced rate applies it is 20% of the rate shown in the table.

STAMP TAXES

Stamp duty	- On shares transferred by physical stock transfer form	0.5%
Stamp duty reserve tax	- On agreements to transfer shares	0.5%
	- On shares transferred to depositary receipt schemes	1.5%

Stamp duty land tax on purchase price / lease premium / transfer value

	2010/11		2009/10	
Rate %	**Residential**	**Non-residential**	**Residential**	**Non-residential**
Zero	£0 - £125,000[(1)(2)]	£0 - £150,000[(3)]	£0 - £125,000[(1)(2)(4)]	£0 - £150,000[(3)]
1	£125,001[(1)(2)] - 250,000	£150,001 - 250,000	£125,001[(1)(2)(4)] - 250,000	£150,001 - 250,000
3	£250,001 - 500,000	£250,001 - 500,000	£250,001 - 500,000	£250,001 - 500,000
4	£500,001 – £1,000,000	Over £500,000	Over £500,000	Over £500,000

Notes (1) A higher threshold of £250,000 applies to purchases by first time buyer completed between 25.3.10 and 24.3.12.

(2) A higher threshold of £150,000 applies to transactions in residential land in disadvantaged areas.

(3) For non-residential property, where the transaction involves a grant of a lease, the zero rate band is not available if annual rent exceeds £1,000.

(4) From 3.9.08 to 31.12.09 a higher threshold of £175,000 applied to residential property. For the period from 3.9.08 to 21.4.09, the higher threshold did not apply to lease premiums where the lease was granted for a term of less than 21 years or assigned with a term of less than 21 years to run.

New leases – Stamp duty land tax on lease rentals[(1)]

Rate (%)	**Net present value of rent**	
	Residential	**Non-residential**
Zero	Up to £125,000[(2)]	Up to £150,000
1%	Excess over £125,000[(2)]	Excess over £150,000

Notes (1) SDLT on the net present value of the rent is payable in addition to SDLT on any lease premium.

(2) A higher threshold of £175,000 applied between 3.9.08 and 31.12.09. For the period from 3.9.08 to 21.4.09, the higher threshold did not apply to leases which were granted for a term of less than 21 years or assigned with a term of less than 21 years to run. In addition, SDLT was payable on the excess of chargeable consideration above £125,000. From 22.4.09 to 31.12.09, the higher threshold applied to all leases of residential accommodation and SDLT was payable on the excess of chargeable consideration above £175,000.

REVIEW FORM

Name: ______________________ **Address:** ______________________

____

How have you used this Workbook?
(Tick one box only)

☐ Home study (book only)

☐ On a course______________________

☐ Other ______________________

During the past six months do you recall seeing/receiving either of the following?
(Tick as many boxes as are relevant)

☐ Our advertisement in *Tax Adviser*

☐ Our Publishing Catalogue

Why did you decide to purchase this Workbook? *(Tick one box only)*

☐ Have used TQT Workbooks in the past

☐ Recommendation by friend/colleague

☐ Recommendation by a lecturer

☐ Saw advertising

☐ Other ______________________

Which (if any) aspects of our advertising do you think are useful?
(Tick as many boxes as are relevant)

☐ Prices and publication dates of new editions

☐ Information on Workbook content

☐ Facility to order books off-the-page

☐ None of the above

Your ratings, comments and suggestions would be appreciated on the following areas of this Workbook.

		Very useful	*Useful*	*Not useful*
Study Period Planners		☐	☐	☐
Study Periods		☐	☐	☐
Progress Tests		☐	☐	☐
Course Exams		☐	☐	☐
Advice on Revision Phase		☐	☐	☐
Sample Paper		☐	☐	☐
Question and Answer Bank		☐	☐	☐
	Excellent	*Good*	*Adequate*	*Poor*
Overall opinion of this Workbook	☐	☐	☐	☐

Do you intend to continue using TQT Products? ☐ Yes ☐ No

Please note any further comments and suggestions/errors on the reverse of this page. The TQT author of this edition can be e-mailed at: suedexter@bpp.com

Please return to: Sue Dexter, Tax Publishing Director, BPP Learning Media Ltd, FREEPOST, London, W12 8BR. BPP Learning Media Ltd is a member of the TQT joint venture.

REVIEW FORM (continued)

TELL US WHAT YOU THINK

Please note any further comments and suggestions/errors below.